Caddo Landscapes
in the East Texas Forests

by

Timothy K. Perttula

with contributions by

Robert Cast, Ross C. Fields, and Tom Middlebrook

AMERICAN LANDSCAPES

Acknowledgements

There are a number of people that I would like to thank for help with this book, but also for their help down the years in working with me on a variety of East Texas Caddo archaeological projects. Foremost among them have been Rodney "Bo" Nelson, Mark Walters, Bob D. Skiles, Linda W. Ellis, and Diane Wilson, as well as Robert Z. Selden, Jr., Chet Walker, Clay Schultz, Shawn Marceaux, Duncan McKinnon and Patti Haskins, but there are too many others to mention individually. I also want to thank the individual contributors to this book: Robert Cast (the Caddo Nation's Tribal Historic Preservation Officer for many years), Ross C. Fields (Prewitt and Associates, Inc.), and Tom Middlebrook (Texas Archeological Steward in Nacogdoches, Texas).

Most of the figures and maps in this book have been prepared by Sandra L. Hannum and Lance Trask. I could not have done this book without their help.

The folks at Oxbow Books have been most gracious and helpful during the book preparation and editing process. I particularly want to thank Julie Gardiner and Pete Topping for the opportunity to write this book.

I also want to thank Mark J. Lynott, who tragically died about a month after he asked me to consider writing this book for the American Landscapes series. I first met Mark and worked with him in Texas many years ago, and then worked with him again a few years later with the National Park Service. The memory of his years as an archaeologist, and his excellent 2014 book on Hopewell Landscapes, spurred me on to complete the book.

My interest in Caddo archaeology was first fostered by Jeff Richner back in the days (1975) when I was working on the Tennessee Colony Lake project for Southern Methodist University. But it was not until I met Dr Alex D. Krieger and Robert C. Dunnell at the University of Washington and Dr Dee Ann Story at the University of Texas at Austin that my long-term research concern with Caddo archaeology really solidified and grew. I am ever appreciative of the time these scholars spent with me while I got on my feet as an archaeologist.

I am also appreciative of the advice, counsel, and support I have received over the years from the Caddo peoples themselves, including past tribal chairmen and chairwomen and Tribal Historic Preservation Office staff, as we have worked on numerous Historic Preservation Fund and Native American Graves Protection and Repatriation grants. In particular, I would like to extend my thanks to LaRue Parker, Brenda Edwards, Cecile Carter, Stacy Halfmoon and Bobby Gonzalez, as well as Robert Cast for those opportunities. I also want to thank Jeri Redcorn and Chase Earles for their support of my work, and for their years spent learning to make, and then excel at making, extraordinary Caddo pottery in traditional ways.

1

Caddo Archaeological Landscapes in the East Texas Forests

The Lives of Things... (Jose Saramago 2012)

This book concerns the cultural and social landscape of the Caddo Indian peoples (*hayaanuh*) and their ancestors that lived in the forests of East Texas from the 9th to the 19th century AD. By cultural and social landscape, I am referring to the various elements of an ancestral Caddo constructed landscape, including earthen monuments or mounds, specialized non-mound structures, domestic settlements and their key facilities – including residential structures, arbors, ramadas and outdoor activity areas – as well as associated gardens and fields (*naht'uh*) for the cultivation of corn (*kisi?*: Caddo words in italics throughout the text are from Kiwat Hasinay Foundation [2001]), beans (*dabas*) and squash, along with trails, and places where salt (*widish*), clay, lithic raw materials, or other materials were collected by Caddo peoples, and the social ties that linked the people together in numerous ways. These places are marked by "things," the artifacts and features of the archaeological record that have been studied by archaeologists since the late 1800s to better understand the native history of Caddo communities and groups. In essence, the Caddo peoples living in East Texas constructed a long-lived historical landscape that was tied to specific places, including community centers marked by earthen mounds and/or community cemeteries, specific social organizations and different traditions/practices. Such landscapes "were created by the intersection of particular cultural practices, resources, economies and environmental settings and the agency of individuals as they lived their lives" (Glowacki 2015: 134).

From the long-term study of the Caddo archaeological record, it is known that this cultural and social landscape existed in East Texas for about 1000 years, and there were continual changes through time in the character and extent of ancestral Caddo landscapes, through times of plenty, risk and hardship, as well as in relationships between different communities of Caddo peoples dispersed or concentrated across the landscape at various points in time. These ancestral Caddo peoples, in all their diversity of origins, material culture, subsistence and rituals and religious beliefs, actively created their societies by establishing places on the land that became home, places where peoples living in individual homesteads and communities across the landscape were dependent upon each other and communicated with each other, leading to the formation of social networks across environments with a diverse mosaic of resources. Established places likely lent

Caddo Social and Political Structure

The Caddo peoples have a matrilineal society, tracing descent through the maternal line rather than the paternal. This is also reflected in the kinship terms used by the Caddo, where the father and father's brothers are called by the same term as the mother and the mother's sister. The Caddo populations were organized into lineages headed by the senior women in the community (Swanton 1942).

Religious and political authority in Caddo society in historic times was situated within a hierarchy of positions within and between the various affiliated communities. The key positions were the *xinesi*, the spiritual leader as well as a political leader; the *caddi*, the principal headman, chief, or governor; and the *canahas*, subordinate headmen or village elders (Newkumet and Meredith 1988: 56–7; Swanton 1942). Other important members of the communities were the *amayxoya*, the war leaders and warriors.

The *xinesi's* position was inherited, as was that of the *caddi*. The *xinesi* had many roles, including: "maintaining the temple containing the sacred perpetual fire; acting as a religious leader for 2 or more of the formally allied villages; mediating between the deities and the people, especially the nominal decision makers for each village; and leading and participating in certain special rites (i.e., first fruits, harvest, and naming ceremonies)" (Wyckoff and Baugh 1980: 234). The *caddi* was primarily responsible for making the political decisions for the community, with the assistance of the *canahas* in governing duties, among them war councils, and conducting the calumet (or peace pipe) ceremony with visitors to the community.

order to the chaotic worlds of people and nature, and they embodied history and the cosmos here on earth.

In creating earthen monuments and settlements across East Texas, the cultural landscape of the Caddo peoples "located themselves in celestial, cosmographic and terrestrial terms. The landscape itself carried inscriptions of Indian history and identity" (Barr and Countryman 2014: 8). The Caddo extended power over geographic space, and "Europeans had no difficulty recognizing the economic and political power behind" (Barr 2015: 18) the mounds, ceremonial centers and associated habitations and trails constructed and used by Caddo peoples, just as did earlier and contemporaneous Indian polities and nations (Barr 2011: 11, 22). These Caddo places – and their narratives about them – provide testimony of the ancestral world of Caddo peoples and communities, a world that has been sometimes glimpsed, but is often hidden, in the Pineywoods and Post Oak Savannah of the East Texas part of the Caddo world that also encompasses southwest Arkansas, northwest Louisiana and southeastern Oklahoma (the southern Caddo area on Fig. 1).

In 1541 when the Spaniards arrived, every place in the Caddo country had, of course, a Caddo name but almost all of those names are gone now, like the people who bestowed them (Schambach 1993a: 7).

Native Americans first settled in East Texas some 13,000 years or more ago, and these mobile hunter-gatherers ranged widely through its forests, grasslands and broad floodplains and wetlands. About 2500 years ago, at the onset of what archaeologists call the Woodland period in this region, these Native Americans

Fig. 1. The Southern and Northern Caddo areas, including East Texas.

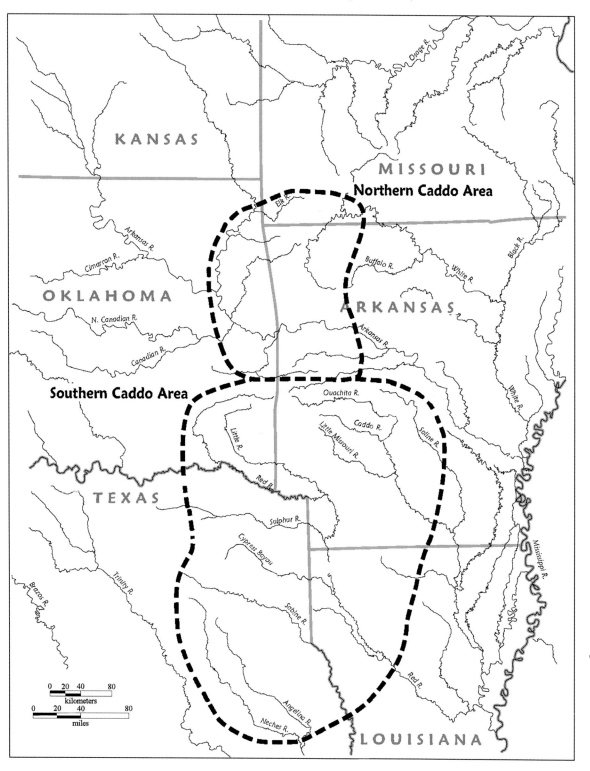

(considered clearly ancestral to the Caddo Indian peoples) began to settle down in recognizable cultural territories across this broad region (e.g., Schambach 2001; 2002; Story 1990), interacted with their neighbors, made a better and more intensive use of native seeds and tropical cultigens such as squash (but not yet growing corn or maize) as well as the bountiful nut mast harvest and white-tailed deer and practised the art of ceramics as part of new technologies of food processing.

It has been common practice by archaeologists since at least the 1940s (e.g. Krieger 1947: 199) to refer to the archaeology of this broad area as "Caddoan" or as the "Caddoan area", even as it was recognized that these terms were problematic, primarily due to the reluctance to link a linguistic label (i.e. "Caddoan") with the archaeological record of indigenous peoples that lived in a specific geographic area in adjacent parts of Oklahoma, Arkansas, Texas and Louisiana. I prefer to employ the term "Caddo" because it directly refers to the peoples that lived in this area beginning more than 1000 years ago, rather than to use the "Caddoan" linguistic term, and also the term "Caddo" can then be employed to refer to the archaeological sites and material remains these people left behind as coming from Caddo archaeological sites. In its broadest sense, the Caddo archaeological and cultural tradition represents "an archaeological concept ... recognizable primarily on the basis of a set of long-standing and distinctive cultural, social and political elements that have temporal, spatial and geographic connotations" (Perttula 1992: 7). The use of the term "Caddo" conveys the idea that the peoples that lived over a large area of four different states, including eastern Texas, northwestern Louisiana, southwestern Arkansas and eastern Oklahoma, centered on the Red River (*Bahtinuh*) and its tributary streams, shared a common cultural heritage and likely shared a common genetic heritage as well, although no ancient DNA studies of Caddo human remains or modern Caddo DNA studies have ever been conducted.

From more than a century of archaeological investigations, it has now been well established that the vibrant and sophisticated prehistoric Caddo culture(s) developed about AD 800–850. Long before Europeans came to what became Texas and the United States, the Caddo Indians had been mound builders, expert traders and artisans, and eventually they also became accomplished farmers. The Caddos were the most socially complex Native American communities living west of the Mississippi River (*Bah Saasin*) and east of the ancestral Puebloan peoples of the American Southwest. These ancestral Caddo peoples constructed mounds across the cultural landscape as a deliberate means to mark the sacred ceremonial and religious places of important priests and chiefs, including burials of priests and chiefs and buildings maintained by priests (Miller 2015: 43). These sacred and ceremonial monuments also mark the places of the "people," or communities, as they "form permanent connections between people and place even as nearby settlements shift and landscapes change" (Rodning and Mehta 2016: 346).

When Europeans came among the Caddo in the late 17th century, they relied on the good will of the Caddo to explore what became Texas, as well as the diplomatic and economic skills of the people (Fig. 2). According to Babcock (2015), the Caddos "constituted the most politically and culturally sophisticated indigenous culture in the region" between AD 1700 and 1800. However, the introduction of European epidemic disease, depredations and territorial dispossession at the hands of French (*Kanush*), Spanish (*Ispayun*), English (*Inkinishih*) and American speculators, mercenaries, priests, traders and land developers, led shortly after 1835 to their abandonment of East Texas. A few Caddo groups continued to live in parts of East Texas until as late as the late 1830s and early 1840s along the western part of the Pineywoods and Post Oak Savannah. They attempted unsuccessfully to cooperatively live and interact with the European and American colonizers of their land (which proved impossible), until they moved, or were removed, to the Brazos River in west central Texas in the 1840s–1850s, and then removed again by the Federal government and the state of Texas to western Oklahoma and Indian Territory in 1859. The Caddo people, now the Caddo Nation of Oklahoma, live to this day (*ka?ischay?ah*) in their new western Oklahoma home, in and around the community of Binger, Oklahoma.

The main purpose of this book is to discuss the character and spatial organization of the Caddo archaeological landscape in the East Texas Pineywoods and Post Oak Savannah, with due consideration paid to the construction of platform mounds, burial mounds and special ritual structures in and outside of mound centers, as well as some of the well-known sites of domestic residences. The Caddo archaeological record is a 1000+ year record of cultural change and continuity at different temporal paces (cf. Hodder 2014: 170–1) among closely related peoples who maintained their own distinctive socio-political and economic dynamic at the same time Mississippian polities in the Southeastern United States fought and competed for power and tribute (e.g. Emerson 2007).

Based on archaeological settlement patterns and cross-cultural comparisons, the development of cultivated plant food systems by Caddo peoples required cooperation among multiple families, probably kin-related, and ultimately led to both the territoriality and sedentary life within settlement and community districts bounded by each other. This began to take place around *c*. AD 800–850 and was associated with both the development of the nuclear family household as the basic social and economic unit, likely based on concepts of private property ownership and inheritance, and continuity of matrilineal household lineages, within over-arching kinship (i.e. a mutuality of being in a group of individuals, see Sahlins 2013: 2), social, religious and political networks led by community and group leaders. The roots of villages and communities in the Caddo area can be seen in these new features of social organization. Rather than interpreting these first horticultural communities in this region as adaptations simply to environmental or population pressures, a larger role for human agency is perhaps more appropriate, thus one where interpretations of resource diversification and intensification in contexts of minimal population pressure and varying resource abundance resulted from deliberate efforts by Caddo peoples to manipulate the environment to enhance resource productivity and predictability. As Smith (2015: 250, 252) hypothesizes, such efforts in plant (and animal) use were part of local efforts to "increase the productivity and predictability of food resources" and most likely took place first in those parts of the Caddo area and East Texas that were "resource-rich ecosystem settings," such as the valleys of the major streams that cross-cut the wooded landscapes of the region.

Archaeological research on the sites and sacred places left behind by the Caddo peoples have rather convincingly demonstrated that the Caddo archaeological tradition should be understood and appreciated through its own long native history. Much attention is given to the Late Caddo period (c. AD 1400–1680) in this book because this span of Caddo native history is well-known, and because this focus provides an excellent opportunity to understand what Caddo groups and communities in East Texas were like before, and immediately after, Europeans explored, invaded, and eventually colonized the area. The archaeology of the Caddo people in the c. 1680–1838 period in East Texas is much more poorly known, however, especially the period after c. AD 1770, but no book on the archaeology of the Caddo peoples would be complete without considering this period as well.

This book takes an archaeological perspective in relating the native history and cultural landscapes of the Caddo Indian

Fig. 2. Painting of a Caddo man (*shuuwi?*), c. 1828, by Jean Louis Berlandier (see Ewers 1969) (image courtesy of Texas Beyond History, Texas Archeological Research Laboratory, University of Texas at Austin)

peoples because this is the best way to experience the long sweep and dense chronicle of an politically and religiously important and astute Native American group. The book begins about 1200 years ago, when the ancestors of the Caddo become recognizable in the archaeological record. The historical accounts, myths and the modern stories of the Caddo are not neglected when they illuminate the broader story and/or cast a more compelling view of particular events, times and places. This chronicle of the Caddo Indian people hopes to bring to light their proud heritage, their creativity and mediating abilities, and their endurance in times of change, calamity and turbulence.

This introductory chapter on Caddo landscapes in the East Texas forests sets the stage for what is to follow by reviewing in broad terms the scope and character of East Texas Caddo archaeology, its temporal and spatial considerations, and architectural contexts. The ceramic traditions and practices of Caddo potters and communities are considered in Chapter 2. Chapter 3 discusses the East Texas environmental setting and paleoenvironmental changes that affected the stability, success and dispersion of Caddo communities. Chapters 4–7 are concerned with characterizing the Caddo landscape during distinct cultural periods (c. AD 800/850–1200, c. AD 1200–1400, c. AD 1400–1680 and c. AD 1680–1838), focusing on settlements and communities, constructed mounds and key sites known at these times. Chapter 8, the concluding chapter of the book, discusses the future of East Texas Caddo archaeology. Appendix 1 describes key Caddo sites to visit in the East Texas forests.

Scope and character of East Texas Caddo archaeology

Archaeological research in East Texas has a lengthy history, with perhaps the 1882–1884 work by the Bureau of American Ethnology at the Winston's Mound and Shawnee Town mound sites the earliest excavations on record (Perttula 2006). A Jesse Martin Glasco, of Gilmer, Texas, also collected Caddo Indian pottery for the Smithsonian Institution between 1859–1861 and 1867–1873 in East Texas (Hawkins and Hicks 2010). The 1898 excavations by W. T. Scott, a local landowner, of the Clements site (41CS25), has also proven to be a significant archaeological investigation for its time (see Perttula *et al.* 2010b).

Substantial archaeological investigations began with the Philadelphia Academy of Natural Sciences expedition in 1911 along the Red River, mostly in northwestern Louisiana and southwestern Arkansas, however. But Clarence B. Moore (1912) recorded several important Caddo mound sites, and conducted excavations at the Moore/Higginbotham site (3MI3/30), located a few miles east of the Texas state line. He chose not to investigate the important Hatchel mound center and village (41BW3), although he was aware of the site.

Much of our knowledge of the ancestral Caddo settlement of East Texas is primarily based on the 1930s excavations by The University of Texas at Austin of aboriginal sites and cemeteries throughout the region, under the direction of Dr J. E. Pearce, and then extensive late 1930s–early 1940s Works Progress Administration investigations at the George C. Davis (41CE19) (Newell and Krieger 1949), Hatchel (Perttula 2005a; 2014a; 2015a), Paul Mitchell (41BW4) (Perttula 2014b; Perttula *et al.* 2016a) and Yarbrough (41VN6) (Johnson 1962) sites. Since then, most of the

Works Progress Administration/Works Projects Administration Archaeology in East Texas

The Works Progress Administration/Works Projects Administration (WPA) was created in 1935 by the administration of President Franklin D. Roosevelt, and lasted until June 1943. It was the principal work relief program in the United States during the time of the Great Depression (Means 2013: 6). The WPA was of great benefit to the study of archaeology in the country because it funded all manner of archaeological investigations. The archaeological work was performed under the direction of professional archaeologists, but the crews were not trained archaeologists, but rather basically unskilled labor drawn from the relief rolls (Means 2013: 9).

In East Texas, WPA crews worked at sites such as the Hatchel Mound center and village (41BW3) on the Red River, the large cemetery at the nearby and culturally associated Mitchell site (41BW4), the Caddo mound center at the George C. Davis site (41CE19) on the Neches River, and the Archaic to Caddo habitation deposits in an alluvial rise at the Fred Yarbrough site (41VN6) on the Sabine River. Archaeological survey of many East Texas Caddo sites was also completed under WPA auspices.

The size of the relief crews allowed for the WPA archaeological work to be extensive and spatially expansive. For example, at the George C. Davis site, the 1939–1941 excavations focused on a 360 × 360 ft (c. 110 m) block centered over and around the Mound A platform mound (Newell and Krieger 1949: fig. 4), exposing a large number of Caddo structures on the mound and in the village while most of the very large platform mound at the Hatchel site was excavated on that WPA project. The spatial scale of these excavations has rarely been duplicated in CRM archaeological investigations of Caddo sites in East Texas, particularly on Caddo mound sites, and thus the WPA work has produced unique and unparalleled data on the character of several key ancestral Caddo sites in the region.

information about the Caddo archaeological record in East Texas first came from a disparate group of privately-funded archaeological research efforts, including: avocational archaeological investigations and Texas Archeological Society field schools, and University of Texas at Austin and Stephen F. Austin State University field schools in archaeology. Since the late 1960s, there have also been extensive professional archaeological work on ancestral Caddo sites in a number of state and federally-funded or permitted reservoirs in the Sabine, Sulphur, Neches, Angelina and Big Cypress drainage basins as well as in large surface lignite mines, and in more recent years excavations of several Caddo sites in the right-of-way of highway development projects across the region.

Temporal and spatial considerations

During the more than 1200 years that the Caddo peoples, and their Woodland period (c. 500 BC – AD 800/850) ancestors, lived in East Texas, they inhabited literally thousands of camp sites, farmsteads, hamlets, villages and civic-ceremonial mound centers over a large area of four different states, including eastern Texas, northwestern Louisiana, southwestern Arkansas and eastern Oklahoma. More specifically, the southern Caddo area is centered on the Red River and its main tributary streams, as well as the Sulphur, Big Cypress, Sabine and Neches-Angelina river basins in East Texas, and includes the Gulf Coastal Plain and Ouachita Mountains physiographic provinces (Fig. 3). The northern Caddo area is centered in the Arkansas River basin in the states of Arkansas and Oklahoma, and includes parts of the adjoining Ozark Plateau and western Ozark Highlands. At its maximum extent, the Caddo archaeological area extends 600 km north to south and 300 km east to west, covering approximately 180,000 km².

There have been several different chronological schemes used by archaeologists since the 1940s in discussing the temporal framework of Caddo settlements in East Texas, and the scheme employed in this book is based on Story (1990; see also Perttula 2012a: table 1-1), with Formative Caddo, Early Caddo, Middle Caddo, Late Caddo and Historic Caddo periods (Table 1). "Within each of these periods are a series of content-based archaeological phases recognized at the scale of the region or locality" (Perttula 2012a: 12) (Table 2).

In the absence of radiocarbon-dated archaeological deposits on sites, ancestral Caddo components have been assigned to one or more of these periods – or a portion of a period – by the character of temporally diagnostic ceramic and/or lithic artifacts, but increasingly Caddo archaeological components are assigned ages based on calibrated radiocarbon dates and age ranges and the data combination process to refine site-specific probability distributions (Selden and Perttula 2013). At the present time, more than 950 radiocarbon dates have been obtained from more than 150 Caddo sites in East Texas (see East Texas Radiocarbon database compiled by Perttula and Robert Z. Selden Jr., http:counciloftexasarcheologists. org/?page_id=27). However, most of these sites have fewer than ten radiocarbon dates, and only 20 ancestral Caddo sites in East Texas have more than ten radiocarbon dates (Selden and Perttula 2013, table 2).

Fig. 3. The Caddo culture areas and sub-regions in the Caddo culture area (map courtesy of Jeffrey S. Girard)

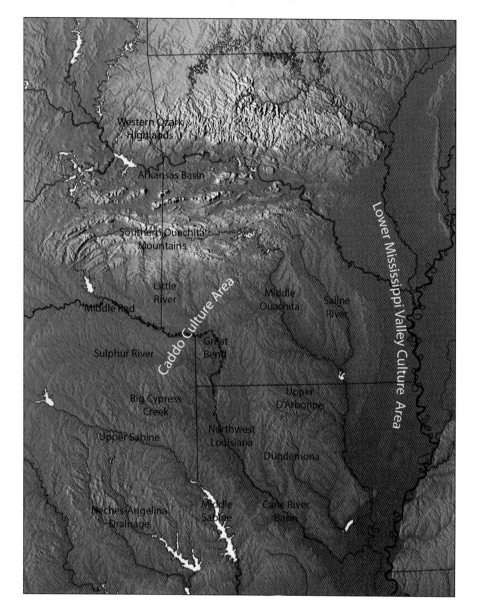

Best known for the distinctive engraved and utility ware ceramic vessels found on mound and habitation sites (see Chapter 2), the Caddo archaeological tradition is characterized by dispersed sedentary settlements of villages, hamlets and farmsteads, the development through time from an horticultural to an agricultural economy dependent upon domesticated corn, beans and squash, and a complex socio-political organization denoted principally by a network of mound centers and the differential treatment of the dead by rank or hierarchy, most notably in burial mound shaft tombs accompanied by elaborate kinds of grave goods, many of exotic origin (Brown 2010; Early 2000a; 2004; Girard 2010; Girard *et al.* 2014).

Although unique Caddo societies developed throughout East Texas, they appear to have formed by the 10th century AD because of social, economic and political interactions between different communities. Increased social integration of these communities was fostered to organize dispersed populations, and the "coordination of construction [of monuments and mounds] and ritual involving extensive spatial parameters and population necessitated leadership" (Girard *et al.* 2014: 37). The social connection of communities into regional polities was led by small groups of individuals in those polities that held political and religious leadership position. Kidder (1998: 132–133) has suggested that the spacing of Caddo mound centers marked "a vertically ranked society with territorially distinct authority over large areas."

Caddo archaeologists have argued that the development of Caddo cultural traditions in prehistoric times took place relatively independently of the emergence of Mississippian cultural developments in the southeastern U.S., though there were contacts between Caddo and various Mississippian polities. Archaeological research conducted over the past 50 years, in combination with the development of radiocarbon dating, has shown that the Caddo archaeological tradition began by about AD 800–850, out of an indigenous Woodland tradition of hunter-gatherer-gardener peoples. Caddo societies shared much with their

Period	Age range (AD)
Formative Caddo	800/850–1000
Early Caddo	1000–1200
Middle Caddo	1200–-400
Late Caddo	1400–1680
Historic Caddo	1680–1840+

Table 1. Chronological Framework for Caddo Archaeology in East Texas

Table 2. Regional cultural sequences in East Texas

Time (AD)	Great Bend of Red River	Middle Red River	Sabine River	Cypress Creek	Neches River	Angelina River
900						
	Lost Prairie					
1000						
1100			Alto		Alto	
1200						
	Haley	Sanders	Sanders			
1300		Mound Prairie			Whelan	
1400		Early McCurtain				
			Titus	Titus	Frankston	early Angelina
1500						
	Belcher/ Texarkana	Late McCurtain	Salt Lick			
1600						
				Titus		late Angelina
1700		Womack			Allen	
	Chakanina					
1800						

Southeastern U.S. Mississippian neighbors, including the adoption of maize and the intensification of maize agricultural economies, an emphasis on monumentality (e.g. Anderson 2012), as well as in systems of social authority and ceremony (e.g. Anderson and Sassaman 2012: 159–163; Blitz 2010; Butler and Welch 2006). Although there are clear socio-political and trade relationships with the Southeast and various Mississippian groups, the people living in the Caddo area are manifestly different in several intriguing ways.

The primary occupation by ancestral Caddo peoples in East Texas in prehistoric and early historic times was by groups that lived in settled horticultural and agricultural communities. These communities were composed principally of farmsteads and small hamlets, but larger villages, as at the Hatchel, Mitchell, Eli Moores (41BW2) and Cabe (41BW14) sites on the Red River, were situated along the Red River bottomlands during much of the prehistoric and historic era (e.g. Creel 1996: 505; R. H. Jackson 2004; Perttula 2005a; Perttula *et al.* 1995; Story 1990). Caddo archaeological sites in the region as a whole are usually located on elevated landforms (alluvial terraces and natural sandy rises, natural levees and upland edges) adjacent to the major streams, as well as along spring-fed branches and smaller tributaries with dependable water (*kuukuh*) flow. They are also located in proximity to arable sandy loam soils, presumably suitable for cultivation purposes with digging sticks and stone celts.

These Caddo groups were powerful theocratic chiefdoms that built earthen mounds for political and religious purposes, functions and rituals, traded extensively across the region as well as with Mississippian and Plains Village groups, and developed intensive maize-producing economies by sometime in the 13th century AD (Perttula *et al.* 2014c; Wilson and Perttula 2013). Due to diseases introduced by Europeans sometime in the latter years of the 17th century, and the later incursions of the Osage (*Waashash*) to obtain deer hides and Caddo slaves, by about 1790, much of East Texas had been abandoned by Caddo groups.

Caddo landscapes and architectural context

At least in East Texas, Caddo communities primarily constructed circular house and temple structures, as well as circular non-mound domestic structures, although there is an impressive diversity in these structures through time and across the Caddo landscape (e.g. Schultz 2010). The range of structure shapes in East Texas Caddo sites includes circular, sub-round, sub-square and rectangular, with each architectural form found in both mound and non-mound contexts. Some of the circular structures associated with platform mounds, such as Feature 111 under Mound B at the George C. Davis site that was 18 m in diameter (Story 1997: fig. 34), the 14 m diameter structure under one of the mounds at the A. C. Saunders site (Kleinschmidt 1982), and Feature 25 at the Hatchel site, 15 m in diameter (Perttula 2014a), were very large in size, at least twice the size of a typical domestic circular structure in a Caddo village.

The study of the architectural character of structures built by late prehistoric and early historic Native American societies in the Southeastern United States has been particularly focused on a better appreciation of the social and symbolic meaning of domestic structures within communities as well as the place of architecture of public buildings "conceived and planned by community leaders" (Hally 2008: 121). These buildings are "a representation of temporal order" (Beck 2007: 20) in social and political realms, and the analysis of architectural structures has provided important insights into Native American views of the cosmos, social practice and cultural identity in post-AD 1000 times. The study of the architecture of specialized buildings – perhaps public in nature, but perhaps more likely of more restricted access – on Caddo sites has also led to insights into how different Caddo societies and communities expressed beliefs in life and death, the cosmos and the place of such buildings as the focus for religious and political rituals and ceremonies (e.g. Kay and Sabo 2006; McKinnon 2013; Perttula 2009a; Regnier et al. 2014; Rogers 1982; Sabo 2012; Schambach 1996; Trubitt 2009).

According to Sabo (1998: 168), Caddo houses are "considered a constituent element of a larger community," and they are "visible symbols of the interconnectedness of families and households comprising villages and communities." A specialized building that may have been used for important political and religious rituals by the social and political elite of a community or polity, or used for mortuary ceremonialism, or used even as an ancestor temple (e.g. Dye and King 2007: 160–1), would stand above and apart in the Caddo constructed landscape. This would be the case with respect to its reflection in certain distinctive kinds of architectural features (i.e. central fires, house size, entranceways, berms and controlled access) of the superhuman power and sacredness principles that would have existed within the social hierarchy of any Caddo community (Sabo 1998: 170), and the specialized rituals and ceremonies that took place in them. This was the case whether they were situated atop a platform mound, as were many structures at the Hatchel site (see Chapter 6) and other Caddo platform mounds, or adjacent to such a mound feature (cf. Schambach 1996: 40; Story 1990: 340).

One kind of structure is of particular interest: extended entranceway structures are a conspicuous and widely distributed architectural construction on Caddo sites in both the southern and northern Caddo archaeological areas; for example, circular extended entranceway structures on the platform mound (in six of the eight mound structure zones) at the Hatchel site are a notable aspect of the construction and use of temples and specialized use structures on this mound (see Chapter 6, below). This type of structure has long been thought to be indicative of an important or specialized Caddo structure, perhaps one lived in by the political or religious elite or used for specialized and restricted purposes. There are other forms of specialized structures on Caddo sites, but J. Daniel Rogers (1982: 49) provides a useful definition of these buildings:

> "Specialized buildings are considered as any of the variety of structures that provided a physical context for the integration of social organization beyond that of the household unit. These may include temples, meeting halls, charnel houses and the residences of chiefs and other officials."

Rogers (1982: 49) goes on to note that specialized buildings are often found in direct association with mounds or have characteristics different from contemporaneous domestic dwellings, including their extra large size; specific and distinctive kinds of construction details; as well as their method of abandonment or disposal (e.g., Early 1988: 160–3; 2000b: 70, 128). Specialized buildings may be found in mound centers as well as "ordinary village context" (Rogers 1982: 49). Brown (1996: 132) points out that since "extended entranceways were employed to restrict the interior access [to structures] suggests the possibility that this architectural restriction in access may well have been reserved for bone houses [charnel houses] or elite residences."

Story (1998: 26) considers special purpose buildings to be structures that were used by special persons for "other than as an everyday family residence." Jelks and Tunnell (1959: 55) had concluded with respect to the extended entranceway structures at the Late Caddo period Harroun site (41UR10) in the Big Cypress Creek basin in East Texas (see Chapter 6) that "because of the consistent pattern of burning, paucity of domestic artifacts, and burial of the house ruins beneath mounds, it is believed that the structures were ceremonial in function and that the burning was intentional." In the same respect, Early (2000b: 128) has identified specialized structures (used for special events or by special people, namely the social and political elite) on Caddo sites in the Ouachita Mountains of southwestern Arkansas because of the special form of treatment they received when they were abandoned (i.e. "the careful burning and burial routine that disposed" of the structures).

Evidence from a wide range of Caddo mound sites with platform mounds in the southern Caddo area indicates that specialized structures of several different shapes were built on one or more mound platform levels. Only a few of the platform mounds have more than one or two mound structure zones buried in them, unlike the Hatchel site with its eight mound structure zones; at the Adair site (3GA1) on the upper Ouachita River in the Ouachita Mountains, however, the main mound had a sequence of nine floors with burned structures, although their shape and size is not known (Trubitt 2009: 241 and table 1). Mound A at the Grobin Davis site (34Mc253) on the Glover River in southeastern Oklahoma also had at least nine different levels of mound construction in the 2 m high mound (Regnier *et al.* 2014), but it is not clear how many of these mound construction episodes (dating from *c.* AD 1230–1500) had structures on the mound summit. Overall in southwestern Arkansas, however, many of the specialized structures found on ancestral Caddo mounds were square or rectangular in shape (Early 2000b: 129–30; Schambach 1996; Trubitt 2009), although circular structures have also been noted on mound platforms (Trubitt 2009: 240–2 and table 1). In other parts of the southern Caddo area, circular temple structures are predominant, but there is considerable architectural diversity. For example, at the George C. Davis site (41CE19) in East Texas, the temple structures on as many as four platform levels in Mound A are mostly circular, as they are at the Hatchel site, although several are sub-square in shape (Newell and Krieger 1949; Schultz 2010; Spock 1977). At the Sanders (41LR2, Jackson *et al.* 2000) and Fasken (41RR14, Prikryl 2008) sites, the temple structures on mound platforms appear to be rectangular in shape, as do specialized structures under mounds at the Holdeman (41RR11, Perino 1995), Fasken (41RR14) (Prikryl 2008) and Sam Kaufman (41RR16, Skinner *et al.* 1969; Perttula 2008b) sites in the mid-Red River basin, and in House 4 under Mound B at the Belcher site on the

Red River in northwestern Louisiana (Webb 1959). There were at least five zones with structures in the West Mound at the Sanders site, including one structure with a burned clay floor (see Jackson *et al.* 2000).

A particularly important part of the archaeological record preserved at many Caddo mound sites is the deposits and features associated with the construction and deliberate destruction of the grass-thatched wood structures occupied by the Caddo elite and domestic commoners. For example, Story (1998: 14) has noted that the destruction and rebuilding of certain structures at the George C. Davis site appears to relate to a cycle of major ceremonies and rituals carried out during the life of the Caddo community; important structures were regularly and purposefully destroyed by fire (Story 1998: 28, 31, 39). Schultz (2010: 326) further noted that by:

> "following such a cycle, the Caddo political elite or ritual practitioners were apparently tapping into the power and authority of the past, as well as integrating the power of the ancestors into their own time and place by appropriating and reusing sacred spaces or other spaces of power. The continued construction and use of specialized buildings atop the floors of earthen mounds, as well as the close vertical alignment of many of those structures with ones that came before, suggests a continuity of traditions related to the construction, use and destruction of sacred spaces."

The use of fire, and its associated smoke and steam, in destroying important buildings has been a characteristic feature of Caddo societies since the 10th century AD (Schambach 1996: 41; Trubitt 2009: 233). Trubitt (2009: 233, 243–4) has commented that "the cleansing properties of smoke continued to be important to Caddo Indians into the twentieth century" for life/renewal ceremonies associated with mortuary rites and the burning of temples. Perhaps structures were burned after the mortuary rites of important individuals "as a way of conveying souls to the world of the dead along an *axis mundi* of smoke …" and temples or the residences of important persons were burned as "a way of terminating the use of it and cleansing the location" (Trubitt 2009: 244). Miller (2015: 43) suggests that the generated smoke "signaled passage between worlds, realms, or dimensions, alerting the dead and immortals to a shift from physical to spiritual conditions."

Two of the better known Caddo mound sites in the southern Caddo area with evidence of the cyclical construction, destruction and burning of temple structures are the Belcher site (16CD13) in northwestern Louisiana (Webb 1959) and the Ferguson site (3HE63) in southwestern Arkansas (Schambach 1972; 1996). At the Belcher site, the structures, covered with wattle and daub, and with grass-thatched roofs, were situated on conjoined Mounds A and B and a connecting low platform or third mound (Webb 1959: fig. 4). The mound platform was about 55 m in length, not much different in length than at the Hatchel site, but the platform was the result of four construction events that took place over apparently more than several hundred years, instead of the nine construction events in the Hatchel platform mound that seemingly took place in less than an estimated 200 years (see Chapter 6). Except for the rectangular structure (House 4) under Mound B, the other seven structures under or on the mounds were circular and ranged from 9.1–12.2 m in diameter (Kelley 2012: 415). The larger structures were on Mound A, and the largest circular structures were built during the post-AD 1500 Belcher phase (Webb 1959: 59). There also seems to have been two structures per mound structure zones at Belcher, not much different than in the mound structure zones at the Hatchel site.

Unlike the circular structures on the platform mound at the Hatchel site, most (89%) of the structures on the conjoined mounds at the Belcher site had central hearth basins filled with ash. Several also had masses of daub (House 1, House 2 and House 4), all in Mound B (Webb 1959), while others had very little daub, much like the structures in the different mound zones in the Hatchel mound. Other distinctive features of the Belcher site structure were ash beds along the walls or in entranceways (Houses 2 and 4, Webb 1959: figs 14 and 23). In House 6, there were large ash beds encircling the walls and an ash-filled trench entranceway covered with sand (Webb 1959: 44 and fig. 32), and House 7 also had a number of ash beds encircling much of the walls (Webb 1959: fig. 39). The extended entranceway to House 8 was a combination of posts and trenches (Webb 1959: fig. 46). Although House 3 is interpreted by Webb (1959: 36) as two different circular structures, it is possible that Houses 3a and 3b represent the construction of a double-walled structure similar to Features 19/20 and 22 at the Hatchel site (Perttula 2014a). The profile of Mound B at Belcher suggests a single House 3 floor level (Webb 1959: fig. 8).

The one rectangular structure and four of the circular structures at the Belcher site had extended entranceways that faced to the northeast (Webb 1959: figs 12, 14, 20, 23, 28, 32, 39 and 46), and the entrances were typically superimposed. The Belcher site mound sequence is distinctive because after the structures had been burned and covered with mound fill and burned structure debris, numerous burial pits, many containing multiple individuals and abundant funerary offerings, were excavated through the debris before another structure was erected over them (Webb 1959: 182–3). There are no such burial pits in the platform mound at the Hatchel site. Webb (1959: 201) suggests that the burning and immolation of houses or temples in the Belcher site mounds was done "in connection with burials of important persons." It appears to be the case that "two structures … stood simultaneously on the conjoined mounds, suggesting that one may have served as a specialized religious structure, while the other was the residence of the caddi" (Kelley 2012: 412).

According to Schambach (1972: 10 and figs 6–9; 1996: 41 and figs 5.8–5.11), Mound A at the Ferguson site was a Middle Caddo period, Haley phase, two stage structure – possibly constructed in the 14th century AD (Ann Early, September 30, 2013, pers. comm.) – with a low northern platform (3 m in height) and a higher (6.5 m in height) southern platform. The northern platform had 10 buildings from five different levels, two per level, "one square building with wattle and daub walls for winter use, and one circular building with thatched walls for summer use" (Schambach 1996: 41). Schambach (1996: 41) suggests these structures were periodically, but accidentally burned (producing considerable amounts of daub and small amounts of carbonized wood) and without obvious ceremony, and that the structures were domestic dwellings. However, I think the context of these buildings – their being situated on one of the platforms on the platform mound – argues against these being domestic dwellings, and it is much more likely the case that they were the residences of a political or religious leader, perhaps the *caddi* or *xinesi* for the community. In any event, these structures on the north platform were apparently occupied at the same time as the series of five structures on the south platform, structures that Schambach (1996: 41) thinks are temples. These southern platform structures "were all square, with extended door passages, thatched roofs and cane matting walls." The structures were represented by great quantities of carbonized logs and other structural debris because they "were all burned and buried according to the same careful ritual" (Schambach 1996: 41), which was to push in the burning walls, quickly cover them with sand (already piled around the walls), thus smothering the fire and leading to the excellent preservation of the carbonized remains. Schambach (1996: 41) also suggests that for:

> "the Caddo, one immediate objective of this ritual may have been to produce the great plume of smoke and steam that must have emanated from each burned and buried building for days or even weeks, as a cord or more of wood was slowly reduced to charcoal."

Caddo horticultural and agricultural economies

The ancestral Caddo groups that lived in East Texas seem to have become horticulturists around *c.* AD 800, cultivating maize and squash, along with several kinds of native seeds (Perttula 2008a), gathered nuts and tubers/storage roots, and were proficient hunters of deer (*da*), fish (*batah*) and many other animal species; they utilized a broad spectrum of resources. The available paleobotanical and bioarchaeological evidence (including stable carbon isotopes on human remains) from the Caddo area; see Wilson 2012) does not indicate, however, that Caddo groups became dependent or reliant upon maize and other domesticated crops until after about AD 1300 (Wilson and Perttula 2013). Only by *c.* AD 1450 did maize apparently comprise more than 50% of the diet of many Caddo groups.

The archaeological and paleobotanical evidence suggests that various cultivated and harvested plants were most intensively grown and used by Caddo peoples beginning after *c.* AD 900. A number of them had been grown and used for at least a millennium before that. By AD 900, the Caddo had begun to live in complex sedentary communities. Intensive food production strategies, however, became most important across almost all of the landscape occupied by the Caddo only after about *c.* AD 1200/1300. As tropical cultigens became the dominant crops, other plant foods, especially naturally gathered plants, were much diminished in use. Stable isotope analyses provide confirmation of the relative importance of maize in ancestral Caddo diets (Wilson 2012). Agricultural strategies and economies (based on domesticated plants and various wild plant foods) were resilient and flexible, apparently designed to suit the changing environments and seasons in East Texas, and were part of their critical understanding of the rhythms of plant growth. The historic Caddo believe they came into the world carrying the seeds of corn and pumpkin (*kunu kakikasaani*).

Ethnographic accounts of plant utilization (Griffith 1954; Swanton 1942; Rogers and Sabo 2004) indicate that the historic Caddo peoples living in East Texas and along the Red River in Louisiana grew two varieties of maize, six varieties of beans, squash, sunflower and tobacco as well as the European introductions of watermelon, peaches (*kaas chuhtuh*) and pomegranates (Swanton 1942: 127–134; Blake 1981). While maize, beans and squash were apparently the mainstays of historic Caddo subsistence, also collected were several key wild plant foods, including hardwood nuts, seeds and greens. Like other Southeastern U.S. tribes (see Scarry and Scarry 2005), the Caddo grew crops in small family plots as well as in larger communal fields, storing the harvests in household granaries and/or large pit features.

The archaeological record attests that a wide suite of plant foods were grown and cultivated by Caddo peoples. This includes the important cultigens maize, common bean and squash, as well as bottle gourd; oily seeds (namely sumpweed and sunflower), and starchy seeds, including chenopod, knotweed, amaranth, maygrass, little barley, and in a few instances in southwestern Arkansas sites, panic grass (see Powell and Lopinot 2000; Fritz 1993). The same range of plant foods are documented in eastern North American sites dating before as well as after *c.* AD 800/900 (Gremillion 2007).

Maize is by far the most common cultigen identified on Caddo sites, although its ubiquity varies considerably both spatially and temporally. The types of races of maize grown include Eastern Eight-Row (also known as "Northern Flint") and Midwestern Twelve-Row; generally speaking, the maize has been grouped with Eastern Complex corn. Beans of several different sizes and kinds have been documented in Caddo sites. Beans are more commonly recovered in post-14th century sites on the Red and Ouachita rivers than elsewhere in the Caddo area. Nevertheless, we know that maize, beans and squash were the principal crops among the Caddo peoples living in East Texas in the late 17th century (Foster 1998: 236, 244). Joutel commented in 1687 that the Nasoni Caddo produced large crops of beans, but that the Caddo did "not make much effort in preparing them; for them it suffices to put them in a large pot, without even removing the strings, then they cover the beans with vine leaves until they are almost cooked" (Foster 1998: 237).

Chenopod, amaranth, knotweed, sumpweed and sunflower are cultigens that exhibited obvious morphological signs of domestication (i.e. increasing seed size and/or thinner seed coats); these seeds do not occur with regularity on Caddo sites anywhere in the larger Caddo Area, however. The maygrass, little barley and panic grass also appear to have been cultivated, based primarily on their occurrence in large numbers at some sites, but they exhibit no morphological distinctions. Powell and Lopinot (2000: 205) suggest that panic grass may be an element of "the native seed complex" in Arkansas sites, primarily because it commonly occurs in prehistoric sites in the American Bottom in southwestern Illinois (cf. Johannessen 1984).

Given the known importance, both before AD 1542, the earliest time of contact between Caddo peoples and the de Soto entrada, and in later historic times, of the cultigens maize, beans and squash to the diet of the Caddo peoples, one of the most critical aspects of the plant husbandry system is that these plants were transported and introduced from habitats (probably from the Southwest and Mexico, see Fritz 2011) where they had been initially domesticated, into an existing southern Caddo area agroecology. Evidence from East Texas and elsewhere suggests that tropical cultigens were introduced independently and sequentially, and that processes of their adaptation were gradual; it was not until some 500–1000 years after the initial introduction of maize in most areas that it became a staple. Furthermore, while native plants such as sumpweed and sunflower were used for a long time before maize was being grown, it was not until after agriculture based on tropical domesticates developed that these native domesticates had their greatest use.

Current evidence indicates that maize was broadly distributed across much of the eastern U.S. after A.D. 200, and was introduced from the northern Southwest. According to Smith and Cowan (2003: 117), "it was only after A.D. 800–900 that this introduced crop took center stage and maize-centered farming appeared across much of the East." Furthermore, "the adoption of maize in eastern North America ... was not straightforward, rapid and uniform across the region, but rather a complex, culturally-variable process" (Smith and Cowan 2003: 122).

The maize introduced into the eastern United States had considerable genetic diversity, both because of the nature of the sources, and gradual environmental and human selection within the area itself (Cutler and Blake 1977: 134–5). Under less stressful climatic conditions (i.e. longer growing season and minimal threat of frost), local selective pressures (including their storability) may have led to the maintenance of row and cob size variability in both hard flint and pop races (Midwestern Twelve Row and North American Pop) rather than a reduction in rows like the Eastern Eight Row.

Evidence from flotation samples from some sites in East Texas indicates that maize is ubiquitous only after AD 950 in Caddo sites (Perttula and Bruseth 1983: 16). Schambach (2002: 105) suggested that "corn horticulture" and/or the gardening of starchy and oily seeds may have been practiced in Woodland period Fourche Maline culture groups by c. AD 400. He based this not on recovered plant remains from Fourche Maline sites along the Red River, but on the appearance of certain types of stone tools that may have been gardening tools, perhaps hoes. Schambach (2002: 106) also argued that corn was present and being used by Fourche Maline groups around AD 800, assuming that late Fourche Maline-Early Caddo groups "added corn gradually to their (still hypothetical) starchy and oily seed horticultural complex, which they almost certainly would have done." He went on to suggest that corn was introduced to the Caddo area from Late Woodland peoples in the American Bottom, and that the corn may have been an accompaniment of foreign prestige goods exchanged between American Bottom societies and Caddo peoples.

Some of the earliest Eight-Row corn in the Eastern United States was initially identified by Jones (1949) from the George C. Davis site in East Texas. Dated originally in the early 1950s at AD 399±162 (C-153, corrected, with a 2 sigma calibrated age range of AD 197–609), it was considered to be significant in terms of discussions about the cultivation of maize in the Caddo area, as well as integral in initial considerations of the development both of the Caddo tradition, and of Mississippian groups in general (Krieger 1948: 158; Newell and Krieger 1949: 231). Jones (1949) suggested that the George C. Davis maize resembled the Northern Flint type, and perhaps originated in Highland Guatemala, rather than in North America. This particular date on maize came from a pit (Feature 31) under the Mound A platform mound at

George C. Davis, but has since been discredited because of (1) the early method of radiocarbon analysis (i.e. solid carbon) that tended to produce older than expected radiocarbon ages, and (2) its archaeological context (Story 1990: 254). The later examination of the Davis site samples and more comprehensive absolute dating (Story and Valastro 1977; Perttula *et al.* 2014c, table 1) indicates that such a temporal affiliation for these corn samples is very unlikely. Small Ten- and Twelve-Row maize were apparently the most common kinds at George C. Davis and throughout the Caddo area on sites of this time period (see Cutler and Blake 1977; 2001).

A few other pre-AD 800 dates on corn come from the George C. Davis site (see Story 1990). The calibrated ages of these six dates range from AD 222 to 773. The OxCal data combination process for these dates indicates that the early dates occur in one group with a 2 sigma calibrated age range of AD 415–606. It is possible that these pre-AD 800 corn dates indicate that corn was being grown in parts of East Texas as early as *c.* AD 400, during the latter part of the Woodland period. But even if these dates are accurate, the cultivation and consumption of corn was sporadic at best during those times.

The most significant aspect of the paleobotanical record for the period between *c.* AD 850 and 1300 is the common appearance of corn in all regions of the Caddo area. Systematically collected paleobotanical assemblages indicate that the introduction and adoption (at least to some extent) of maize as a food source was generally accomplished by *c.* AD 900. The record of its utilization is sporadic at best prior to that time. At the George C. Davis site pre-Mound A (Jones 1949) and Early Village (*c.* AD 850–1050) samples from features contained maize from small 8–10-rowed varieties. Quantification of maize remains from village excavations suggests that maize was more prevalent, however, only in the Late Village (AD 1050–1300) occupation. Such a trend in maize has also been documented at the Oak Hill Village site (41RK214), where maize ubiquity increased from 31.6% in the Early Village (dating *c.* AD 1150–1250) to 96.9% in the Late Village (*c.* AD 1350/1375–1450) (Dering 2004, table 88).

Most of the dates on corn from East Texas Caddo sites are from only a few sites (Perttula *et al.* 2014c, table 1), including dates from Formative Caddo, Early Caddo and Middle Caddo period components at the George C. Davis mound center and village site (n=12 dates) (Story 2000). These corn dates fall into two groups, one with a 2 sigma age range of AD 898–1020 (five dates) and AD 1173–1277 (seven dates). Other sites with common corn dates are a Late Caddo period Titus phase component with a single mound and village areas at the Pilgrim's Pride site (n=6, Perttula 2005b) in the Big Cypress Creek basin, a Titus phase component at the expansive Pine Tree Mound site (n=10) (Fields and Gadus 2012a; 2012b), a Middle Caddo period component at the Oak Hill Village site (41RK214) on a tributary to the Sabine River (n=5, Rogers and Perttula 2004; Perttula and Rogers 2012) and the George E. Richey (n=10), William A. Ford (n=22) and James E. Richey (n=6) sites in the Big Cypress Creek basin (Fields *et al.* 2014). Notwithstanding possible sample size issues, the summed probability distribution of all the corn dates from East Texas indicates that the majority of the calibrated ages in the 2 sigma range fall after AD 1300. There are notable temporal peaks at *c.* AD 1350 and 1450 in the summed probability distribution, and then a plateau in probability density after *c.* D 1500. Plotting median calibrated ages in ten-year intervals illustrates the same temporal trends in corn dates from Caddo sites. That is, corn is present in low numbers of dated samples from as early as *c.* AD 900 until *c.* AD 1300, but there are significant increases in dated corn samples from *c.* AD 1330–1580. Furthermore, there are notable peaks in the calibrated age range of the summed probability distribution of dated samples of corn at cal. AD 1341–1350 (in the latter part of the Middle Caddo period), cal AD 1421–1430 at the beginning of the Late Caddo period, and cal AD 1561–1570 later in the Late Caddo period.

Corn remains from Caddo sites are variable in terms of cob size and row numbers, and this is also reflected in median cupule widths between different assemblages. Cupule width of maize may be a good proxy for large kernels, and larger corn yields; that is "corn varieties with larger cupules will tend to support larger kernels, thus resulting in greater yields" (Diehl 2005: 364). In East Texas, the largest cupule widths are reported from a historic Caddo site: the early 19th century Timber Hill site (41MR211) (Goldborer 2002), while the smallest (3.2 mm) are in Middle Caddo archaeological deposits at the Oak Hill Village (Elson *et al.* 2004). Most Caddo Area corn is from 10-, 12- and 14-rowed ears resembling Northern American Pop and Midwest Twelve-Row races. These are corn varieties with small cobs and cupules, and longer than wide kernels (Blake and Cutler 1979: 53). Archaeological samples of maize dating before AD 1400 are dominated by 8- and 10-rowed varieties. The maize varieties grown by peoples of different regions were quite similar to one another in character.

Fritz (1986: 214–15) has pointed out that chenopods, maygrass and sumpweed domesticates became scarcer as maize became the most important plant food source, and other domesticates were introduced, including beans and domesticated amaranth. She suggested that:

> "as maize became what would seem to have been the most productive crop, husbandry of the previous staples appears to have become more casual. Introgression from the by then probably highly evolved weedy companions may have been permitted to the point that something akin to a gradual reversal of the domestication process went into effect."

The Caddo paleobotanical record for the utilization of weeds for their seeds is consistent with these general changes in plant exploitation patterns, although the total evidence is considerably more limited outside of the northern Caddo regions (e.g. Fritz 1990).

Perhaps the best measure of the importance of maize in the diet of Caddo peoples comes from stable isotope analyses of preserved human remains from sites throughout the Caddo area (see Rogers 2011; Rogers *et al.* 2003; Rose *et al.* 1998; Wilson 2012; Wilson and Perttula 2013). The stable carbon isotope information from burials recovered from single and multiple mound centers, cemeteries, villages, farmsteads and hamlets at more than 55 sites in both the southern and northern Caddo regions indicates that after around AD 1200, there was a significant increase in the consumption of maize, and an increase in diet variability, as marked by C_4-enriched collagen and apatite samples (Wilson and Perttula 2013). Apatite signatures in particular indicate that maize consumption remained at a consistent level from the Formative Caddo through Middle Caddo periods. Not until the Late Caddo period is there a significant increase in maize contribution to the overall diet. Isotopic values in these later samples suggest that the importance of maize continued to increase in the diet, peaking after *c.* AD 1650 (Wilson 2012). Based on apatite values, the percentage of C_4-based foods in diets was as much as 66–72% in Caddo peoples living in sites dating after *c.* AD 1400.

Wilson and Perttula (2013) have noted that Caddo populations did not consume the amount of maize that other Mississippian and related populations did in Illinois, Missouri, the Ohio River valley and Fort Ancient populations, even though there is dietary heterogeneity. The Southern Caddo stable isotopic findings parallel the maize contribution to protein noted in Middle Mississippian populations, although the maize contribution is consistently lower among the Southern Caddo. Stable isotope research shows that the Caddo had less C_4 plant foods in their diet and intensified maize production centuries later than did Mississippian cultures.

Long distance trade

The development and maintenance of long-distance trade networks for both economic, social and religious purposes was a notable feature of the ancestral Caddo tradition from its very beginnings. Bison (*tanaha*) hides, salt, raw materials such as copper, galena, stone and marine shell, and finished objects such as pottery vessels (and their contents), were part of the trading system. Indeed, the possible trade in bison hides and bows (*chaway*) made from bois d'arc (*Machura pomifera*, commonly known as Osage Orange) with Mississippian populations in the central Mississippi River valley seems to have played a large part in recent arguments establishing the paramount importance of the Spiro center on the Arkansas River in eastern Oklahoma as a trading entrepot (see Schambach 1993b; 1997; 2000). In fact, Frank F. Schambach has suggested that the Cahokia polity had a monopoly on the source of bois d'arc, and this may have been a key to its apparent military power. The Spiroans are thought to have obtained the bois d'arc bows from restricted sources along the Red River in East Texas and the western Ouachita Mountains (see Schambach 2003).

Much of the archaeological evidence for the Caddo long-distance trade and exchange networks occur in contexts dating from *c.* AD 800–1400, with long-distance trade declining after that time. Certainly the best known examples of Caddo long-distance exchange are seen in the grave offerings from mound burials from the premier civic-ceremonial centers like Spiro, Crenshaw, Gahagan, Mounds Plantation and Mineral Springs in eastern Oklahoma, southwestern Arkansas, and northwestern Louisiana (see Girard *et al.* 2014), respectively, and George C. Davis in East Texas. Exchanged goods in components dating from *c.* AD 1000–1300 – the apex of the long-distance trade network – include a wide variety of prestige goods such as ceramic vessels, ceremonial tools, marine shell gorgets and conchs, shell columella beads, stone pipes, copper masks and repoussé, copper-covered ornaments and large chert bifaces. The most prodigious mortuary deposit of exotics are found in Harlan and Spiro phase contexts in the Craig Mound at the Spiro site in the northern Caddo area (see Brown 2012), particularly in the *c.* AD 1400 Great Mortuary.

Evidence of this trade and exchange is clearly denoted by the wide distribution of Caddo ceramic vessels from: Mississippian sites in Missouri, Arkansas, Louisiana and Alabama (see Steponaitis 1983: 331 and fig. 65d); Plains Village sites in the Central and Southern Plains (i.e. the Washita River, Great Bend of the Arkansas River, Great Oasis and Mill Creek cultures), and among hunting-gathering groups in the Texas Panhandle, Caprock Canyonlands and Central Texas. Ceramic petrographic investigations also document the intra-regional exchange of ceramic vessels among Caddo groups in East Texas. When the de Soto-Moscoso entrada encountered Caddo groups in East Texas in 1542, and then in later 17th century entradas (Foster 2008: 201–2), the chroniclers did note the presence of cotton and turquoise that must have come from the Southwestern Pueblos, indicating that Caddo interregional trade and exchange continued into the 16th and late 17th centuries.

Population densities and estimate

The southern Caddo area was well populated in both prehistoric and early historic times, until the effects of European introduced diseases drastically reduced their populations and led to the extinction of some East Texas Caddo groups. Around 1700, European chroniclers estimated the population of East Texas Caddo groups as a whole at about 10,000 individuals (see Chapter 7).

The Caddo area of East Texas covers *c.* 59,000 km^2 (*c.* 330 km north–south and 180 km east–west), and perhaps as much as 90% of the land was habitable. Using figures provided by Gautney and Holliday (2015, table 3) for mean population density estimates for hunter-gatherers – 0.1223 individuals per square kilometer – prior to the development of sedentary life by ancestral Caddo peoples of the Woodland period in East Texas (before *c.* AD 800), around 7000 Native Americans may have lived in the area at any one time.

Regional population estimates for the sedentary and increasingly maize-based agricultural societies of the East Texas Caddo area can be proposed from population densities that ranged from 0.31 individuals per square kilometer to 1.1 individuals per square kilometer (see Milner and Chaplin 2010: fig. 4; Milner *et al.* 2013: fig. 2). Population trends from *c.* AD 800 to 1200 most likely were at the low end of this range, while after *c.* AD 1300–1400, higher population densities would have been prevalent in a number of East Texas Caddo communities. Again assuming that at least 90% of East Texas was habitable by Caddo peoples, population sizes could have ranged from about 18,000 to 60,000 individuals prior to mid-16th and later 17th century contact with Europeans. After sustained European contact in the later 17th century, and the deleterious effects of the many introduced epidemic diseases (Derrick and Wilson 2001), beginning perhaps with the 1691 smallpox epidemic (see Jones 2014: fig. 4; Smith 2014: 51), Caddo populations declined precipitously (Perttula 1991; 1993a; 1993b). Before that time Caddo peoples were demographically stable.

2

Everyday Things: the Character of Prehistoric and Early Historic Caddo Ceramics

The most distinctive material culture item of the Caddo groups living in East Texas were the ceramic vessels they made for cooking, storage and serving needs (Fig. 4), and also they then included them as necessary funerary goods. The styles and forms of ceramics found on sites in the region hint at the variety, temporal span and geographic extent of a number of ancestral Caddo groups spread across the landscape. The diversity in decoration and shape in Caddo ceramics is substantial, both in the utility ware jars and bowls (*kahwis*), as well as in the fine ware bottles, carinated bowls and compound vessels. These characteristics are related to distinctive communities of identity and practice and the recognition of social networks from these ceramic assemblages, where potters shared a group identity that can be reconstructed through the analysis of suites of technological and stylistic attributes (cf. Eckert *et al.* 2015: 2).

Caddo potters made ceramics in a wide variety of vessel shapes, employing distinctive technological traditions of temper choice, surface finishing techniques and firing conditions, along with an abundance of well-crafted and executed body and rim designs and surface treatments. From the archaeological contexts in which Caddo ceramics have been found, as well as inferences about their manufacture and use, it is evident that ceramics were important to ancestral Caddo peoples in: the cooking and serving of foods and beverages, in the storage of foodstuffs, as personal possessions, as beautiful works of art and craftsmanship (i.e. some vessels were clearly made to never be used in domestic contexts) and as social identifiers; that is, certain shared and distinctive stylistic motifs and decorative patterns marked closely related communities and constituent groups. Other motifs may have originally been more personal, perhaps deriving from body tattoo motifs.

The Caddo made both fine wares (with very finely crushed temper) with engraved, trailed and slipped decorative elements, with burnished or polished surfaces, including bottles and many bowls of different forms, and utility wares (some of the simple bowls, as well as the jars that were made in a variety of sizes) with wet paste decorative elements (i.e. brushed, incised, punctated, etc., decorations made before a vessel was fired). These kinds of ceramics were designed to serve different purposes within Caddo communities and family groups – from that of a cooking pot to the mortuary function of a ceremonial beaker – and this is reflected in differences in paste, surface treatment, firing methods, decoration and vessel form between the two wares.

Almost without exception, Caddo ceramics were tempered with grog (crushed sherds) or bone, although burned and crushed shells were commonly used as temper after *c.* AD 1300 among most of the Red River Caddo groups and on later Caddo sites in the lower and upper Sulphur River basin in East Texas (see Perttula *et al.* 2012b). After adding the temper to the clay, the kneaded clay was formed into clay coils that were added to flat disk bases to form the vessel, and the coils were apparently smoothed with a round river pebble to create the finished vessel form. Decorations and slips, both red (*hatinu*) and black (*hadikuh*), were added before, as well as after, baking in an open fire, and commonly the vessels were then burnished and polished; red ochre and white (*hakaayuh*) kaolinite clay pigments were often added to the decorations on a variety of vessel forms, primarily on bottles and carinated bowls.

Fig. 4. A selection of East Texas Caddo pottery (image courtesy of the Texas Archeological Research Laboratory, University of Texas at Austin)

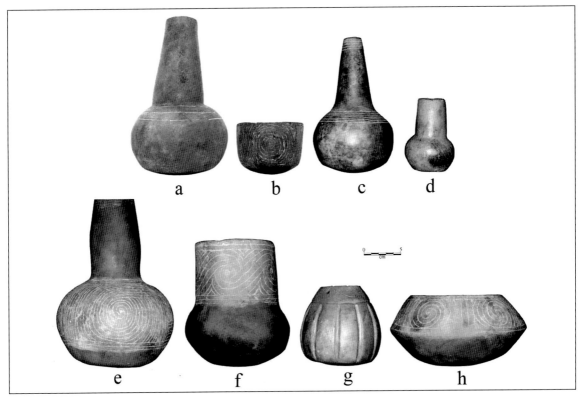

a   b   c   d

e   f   g   h

Fig. 5a

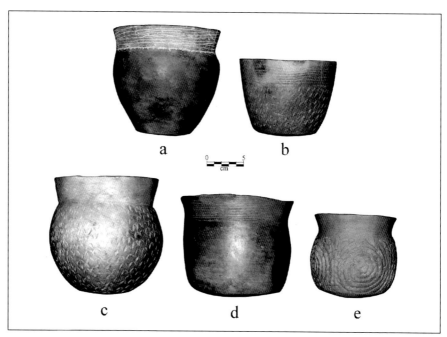

Fig. 5b

Fig. 5. Examples of Early Caddo period fine ware and utility ware vessels from mortuary features at the Boxed Springs (a–b), T. N. Coles (c–d), and R. L. Jaggers (e–f) sites: a fine wares; b. utility wares; c. Holly Fine Engraved bottle; d. Spiro Engraved conjoined vessel; e. Hickory Engraved jar; f. Spiro Engraved bowl (courtesy of the Texas Archeological Society)

Fig. 5c

Fig. 5d

Fig. 5e

Fig. 5f

The earlier (pre-AD 1200) Caddo fine ware designs are comprised of curvilinear, rectilinear, and horizontal elements, and frequently cover the entire vessel surface; other fine ware designs simply are placed on the rim, or sometimes on the interior rim surface. In general, the earlier Caddo fine wares across East Texas (and indeed extending across much of the Caddo area itself) are quite uniform in style and form within specific regions, suggesting broad and extensive social interaction between Caddo groups living within particular regions. The use of a red hematite slip on interior and/or exterior surfaces of carinated bowls and bottles began to occur with some regularity in *c.* AD 1200–1400 ceramic assemblages in various parts of the region (particularly the upper Red, Sabine and Big Cypress drainage basins), continuing as a decorative method in post-AD 1400 assemblages in the western part of these basins, and in the case of Maxey Noded Redware vessels made during that time, the squat, long-necked bottles also have appliqued and/or punctated designs below the neck of the bottle.

Early Caddo ceramic types include Davis Incised, Dunkin Incised, Weches Fingernail Impressed, Kiam Incised, Crockett Curvilinear Incised, Pennington Punctated-Incised, Hickory Engraved, Spiro Engraved and Holly Fine Engraved types (see Suhm and Jelks 1962). Sherds of Coles Creek Incised, *vars. Coles Creek* and *Hardy* vessels are also present in some assemblages, along with plain ware vessels (Fig. 5) (Girard 2014: 75–6).

In the Middle Caddo period, ceramic vessels were of a wide range of vessel forms, sizes and decoration, and the well-crafted character of the vessels for both everyday and sacred uses is evident (Fig. 6). Bottles were particularly well-made, and the engraved rattlesnake motif is one of the more distinctive motifs of the period (Fig. 7a–b).

Rattlesnakes as figural representations in Caddo material culture

The engraved rattlesnake motif on Caddo water bottles (see Fig. 6a–b) appear to be portrayals of the canebrake rattlesnake that had ritual or social significance to various communities in East Texas (see Hart and Perttula 2010: fig. 2). The motif has entwined or interlocking tails, sinuous bodies that "rotate around a center or axis" (Gadus 2013: 223), and rounded heads that curl around the body; the snake heads have forked tongues, and lines and dots for the eyes and nose; Hart and Perttula (2010, 206) suggest that the forked tongue element resembles the head of the Scorpio constellation, known also to many aboriginal groups in eastern North America as the "Great Serpent" or the "master of the Beneath World." The snake body has cross-hatched engraved chevrons (Gadus 2013, 223; Walters 2006, 17–19).

The engraved rattlesnake motif certainly had iconographic meaning for the Caddo that made and used these engraved bottles (see Lankford 2007). That meaning is related to a multi-level view of the world – middle world, upper world, and lower world (from which the people came) – where powerful beings moved or danced around a sacred pole at the center of the world or had activities within a particular world. Rattlesnakes were part of the lower world that was ruled by the Great Serpent (Gadus 2013: 227, 235, 239). Dorsey (1905: 46–7) relates a Caddo story with snake-like water monsters from the lower world, and other stories "connect rattlesnakes with the mythical Snake Woman, who provided maize to the Caddo, but who also condemned those who broke taboos surrounding maize growth and harvesting to rattlesnake bites" (Hart and Perttula 2010: 221).

The Middle Caddo period vessels at sites in the Sabine River basin include Washington Square Paneled carinated bowls; Haley Engraved bottles; Maydelle Incised and Bullard Brushed jars; Killough Pinched jars; possible Handy Engraved carinated bowls; and Nacogdoches Engraved bottles with a rattlesnake motif (Fig. 8). Washington Square Paneled carinated bowls have horizontal interlocking incised scrolls with upper, lower and vertical incised bands filled with tool punctates. This particular decorative style has a considerable distribution on Middle Caddo period sites in the mid-Sabine River basin and tributaries as well as in contemporaneous Caddo sites in the Angelina River basin.

Other fine ware vessels (carinated bowls and bottles) have diagonal and vertical engraved zones and pendant triangles, rectangular panels and pendant triangles, concentric ovals and scrolls and open circles. Engraved vessels from a Middle Caddo interment at 41HS718, about 25 km downstream and in the Pine Tree Mound community in the Sabine River basin (see Fields and Gadus 2012a: figs 9–10) have panels, spurs, hooked elements and concentric ovals as well as hatched pendant triangles.

The later (after *c.* AD 1400) Caddo fine ware designs in East Texas include scrolls (horizontal, horizontal-vertical and slanted in orientation across the rim panel), scrolls with ticked lines, scrolls and circles, negative ovals and circles, pendant triangles, diagonal lines and ladders and S-shaped motifs. These kinds of decorative elements continued in use in historic Caddo ceramics (that is, until about AD 1800

Fig. 6. Middle Caddo period vessels: a–b. Nacogdoches Engraved bottle with rattlesnake motif; c. Nacogdoches Engraved bottle; d. Haley Engraved bottle; e. Maxey Noded Redware bottle; f. Nacogdoches Engraved compound bowl; g. Tyson Engraved compound bowl; h. Haley Complicated Incised jar. Provenience: a–c, f, Washington Square Mound site (41NA49); d, h, Haley site, Southwest Arkansas, from Moore (1912, pls 39 and 40); e, Woodbury Creek site (41RA49: image courtesy of Lance Trask); g. Tyson site (41SY92: image courtesy of Tom Middlebrook)

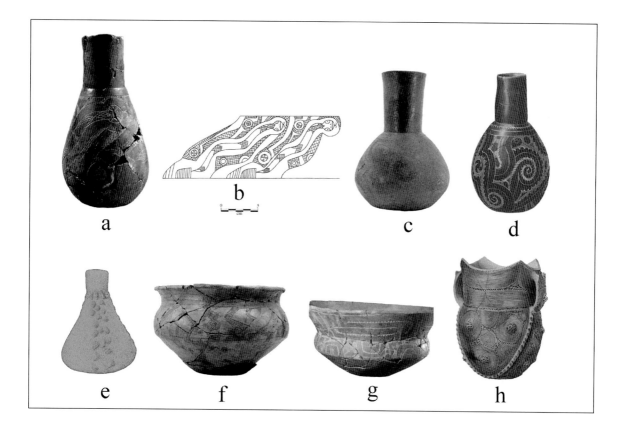

Fig. 7. Selected vessels from Features 31 and 95 at the Washington Square Mound site: a. Vessel F31-9; b. Vessel F95-8

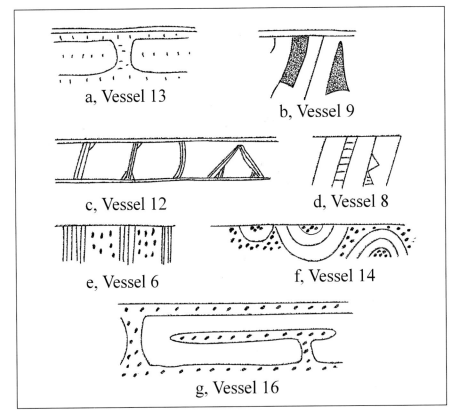

Fig. 8. 41GG5 Vessel motif drawings: a. Vessel 13; b. Vessel 9; c. Vessel 12; d. Vessel 8; e. Vessel 6; f. Vessel 14; g. Vessel 16

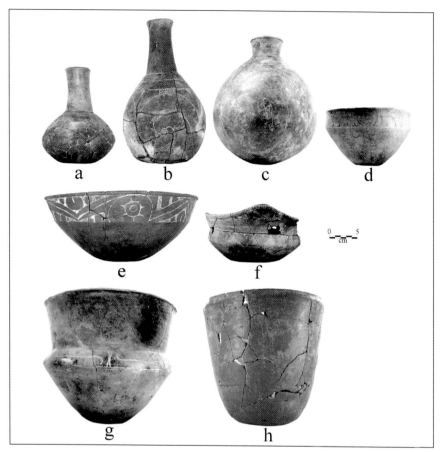

Fig. 9a

Fig. 9. Ceramic wares from Titus phase sites: a. fine ware vessels; b. utility ware vessels (images courtesy of the Texas Archeological Society)

Fig. 9b

or later). They are best exemplified by the intricate scrolls, ovals and circles on Hudson Engraved and Keno Trailed bottles and Natchitoches Engraved bowls among Red River Caddo groups; Hodges Engraved bottles; the scrolls and ticks of Patton Engraved among Hasinai Caddo groups south of the Sabine River; and the pendant triangles and engraved scrolls on Womack Engraved bowls on the upper Sabine and the middle Red River.

The later Caddo fine wares are also more stylistically diverse across East Texas, and there are very specific differences in vessel shapes, designs and decorative attributes between Caddo ceramics in individual drainages, or even within specific smaller segments of river and creek basins. The stylistic and functional diversity in Late Caddo Titus phase, Frankston phase and McCurtain phase fine ware and utility ware ceramics is illustrated in Figures 9 and 10. This diversity can be reasonably interpreted to be representative of the ceramic traditions of specific Caddo social groups.

Fine wares in McCurtain phase sites include Avery Engraved, Hudson Engraved, Keno Trailed and Simms Engraved bottles, bowls and carinated bowls, along with a plain red-slipped fine ware (Clement Redware), while the utility ware jars are from Nash Neck Banded and Emory Punctated-Incised types (Fig. 11). Simms Engraved, *var. Darco* is a post-AD 1650 fine ware style present in late McCurtain phase contexts as well as other East Texas sites in the lower Red River and Sabine River basins. Clay elbow pipes were made, used and discarded in the different village areas and farmstead compounds as well as placed in graves as funerary offerings.

Fig. 10. Frankston phase fine ware and utility ware vessels (image courtesy of the Texas Archeological Society)

Fig. 11. McCurtain phase fine ware vessels: a, d, h. Avery Engraved; b. Hudson Engraved; c. Simms Engraved; e. Simms Engraved, *var. Darco*; f–g. Engraved jar; i. engraved effigy bowl. Provenience: a. Foster Place (3LA27; from Moore 1912, pl. 43); b, e–f, Sam Kaufman (41RR16); c–d, g, i, Boyce Smith collection from Red River sites; h. Jim Clark site, Red River County, Texas

In historic Caddo times, ceramic vessel forms and decorations are considerably more homogeneous across much of the Caddo area, suggesting extensive intraregional contact and social networking between contemporaneous Caddo groups. In the late 17th–early 18th century component at the Clements site (41CS25), for example, vessels include Cass Appliqued and red-slipped jars, Hodges Engraved and Hatinu Engraved bottles, a Keno Trailed bowl and Taylor Engraved and Simms Engraved, *var. Darco* carinated bowls (Fig. 12).

Fig. 12. Ceramic vessels from the Clements site (Image courtesy of the Texas Archeological Society)

Womack Engraved is a *c.* AD 1680–1730 ceramic type among Womack phase Caddo groups in the upper Sabine and Red River drainages (Fig. 13). Historic Allen phase types include several varieties of Patton Engraved as well as Poynor Engraved, *var. Freeman* and Bullard Brushed, La Rue Neck Banded, Lindsey Grooved and Spradley Brushed-Incised (Fig. 14a–b). Patton Engraved is the youngest of the fine ware types in the upper Neches River basin.

One temporal trend in Caddo ceramics from parts of the Red River valley (in northwestern Louisiana) below the Great Bend, the middle Sabine River basin and the Neches-Angelina river basins is for larger portions of vessel surfaces to be decorated, particularly with the introduction of brushing marks on the bodies of utility jars. Consequently, through time, ceramic assemblages have lower proportions of undecorated sherds (using a plain to decorated sherd ratio) in domestic sherd assemblages. Just the opposite trend is apparent, however, on the middle Red River in Late Caddo period contexts, as the plain/decorated sherd ratio in McCurtain phase assemblages at the Sam Kaufman site is at least 40–50 times higher than in post-AD 1400 Big Cypress, Sabine and Neches-Angelina Caddo sites. This clearly indicates that the McCurtain phase ceramics are from a different Late Caddo stylistic tradition than other contemporaneous East Texas Caddo traditions, one where assemblages are predominantly comprised of plain vessels, and large rim-decorated vessels with plain bodies.

There is an impressive diversity of vessel forms among the Caddo fine wares. This includes carinated bowls, deep compound bowls, double and triple vessels (joined bowls and bottles), bottles, ollas, zoomorphic and anthropomorphic effigy bowls and bottles, ladles, platters, peaked jars, gourd and box-shaped bowls and chalices (distinctive vessels with a pedestal base).

The Caddo utility vessels usually have a coarser paste, a rougher surface treatment and thicker body walls than the fine wares, probably related to the performance needs of the cooking jar to withstand thermal shock and cracking during use. Typical utility vessel shapes included small to large jars, as well as a variety of conical and simple bowl and bottle forms, most of the latter in the earlier Caddo ceramics (and the historic Caddo ceramics) being plain and unpolished. The utility vessels have carbon encrustations, food residues and soot stains, suggesting they were employed by the Caddo as cooking vessels, probably to cook maize (cf. Briggs 2016: 329). Some of these kinds of vessels may have been used primarily for storage (those with large orifice diameters and vessel volumes) of foodstuffs and liquids.

While plain utility vessels were commonly used by Caddo groups in East Texas, particularly before

Fig. 13. Womack Engraved vessel from the Womack site (image courtesy of the Texas Archeological Research Laboratory at the University of Texas at Austin)

Fig. 14. Patton Engraved
vessels from the Richard
Patton site: a. Patton
Engraved, *var. Patton*
carinated bowl; b. Patton
Engraved, *var. Freeman*
globular bowl

c. AD 1300–1400, they were also decorated in a variety of ways. As noted above, brushing of vessel bodies is a form of surface treatment that is notable after *c.* AD 1300 in the Big Cypress Creek basin, and in sites on the middle reaches of the Sabine River and on the lower Sulphur River. Other types of decorations and/or surface treatments on later Caddo utility vessels included neck-banding or corrugation, ridging, appliquéd elements and combinations of zoned and diagonal incised and punctated designs on the rim and body of jars. In historic Caddo times, dating after *c.* AD 1680, rows of fingernail punctations on the rim of everted-rim Emory Punctated-Incised jars are also a common decorative treatment in Caddo sites along the Red River and in the upper part of the Sabine River basin. Handles and lugs were present on some of the utility vessels.

Caddo ceramics were apparently widely traded or exchanged in Texas, as they have been found in significant quantities on North Central, East Central, Central and inland Southeast Texas archaeological sites. The earlier Caddo ceramics (dating before *c.* AD 1200) were most widely distributed in the upper Trinity and Brazos River basins of North Central Texas, and in inland Southeast Texas, while the Late Caddo ceramic wares appear to have been most commonly exchanged with East Central and Central Texas groups after *c.* AD 1200–1300, as well as with peoples living along the Trinity River in inland Southeast Texas. Caddo ceramic fine wares were also traded or exchanged extensively in parts of the Midwest and Southeastern U.S., most notably after *c.* AD 1300–1400, with Native American groups living in the Lower Mississippi Valley of Arkansas and Louisiana, as well as far afield to the north, such as central Kansas and Iowa (Perttula 2002). Based on decorative styles, Caddo pottery may have been made at Cahokia (Pauketat 2015: 14), as it appears that Caddo peoples were living at Cahokia by the 11th century AD (Slater *et al.* 2014).

Other types of ceramic artifacts manufactured by ancestral Caddo groups include ceramic ear spools and disks, figurines and a variety of pipe (*tankuh*) forms. The earliest types of Caddo clay pipes were plain, tubular and cigar-shaped forms, followed by the long-stem "Red River" pipes with burnished and polished stems and small bowls; rectangular platform pipes have also been recovered in Caddo sites dating before AD 1200/1300. The later Caddo pipe forms in East Texas are biconical and elbow pipe forms with larger bowl and stem diameters; many of these elbow pipes were decorated with bands of incised or engraved lines or punctations.

One recent advance in the study of ancestral Caddo ceramics that has increased knowledge about stylistic, technological and functional changes in this material culture, is compositional analysis. Compositional analyses using petrographic and chemical characterizations (primarily instrumental neutron activation analysis) are now being used on samples of Caddo ceramics to discern manufacturing techniques, the source and regional distributions of particular wares (Selden and Perttula 2014), and the functional characteristics of different kinds of vessels. Analyses of the chemical and petrographic constituents in the pastes of Caddo ceramic assemblages in the Sabine River, Big Cypress Creek and Sulphur River basins has shown that there appear to be consistent paste differences between the ceramics in each of the river and creek basins. This is turn seems to reflect the local basin-specific production by Caddo groups of ceramic vessels from locally available clays, with limited evidence for the exchange of vessels from one group to another in different basins. This type of analysis will undoubtedly continue to be used for considerations of cultural affiliation, and trade and exchange between Caddo and non-Caddo groups, as well as for discerning manufacturing techniques, raw material use, source/regional distributions of particular wares and specific functional characteristics of different kinds of vessels.

3

Environmental Setting and Paleoenvironmental Changes

Habitats

East Texas has three main biotic communities: the Post Oak Savannah or Oak Woodlands, the Blackland Prairie and the Pineywoods (Fig. 15). The Caddo lived mainly within the modern distribution of the Pineywoods and the Post Oak Savannah, and the small portion of the Blackland Prairie that lies at the western margins of the region was periodically used for the hunting of bison (*tanaha*) before and after the Caddo peoples had horses (*kawaayuh*).

The Post Oak Savannah is a narrow southwest to northeast trending woodland belt that marks a natural transition zone or ecotone between the drier Blackland Prairie to the west and the moister Pineywoods to the east (see Diggs *et al.* 2006: fig. 2). Both the Post Oak Savannah and the Pineywoods have medium-tall to tall broadleaf deciduous forests, and shortleaf and loblolly pines are common in the Pineywoods on upland fine sandy loam soils with adequate moisture. Bottomland communities contain a hardwood and swamp forest (including cypress, tupelo and sweet gum), with natural levees and alluvial terraces, point bar deposits, old stream channels, oxbow lakes (*hikut*) and backwater swamps (Fig. 16). A less diverse bottomland hardwood community is present along creeks and tributaries.

In the mid-19th century, uplands, especially in settings with very deep and well-drained sandy soils, would have had a forest overstory consisting of a mixture of pine and oaks, including blue oak (*Quercus incana*), blackjack oak (*Quercus marilandica*), post oak (*Quercus stellata*) and red oak (*Quercus rubra*). Some portion of these landform-soils settings probably had pure stands of pine. In upland settings with thinner sandy sediments that are not as well-drained, the overstory probably consisted of a variety of oaks (post oak, red oak, blackjack oak, bluejack or blue oak) and chinquapin oak (*Quercus muehlenbergii*) and hickory (*Carya* sp.). Abundant nut mast would have been available in these upland habitats on an annual basis. On landforms with deep and well-drained loamy fine sand, such as more mesic lower valley slopes, toe slopes and elevated alluvial landforms, the vegetational overstory would have had red oak and post oak trees (*kahdachah*).

Small areas of tall grass prairie may be present in both communities throughout the region. Bottomland communities along the Red, Sulphur, Sabine, Cypress,

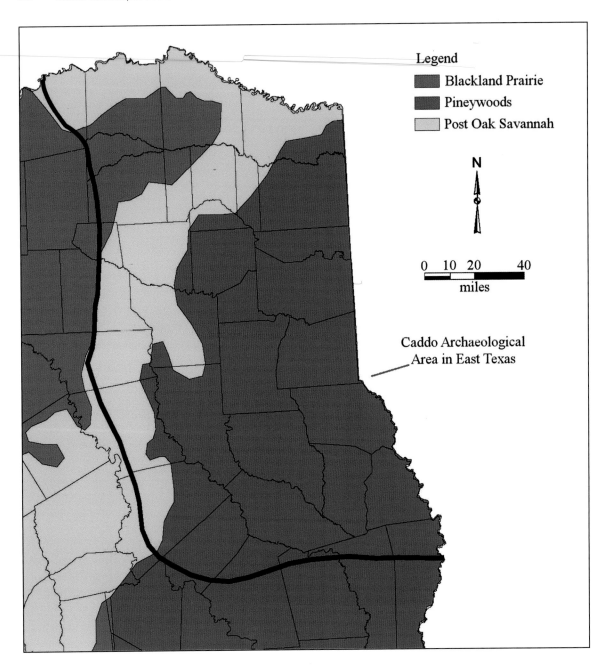

Fig. 15. East Texas biotic habitats and the Caddo archaeological area

Neches and Angelina drainages contained a diverse hardwood and swamp forest, with natural levees, point bar deposits, old stream channels, oxbow lakes and backwater swamps.

The modern climate of the region is humid, with a mean annual precipitation of at least 120 cm; periods of maximum rainfall occur in the spring (*hashnih*) and fall (*nasakaabasdawih*) seasons. Droughts are not uncommon, some lasting several

Fig. 16. Caddo Lake in East Texas

decades, and dendrochronological analyses of tree rings for the last 1000 years suggest there were numerous wet and dry spells during that era.

Pollen and tree ring records and paleoenvironmental change

Three broad climatic periods can be defined for this area over the last 4000+ years from temperature and precipitation reconstructions, pollen records and tree ring data (Perttula 2005b: 16–24). Period I lasts from *c.* 4030–2300 years ago, in the Late Archaic period and the early years of the Woodland period. It is a time of wetter and periodically cooler temperatures, with climatic minima (i.e. coolest and drier conditions) at *c.* 2700 and 2300 years ago (Fig. 17a–c). Climatic conditions were generally equitable. A period of increased fire frequency around 3200–3300 years ago suggests drier conditions (an estimated 2 inch (5.1 cm) decrease in precipitation). Period II extends from 2300–580 years ago, and it is a period of fluctuating climates, from very dry and cooler conditions from 2300–1800 years ago (with at least a 2 inch/5.1 cm) drop in precipitation annually and a 1° drop in average temperature) to more mesic (warmer and wetter) intervals, especially after 900 years ago. Cooler and drier climatic minima occurred around 1700, 1500, 1200, 1150 and 900 years ago, demonstrating the rapid and widely fluctuating character of climate during this time. There was an increased frequency of fire throughout much of Period II, particularly from *c.* 2270–960 years ago. There is also a period of heightened soil instability around 950-920 years ago that may correlate with a period of colder and wetter weather patterns across East Texas.

The final climatic period (Period III) lasts from 580–220 years ago, during the

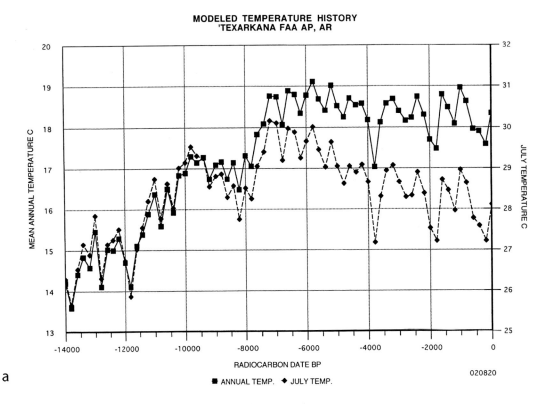

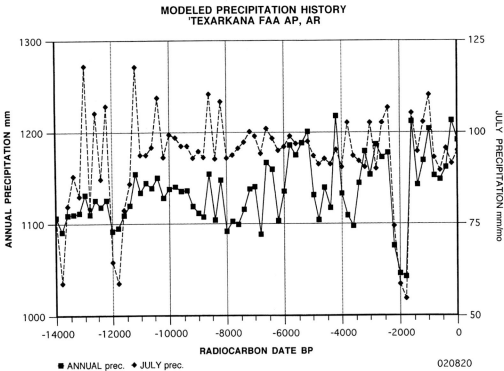

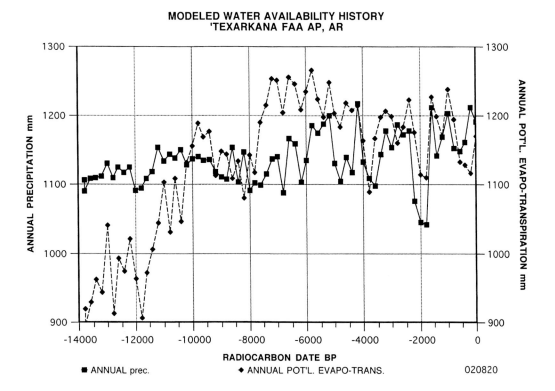

MODELED WATER AVAILABILITY HISTORY
'TEXARKANA FAA AP, AR

C

■ ANNUAL prec.   ◆ ANNUAL POT'L. EVAPO-TRANS.   020820

Fig. 17. East Texas paleoenvironmental models: a. modeled temperature history; b. modeled precipitation history; c. modeled water availability history (graphs provided courtesy of Dr Reid A. Bryson at the Center for Climatic Research, University of Wisconsin-Madison)

latter years of the Middle Caddo period, as well as through the Late Caddo and the early years of the Historic Caddo period. During this time it was generally drier and colder, with much drier and colder climatic minima at *c.* 500 and 300 years ago as identified by changes in reconstructed solar radiation as well as tree rings. Based on soils data, there was a period of heightened soil instability that occurred between about 580–420 years ago, with peaks of instability clustering around 570 years ago, 480 years ago and 430 years ago. There are mesic intervals during Period III, particularly after 410 years ago, and from tree-ring data, the driest conditions during this period (and indeed over the last 1000 years ago) occurred around 540–570 years ago (*c.* AD 1440–1475) (Fig. 18). During this time, particularly after 600 years ago, it is likely that Caddo farmers in the area created larger cleared areas through their agricultural practices, and also used deliberately-set fires to open forest lands.

The wetter years would likely have been optimal growing years for Caddo farming groups dispersed across a wooded landscape, assuming a correlation between crop production and spring precipitation values. Generally warmer and wetter conditions are optimal for increasing the yield and predictability of the maize crop. The wetter rainfall conditions would also likely have led to an increase in the extent of swamp and wetland habitats in the major river basins, and a concomitant expansion in the carrying capacity of woodland-favoring plants and animals in the region.

These drought periods, especially those periods that exceeded 2 years in length, may well have been times when there were stressed food supplies, limiting the

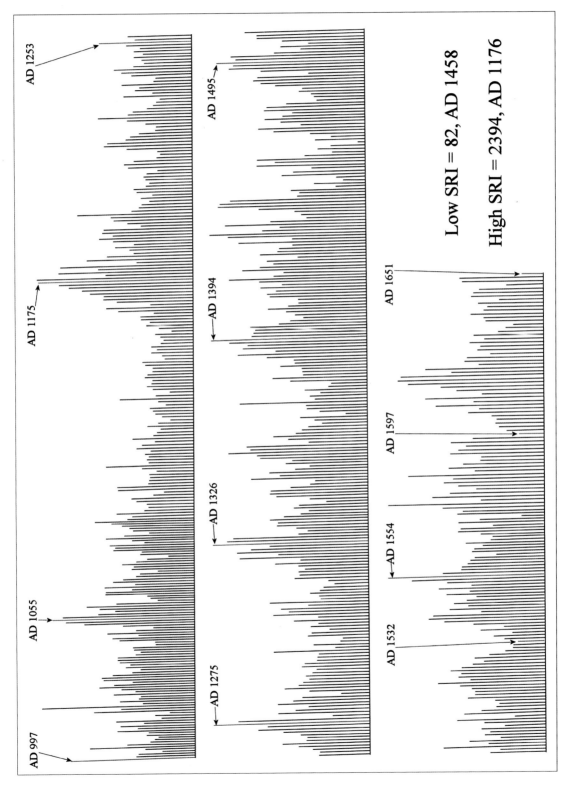

Fig. 18. Big Cypress Bayou in Northwest Louisiana tree-ring data, AD 997–1651

Fig. 19. Northwest
Louisiana tree ring data
with 20 year moving
averages (provided
courtesy of Dr Jon Lohse)

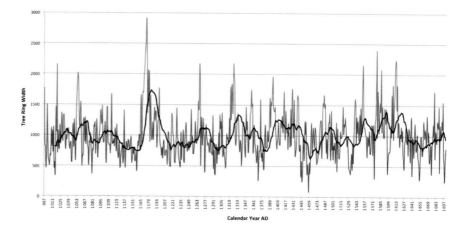

ability of Caddo groups to produce sufficient and predictable food reserves from
the cultivation of tropical cultigens, to maintain seed stocks for future crops,
and these extended droughty periods would have hindered the success of maize
harvests. These droughts probably also affected the constancy of flow in the
numerous upland springs in the area, which in turn would have influenced the
relative quantity and diversity of naturally available animal and plant foods in
floodplain and upland forested habitats.

Dry conditions and the worst droughts (Fig. 19) apparently occurred in the
late AD 1200s (AD 1271–1297), in the mid-1400s and 1600s, and then again in the
mid-1700s. The period between AD 1549–1577 has been suggested to have been

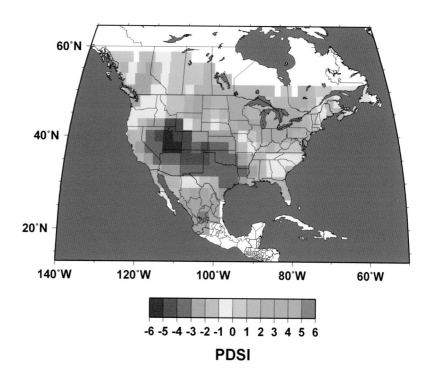

Fig. 20. AD 1450 Tree-ring
reconstructed drought

the worst June drought in the past 450 years (Stahle *et al.* 2000; Stahle and Dean 2010: fig. 10.12), but the dry conditions that prevailed at that time were primarily centered in the southwestern part of North America, northern Mexico and the North American Great Plains (Cook *et al.* 2016: fig. 4c). There was instead a very significant and spatially extensive droughty period that occurred between *c.* AD 1435–1478 (Fig. 20) (Cook *et al.* 2016: fig. 4b). More favorable crop growing conditions were probably prevalent during the intervening years, especially between *c.* AD 1390–1435, then in the latter part of the 16th and early 17th century, and finally, at the beginning of the 18th century when Spanish and French colonists settled amongst the Caddo peoples in earnest. These climatic fluctuations must have affected the predictability and success of the maize harvests during the Caddo occupation of the Pineywoods and Post Oak Savannah. Certainly similar short-term climatic changes in the Holocene period (the last 10,000 years) also affected the range, distribution and abundance of naturally occurring plants and animals during the long Native American settlement of East Texas.

Drought indices

Reconstructed Palmer Drought Severity Index values by Cook and Krusic (2004; see also Kemp 2015: fig. 159) for East Texas between AD 996–1800 indicate that there were several especially dry periods during the Caddo settlement of the region. These periods were in the first half of the 12th and 13th centuries, ending by AD 1250; the late 14th century (AD 1360–1390); and the mid-15th century, as well as during the mid- to late 16th century, the early to mid-17th century and the late 18th century. The most droughty periods were between the AD 1440s–1450s and the AD 1560s. Although there were many droughty periods – as well as corresponding and succeeding wet periods – there is no evidence that any of these droughts were severe enough to lead Caddo groups and communities to choose to abandon East Texas in any meaningful measure, nor are there archaeological data available to indicate either population aggregation or a more widely dispersed community structure during known periods of droughty conditions. There were some parts of East Texas, however, especially along the margins of the Post Oak Savannah and the Blackland Prairie, and in parts of the upper Sabine River basin, that appear to have been abandoned after the 15th century AD by Caddo peoples that relied on agricultural crops.

4

The Beginnings of Caddo Groups and Communities, c. AD 850–1200

Woodland period ancestors

I begin this chapter with a consideration of the archaeology of the Woodland period ancestors of the Caddo peoples that lived in East Texas, to set the stage for the beginnings of Caddo groups and communities there. Woodland period sites in this region date between c. 2450 and 1100 years ago, based on radiocarbon dates and ceramic stylistic comparisons with Lower Mississippi Valley ceramics from a number of different sites in the region (see Ellis 2013; Ellis *et al.* 2013). Sites occupied by Woodland peoples in East Texas took place during times of generally cooler climates than modern times, but with periods of widespread vegetation change, and with a very dry and cool episode c. 2300–1800 years ago. After c. 1650 years ago, there was a climatic amelioration with peaks and valleys in temperature and precipitation, with warm periods culminating around 1000 years ago (see Chapter 3).

Within East Texas, three different Woodland period cultures have been defined, from north to south: Fourche Maline (Schambach 1998; 2002); Mill Creek (Ellis 2013); and Mossy Grove (Story 1990) (Fig. 21). Caddo cultures evolved from these Woodland period ancestors sometime after c. AD 800–850, although the mechanisms of culture change are not well understood. The more regular use of cultivated plants, and population increases associated with the development of sedentary communities across the landscape were clearly important aspects in what comprises the beginnings of East Texas Caddo cultures that had not been apparent in the preceding Woodland period.

There has been a general consensus of opinion for years among archaeologists that specialize in Woodland and Caddo archaeology that the Fourche Maline culture "evolved into Caddo culture" around AD 800 or so (Schambach 2002: 91). However, we now know that Caddo "culture" or "cultures" evolved from several different Woodland period cultures, not just the Fourche Maline culture, and that each Woodland period culture had different material culture assemblages as well as mound building practices and settlement complexity.

Frank Schambach (2002: 108) has indicated his belief that "most archeologists interested in Caddo culture" share his opinion that the Fourche Maline culture

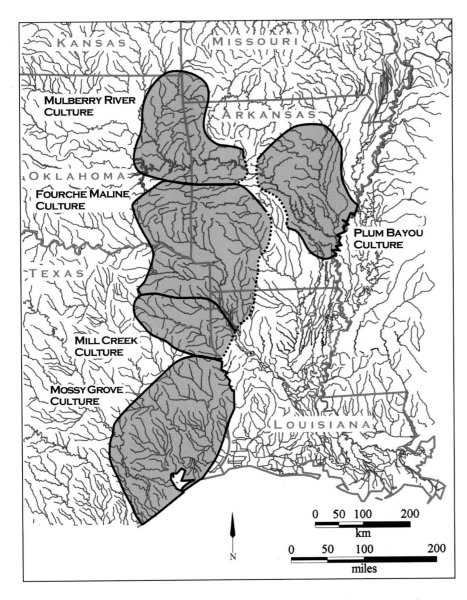

Fig. 21. Map of Woodland period cultures in East Texas and surrounding states

is ancestral to Caddo culture in northeastern Texas, southwestern Arkansas, northwestern Louisiana and southeastern Oklahoma, the traditional Caddo homelands (see also Story 1990). From comprehensive bioarchaeological studies of Woodland and Caddo skeletal remains, it has also been concluded that there is "not even a hint that the southern Caddo populations did not derive from the preceding Fourche Maline inhabitants" (Rose *et al.* 1998: 115). Nevertheless, the recognition that there are three different Woodland period archaeological cultures in East Texas clearly indicates that ancestral Caddo populations did not evolve from just one culture.

Ceramics occur on all Woodland period sites in East Texas, and these consist primarily of plain wares of grog-tempered Williams Plain and sandy paste Goose

Creek Plain vessels (see Ellis 2013), along with a few lower Mississippi Valley ceramic vessel sherds. This occurrence points to the development of some occupational tethering to certain locations and a repeated and consistent use of those locations. A study of the use of ceramics among residentially mobile hunter-gatherers has suggested that "the degree of occupational redundancy in areas with resources suited to mass collecting and boiling [are]... correlated with pottery use" (Eerkens 2003: 736). This occupational redundancy may actually promote long-term trends in decreasing mobility and increasing sedentism, and in such settings the use of pottery may be also "associated with incipient agricultural strategies" (Eerkens 2003: 736). In the case of inland Mossy Grove and Mill Creek culture sites like Herman Bellew (41RK222) or Hawkwind (41HS915), pottery development and use seems related to the mass processing of hickory nuts for their oil. Through time, beginning in the Woodland period, the Native American groups in this part of Texas became less mobile, as evidenced by the development of midden deposits on a number of habitation sites, and they also developed distinctive territories within which diverse settlement and subsistence patterns began to fully develop.

The best known Fourche Maline site is the Crenshaw site (3MI6) on the Red River in the Great Bend area of southwest Arkansas. Its Fourche Maline village and extensive mound and cemetery complex is unprecedented in size and archaeological complexity in the Caddo area (Schambach 1982a; 1982b; 2002). There are extensive Fourche Maline habitation deposits at the site, estimated at 8 ha (Schambach 1982a: 150), several cemeteries, and six earthen mounds (Mounds A–F), at least three of which (Mounds C, D and F) were constructed in Fourche Maline times. The village and cemetery deposits, as well as the funerary offerings included in burials under or in the various mounds, indicate that Woodland Fourche Maline and Caddo peoples used the site for habitation and/or mortuary purposes for at least 550 years. The most extensive occupation of the site was during what is the late Fourche Maline period, which Samuelsen (2014) dates from c. AD 850–1000.

In Mound D, the late Fourche Maline burials "were found on the thin layers of clay indicating that the mound had been built by stages, an additional layer being added as a burial or group of burials were made" (Lemley 1936: 30); this includes burials with funerary offerings in the basal mound layer and Burial 3. Sometime after the mound was completed, two deep Middle Caddo shaft tombs (Pits 1 and 2) were dug from the top of the mound remnant and penetrated into the subsoil under the mound and the late Fourche Maline midden deposits (Lemley 1936: 35). There were off-mound burials dating to the late Fourche Maline at the site. According to Schambach (1982a: 152), the late Fourche Maline burials in the off-mound cemeteries, including Cemetery 3, were in "generally single extended supine internments in shallow graves dug 30 to 50 cm below the midden surface." Grave offerings generally consist of one or more ceramic vessels placed near the head.

These vessels are dominated by Williams Plain jars and bowls (28%), several varieties of Coles Creek Incised (40%), mainly bowls, and particularly *var. Greenhouse* and *var. Chase*, as well as French Fork Incised (16%) bowls, jars and a carinated bowl. There are also a number of Coles Creek Incised-French Fork Incised hybrid vessels (i.e. these have design motifs from both types on the same vessel), which have been named Agee Incised by Frank Schambach (see discussion in Brown

1996). The main vessel forms in late Fourche Maline contexts are bowls and jars, with only a few plates and carinated bowls. There are also gourd-shaped ladles or bowls and boat-shaped bowls. About 31% of all the vessels are plain wares. Other distinctive attributes of the late Fourche Maline vessels include vessels with rim collars. More than 15% of the vessels have square bases, primarily the Williams Plain jars, and one bowl has suspension holes. Finally, a white kaolin clay pigment was used as a decorative embellishment on one bowl. Another vessel had red pigment staining, indicating a hematite-rich clay pigment had been stored in it before it was placed in a burial.

In East Texas, Fourche Maline sites are present in the Red and Sulphur River basins, and none are known that have constructed mounds. Rather, they are marked by pits and hearth features, burials (in small numbers) and midden deposits (Ellis *et al.* 2013, table 4), and no clear post-hole patterns have been identified in these sites. The most characteristic aspect of the material culture assemblages in East Texas Fourche Maline sites are thick grog-tempered Williams Plain sherds and vessels, few bone-tempered vessel sherds and rare lower Mississippi Valley Marksville and Coles Creek sherds. Burials at the Snipes site (41CS8) had a small late Fourche Maline (*c.* AD 550–700) cemetery with nine individuals placed in graves in an extended supine position; several were accompanied by ceramic vessels (Jelks 1961).

The Herman Bellew site on Mill Creek, a tributary to the Sabine River, is a well-studied Mill Creek culture site. The site was occupied by Woodland period hunter-gatherer groups at least twice between *c.* AD 100–700; the post-AD 400 occupation appears to have been the most extensive (Rogers *et al.* 2001). Although no structures were identified in excavations, there were numerous features found there, including three scatters of burned rocks discarded from hearths or cooking ovens, seven rock-lined hearths or earth ovens and seven pits; several of the pits had a charcoal-rich fill, probably from their use as cooking pits, while one large pit (2.5 m³ of fill) may have been originally intended for use as a storage pit. Such storage pits, and the range of features in use at this Woodland encampment, hint at the possibility of extended stays by certain groups that occupied the site because the storage of food "can be seen as evidence for close attachments and significant investments by a group or groups of people in particular points within a landscape" (Rodning 2010: 186). Few charred plant remains were recovered in the archaeological deposits. These included 220+ seeds of bedstraw (*Galium* sp.), goosefoot/pigweed (*Chenopodium* sp.) and grass (Poaceae sp.), hickory nutshells, walnut nutshells and a small amount of wood charcoal, including oak wood. There was a considerable dependence on nut plant foods, but not on cultivated plant foods.

The Woodland period occupations in the southern part of East Texas are components of the Mossy Grove culture, specifically inland groups of that culture that lived in the Neches and Angelina river basins in East Texas (see Story 1990).

Woodland period sites in this area are marked by a low density scattering of lithic tools, dart points, and debris, some sandy paste ceramic sherds (Goose Creek Plain, *var. unspecified*) as well as sherds from incised and punctated vessels, fire-cracked rock and ground stone tools. Features are rare, and midden deposits are absent at this time on even more intensively occupied components. These characteristics suggest periodic use of sites over more than ten centuries by mobile hunting-gathering foraging groups. The presence of ceramics hints at the beginnings of a more settled way of life, as the manufacture and use of ceramic vessels for cooking, storage and food-serving implies that more extended stays may have occasionally taken place at the sites, perhaps after c. AD 500/600. It is hard to disagree with the notion that these Woodland period settlements represent temporary encampments by small groups of people over a lengthy period of time.

The Mossy Grove Culture encompasses Woodland period archeological sites from the upper Texas Coast well into East Texas (see Fig. 21). The prehistoric peoples that we refer to as the inland groups of the Mossy Grove culture are considered likely to be ancestral to the prehistoric Caddo that lived in this part of East Texas after c. AD 800. Certainly not all Mossy Grove culture groups living in southeastern and East Texas are ancestral to the Caddo, however, and James A. Corbin (1989a; 1998) has suggested that Mossy Grove groups were contemporaries with the earliest Caddo to live in East Texas, and that gradually over time these groups adopted Caddo lifeways.

Woodland period groups of the Mossy Grove culture that lived in the Neches-Angelina river valleys did construct burial mounds. These mounds were first built over central pits containing cremated human bone, as well as "small additional deposits of prestige goods that had been laid on intermediate surfaces, probably along with fragmentary human remains, and covered with soil as the mounds were built" (Schambach 2002: 111). After c. AD 100, building mounds over central cremation deposits apparently ceased, but caches of prestige artifacts (vessels and copper ornaments, quartz crystals and quartz pendants), cremated human remains and parts of non-cremated remains were incorporated into the mounds, as at the Jonas Short site (41SA101), as they were built up.

The use of quartz crystals and quartz ornaments was important in some Woodland period contexts, as shown by the placement of a quartz pendant and crystals from caches at the Jonas Short site and a polished quartz figurine from the Coral Snake mound (16SA48) in northwestern Louisiana (see McClurkan et al. 1980); the source of these quartz crystal artifacts is not known. Quartz crystals and other artifacts made from quartz may have been a source of power for the Woodland period individuals or groups that possessed them (and then buried them) at the Jonas Short site, just as they were for other Southeastern U.S. Native American groups. Charles M. Hudson (1976) has noted that quartz crystals were aids in hunting and in predicting the future, and "had to be handled carefully. They were hidden in a dry place until they were actually used, and they were never kept inside one's house" (Hudson 1976: 356–7). Because quartz crystals were considered "underworld" objects, they gave the owners power, but a power that had to be carefully controlled by caring for the crystal: "When the owner died it [the quartz crystal] was buried with him or else it would roam free, seeking the lives of men" (Emerson 1989: 82). The use of quartz crystals and quartz ornaments has also been attested to in ancestral Caddo burials in a number of sites in East Texas, southwestern Arkansas and northwestern Louisiana.

Formative to Early Caddo settlements and communities

By about *c.* AD 800–900, at the end of the Woodland period, the stone tools and ceramic vessels found on sites in East Texas clearly identify them as being made by ancestral peoples culturally affiliated to the modern-day Caddo Nation of Oklahoma. These Caddo peoples, in all their diversity of origins, material culture, subsistence and rituals and beliefs, their "doings" (cf. Fowles 2013: 104), essentially created the character and structure of their own societies by establishing places on the land that became home. As Pauketat (2007: 198–9) has commented, established places "lent order to the chaotic worlds of people and nature. They were embodiments of history and the cosmos here on earth."

Up until *c.* AD 1000 in East Texas, the weather was relatively warm and wet, with cooler and drier climatic minima around AD 800 and 1050 (see Chapter 3). From about AD 1370 to 1730, it was generally drier and colder than the warmer and wetter conditions in the years between *c.* AD 1050–1370.

These Caddo lived in permanently occupied settlements, eventually successfully growing maize and other cultigens (beans and squash, with beans apparently becoming important after *c.* AD 1300) in varying quantities (see Perttula 2008a; Perttula *et al.* 2014c), and lived primarily in dispersed communities led by a social hierarchy of priests, civic leaders and other elites. These leaders lived at the civic-ceremonial centers placed at key locations across the landscape: major river crossings, and at the intersection of trails and major foot paths. Caddo sites are situated primarily on elevated landforms (alluvial terraces and rises, natural levees and upland edges) adjacent to the major streams, as well as along minor tributaries and spring-fed branches, and with proximity to arable sandy loam soils because of good drainage for habitation and cultivation purposes.

The majority of these Caddo sites are:

> "permanent settlements that have evidence of the structures, including posts, pits and features marking their residency, along with the cemeteries and graves where the dead were buried; the middens where the animal and plant food refuse was discarded amidst broken stone tools and pottery vessels; and the material remains of tools and ceramics used in the procurement and processing of the bountiful resources of the region. They represent the settlements of ... communities and sociopolitical entities, and the civic-ceremonial centers that were their focus" (Perttula 1993c: 125).

The distribution of Caddo settlements across the landscape suggests that all habitats were used to some extent, either intensively as locations for the sedentary communities and farmsteads (that may have been occupied for single or multiple generations), or periodically by groups in logistical camps where specific natural resources could be procured by the Caddo in bulk (i.e. hardwood mast or stands of wild plants). Along the Red River, and probably on the other large streams or rivers in the Pineywoods, a particular focus of settlement was along natural levees in recently abandoned meander belts, and these habitats "served as an ideal context for a dispersed community" in a major floodplain landscape (Girard 1997: 156).

The most common types of Caddo settlements in the region during these periods of time appear to be small year-round hamlets and farmsteads with circular to rectangular residential structures. These settlements sometimes occur in association with small household cemeteries, and occasionally with a larger cemetery (>10 burials). Larger communities (covering more than 10 acres/c. 4.4 ha) have also been recognized that occur in association with mound centers, such as the large settlements at the George C. Davis (41CE19), Boxed Springs (41UR30) and Hudnall-Pirtle (41RK4) sites.

Constructed mounds

Both temple and burial mounds were built by these Pineywoods and Post Oak Savannah Caddo groups, from as early as the 9th century to the late 17th century AD. Such mounds may be seen as expressions of power, as their construction was part of the strategy used by elites to secure and consolidate their power over a group of people or a community. Rafferty (2015: 210–13) suggests, on the other hand, that the aboriginal construction of mounds in southeastern North America represent forms of costly signaling and bet-hedging, where the "person or group involved has resources to waste, by giving them away, or by emphasizing effort and energy expended in obtaining the display items."

Such monumental constructions may also be seen as efforts to insure "intensely cooperative human behaviors," as the development of elaborate rituals at such places "inspired gods and created social solidarity" (Norenzayan 2013: 126, 132). Norenzayan (2013: 132–3) has noted that in the archaeological record:

> "the expansion of regularly performed rituals and the construction of religiously significant monumental architecture emerged within the same period with increasing societal size, political complexity, and reliance on agriculture...powerful and moralizing gods likely coevolved with costly regularized rituals, creating a mutually reinforcing package capable of enhancing internal cooperation and harmony, will providing opportunities to outcompete smaller and less well-organized outgroups."

The larger Caddo sites are important civic-ceremonial centers containing multiple mounds and associated villages, and these generally date after c. AD 900 across the major river valleys in East Texas; the smaller mounds at sites such as the Early Caddo Mound Pond site in the Big Cypress Bayou basin appear to represent mounds built over temple structures with sacred fires or other specialized buildings that were periodically burned, destroyed and covered over with mound fill (see Trubitt 2009). The multiple mound centers are rather evenly spaced along the Red River, Sabine River and Big Cypress Bayou, and those that are contemporaneous may represent hierarchical systems of an "integrated ... regional network of interaction and redistribution" (Thurmond 1990: 234).

The distribution, number and spacing of mound centers, particularly the sites with multiple mounds (Fig. 22), in East Texas and adjoining parts of southwestern Arkansas and northwestern Louisiana clearly indicates that the Caddo peoples who built and used these mounds were integrated into societies of considerable socio-political complexity. Shaft burials of high status individuals have been documented in Early to Middle Caddo period mound contexts at George C. Davis (Story 1997;

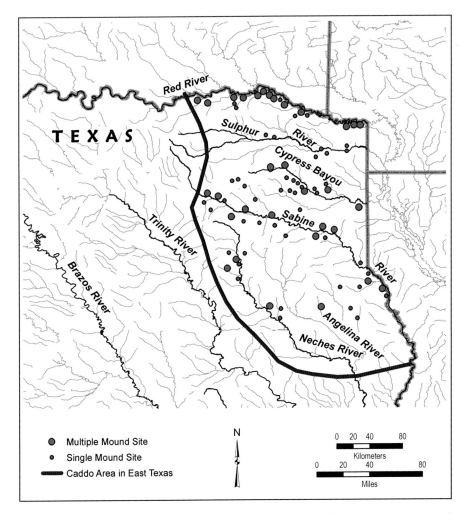

Fig. 22. The distribution of single and multiple mound ancestral Caddo sites in East Texas.

1998; 2000) and a few other mound centers (such as Washington Square, Boxed Springs and Sanders [41LR2]; see Corbin and Hart 1998; Hamilton 1997), as well as Late Caddo period mound contexts at the Pine Tree Mound site (Fields and Gadus 2012a; 2012b) and the Morse Mound site (Middlebrook 2014) in the Sabine River basin, and they also occur in non-mound contexts at several sites along the Red River during this period of time (see Bruseth 1998).

The Early Caddo sites with constructed mounds were likely the nexus of different Caddo communities, as they contained evidence of mounds and ritual buildings (on top of as well as underneath the mounds), and religious practices and ceremonies that were conducted at the sites and in the temples and other important buildings on the mounds, were key to integrating different farmsteads and households in different East Texas Caddo communities and binding them together. The construction of earthen mounds at these Caddo sites was certainly an important part of religious life and ritual in these East Texas Caddo societies. The rituals that were carried out in important structures at these mound sites not only would have fulfilled religious obligations (see Miller 1996), but as Spielmann

(2009: 179) notes, these rituals would have been a source of political power, "in that people with ritual knowledge have political influence. In addition, those who are able to organize elaborate ritual performances and feasts gain a measure of prestige within their societies." Such rituals would also be the context for much social interaction between members of the Caddo communities that frequented the mound centers and viewed them as key places in the landscape of their communities.

Anderson and Sassaman (2012: 168) have noted that the construction of monumental earthen architecture was an important aspect of post-AD 900–1000 life in eastern North American, as it was in the Caddo area. In fact, Steponaitis *et al.* (2015: 15) suggest that ancestral Caddo communities adopted a mound architectural pattern from Coles Creek cultural groups in the lower Mississippi Valley, a pattern "in which ceremonial centers typically consisted of two to four platform mounds arranged around an open plaza ... The newer platform mounds tended to be larger than their predecessors and show more stages of construction, suggesting greater continuity of use."

Accordingly, mounds are a key aspect of the archaeological record that has been used to assess and judge the complexity and socio-political organization of aboriginal peoples (see Anderson 2012) and the relationships of peoples to "creation, the sources of life, and the intersection of cosmic and human fields" (Pauketat 2013: 165). The archaeological evidence gathered from the mound sites can lend insights into such realms (e.g., what Pauketat (2013: 164) refers to as cosmic deposits).

It is apparently the case that at a number of the Caddo sites with multiple mounds, the mounds were constructed in a northeast to southwest alignment that likely corresponds to the lunar cycle of maximum moonrise and maximum moonset. This practice was common in Mississippian sites in the Southeast and in the Cahokia region (see Pauketat 2013; forthcoming; Pauketat *et al.* 2017; Romain 2015). The Caddo peoples had a special relationship to the Moon, and their chief priests were known as *xinesi* (or *tsah neeshi*), translated as Mr Moon (Miller 1996: 256). As Emerson (2015: 58) notes, the Caddo peoples "had strong ties to Earth Mother and her association with death, the moon and the evening star." The Earth Mother was linked "with snakes and death, agricultural abundance, the moon and the bringing of domesticates and farming skills." The Morning Star and Evening Star are also important parts of Caddo creation myths (see Dorsey 1905; Emerson *et al.* 2016: 421).

Many of the mounds at Early Caddo sites were platforms built to elevate and/or cap important structures that were used for religious and political rituals and ceremonies conducted by religious and political leaders in Caddo communities, and the actual construction of the mounds using different colored and textured mound fills had important ritual and symbolic meanings, such that "the act of construction itself was a ritual process intended to serve its own religious and social purposes" (Kidder and Sherwood 2016). The volumes of the mounds likely indicate that their construction required "the cooperative activity of ... larger numbers of people and presumably multiple social groups" (Anderson and Sassaman 2012: 167).

Other Early Caddo mounds were often constructed to hold burials, usually multiple interments, and are very similar to shaft tombs at the Gahagan (Webb and Dodd 1939) and Mounds Plantation (Webb and McKinney 1975) sites on the Red River in northwest Louisiana, the Crenshaw site on the Red River in southwest Arkansas (H. E. Jackson *et al.* 2012; Perttula *et al.* 2014b; Samuelsen 2014; Schambach 1982b), and the George C. Davis (Story 1997; 1998) and Boxed Springs (Perttula 2011a) sites on the Neches and Sabine rivers in East Texas.

Specifically, Early Caddo period multiple mound centers were present on the Sabine River at the Boxed Springs (41UR30) and Hudnall-Pirtle (41RK4) sites, and more than 40 miles/64 km to the southwest at the George C. Davis site (41CE19) on the Neches River (see Fig. 3). The distance between mound centers in Early Caddo times suggests that the local region was not heavily populated since there are actually few Caddo habitation sites of this age even known in East Texas.

Certainly the most thoroughly studied Formative Caddo and Early Caddo period site in East Texas is the George C. Davis site, a large village and mound center (covering *c.* 120 acres/48.5 ha) on a fertile alluvial terrace of the Neches River, just east of the river crossing on El Camino Real de los Tejas, an ancient Caddo trail (Figs 23–24). This mound center has extensive habitation areas, plazas, and spatially restricted temple platform and burial mound locales (Newell and Krieger 1949; Story 1997; 1998; 2000). Shaft burials of high status individuals (i.e. the political and religious elite) have been documented in mound contexts during a 250 year period of the site's occupation.

There were three mounds at the George C. Davis site, including Mound A (a flat-topped platform), Mound C (burial mound) built over a large pre-mound burial pit in the latter part of the Formative Caddo period and containing an estimated 25–30 elite burial pits (with 75–100 individuals interred in those deep burial pits), and Mound B, a second flat-topped platform; this platform was constructed about AD 1200 or slightly earlier over a large circular structure, likely a fire temple. Calibrated radiocarbon dates from village and mound contexts establish that the site was occupied beginning by about the mid-9th century AD, and then was apparently continuously settled until the end of the 13th century, although the settlement became smaller and less complex sometime in that century (Fig. 25a–b).

A large number of structures were built on, and adjacent to, Mound A (*c.* 90 × 80 m in size,

Fig. 23. Early Caddo sites mentioned in the text: 1. George C. Davis; 2. Boxed Springs; 3. Hudnall-Pirtle; 4. Oak Hill; 5. Hale; 6. Mound Pond; 7. T. N. Coles; 8. A. C. Mackin; 9. Joe Meyer Estate #1; 10. Taddlock; 11. Henry Chapman; 12. R. L. Jaggers; 13. Spider Knoll; 14. Bentsen-Clark; 15. Ray.

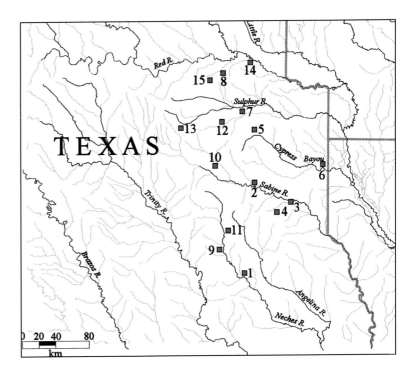

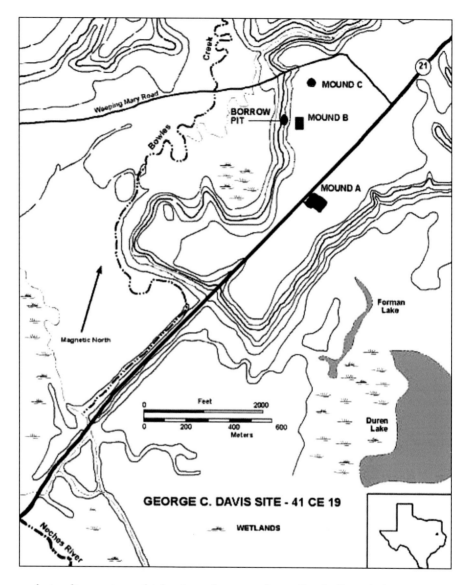

and standing *c.* 4.5 m high when the mound was finished), and the extensive structure rebuilding there indicates the area (referred to as an Inner Precinct) was preferred for settlement by the Caddo (Fig. 26). Several special purpose structures (i.e. temples or public buildings) had also been constructed on the terrace surface, and when they were no longer in use the first platform of Mound A was built over their remains. All told, an estimated six different buildings stood on the mound platforms as they were continually being built and rebuilt; there were eight buildings under the mound that were covered up by the first platform stages, and 26 other structures were built in the immediate vicinity of the platform mound.

Mound B, about 37 × 31 m in size and 2 m in height, was constructed in several platform stages over the top of at least two large circular wood and grass-covered structures or temples with prepared clay floors that were built on the ground

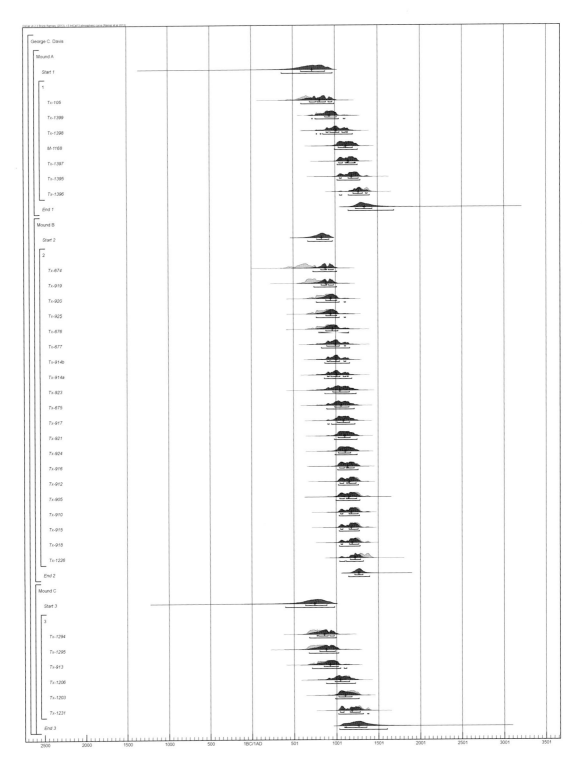

Modelled date (BC/AD)

a

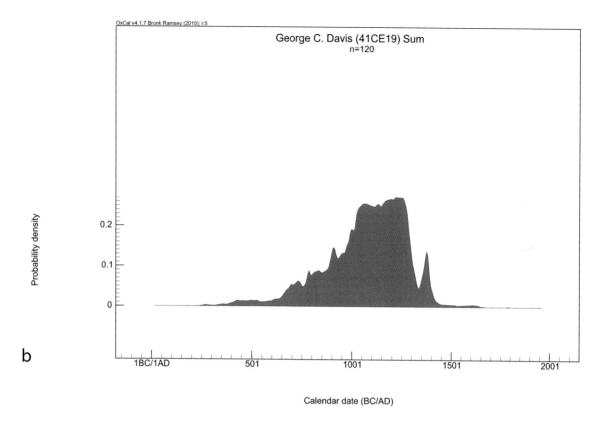

OxCal v4.1.7 Bronk Ramsey (2010); r:5

George C. Davis (41CE19) Sum
n=120

Probability density

Calendar date (BC/AD)

b

Fig. 25. Calibrated radiocarbon dates from the George C. Davis site: a. calibrated dates from Mounds A–C; b. the probability density of calibrated radiocarbon dates (images provided courtesy of Robert Z. Selden, Jr)

surface (Fig. 27); it is possible that other structures stood on these platforms. One of the structures was very large (18 m in diameter), and had been deliberately burned and then capped with mound fill. Ramps were built on three sides of the mound to reach the platform top.

Mound C is a flat-topped (46 × 38 m in size, and 6 m in height) burial mound and special mortuary that was used by the Caddo community for the burial of the social, political and religious elite (Story 1997: 64–5). Six stages (I–VI) of tombs were found within the mound. The first stage (Feature 134) is a sub-mound burial, and Stages II–VI represent mound surfaces from which different shaft tombs originated. Although the burial features and construction of Mound C are not well dated by radiocarbon assays, the six stages of burials and mound surfaces may have been in use for *c.* 250 or more years, from perhaps as early as cal. AD 903–1157 (2 sigma) to at least cal. AD 1163–1299 (2 sigma).

The mortuary program of burial tombs (some as large as 9 × 7.5 m in size, and 7 m deep) of these individuals began with a sub-mound burial crypt or log tomb (Feature 134), surrounded by a yellow clay berm, that had eight individuals (some probably sacrificed retainers) laid out in it. Once this tomb collapsed, creating a depression in the area enclosed by the berm, it was covered by the first of five stages of mound fill. Other shaft tombs were eventually excavated by the Caddo from four of the flat-topped burial mound platforms, followed by a final sediment capping event, and the mound platforms were marked by different kinds and colors of fill

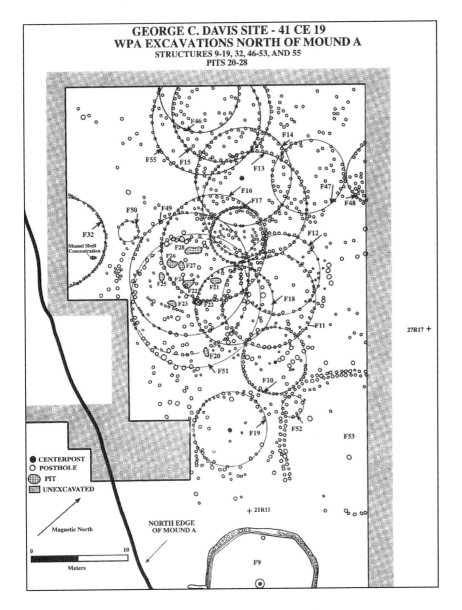

GEORGE C. DAVIS SITE - 41 CE 19
WPA EXCAVATIONS NORTH OF MOUND A
STRUCTURES 9-19, 32, 46-53, AND 55
PITS 20-28

● CENTERPOST
○ POSTHOLE
⊕ PIT
▨ UNEXCAVATED

Magnetic North

NORTH EDGE
OF MOUND A

0   10
Meters

Fig. 26. Area of overlapping structures adjacent to Mound A at the George C. Davis site (Story 1998: 29 and Fig. 2-14: reproduced courtesy of Texas Archeological Research Laboratory, University of Texas at Austin)

"perhaps to symbolize the uniqueness of each mound-building event and the associated burials. These contrasts also ... may have served as a visual indicator for the succession of individuals who for over perhaps 10 or more generations supervised the mound construction" (Story 1998: 14).

Many of the offerings placed with the individuals in the tombs include caches of marine shells, copper (in Stage I–IV burials), stone tools, celts and other artifacts that were made from exotic raw materials, indicating the importance to the Caddo religious, social and political elite of obtaining unique and exotic goods to symbolize their paramount authority within the community. The range of offerings is striking, including clusters of ground stone celts (n=19) and caches of

Fig. 27. *(opposite top)* Excavations in Mound B at the George C. Davis site

Fig. 28. *(opposite bottom)* Ritual caches of Alba arrow points and Gahagan knives in Feature 134, George C. Davis site (image courtesy of the Texas Archeological Research Laboratory, University of Texas at Austin)

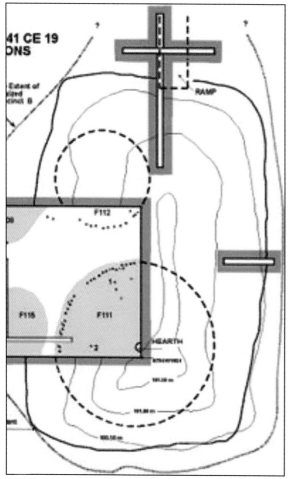

arrow (*ba?*) points (n=353), some in quivers (*chaba?*); large Gahagan bifaces (n=20) (Fig. 28); boatstones (n=3) and plummets (n=1); a notched axe; stone ear spools (n=14, and sometimes copper-covered); grooved and ungrooved sandstone tablets (n=20); a sandstone disk; a sandstone abrader; polished pebble stones; a perforated discoidal or chunky stone; a copper ornament that may have been in the hair or on a headdress; a copper, wood and conch shell disc-shaped ornament or badge; ceramic vessels (primarily of the Holly Fine Engraved type, n=12); a long-stemmed Red River clay pipe (see Hoffman 1967); marine conch shell containers or dippers (n=2) and beads; a marine gastropod bead waist band; pearl beads in necklaces and bracelets; mussel shells (including perforated valves and ornaments); tortoise shells (including part of a rattle); bone pins (n=75); a bison bone rib; deer ulna flaking tools and awls (n=4); beaver and bear (*?nawtsi?*) teeth; *Lithospermum* seed beads; wood objects (including ear spools) covered with thin sheet copper; several stone human and bird effigy pipes; red ochre; and clay pigments of several different colors (see Story 1997: 21–53).

Recent remote sensing investigations (Fig. 29) indicate that there are more than 78 structures (and as many as 84, based on partial structure arcs visible in the remote sensing data) in the village areas around the three mounds, including structures with four center posts around a central hearth (Fig. 30a–c) (see Creel *et al.* 2005; 2008; Osburn *et al.* 2008; Walker 2009). Previous excavations in the 1940s, and then in the 1970s and later, had uncovered more than ten structures in various other places across the site. Most of these structures were circular in shape, and were apparently grass- and thatch-covered wood pole domiciles (Fig. 31a–b), with central hearths, but there are rectangular and sub-square structures as well as several possible granaries. In the village areas, there may be several courtyards or small plazas between structures, and these common areas may represent the compounds of kin- or clan-related families.

The George C. Davis site was apparently the premier civic and ceremonial center for Caddo groups in the Neches-Angelina River basins for

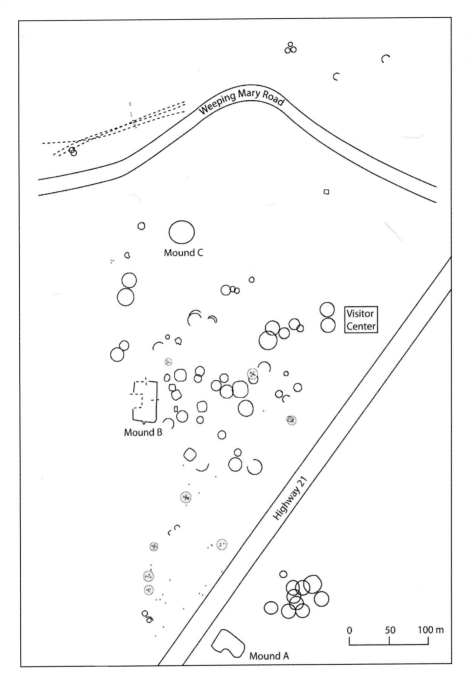

Fig. 29. Structures recorded as part of the TARL/UT magnetometer survey of the George C. Davis site (from Schultz 2010: fig. 132)

more than 300 years. The radiocarbon dating of the George C. Davis and Washington Square Mound (41NA49) sites, the main multiple mound centers in the basins, suggests that the Washington Square Mound center began to flourish about the time (after *c.* AD 1250) the George C. Davis site was diminishing in power and social authority (see Chapter 5). The Caddo community that built and used the Washington Square Mound site likely achieved pre-eminence at the expense of

Fig. 30. Archaeological and remote sensing features from the George C. Davis site magnetometer data: a. example of circular structure (Feature 125); b. Feature 242 "Button House"; c. Feature 237 "Button House"

Fig. 31. Experimental Caddo structure built at Caddo Mounds State Historic Site (the George C. Davis site) using traditional materials (see Perttula and Skiles 2014): a. wood pole framework; b. grass lashed to the wood pole framework

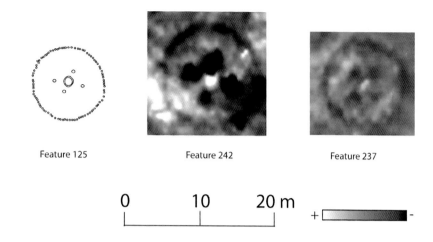

Feature 125   Feature 242   Feature 237

0   10   20 m

the long-lasting polity on the Neches River. The George C. Davis site was essentially abandoned as a mound center by the early 14th century.

One of the largest of the Early Caddo multiple mound centers in East Texas is the Hudnall-Pirtle site on an alluvial terrace of the Sabine River. The ancestral Caddo settlement covers more than 50 acres/20.2 ha of the terrace (Bruseth and Perttula 2006).

The site has eight constructed mounds (A–G), likely platform, house and burial mounds, around a large central plaza (Fig. 32), extensive habitation area in a broad circular area near and outside the mounds and plaza, and several large borrow pits (Bruseth and Perttula 2006; fig. 30). Other than a looter trench in Mound C, thought to have been the burial mound for the social and political elite in the community, the only other excavation in the mounds at the Hudnall-Pirtle site was a trench in Mound F. This trench excavation disclosed the remnants of a burned house with 2 sigma calibrated radiocarbon dates that range from AD 1014–1275.

Habitation debris is extensive at the Hudnall-Pirtle site, particularly sherds from plain, fine and utility ware vessels, long-stemmed Red River clay pipes, and ceramic ear spools. Identified ceramic types are consistent with other Early Caddo sites in the southern part of East Texas, and this led Story (2000: fig. 5) to include it in the Early Caddo Alto phase along with the George C. Davis site. Approximately 78% of the decorated sherds are from wet paste-decorated utility wares.

Lithic artifacts are dominated by unifacial expedient flake tools and chipped stone arrow points (primarily of the Alba type, but also including Colbert, Homan and Catahoula types),

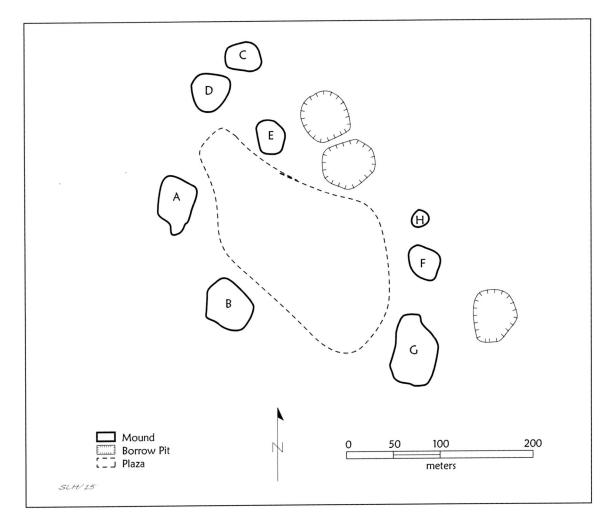

Mound
Borrow Pit
Plaza

0   50   100   200
meters

N

SLH/15

and there are also Gahagan bifaces and celts in the tool kit, along with grinding slabs and manos. The wide variety of chipped and ground stone tools at the Hudnall-Pirtle site indicates that a diverse range of domestic tasks took place in each part of the site during the Early Caddo occupation. Local cherts were the most common raw material in the habitation areas, but non-local lithic raw materials were best represented in the southwestern part of the village; these materials included novaculite and baked/fused chert from the Manning Formation in the southern part of East Texas (see Brown 1976). A single copper bead was found in midden deposits in the southwestern part of the village areas; this is one of the few instances in the southern Caddo area where copper artifacts are found in non-mound and non-burial contexts (see Girard and Perttula 2016, table 1).

Fritz's (2006; 133–7) analysis of the recovered paleobotanical remains from features in the village at the Hudnall-Pirtle site indicates that maize was common in the plant assemblage, along with hickory and acorn mast. Edible native seeds were very uncommon, leading Fritz (2006: 137) to note that

Fig. 32. Plan of the mounds, plaza and borrow pits at the Hudnall-Pirtle mound center

"there is no evidence for serious use of starchy temperate seed crops...in northeastern Texas at any point in time. This distinguishes the southern Caddos from societies in the Arkansas River valley, such as Spiro and Toltec..., from groups in the Ozarks..., and from peoples in the central Mississippi River valley."

The Boxed Springs (41UR30) mound center is another Early Caddo multiple mound center on terrace and upland landforms immediately adjacent to the Sabine River, situated just upstream from the confluence of Big Sandy Creek with the river. The site had been known since the late 1950s–early 1960s, and avocational archaeologists had conducted excavations in Mound A, a burial mound, as well as several other mounds that apparently were built to cover burned special purpose structures (Perttula and Wilson 2000). A large Early Caddo period cemetery in the northern part of the site, with more than 100 interments, was looted there in the 1980s by local East Texas pothunters.

The Early Caddo occupation at the Boxed Springs site consists of four earthen mounds, one used for shaft tomb burial, the large cemetery well away from the mounds and habitation debris, and a number of habitation areas dispersed across this +30 acre/+12 ha civic-ceremonial site; whether these habitation areas are domestic locales, or the locales of the social and political elite, has not been determined (Fig. 33). Important and powerful individuals lived in the Boxed Springs community, and were buried there. The four mounds apparently included two low "structural" or house mounds with prepared clay floors at the southeastern and southwestern ends of the plaza, one burial mound about 12 × 8 m in size and 1 m in height at the northwestern plaza edge, and a flat-topped mound of unknown function at the northeastern end of the plaza. There were borrow pits, and occupation areas/midden deposits along the uplands at the southern edge of the site as well as north and northwest of one of the mounds.

Excavations in Mound A encountered a cremated burial of a single individual at a depth of c. 1.1 m below surface (hereafter

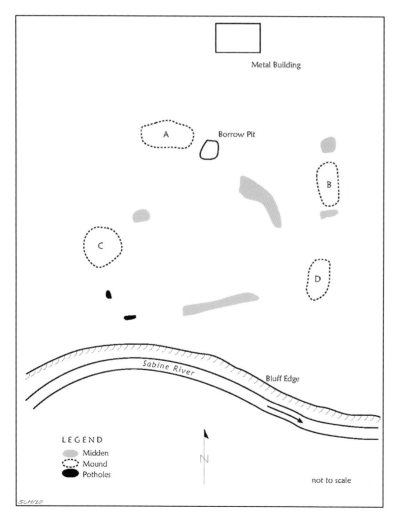

Fig. 33. Map of the Boxed Springs site (41UR30) in the Sabine River basin

bs); the mound was a maximum of 1.83 m in height and 10.7 × 13.1 m in length and width. With the removal of all the mound fill, a large circular clay berm was exposed near the base of the mound (Fig. 34). This red sandy clay berm was 0.6 m in width and 16 cm thick, and marked the area around a large clay- and sand-filled pit that extended approximately 0.9–1.2 m below the original ground surface under the mound; the top of the berm was between 0.6–1.2 m below the top of the mound (Fig. 35). The pit was 3.8 × 4.1 m in size, and had rounded corners and slightly sloping walls. The upper and central portion of the pit had a white sand

Fig. 34. Clay berm at the base of Mound A at the Boxed Springs site

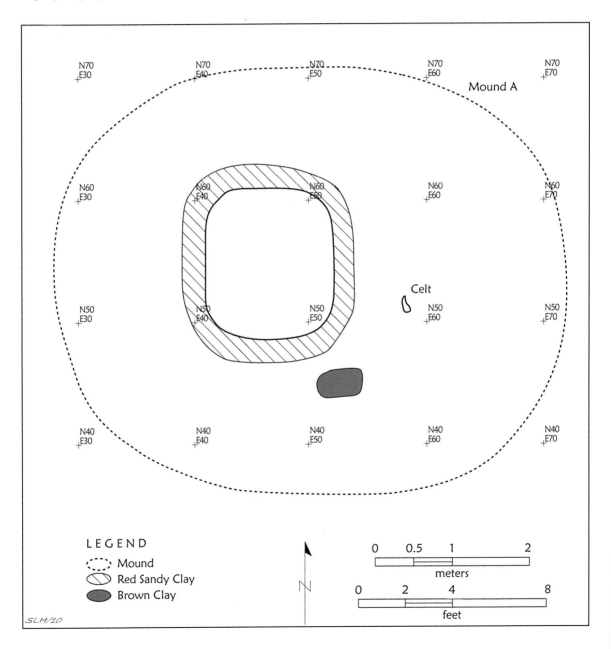

LEGEND

- Mound
- Red Sandy Clay
- Brown Clay

0   0.5   1   2
meters

0   2   4   8
feet

SLH/10

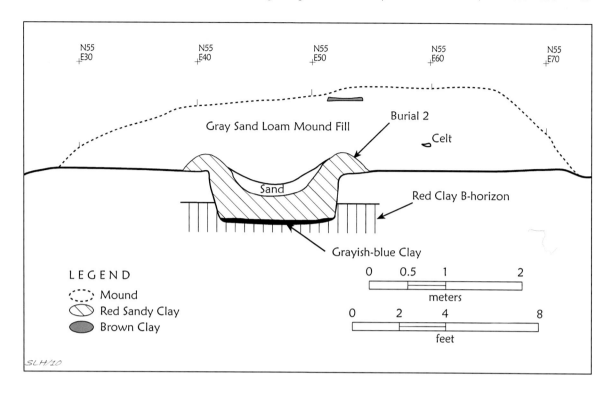

Fig. 35. Profile of Mound A and Burial 2 at the Boxed Springs site

fill, with the remainder of the fill and berm grading from a sandy red clay to a very dense red clay just above the floor. The pit floor was covered with a 2.5–5 cm thick lens of bluish-gray clay, probably obtained from Pleistocene alluvial deposits along the Sabine River.

The pit feature at Boxed Springs, Burial 2, contained three sets of teeth enamel along the eastern side of the pit (Fig. 36). The broad spacing of the teeth (*ta?uh*) enamel suggests that Burial 2 contained the bodies of three individuals that were laid out east-west, with their heads (*kantuh*) facing west. Most of the artifacts placed on the floor of the burial pit were along the north side of the feature, north of the third set of teeth enamel, although three of the clusters of arrow points were in the central and southern part of the feature, and one ceramic vessel (V. 5, a plain bottle) was near the eastern pit wall. Overall, funerary objects placed in Burial 2 included two large chipped stone bifaces, five ground stone celts, several polished stones, a ferruginous sandstone tool, four clusters of arrow points and seven ceramic vessels (V. 1 through V. 7).

Burial 2 in Mound A likely represented a tomb of a powerful individual within this Early Caddo community. He or she was buried with two individuals or retainers, along with many material items, including perishable things, that were intended for the use of this individual in the ancestral world. There were several other important people in the community, as there were individuals buried in the non-mound cemetery that were accompanied with Gahagan bifaces, arrow point clusters and ear spools, markers of social rank.

The large and well-made chipped stone bifaces were found together on the

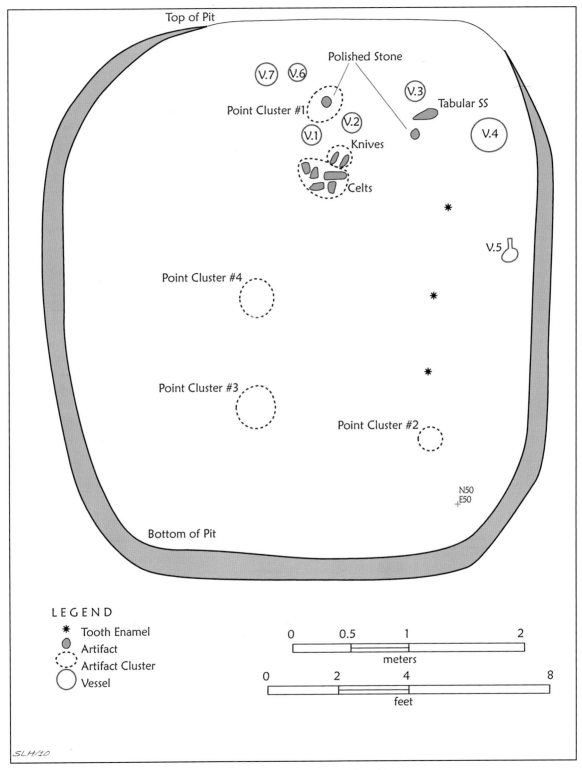

Fig. 36. Plan map of Burial 2 in Mound A at the Boxed Springs site

northern side of the pit, and immediately next to five ground stone celts. Both of the large bifaces appear to have been made from non-local cherts from Central Texas sources. The larger biface (about 16 cm in length) is a Gahagan biface (Shafer 1973: 224 and fig. 19), while the other compares well with the Group 2 bifaces at the George C. Davis site (Shafer 1973: fig. 19w).

The ferruginous sandstone tool is a tabular piece about 20 cm in length and 4 cm in width, with straight and smoothed edges. The Boxed Springs tool resembles tabular sandstone saws recovered in Early Caddo contexts at the George C. Davis site (Shafer 1973: 317 and fig. 25h–i). It was placed between V. 3 and V. 4, and near a polished pebble.

The two polished stones are pebble-sized pieces of chert that may have been used to polish ceramic vessels after they had been successfully fired. One of the polished stones was near the ferruginous sandstone tabular tool, and the other was amidst arrow point cluster #1 in the northern part of the burial pit. One mano was apparently found in close association with Burial 1.

The five celts in Burial 2 were found cached together near the northernmost set of teeth enamel, and immediately south of the two large chipped bifaces and V. 1, a plain bottle. The celts were made from non-local metamorphic or igneous raw materials originating in the Ouachita Mountains of southeastern Oklahoma and southwestern Arkansas, and at least one may be diorite or Hatton tuff.

There were four clusters of arrow points in Burial 2. Cluster #1, at the northern end of the pit, had 55 specimens. They apparently were not on shafts or in a quiver when they were placed in the burial pit, because they were turned in various directions. Arrow point cluster #2 had four specimens, while cluster #3 had 36 points and cluster #4 had five arrow points. All the cluster #3 points were pointing south and probably were shafted and in a quiver. The direction of the cluster #2 and #4 arrow points was not determined. These three arrow point clusters were placed in the central and southern parts of the pit, in apparent association with the central and southern sets of tooth enamel.

Stylistically, the arrow points from Burial 2 at Boxed Springs are rather morphologically homogeneous. Most have square or parallel stems with squared barbs and flat bases, or have square/parallel stems with concave bases (Alba type) or expanding stems and flat to convex bases (Homan) (Fig. 37). Several of the square stemmed points have more sweeping barbs, similar to the Catahoula type, and there are a few specimens with a diamond-shaped stem comparable to the Hayes type. A variety of raw materials were used in the manufacture of the Boxed Springs arrow points, including fine-grained and coarse-grained quartzite, local cherts of brown (*hakuunu?*) and yellow hues, and high quality cherts that probably originated in the Ouachita Mountains and/or Red River gravels (see Banks 1990).

The seven ceramic vessels in Burial 2 cluster in the northern end of the pit. Vessel 1 is a plain bottle, and Vessel 2 is a small (*c.* 10 cm in height) Spiro Engraved beaker. These vessels were placed between arrow point cluster #1, the two large chipped bifaces and the five celts. Vessel 3 is a 13 cm tall everted rim jar with a pinched body and a zoned incised-cane punctated decoration on the rim. It was placed immediately north of the tabular ferruginous sandstone tool and 0.60 m east of arrow point cluster #1. Vessels 4 and 5 lay along the eastern side of the

Fig. 37. Homan arrow points from Burial 2. The material is claystone with the exception of DD, which is Boone chert, and II, which is siltstone (images provided by the Texas Archeological Research Laboratory at University of Texas at Austin)

burial pit, between the pit wall and the central and northernmost sets of tooth enamel. Vessel 4 is a large plain carinated bowl, and Vessel 5 is a plain bottle with a straight neck and a globular-shaped body. The bottle stands *c.* 23 cm tall. Vessels 6 and 7 were placed next to each other at the northern end of the Burial 2 pit, between 15–30 cm north-northwest of arrow point cluster #1. Both are plain jars.

Domesticated corn was grown at the site, based on the recovery of charred plant remains from features (Bush 2011), and a variety of wild plants and animals also were collected as part of the diet of the Caddo people that lived there. The site appears to be contemporaneous with the earliest part of the Alto phase component at the George C. Davis site on the Neches River, dating as the latter does from the mid-9th to the mid-11th century AD, but may have been occupied through the end of the 13th century.

The ancestral Caddo occupation extends north–south distance *c.* 800 m, beginning at the Sabine River bluff line on the south, and ranged between *c.* 100–180 m east–west. Based primarily on the distribution of more than 100 shovel tests with Caddo material remains, the highest densities of ceramic vessel sherds occur in eight different habitation areas (Areas I–VIII) across the site. These areas occur on low sandy rises and narrow ridges across the landform, and they ranged in size from 300–4900 m². One area had midden deposits (Area I), two others (Areas IV and V) were situated by an open community area or possible plaza between the four known mounds, and Area VII was situated on a landform that juts out towards the Sabine River floodplain (Fig. 38).

A comparison of the Boxed Springs site ceramic assemblage to other Early Caddo period sites in East Texas, northwest Louisiana and southwest Arkansas, suggested that the ceramic assemblages from these sites are diverse in decorative treatment

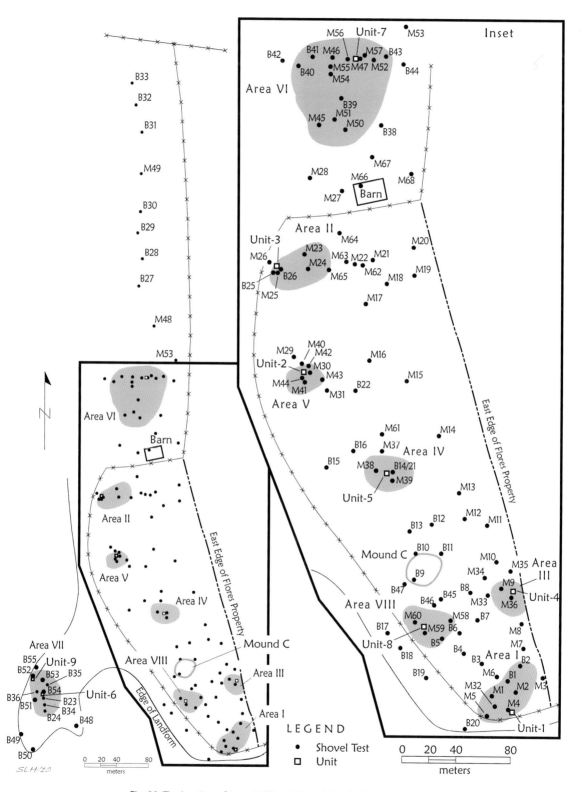

Fig. 38. The location of Areas I–VIII and Mound C at the Boxed Springs site

as well as in the relative abundance of both plain wares and engraved wares, particularly from east to west across the area from the Red River to the Neches River (Perttula 2011a). This diversity in vessel decoration (and likely also a diversity in vessel forms) would support the notion that there were several different Caddo groups and their associated ceramic traditions in this region between *c.* AD 850/900 and up to *c.* AD 1200 that were developing their own social and ceramic stylistic expressions and practices. Coles Creek Incised sherds are present in several Early Caddo sites in East Texas including Boxed Springs. The most common variety is *var. Coles Creek* (Phillips 1970), and this variety apparently dates from *c.* AD 900–1050 in Early Caddo contexts as well as in sites in the lower Ouachita River valley in the Lower Mississippi Valley. The presence of Coles Creek Incised, *var. Coles Creek* vessels and decorated sherds at the Boxed Springs site may be the best evidence currently available that some part of the Early Caddo occupation there may have taken place primarily before AD 1050.

The occurrence of two other pottery types in several East Texas, northwest Louisiana and southwest Arkansas sites provided insights into the age of the Caddo settlement at Boxed Springs: Crenshaw Fluted ceramic sherds and vessels and Hollyknowe Ridge Pinched sherds; both types were identified in the ceramic assemblage at Boxed Springs. Crenshaw Fluted vessels were present in the Early Caddo component at the Crenshaw site, with radiocarbon dates that range from cal. AD 1150–1222 (2 sigma). Calibrated radiocarbon-dated East Texas and northwest Louisiana sites with Hollyknowe Ridge Pinched sherds and/or vessels have age ranges of cal. AD 978–1260 (Hanna), cal. AD 980–1250 (Hudnall-Pirtle), cal. AD 989–1146 (Mounds Plantation, Mound 2) and cal. AD 1150–1222 (Crenshaw, Early Caddo component); together, these range from cal AD 978–1222. The two radiocarbon dates from the Boxed Springs Caddo occupation range from cal. AD 990–1230 (Perttula 2011a).

The lithic artifacts from the Boxed Springs site provide important assemblage-specific as well as comparative information about the character of lithic tools, tool production and the access to non-local lithic raw materials at an Early Caddo ceremonial center. The various tools in the assemblages included 165 arrow points (mainly Homan and Alba points); six Gahagan bifaces, one Ramey-like knife; bifaces (n=3); adzes and perforators (n=2); flake tools and scrapers (n=2); hammerstones and hammerstone/anvils (n=3); abrader-saws (n=3); slabs (n=1); celts (n=13); and polishing stones (n=4). There were also 13 cores and 526 pieces of lithic debris. The extra-territorial connections represented in the tools and lithic debris are strikingly different when compared to sites such as George C. Davis in the Neches River basin, or Bentsen-Clark on the Red River. The ceramic stylistic data discussed above suggest that the Boxed Springs socio-cultural relationships strongly point toward the Caddo peoples living along the Red River above its Great Bend.

Shafer (2011) determined that the Boxed Springs settlement, like most Caddo settlements in East Texas, was a consumer of stone tools, rather than a producer. This was the product of the poor locally available lithic resources, which included small pebbles of orthoquartzite and chert from reworked Uvalde gravels and reworked orthoquartzites and Ouachita Mountain cherts from gravels. Prestigious items such as the Gahagan knives (*kat*) and celts made on non-local lithic raw

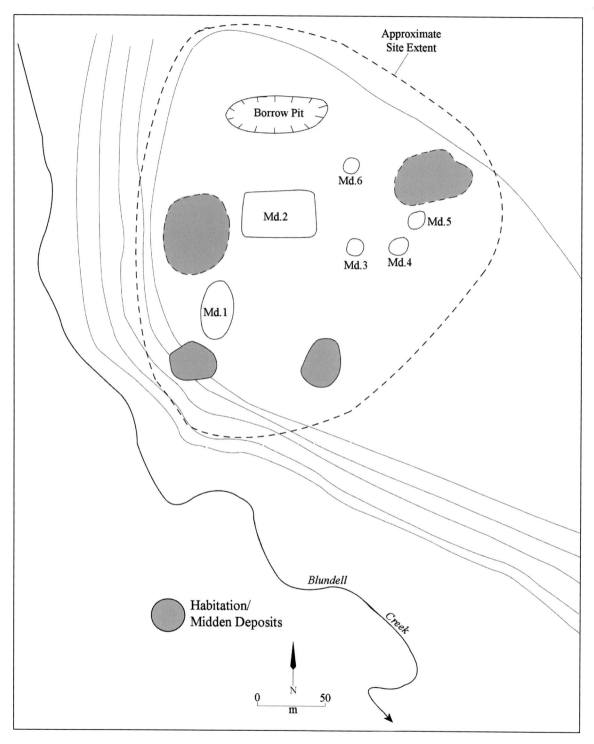

Fig. 39. Map of the L. A. Hale site (41TT12) showing relationship of constructed mounds, habitation/midden deposits, and borrow pit area

materials had to be either exchanged through trade or acquired through gifting. These lithic artifacts were found in tombs of important people at Boxed Springs. As Shafer (2011: 103) noted: "[t]hese were people of power in their societies, wielded power over their people, and were revered, or feared, by their rivals." The different kinds of non-local lithic artifacts came from sources along the Red River and in southeastern Oklahoma, as well as Central Texas, in the case of the Gahagan and Ramey-like knives. The raw material and style of the arrow points in tombs at Boxed Springs also points toward the Red River as a source area.

The L. A. Hale Mound site (41TT12) is situated on a broad alluvial terrace of Blundell Creek, a southward-flowing tributary to Big Cypress Creek. The excavations at the site by the University of Texas at Austin (UT) were completed in May 1934. The principal component at the site is an Early Caddo mound center with extensive midden deposits. There are six mounds at the site, two large platform mounds (Mounds 1 and 2) and four low mounds that cover occupational deposits and burned house structures. There are also four large midden areas adjacent to the earthen mounds as well as at least one borrow pit. UT excavations were in the two platform mounds and three of the small mounds (Mounds Nos 3–5) (Perttula 2014c) (Fig. 39).

The mounds at the Hale site likely were built at different times to elevate and/ or cap important structures that were used for religious and political rituals and ceremonies conducted by religious and political leaders in a Big Cypress Creek basin Caddo community. The mounds were constructed between the 11th and 13th centuries and required the cooperation of large numbers of people and likely multiple social groups. Mound No. 1 at Hale had structural deposits in several zones, marked by concentrated ash zones, a large pit or hearth in association with a thick brick-hard burned soil, and a burned structural zone likely atop the original ground surface; there was also one human cremation in the lower depths of the mound deposits. Mound No. 2 was built over a burned house or temple floor marked by a c. 20 cm thick zone of hard-packed ash. Very little evidence of occupational debris was encountered in any of the Mound No. 2 zones. Mound No. 3 was built over another important burned Caddo structure. On archaeological grounds, primarily the decorated ceramics, ceramic pipe sherds, and Alba arrow points, the Hale site mounds were built and occupied as early as cal. AD 1050 and as late as cal. AD 1200.

The analysis of recovered ceramics from the Hale site indicates that most are from grog-tempered plain and utility ware vessels. Approximately 43% of the rims in the ceramic assemblage are from plain wares (from carinated bowls, simple bowls and jars). Utility ware sherds are dominated by sherds from incised, punctated and incised-punctated vessels. Utility ware types identified in the assemblage include Coles Creek Incised, *var. unspecified*, Canton Incised, Crockett Curvilinear Incised, Davis Incised, Dunkin Incised, Kiam Incised and Weches Fingernail Impressed, *var. Weches*. The engraved sherds from the Hale site are from bowls and carinated bowls as well as bottles. The fine ware sherds are primarily from Holly Fine Engraved and Spiro Engraved vessels. There is a rim from an engraved variety of East Incised, and there are also rims from Hickory Engraved bowls. There are red-slipped sherds from Mound No. 1 and Mound No. 5 excavations.

Other material culture remains from the Hale site include Red River long-stemmed pipe sherds, a possible clay figurine fragment, bone tools (from Mounds No. 1 and No. 5), an alligator (*kuhuh*) tooth pendant from Mound No. 1, and a variety of stone tools, a quartz crystal pebble and cobble-sized pieces of stones and clay used as pigments; the latter are all from Mound No. 1. Among the chipped stone tools are Alba and corner-notched arrow points, and one finished biface. A single ground stone celt was found on the surface of the site.

The Mound Pond site (41HS12) lies on the south, or right, bank of Big Cypress Creek in the upper reaches of Caddo Lake. This is within 50 m of a small meander lake (a relict channel of Big Cypress Creek) known as Mound Pond, and approximately 300 m from a horseshoe bend in the creek to the northwest.

The site is marked by a low, flat-topped earthen mound and habitation areas both near the mound and more than 50 m from it. The mound was *c.* 30 m in diameter and 1.85 m high at the mound center. Another earthen mound (41HS29) is approximately 200–300 m west of Mound Pond. The mound there was conical, about *c.* 18.4–21.4 m in diameter and *c.* 2.7–3.0 m in height.

Excavations in the mound at the Mound Pond site disclosed that a structure had been built on the alluvial terrace surface, along with some midden deposits, then the structure was burned, followed by the construction of a small sandy mound (16–18 m in diameter and *c.* 1 m in height) over the burned structure (Goode *et al.* 2015); a semi-circular sand berm was built along the eastern half of the mound. After some years, Caddo peoples returned and enlarged the mound. This was the second stage of mound building, and it appears that only the margins were added to while the central portion was left as it was. The Stage 2 mound likely served as a platform for the first structure on the mound. The third stage of mound building was the most complex, as it encompassed several alternating lenses of clay and sand. A second structure was constructed on the mound platform in Stage 3, the final construction stage in the mound (Fig. 40).

Fig. 40. View to the north of the north wall and floor of block excavations at the Mound Pond site after removal of the midden and the structure floor. This is a work shot without a scale, but the length of the shovel is 140 cm

The assemblage of lithic tools and debitage from Mound Pond consists primarily of debitage from siliceous pebbles from local and regional sources. Red River jasper is the dominant material, the majority acquired from the Red River drainage approximately 30 km to the east. Much smaller samples of most of the lithic resources common to East Texas occur at the site, as well as only one or two specimens of much more distant resources such as novaculite and Central Texas chert.

The most common tool form is the arrow point; blanks and preforms (mostly failures) also contribute to the arrow point-related assemblage (Fig. 41a–c). Among

Fig. 41. Selected tools from Mound Pond: a, arrow point; b–c, arrow point preforms; d–h, utilized flakes; i–j, chipped pebble fragments; k–l, ground stone tool fragments; m, chipped and smoothed hematite; n–o, hammerstones.

the identified arrow points are several of the types common to the Early Caddo period, including Alba and Colbert. Other stone tools, few in number, include utilized flakes for use in cutting and scraping tasks, and possible gravers. Ground, battered and polished tools include a possible axe fragment, two small hammerstones and a few pitted stones and grinding slab fragments.

The mound vs. sub-mound midden deposits have distinctive ceramic assemblages, with a particular abundance of Coles Creek Incised sherds from the sub-mound deposits (Goode *et al.* 2015), although the available radiocarbon dates from the site indicate that there is not that much of a temporal difference between the two assemblages. Two sigma calibrated age ranges for two samples of charred *Carya* sp. nutshells from sub-mound midden deposits range from cal. AD 1030–1220. The mean of the 2 sigma calibration range of the averaged dates is cal. AD 1024–1212. The principal peaks in probability for both dates range from cal. AD 1025–1169 and cal. AD 1150–1220.

A large assemblage of ceramic sherds (n=3063) was recovered from the mound and sub-mound midden deposits. The midden deposits under the mound are dominated by sherds from incised vessels, many of the Coles Creek Incised type, as well as sherds from vessels with incised lines and impressed triangles (also Coles Creek Incised), and a few engraved, pinched, punctated and incised-punctated vessel sherds (Fig. 42a–b). At the Mounds Plantation site on the Red River in Northwest Louisiana, in pre-AD 1050 archaeological deposits, sherds of Coles Creek Incised comprise between 91.6–100% of the decorated sherds, not much different than in the sub-mound midden deposits at the Mound Pond site. At the 9th to late 11th century James Pace mound site (16DS268) on the Sabine river, Coles Creek Incised pottery accounts for 72% of the decorated sherds (Girard 2014).

Incised sherds remain common in both the Mound and Area B assemblages, but with few Coles Creek Incised vessel sherds. More common in these two assemblages, which both date sometime later than the sub-mound midden deposit, are incised-punctated, punctated, band punctated, engraved and slipped sherds. Similar decorated sherd assemblages have been dated to as late as cal AD 1260 at the Boxed Springs site, but engraved sherds constitute 35% of the decorated sherd assemblage there. At Mound Pond, only 8.7% of the decorated sherds are from engraved and/or slipped fine ware vessels (Fig. 43). In northwest Louisiana ceramic assemblages such as that from the Mounds Plantation site, and the Crenshaw site, fine wares are not common before cal AD 1000, and even after that date, engraved wares are not as well represented in these sites compared to contemporaneous East Texas Caddo sites; Mound Pond is thus an important exception when it comes to the use of engraved wares.

The ceramic assemblages from the sub-mound midden and mound deposits at the Mound Pond site are culturally distinctive. The sub-mound midden deposits are defined by the high frequencies of horizontal incised vessels, many of them identified as several varieties of Coles Creek Incised. Very similar Northwest Louisiana ceramic assemblages appear to date from the late 10th to the mid-11th century. The ceramics from the mound deposits at Mound Pond resemble Early Caddo assemblages from both East Texas and northwest Louisiana, with a

Fig. 42a. Coles Creek Incised sherds from the Mound Pond site: a. Coles Creek Incised, *var.* Chase from the sub-mound midden deposits; b. Coles Creek Incised, *var.* Blakely carinated bowl; c–d. Coles Creek Incised, *var.* Mott from the sub-mound midden deposits

considerable number of incised, punctated and incised-punctated vessel sherds, and relatively low frequencies of engraved fine ware sherds.

In comparing the technological character of the mound vs. sub-mound midden ceramic assemblages, grog temper was the preferred temper in the decorated sherds in both ceramic assemblages, although its use is more common in the sub-mound midden deposits. Crushed pieces of burned bone and hematite were also used as tempering materials, particularly in the mound deposits. Data on the firing conditions observed in the decorated sherds from both mound and sub-mound midden contexts indicate that they are from vessels most commonly fired (80–85.8%) in a reducing or low oxygen environment. In the plain wares,

Fig. 42b. Coles Creek Incised, *var. Coles Creek* and Coles Creek Incised, *var. unspecified* rim sherds in the midden deposits at the Mound Pond site: e–f Coles Creek Incised, *var. Coles Creek*; g. Coles Creek Incised, *var. unspecified*

62.0–72.9% of the sherds are from vessels fired in a reducing environment. Finally, sherds from sooted, smudged, or reheated vessels are more common among the decorated wares than they are among the plain wares. These differences in firing conditions between the mound and sub-mound midden deposits, and between the plain and decorated wares, likely relates to the differences in the intended functions and uses of the Mound Pond ceramic wares for cooking, food serving and as containers for liquids in the community.

The T. N. Coles site (41RR3) is an Early Caddo period site with a single burial mound constructed on a tributary to the Sulphur River in East Texas. The mound

Fig. 43. Red-slipped, engraved, and a finely-made Crockett Curvilinear Incised rim sherd from the Mound Pond site: a. exterior red-slipped; b–c. Holly Fine Engraved; d. horizontal and hatched engraved diagonal zone rim; e. Crockett Curvilinear Incised rim sherd

measured 23 m in diameter and stood 3.6 m high. A pit excavated to *c.* 3.6 m below the surface in the mound encountered a large burial pit with multiple interred individuals, including at least two ancestral Caddo individuals with cranially modeled skulls (cf. Derrick and Wilson 1997); these individuals had their skulls bound when they were children to shape or model the cranium in several culturally prescribed ways. Found associated with these individuals were a number of ceramic vessels of the Pennington Punctated-Incised, Holly Fine Engraved, Spiro Engraved and Hickory Engraved types, two conch shell beads, fragments of hammered sheet copper and a large chipped knive (i.e. a Gahagan biface). The range of funerary offerings in this burial feature would seem to indicate that it was clearly associated with the death and interment of important religious or political individuals/leaders in the local Sulphur River Caddo community, as has been the case at a number of burials and tombs in Early Caddo mound centers in much of the southern Caddo area.

An important mound center was built at the A. C. Mackin site (41LR39) by an ancestral Caddo community during Early Caddo period times. The site is on a tributary to Little Pine Creek in the Red River basin (Mallouf 1976), and in addition to two constructed mounds (one of which was apparently built in the 13th century AD, in Middle Caddo period times), there are habitation deposits over *c.* 45 acres/+18 ha of an alluvial landform.

Mound A, 36 × 48 m in length and width and 2.5 m in height, was a platform mound built over a burned rectangular structure on the original and pre-mound surface. The burned structure has calibrated radiocarbon ages that range from AD 967–1162. Once the structure was covered up with the first main platform mound stage, another structure (Feature III) was built on the mound, atop a clay cap, about 100 years later. This structure also was eventually burned, and was marked by hearths, pits, post-holes, ash and daub concentrations. The material culture remains recovered in the mound excavations included Alba arrow points, sherds from long-stemmed Red River pipes, and sherds from typical Early Caddo ceramic types: Crockett Curvilinear Incised, Pennington Punctated-Incised, East Incised and Spiro Engraved, as well as red-slipped wares; these latter are a common fine ware in ancestral Caddo Red River communities.

Key non-mound sites

The Joe Meyer Estate #1 site (41SM73) is an ancestral Caddo settlement covering 3–5 acres (1.2–2 ha) and cemetery on an upland landform west of Saline Creek, a southern-flowing tributary of the Neches River in the upper Neches River basin. In the spring of 1957 members of the East Texas Archeological Society located the site and commenced excavations. The site had substantial midden deposits between 60–100 cm in thickness, with abundant sherds, animal bones and pieces of mussel shell. In one part of the midden, seven ancestral Caddo burial features dating to the Early Caddo period were identified and excavated (Burials 1–6 and Multiple Burial 1). Funerary offerings were present with each of the burial features.

Six of the burial features at the Joe Meyer Estate #1 site are individual burials (Burials 1–6) placed in a single north-south row in an extended supine position with the head of the deceased facing generally west (Burials 1–5) or northwest (Burial 6) (Fig. 44) towards the House of Death in the Sky (hereafter, House of Death, see Hatcher 1927: 162; Perttula *et al.* 2011: 403–33). The area excavated to expose the burial features was *c.* 6 m (north–south) × 9 m (east–west) in size. These burials lay in the lowest part of the midden deposits, from *c.* 81–102 cm bs. Funerary offerings with the burials included 12 ceramic vessels – 1–4 vessels per burial; one of the vessels contained a green (*hasikuh*) clay pigment and mussel shells. The multiple burial west of Burials 5 and 6 had four individuals laid out in an extended supine position, with their heads facing west. The multiple burial was in the upper part of the midden, with a bottom depth of only *c.* 61 cm bs. Based simply on the depth of this burial feature and the likelihood that the burial pit encountered and disturbed Burials 5 and 6, it is probable that the multiple burial was the latest burial feature interred by the Caddo in this cemetery.

The 15 ceramic vessels or portions of vessels in the burial features include bottles (n=4), jars (n=2), bowls (n=6) and carinated bowls (n=3). Most of the vessels are plain (67%), but those that are decorated include a Canton Incised bowl in Burial 4 (Fig. 45f); a carinated bowl in Burial 3 with a reworked rim that has alternating series of ovals with excised and cross-hatched engraved zones; a bottle in Burial 5 with short and widely-spaced pinched ridges on its body (Fig. 45h); a Hickory Engraved bottle in the Multiple Burial (Fig. 45l); and a Weches Fingernail Impressed carinated bowl in the Multiple Burial (Fig. 45m).

The ancestral Caddo occupation at the Joe Meyer Estate #1 site was intensive, as a large and relatively thick midden deposit accumulated on the landform. It is likely that there are house structural features preserved in the archaeological deposits here.

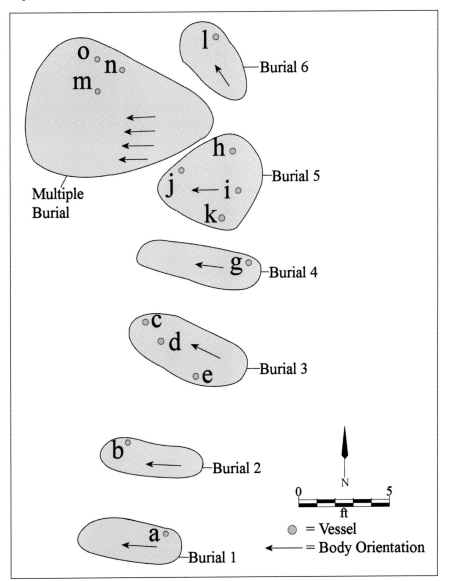

Fig. 44. Plan of the cemetery at the Joe Meyer Estate #1 site (41SM73)

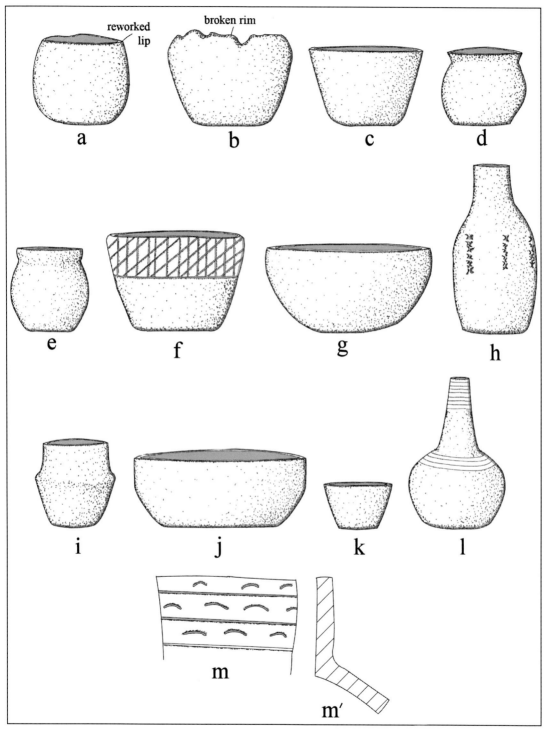

Fig. 45. Vessels from Burials 1–6 and Multiple Burial at the Joe Meyer Estate #1 site: a. Vessel A, Burial 1; b. Vessel B, Burial 2; c. Vessel C, Burial 3; d. Vessel D, Burial 3; e. Vessel F, Burial 3; f. Vessel G, Burial 4; g. Vessel H, Burial 5. h, Vessel I, Burial 5; i. Vessel J, Burial 5; j. Vessel K, Burial 5; k. Vessel L, Burial 6; l. Vessel M, Multiple Burial; m'. Vessel O. Multiple Burial

The Taddlock Site (41WD482) is an Early Caddo period sedentary settlement located in the upper Sabine River basin. It lies on both an upland landform remnant and alluvial terrace in the valley of Lake Fork Creek, a major tributary of the Sabine River. It was excavated in 1978 as part of a Southern Methodist University archaeological program to mitigate the effects of reservoir construction on the cultural resources found at Lake Fork Reservoir (Bruseth and Perttula 1981). The Caddo occupation was concentrated in a 1200 m² area on the highest elevations of the upland remnant.

The calibrated radiocarbon dates from the Taddlock site indicates that the occupation took place between AD 889–1219 (2 sigma). The Caddo occupational debris was concentrated in a crescent-shaped area around an open courtyard where cultural features and activity areas were not present. A storage pit and evidence of a single burial were recorded adjacent to one of two probable house locations. The two house locations were marked by shallow circular middens that were 9 m in diameter, in which were such features as post-holes and circular burned areas of charcoal and ash, interpreted as remains of hearths. A third midden deposit was discovered in a gully about 10–20 m down slope from the house locations. This midden was a thick trash deposit 50 cm deep, where abundant bone, plant remains, broken lithic tools and ceramic vessel fragments were discarded by the site's Caddo occupants. The two house locations and the trash midden were used contemporaneously; sherds from the trash midden were refitted to sherds from broken vessels found in the house deposits.

Over 18,000 ceramic sherds were recovered from the Taddlock site. They represent several hundred different vessels made by skilled potters, including carinated bowls, simple bowls, large cylindrical jars and bottles used for food storage, preparation and consumption. Decorated ceramic types include Canton Incised, Sanders Engraved, Davis Incised and East Incised, indicating that they were part of an Early Caddo ceramic tradition seen along the Red River and other sites in the upper Sabine and Sulphur river drainages. A hematite-rich clay slip frequently covered the engraved and noded ceramics as another means of decoration. Additional ceramic artifacts included pipes, particularly the long-stemmed or Red River pipe style. Native tobacco, or mixtures of tobacco and other plants, may have been smoked in these pipes. The lithic assemblage is dominated by small arrow points, flake tools and celts, used for hunting, butchering, scraping and woodworking. Most of these tools were manufactured from cherts available in Central Texas and southeast Oklahoma, rather than from poorer quality local materials.

A faunal sample of more than 13,000 identifiable elements was recovered in the trash midden. Animals from all vertebrate classes were represented, including a minimum of 267 individuals of all classes. Deer (da?) contributed most meat (ka?uhtuh) to the Caddo diet at the Taddlock site. Other utilized species include carp, catfish, opossum (tsatawin?), turkey (nu?), squirrel (shiwah), jackrabbit, freshwater drum, raccoon (ut) and beaver. Plant foods found at Taddlock include wild plant seeds, nuts from black walnut, oak, hickory and pecan and corn. Floral remains that were better preserved in the nearby Spoonbill site (41WD109) suggest that the collection of wild plant foods was important in the Early Caddo economy and was apparently supplemented by the use of corn and cultivated seeds (Perttula and Bruseth 1983).

In the mid-1950s, Sam Whiteside, an avocational archaeologist, conducted excavations at the Henry Chapman site, (41SM56), on Prairie Creek in eastern Smith County, Texas. Prairie Creek is an eastward-flowing tributary to the Sabine River. The Henry Chapman site is a small (0.4 acres/0.16 ha) Early Caddo period hamlet on an alluvial terrace of the creek (Walters 2009: 11–35).

Excavations uncovered three roughly circular 6–9 m diameter areas (I, II and III) marked by increased artifact concentrations and darker carbon-stained soils (Fig, 46) that appeared to represent circular house locations. Area I had relatively deep midden deposits along with a large trash pit (Feature 2). Area II was marked by increased artifact densities; an arc of possible post-holes (Feature 11); and several pit features. Soils were thinner in Area II and post-holes were detected only when they extended into the clay subsoil. The Caddo house in Area III may have been burned since a fired mud dauber nest with grass (*kuhut*) and reed impressions on one side was found in the excavations there. Such nests are often constructed in protected locations inside structures or along exterior structure walls. Pieces of daub with grass/cane impressions were also found in Area III, along with portions of an unfired vessel that had been distorted by intense heat.

The three or more permanently constructed houses were either all occupied at one time or occupied sequentially by one or more family groups. The total Caddo population at the site probably did not exceed 20–25 people. The house structures would not have been occupied for more than 10–15 years at a time, as the wood poles used to construct the structure would deteriorate and rot, eventually leaving the structures unlivable. Thus, the Henry Chapman site may have been occupied by a Caddo group of kin-related families for no more than *c.* 10-15 to 30–45 years.

Several features were recorded during the excavations at the Henry Chapman site, mainly associated with the three areas identified as possible house locations with associated pits and hearths. Large pits probably represent food storage facilities reused as trash receptacles after they were emptied of their intended contents. Hearths occur inside structures or in outdoor activity areas. There were two burial features (see Fig. 46); one was a partial cremation (Feature 3) that was associated with the Caddo occupation; the cultural affiliation of the other burial (Feature 5) has not been determined.

The artifacts from the site are indicative of a domestic occupation. They are dominated by sherds from grog- and bone-grog-tempered utility ware jars decorated with punctated, incised and punctated-incised designs; these comprise more than 70% of the decorated sherds in the artifact assemblage. There are also sherds from plain bowls, bottles, jars and carinated bowls and engraved carinated bowls and bottles; Holly Fine Engraved and Hickory Engraved vessel sherds are especially noteworthy. Evidence of the use of large utility vessels at the site is indicative of the major transformative changes by Caddo peoples after *c.* AD 850 from a hunting-gathering to a more sedentary lifestyle with the storage of foodstuffs, including domesticated plants. Large carinated bowls (used for serving foods) at the Chapman site may also indicate that feasting by Caddo living there also played a role in their social life.

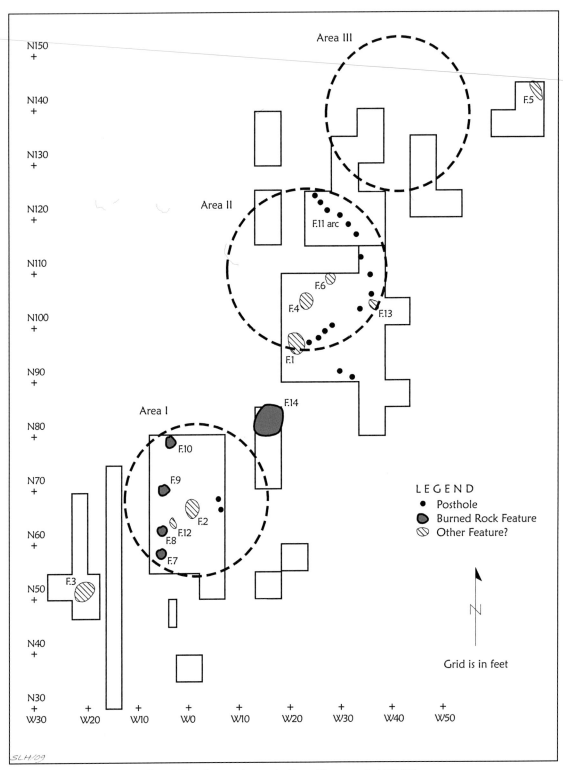

Fig. 46. Plan of excavations at the Henry Chapman site (41SM56)

The lithic tools in use at the Henry Chapman site by the Caddo families included chipped arrow points, flake tools used for scraping, cutting and shredding tasks and a bifacially-flaked perforator. They appear to have been made from non-local cherts. Ground stone tools in the assemblage were represented by five celts used to chop wood and three abraders for grinding and shaping wood shafts and bone tools.

The R. L. Jaggers site (41FK3) is an Early Caddo period settlement and cemetery in the Sulphur River basin Pineywoods. UT completed archaeological investigations at the site in 1930. UT archaeologists investigated a *c.* 13.7 × 15.2 m area of the terrace and in addition to discovering habitation deposits of Late Archaic, Woodland and Early Caddo period age, they identified four burial features (Burials 1–4). The Early Caddo occupation included some habitation debris – primarily sherds from plain ware, utility ware and fine ware vessels – and the four burials; burials dating to this period are rare from non-mound sites in East Texas, so they provide unique information on the character of mortuary practices from habitation sites.

Burials 2–4 at the R. L. Jaggers site were extended supine interments, but in each case the burials were oriented in different directions, with the head of the deceased either facing southwest (Burial 2), south (Burial 3), or west-northwest (Burial 4) (Jackson 1930: 2–3). Burial 2, discovered at a depth of *c.* 76 cm bs, had four associated ceramic vessel funerary offerings (two fine ware vessels and two plain vessels). Burial 3 was at a depth of *c.* 63 cm bs; the funerary offerings included three vessels (one fine ware vessel and two utility ware vessels), a celt and one Gary dart point. Burial 4 was buried only at a depth of *c.* 41 cm bs. Funerary offerings included a cache of ten lithic flakes and two Gary dart points.

There are 13 Early Caddo period vessels from the excavations at the R. L. Jaggers site. The include an engraved-punctated bottle, two Hickory Engraved jars, four Spiro Engraved carinated bowls and bottles, two Davis Incised jars, a Kiam Incised bowl and plain carinated bowls and jars.

The Spider Knoll site (41DT11) is an Early Caddo habitation site on the slopes and crest of a Pleistocene alluvial terrace just north of the channel of the Middle Sulphur River, in the modern Blackland Prairie vegetational zone. The site was investigated primarily in the early 1990s before it was inundated by the construction and operation of Cooper Lake. The main set of calibrated radiocarbon dates from the site (n=16) have a 2 sigma age range of AD 995–1045 (Selden and Perttula 2013, table 3).

The excavations showed that there were deep and well-preserved midden deposits on the southern slopes of the landform, with different kinds of habitation features (pits, post-holes and hearths) on the crest of the terrace. "Well-defined posthole patterns representing substantial houses were not present, and it appears that the structures built there were ephemeral" (Fields *et al.* 1997: 20). These structures were circular in shape and roughly 8–10 m in diameter. Other post-holes may represent the remains of wood arbors and drying racks that were situated amidst an outdoor work area north of the possible structures (Fig. 47).

The Caddo occupants of the site grow some corn and squash, but they were not a major part of their diet. Rather, they consumed a variety of wild plant foods, among them hickory nuts and pecan nuts, seeds of pigweed, sedge, honey locust, sunflower, sumpweed, wood sorrel, maygrass and knotweed, fruits such as wild

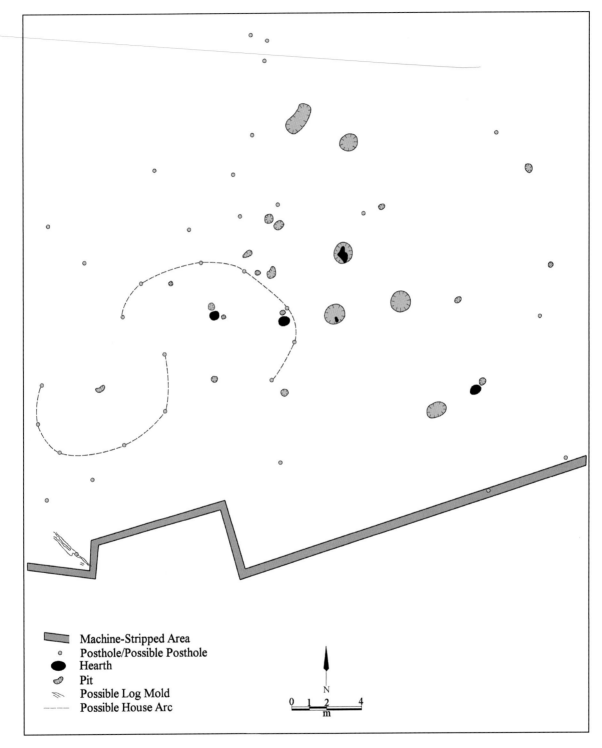

Fig. 47. Plan of features at the Spider Knoll site (from Fields *et al.* 1997: fig. 35)

plum and grape and roots/tubers. Turtles (*chayah*), white-tailed deer, rabbit and mussels were important faunal species that were gathered and consumed during the Spider Knoll occupation; pronghorn and elk were also hunted.

The ceramics recovered at the site are consistent with a domestic occupation by a small group of people, perhaps one that was seasonal and spanned no more than 20–30 years in total that the site may have been periodically occupied. "The early Caddoan sites at Cooper Lake represent occupations by single, small social groups, and there is no evidence for aggregation of populations into multifamily hamlets or villages" (Fields *et al.* 1997: 90). Fields *et al.* (1997) also suggest that the Cooper Lake Caddo population was not fully integrated "into the Caddo culture as were groups in adjacent areas," such as groups in the Red River to the north, or in the Sabine and Big Cypress drainages to the south.

Most of the sherds are from grog- and bone-tempered wares, with a high proportion of plain ware bowls and jars. Cooking jars as well as serving vessels had simple incised as well as curvilinear zoned incised and punctated decorations (including sherds from Crockett Curvilinear Incised and/or Pennington Punctated-Incised vessels), and these represented only 10% of the ceramic sherd assemblages. Sherds from engraved fine ware vessels comprise another 7%, among them several possible Spiro Engraved sherds. Chipped stone tools include stemmed arrow points of the Colbert, Steiner, Friley and Catahoula types, arrow point preforms (indicating that these tools were being manufactured on site), as well as flake tools. These tools were overwhelmingly made from abundant local lithic raw materials, including quartzite and petrified wood.

Another distinctive non-mound Early Caddo site in East Texas is the Bentsen-Clark site (41RR41) on an alluvial terrace along the south bank of the Red River (Banks and Winters 1975). The site contained two large shaft tombs (Features 1 and 3) and a daub and midden concentration (Feature 4) marking the location of a burned structure and habitation deposits. Feature 6 is a burial with three or four individuals that was exposed *c.* 15 cm bs; the only obvious funerary offering with this burial feature was a piece of rolled copper (Banks and Winters 1975: 66).

Feature 1 was a large (*c.* 4.1 m in diameter) and deep (3.8 m bs) shaft tomb with eight individuals placed on split cane matting on the floor of the shaft tomb. An impressive and diverse number of funerary offerings were placed in the tomb, including cougar and bear teeth; deer antlers and bone tools, including a bone hairpin overlaid with copper; conch shell dippers, ear spools and beads; *Marginella* shell beads; mussel shell hoes and pendants; long-stemmed Red River ceramic pipes and a limestone pipe; a limestone effigy pipe; stone ear spools; celts; Gahagan bifaces; 40 arrow points, including Alba, Hayes and Scallorn types; and 61 ceramic vessels (Banks and Winters 1975: 19–52). The predominant kinds of vessels in the Feature 1 shaft tomb are fine ware bottles, bowls and carinated bowls: Spiro Engraved (n=24); Holly Fine Engraved (n=2); and Hickory Engraved (n=2). Other vessels are utility wares, comprised of Crockett Curvilinear Incised bowls (n=3), a Kiam Incised jar, two East Incised bowls and a Hollyknowe Pinched jar. Sixteen vessels are plain wares, among them bottles, jars and carinated bowls.

Feature 3, the other Early Caddo shaft tomb at the Bentsen Clark site, was approximately 3.6 m deep and also contained multiple individuals, including some that had modeled and deliberately-shaped skulls (Banks and Winters 1975: fig. 25b); one individual had copper stains on the back of the skull that suggests this person was wearing a copper head ornament at the time of placement in the shaft tomb. The associated funerary offerings were not as lavish as in Feature 1, but did include 16 ceramic vessels, among them Spiro Engraved bowls and bottles, a Hickory Engraved bottle, two Crockett Curvilinear Incised carinated bowls, a Kiam Incised jar and plain bottles and carinated bowls (Banks and Winters 1975: 59–61). A single long-stemmed Red River pipe had also been placed in Feature 3.

These shaft tombs at the Bentsen-Clark site are indicative of considerable social ranking among the Early Caddo period community in this part of the Red River basin in East Texas. Both burials contained multiple individuals, and it is likely these tombs represent the burial of a person of social or religious prominence accompanied by a number of retainer burials.

Finally, the Ray site (41LR135) is a c. AD 1000–1200 Early Caddo period residential settlement on an upland ridge near a tributary of Big Pine Creek in the Red River basin; there are also c. AD 800–1000 archaeological deposits, but they are not substantial (Bruseth *et al.* 2001). Post-holes and small to large pit features were documented in two block excavations that were associated with several partially defined circular house structures (Bruseth *et al.* 2001: fig. 31). Calibrated radiocarbon dates on charred nutshells and corn from features in these excavations primarily range from AD 1020–1215.

The material culture remains associated with this ancestral Caddo component include ceramic sherds from straight and thick-walled Williams Plain jars with outflaring rims and simple bowls tempered with grog or burned bone, mainly undecorated, and a large number of long-stemmed Red River style pipes, primarily *var. Miller's Crossing* (Hoffman 1967: 9). The few decorated sherds (c. 2% of the 5719 vessel sherds) are from Crockett Curvilinear Incised, French Fork Incised, and possible Coles Creek Incised and East Incised vessels. The assemblage also has many Early Caddo style arrow points of the Alba, Homan and Scallorn types made on both local and non-local lithic raw materials, including Red River gravels.

5

Caddo Dispersion Across the East Texas Forests, c. AD 1200–1400

Settlements and communities

Caddo archaeological sites of Middle Caddo period age are quite common throughout East Texas (Fig. 48), including both mound centers and habitation sites. These sites are situated primarily on alluvial terraces and rises, natural levees and upland edges adjacent to the major fresh water streams and spring-fed branches. Arable sandy loam soils were preferred for settlement locations because of good drainage for habitation, and because the soils were suitable for cultivation purposes. The majority of these Caddo sites are permanent settlements that have evidence of the structures, including posts, pits and features, that mark their residency, along with the cemeteries and graves where the dead were buried. They also have middens where animal and plant food refuse was discarded amidst broken stone tools and pottery vessels, the material remains of stone tools and ceramics used in the procurement and processing of the bountiful resources of the region. They represent the settlements of distinct Middle Caddo communities and socio-political entities across the landscape; the civic-ceremonial centers were their focus.

The distribution of Caddo settlements at this time remained dispersed across the landscape, suggesting that all environmental habitats were used by sedentary communities and farmsteads that may have been occupied for single or multiple generations, say between 10–30 years. The most common types of Caddo settlements in the region during this period of time appear to be small year-round occupied hamlets and farmsteads with circular to rectangular structures. These settlements sometimes occur in association with small household cemeteries.

The development of distinctive ceramic style zones is a characteristic feature of Caddo groups in East Texas during the Middle Caddo period (Hart and Perttula 2010: 203–4). This appears to be related to the fact that Caddo communities at this time "became economically, as well as socially and politically, more autonomous" (Girard 2010: 205), thanks to the development of stable agricultural economies across the region, along with local control of newly-formed communities by the religious and political elite.

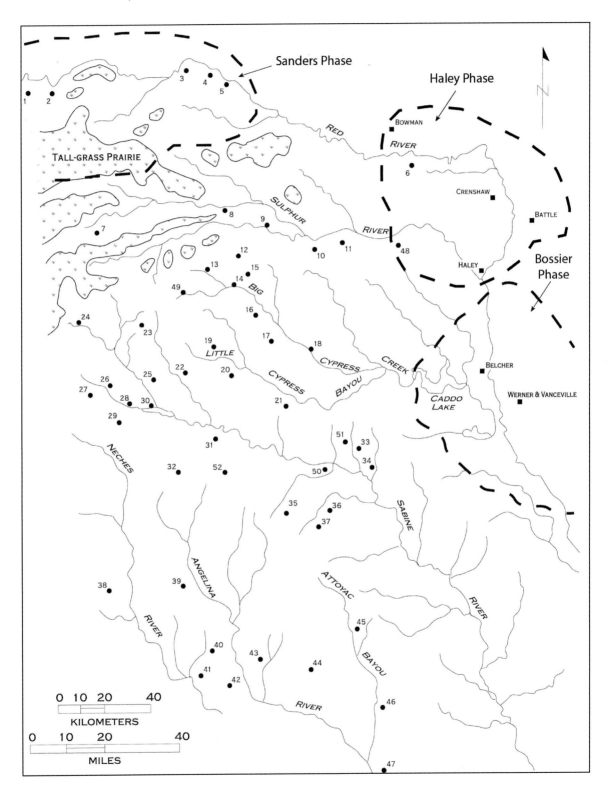

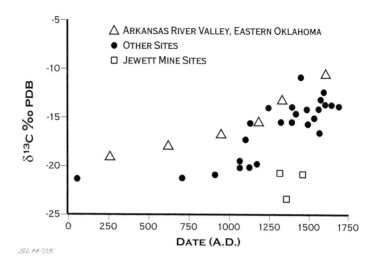

Fig. 49. (*above right*) Stable carbon isotope values from East Texas Caddo sites, Arkansas River basin sites, and non-Caddo sites at Jewett Mine in East-central Texas

During this period, the cultivation and use of maize continued to increase, such that by *c.* AD 1300, maize was the most important part of ancestral Caddo diets in East Texas (see Perttula 2008a; Perttula *et al.* 2014c; Wilson 2012; Wilson and Perttula 2013) (Fig. 49). These Caddo groups cultivated maize and squash, along with several kinds of native seeds, gathered nuts and tubers/storage roots, and were proficient hunters of deer, fish and many other animal species. The available paleobotanical and bioarchaeological evidence – including stable carbon isotopes on human remains – from East Texas (and elsewhere in the Caddo area) does not indicate, however, that Caddo groups became dependent upon maize and other domesticated crops until after about AD 1300; by *c.* AD 1450, maize comprised more than 50% of the diet. In portions of the middle and upper Sulphur River basin, however, the use of cultivated plants appears to have been rather limited during this period, with only small amounts of maize and squash being recovered from the flotation of feature contents (see Fields *et al.* 1997; Perttula 1999).

Constructed mounds

Both temple and burial mounds were built by East Texas Caddo groups during the Middle Caddo period. The larger sites are important civic-ceremonial centers containing multiple mounds and associated villages. The multiple mound centers are rather evenly spaced along the Red River, the Sabine River and Big Cypress Bayou and those that are contemporaneous may represent an integrated regional network of interaction and redistribution of goods between socially related peoples.

There are only a few widely dispersed Middle Caddo period mound centers in the Neches River basin. The Pace McDonald site (41AN51) is one of these ancestral Caddo mound centers; it is situated on Mound Prairie Creek in the upper Neches River basin. The site overlooks Mound Prairie Creek, has evidence of a settlement that covers at least 11 acres (*c.* 4.5 ha), and at least two (Mounds Nos 1 and 2), and as many as five, earthen mounds were constructed there by the Caddo (Fig.

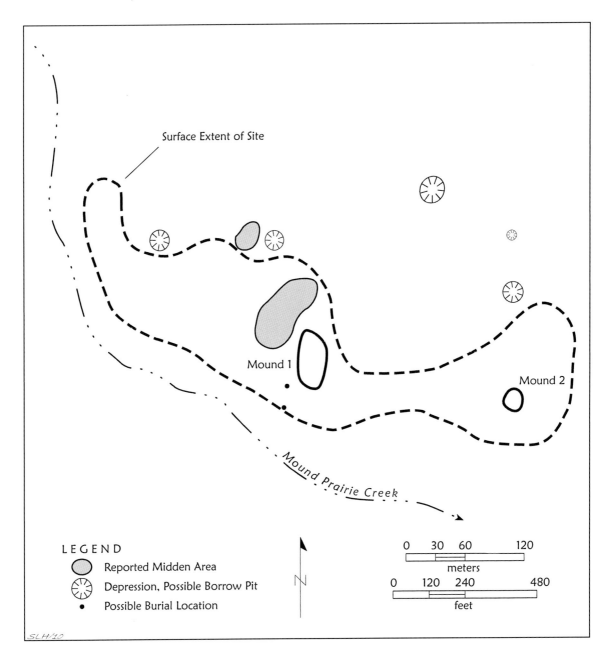

Surface Extent of Site

Mound 1

Mound 2

Mound Prairie Creek

LEGEND

Reported Midden Area

Depression, Possible Borrow Pit

• Possible Burial Location

N

0   30   60   120
meters

0   120   240   480
feet

SLH/10

50) (Perttula 2011a; 2011b; Perttula *et al.* 2012b). There is a large and associated habitation area (including several middens), and probably at least one associated cemetery area. There are also a number of small depressions (*c.* 6–12.5 m in diameter), with an average depth of 30–60 cm, visible on the landform that may represent borrow pits for sediments used by the Caddo to build the two earthen mounds (Mounds No. 1 and No. 2) that were constructed over special purpose structures with significant accumulations of ash.

Fig. 50. Map of the Pace McDonald site (41AN51), based on a 1978 sketch map by Ulrich Kleinschmidt and Pete Thurmond, and other information in the Texas Archeological Research Laboratory, University of Texas at Austin files

An examination of the decorated sherds in the assemblage, ceramic pipes and arrow points from the Pace McDonald site indicate that it was first occupied sometime before the 13th century AD – based on the predominance of Alba arrow points and some of the decorated utility ware ceramics – contemporaneous with some part of the lengthy Caddo occupation at the George C. Davis site. The end of the Caddo occupation at the Pace McDonald site was c. AD 1350–1400, based on the presence of 14th and 15th century L-shaped elbow pipes in the assemblage, and perhaps also by one red-slipped Redwine mode rim that also dates to this time period at other East Texas Caddo sites. Temporally speaking then, the Pace McDonald site is best viewed as an Middle Caddo period mound site whose occupation overlapped with that of the long-occupied George C. Davis mound center (most likely the component there associated with the construction of the Mound B platform around c. AD 1200), but apparently continued after the George C. Davis mound site was abandoned in the early 1300s. In cultural terms, the Pace McDonald site was an important mound center built by a Caddo group that was apparently related to others of similar socio-political character in the upper Neches, middle and upper Sabine and the Angelina River basin (see Story 2000).

Another Middle Caddo period mound center in the upper Neches River basin is the M. S. Roberts site (41HE8) in the Caddo Creek valley. The site has a single earthen mound about 24 × 20 m in length and width, and it stood more than 1.7 m in height. A likely borrow pit depression was noted just to the west of the mound. 1931 trench excavations by University of Texas archaeologists (Fig. 51a) determined that the mound rested atop a clay floor (114–122 cm bs) from a burned Caddo

Fig. 51. The M. S. Roberts site: a. 1931 excavations on the mound summit; b. geophysical anomalies interpreted as 1931 excavation trenches (provided courtesy of Duncan P. McKinnon)

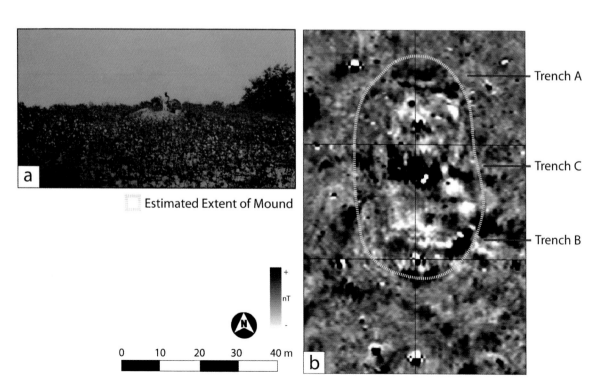

Estimated Extent of Mound

Trench A

Trench C

Trench B

0   10   20   30   40 m

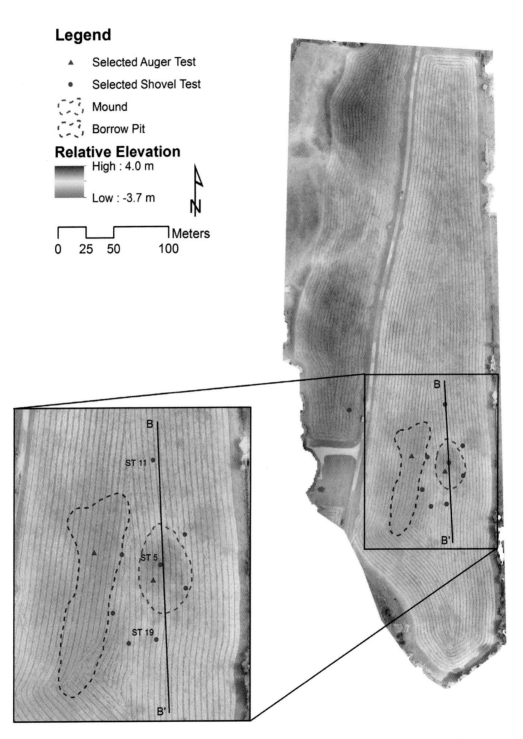

Fig. 52. Map showing the DEM and orthophoto overlay of the M. S. Roberts site (41HE8) study area. The locations of representative shovel tests and an artificial cross section (B) through the mound and low lying area to the north are also shown (image courtesy of Arlo McKee)

structure, and this clay floor was placed atop the first mound fill zone, a yellow sand (122–146 cm bs) that also had unspecified associated midden materials. These first mound deposits were constructed on top of the natural ground surface, a brown sandy loam A- and E-horizon (146–196+ cm bs). The mound at the M. S. Roberts site was undoubtedly built to cover an important Caddo structure, most likely a structure used for political and religious ceremonies or used as the residence of an important and elite member of the local Caddo community.

Renewed investigations of the site in 2015 disclosed that the mound now stands about 1.8 m in height (Figs 52–3). and it is associated with a substantial settlement and habitation area (Perttula 2016a; 2016b). Auger probes in the mound indicated that there is a very dark sandy loam zone between *c.* 102–135 cm bs that likely represents the remains of a burned Caddo structure.

Over 79% of the decorated sherds from the site are from utility ware vessels. Most of these have incised, punctated, or brushed decorative elements, including sherds from Maydelle Incised and Bullard Brushed vessels. The proportion of brushed sheds in the assemblage, the proportion of other wet paste decorated sherds, the amount of bone used as temper in vessel manufacture, and other ceramic metric attributes suggest that the Caddo occupation of the M. S. Roberts site may well have begun in the 14th century, perhaps after *c.* AD 1300, and likely ended in the early 15th century (Perttula *et al.* 2016d). Calibrated radiocarbon dates from both mound and non-mound habitation areas range at 2 sigma from AD 1294–1405.

In early 2016, additional investigations were conducted at the M. S. Roberts site, including remote sensing (McKinnon 2016) of a 2.8 acre (*c.* 1.1 ha) area over and around the mound, as well as more shovel tests and the excavation of several 1 × 1 m units. The purpose of this archaeological work was to better define the spatial extent of non-mound archaeological deposits; locate and sample well-preserved non-mound habitation deposits and obtain charred plant remains for AMS dating; and investigate the stratigraphic character of the mound deposits, identify cultural features in the mound, and obtain charred plant remains or unburned animal bones from these deposits for AMS dating.

The remote sensing of the mound documented the locations of at least two 10 m diameter Caddo structures on the northern and southern ends of the mound

Fig. 53. Images showing the vertical exaggerated 3D orthophoto and DEM showing the mound and borrow pit viewed from the northeast (image courtesy of Arlo McKee)

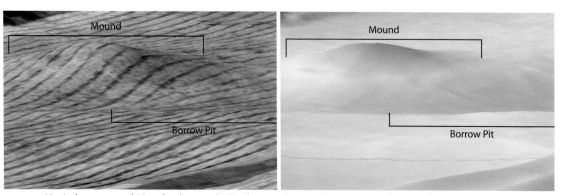

Vertical exaggerated 3D orthophoto and DEM showing the mound and borrow pit viewed from the northeast.

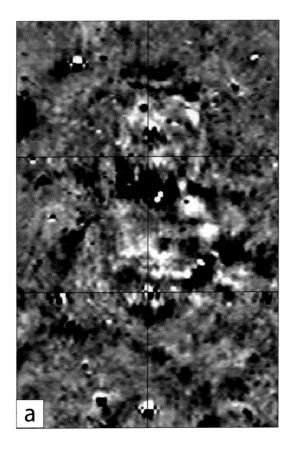

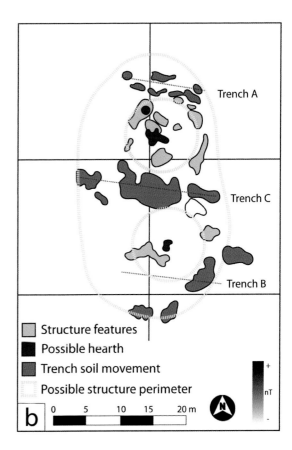

(McKinnon 2016: fig. 9), both with possible central hearths and other internal cultural features (Fig. 54); as previously discussed, this duality of structures is a common feature in a number of constructed Caddo mounds in the region. Because of the magnetic signatures, these structures were apparently "thatch style ... with little or no wattle and daub" (McKinnon 2016: 12). Excavations have identified the remains of at least two stratified burned structures in the northern part of the mound, with a well-preserved upper mound zone that represents the remains of a burned Caddo building (Fig. 55); a large piece of a burned mud dauber nest was recovered *in situ* in this zone (Zone 2b) at 31 cm bs (mud dauber wasps tend to build dirt nests on or under the eaves of structures and these nests are preserved when a structure burns down). Mound zones were a combination of sandy loam and clay fills obtained from the nearby borrow pit, and are roughly comparable in character from one end of the mound to the other, except that no evidence for burned Caddo structures was apparent in the southern part of the mound; these remains may lie deeper in the mound, as was suggested by auger holes excavated to 140 cm bs in the mound in 2015.

There are habitation areas both north, south and east of the mound over *c.* 4.5 acres (*c* 1.8 ha) of the landform. The best preserved habitation deposits are in a *c.* 35 × 35 m area south and southeast of the southern end of the mound. Remote

Fig. 54. Geophysical anomalies of ancestral Caddo origin at the M. S. Roberts site: a. extent of survey covering the mound; b. interpreted mound structures and associated anomalies (provided courtesy of Duncan P. McKinnon)

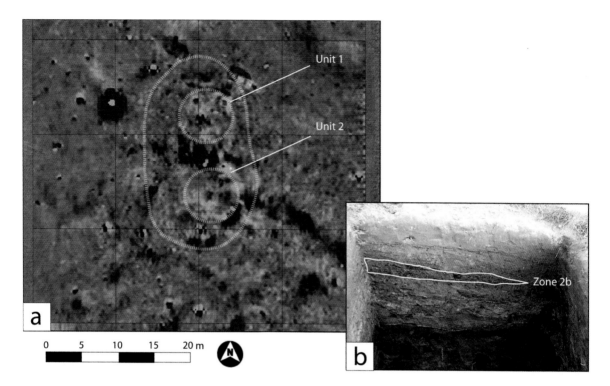

Unit 1

Unit 2

Zone 2b

a

b

0   5   10   15   20 m

Fig. 55. Comparison of magnetic gradient and excavation unit at the M. S. Roberts site: a. magnetic gradient overlain on aerial survey and showing location of Units 1 and 2 (provided courtesy of Duncan P. McKinnon); b. profile of the north wall of Unit 1 (Perttula *et al.* 2016b, fig. 5b)

sensing work in this part of the site also suggested that there were likely cultural pit features in this area (see McKinnon 2016).

The Washington Square Mound site (41NA49) is a Caddo multiple mound center located on an upland interfluve between Banita Creek on the west and La Nana Creek on the east, in the Angelina River basin, within the city limits of Nacogdoches, Texas (Corbin and Hart 1998; Perttula 2009b). The site appears to have been primarily occupied by ancestors of the modern-day Caddo Indian peoples between *c.* AD 1250–1425. During this occupation, the Caddo erected at least three mounds, the University Mound or Mounds 1/2, Mound 3 and Mound 4 or the Reavely-House Mound. Mound 1/2 was constructed by the Caddo over an important building, as was apparently also the case for Mound 3, the largest of the known mounds at Washington Square.

Extensive excavations documented a circular structure under Mound 1/2, an assortment of pits and post-holes in non-mound contexts, and several large burial pits in a mortuary mound (the Reavely-House Mound). No clear evidence for on-site permanent Caddo habitation was identified at Washington Square, although there were an assortment of large sherd-filled pits (representing many vessels) encountered in one area between Mound 1/2 and the mortuary mound. These may represent deposits from public feasting activities led by the Caddo elite that used the Washington Square mound site as a ceremonial center in the 13th and 14th centuries (Hart and Perttula 2010).

Mound 4, the Reavely-House Mound, is a Caddo burial mound with at least six known burial pits, based on archaeological investigations by Stephen F. Austin

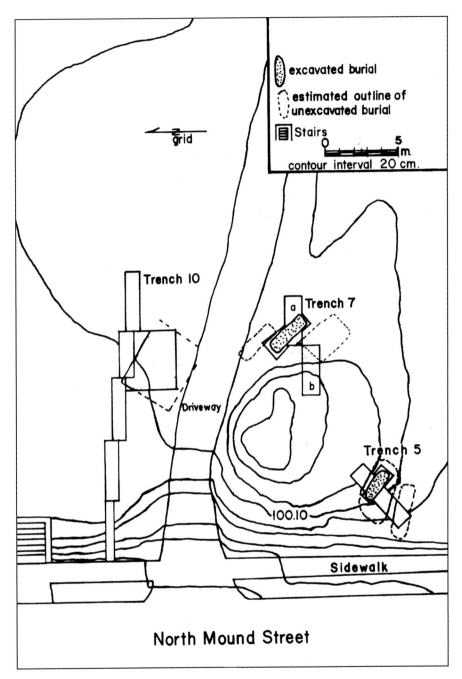

Fig. 56. Excavations at the Reavely-House Mound at the Washington Square Mound site, reproduced from Corbin and Hart (1998: fig. 26) (courtesy of the Texas Archeological Society)

State University in 1979 and 1981. During the course of that work, two burial features were identified and excavated in the mound: Feature 31 and Feature 95 (Fig. 56). Based on the richness and diversity of funerary offerings placed with the Caddo individuals in these two burial features, and their interment in a specially constructed burial or mortuary mound, there is no doubt that the individuals in Features 31 and 95 were amongst the "highest ranking individual(s) in the society"

(Story 1990: 339) that lived around the Washington Square Mound, and used the mound site for both religious and political ceremonies.

The ancestral Caddo burials associated with earthen mounds like those from Washington Square were lavish and expensive (in terms of the exotic funerary offerings placed with the burials and the labor expended to excavate the shaft burial as well as construct the mortuary mound). They also had "the distinction of being placed in a relatively large and deep pit dug into, or capped by, a mound … these burials were embellished by numerous offerings, many of materials indicating the existence of long distance trade networks possibly controlled by elites" (Story 1990: 339).

Feature 31 is the burial of an apparently young adult male Caddo individual placed near the southwestern part of the mound. The deceased was laid to rest in a 160 × 105 cm pit, with the head at the southeastern end of the burial. Fifteen ceramic vessels were placed around the edges of the burial feature, along with 13 marine shell columella beads with some around the wrist area, probably having been worn as a bracelet, and a cache (probably inside a leather bag) of 11 lithic artifacts near what would have been the feet of the deceased (Hart and Perttula 2010: 209).

There were several darkly-stained soil patches in the central part of the burial pit, and these may mark decayed organic materials, probably baskets or matting. There was a small area of charred wood and fire-reddened earth by one of the vessels, indicating that a small fire had been constructed in the burial pit before the vessel was laid down on it. This fire's purpose may have been to burn food offerings placed in the grave during the burial ceremonies (see Gonzalez 2005).

Feature 95 was located along the eastern part of the Reavely-House Mound, more than 5 m from Feature 31 (Hart and Perttula 2010: 210-11). Two individuals were placed in the burial pit, an adult female on the pit floor, and a sub-adult male (*shuuwi*) laying atop the woman (*nattih*). The burial pit measured 280 × 130 cm in length and width. Both individuals had cranially modeled skulls, a distinctive Caddo cranial treatment (Derrick and Wilson 1997). This burial feature has a northwest–southeast orientation, with the heads of both deceased near the eastern end of the pit.

The floor of the burial pit was signified by a bright yellow clay strata, especially near the two bodies; underneath was a red clay C-horizon. The yellow clay may have been obtained from a nearby Weches Formation bedrock outcrop. The remainder of the burial fill was a red clay.

The burials and funerary offerings (primarily ceramic vessels) were laid on a 6–8 cm thick organic layer (matting?) placed on this yellow clay. "Organic staining and debris in and around the vessels and skeletal remains suggest that the individuals were both covered with some material distinct from clothing at the time of interment" (Corbin and Hart 1998: 69).

Funerary offerings in Feature 95 include 32 vessels (see Hart 1982; 2014; Perttula *et al.* 2010b), among them a Nacogdoches Engraved vessel with an engraved rattlesnake motif on the vessel body, pigments of various colors in a number of vessels, marine shell columella beads on the wrists of the adult female, a marine shell pendant from the chest area of the adult female, and a shell disc. A number

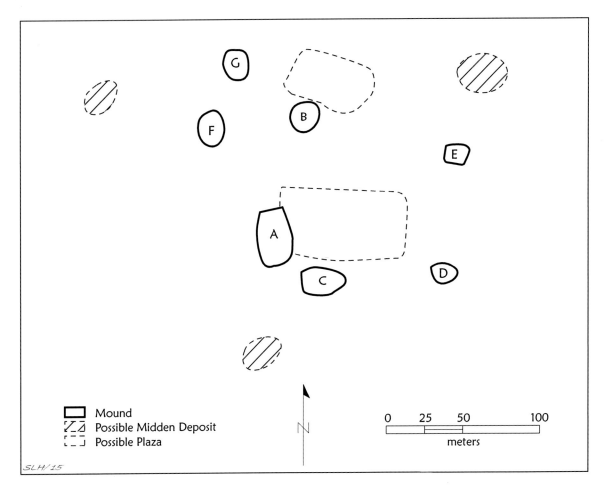

Mound
Possible Midden Deposit
Possible Plaza

0   25   50   100
meters

SLH/15

of vessels had clay pigment placed in them, as well as small amount of the same yellow clay that covered the burial pit floor.

Fig. 57. Recorded mounds and possible midden areas at the Jamestown site

In the Sabine River basin, the Jamestown site (41SM54) is a multiple mound center (Fig. 57) with seven or eight mounds and village deposits covering c. 15 acres (c. 6.1 ha). This mound center represents the apex of a c. AD 1200–1400 Caddo community (Perttula and Walker 2008). During 2007 remote sensing investigations at the Jamestown site, several geophysical anomalies (A–D) were identified in the field east of Mounds A and B, and in the vicinity of two proposed plazas between several of the mounds. Perttula and Walker (2008: 15) suggested that Anomalies A, C and D may represent burned Caddo houses or burned habitation surfaces about 8–10 m in diameter. Anomaly B may be an area of intense burning, perhaps associated with the immolation of a special purpose structure (Perttula and Walker 2008: 21).

Then there are the smaller mound centers in the Sabine River basin. The McKenzie (41WD55) site in the middle Sabine River drainage has a single sub-structural mound that dates between cal. AD 1208–1468, and there are contemporaneous mounds covering structures with extended entranceways at the Redwine (41SM193), Cox (41WD349) and Bryan Hardy (41SM55) sites. At the Bryan Hardy site, on Harris Creek in the Sabine River basin, in Middle Caddo period times, the ancestral Caddo community constructed a circular house (5.5 m in diameter) with a 3.7 m extended entranceway. A small mound was constructed over the house after it had been burned. A calibrated radiocarbon date obtained from a charred post from the house ranges from AD 1278–1398 at 2 sigma. Portions of two other circular houses, 9.75–10.4 m in diameter, were excavated at the site in the 1950s (Walters and Haskins 2000); neither of these structures had been burned or covered with mounds.

Within the same drainage as the Bryan Hardy site is another Middle Caddo period mound site, the Redwine site. Investigations (see Walters and Haskins 1998: 22–5) disclosed a circular house with an extended entrance that appears to have been burned and subsequently covered with approximately 1 m of undifferentiated soil. There also was an intentional mounding of soil or clay as berms around part of the structure. The one calibrated 2 sigma radiocarbon date from this site ranges from AD 1312–1423. The 14th century occupation at the Redwine site (Walters and Haskins 1998) also included an extensive midden deposit, hearth and pit features and a small cemetery with extended supine burials; the latter contained ceramic vessels, ceramic pipes, and numerous arrow points (primarily the Perdiz type) per burial.

The Oak Hill Village (41RK214), on a tributary (Mill Creek) to the Sabine River, is one of the few archaeological examples of a Caddo village in East Texas that has been exposed through expansive and controlled excavations. Estimated to have been occupied at several times between *c.* AD 1150–1450 – a temporal interval of significant cultural changes among southern Caddo peoples in subsistence, settlement and mound-building – the site has at least 43 circular and rectangular structures (Fig. 58), many pit features, and a large assemblage of Caddo ceramic and lithic artifacts (Rogers and Perttula 2004; Perttula and Rogers 2007; 2012). The village was fully uncovered in the mid-1990s prior to proposed strip mining of lignite coal. The village evolved over a 300-year period, in three different and distinct village eras, termed the earliest (AD 1150–1250), middle (*c.* AD 1250–1350/1375) and latest village (*c.* AD 1350/1375–1450). The estimated population during each of the village areas ranges from 54–71 people (early village), 74–95 people (middle village) and 25–35 people (latest village).

Some of the structures had been rebuilt and some overlapped earlier structures, particularly at the northwestern end of the ridge and plaza, and they were arranged in several distinct clusters over the 3.5 acre (*c.* 1.4 ha) village in a circular pattern around a central plaza area that was apparently established during the middle village era (Fig. 59). The single earthen mound was built on the northern end of the site over the locations of three houses, at least one of which had been burned. The structure entrances opened into the plaza. Several small structures (1.6–3.0 m in diameter) on the eastern side of the plaza have been identified as possible granaries for the storage of harvested corn. The middle era village was occupied during a time of favorable climatic conditions, but after *c.* AD 1375, the climate became colder and drier, with a likely shorter growing season (see Chapter 3).

The structures themselves include a number of rectangular and circular

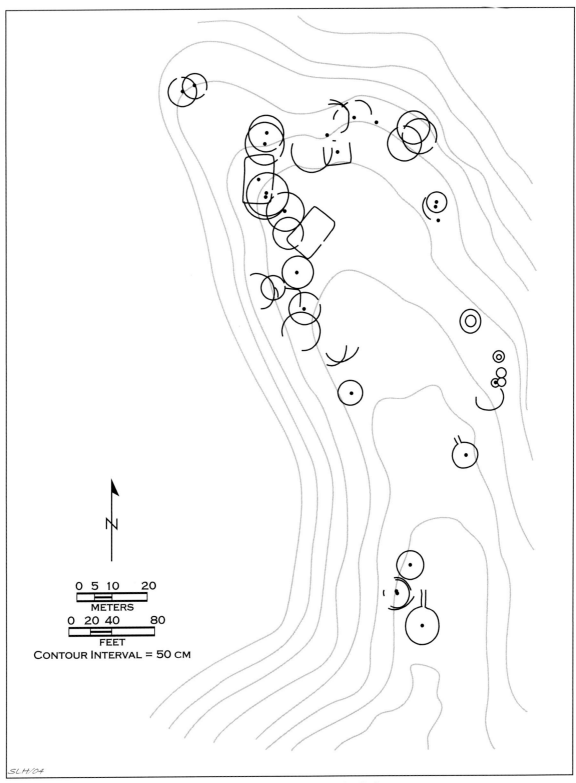

Fig. 58. Plan of structure features at the Oak Hill Village site

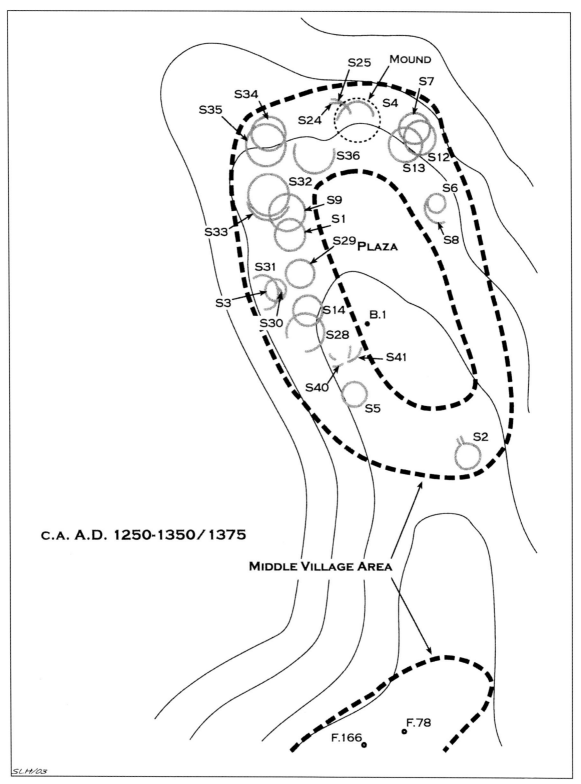

Fig. 59. Distribution of structures in the postulated middle-era village at the Oak Hill Village site

household structures, a few circular structures with extended entranceways, and several small (less than 3 m in diameter) structures that likely served as above-ground granaries (Fig. 60). The rectangular structures ranged from 6.5 × 9 m (Structure 43) to 8 × 12 m in size (Structure 37). The mean enclosed area of the four rectangular structures is 84.25 m². The 32 circular structures without extended entranceways range from 5.25–11 m in diameter; the circular structures were intended for domestic use based on their archaeological context and general architectural, artifactual and feature characteristics, and are found widely across the site. Two unique circular structures (Structures 2 and 18) at the site had 3–4 m long extended entranceways that opened either to the north or northwest towards the plaza. These are likely important structures, probably the residences of elite members of the village: (a) they are set apart (on a higher elevation) or isolated from the remainder of the structures; (b) construction details are different on them in comparison to the typical domestic residence; (c) the extended entranceway would have restricted ready access to the structure interior; and (d) Caddo structures in East Texas with extended entranceways tend to be found almost exclusively in special contexts, such as earthen mound platforms, or are found buried beneath small earthen mounds (see Perttula 2009a). The special form and orientation of these extended entranceway structures suggests they are probably either public buildings used by the Oak Hill Village community and/or elite families for special purposes. Ceramic analyses and extensive radiocarbon dating indicate these structures were built after c. AD 1350/1375 during the Late Village era. The site was abandoned around AD 1450, during a time of some regional population movements and localized territorial abandonment in the Sabine River basin.

Ceramic stylistic changes around this time also suggest that local communities were beginning to develop their own distinctive stylistic and social expressions by the time the middle village was occupied, while Caddo area-wide subsistence and bioarchaeological information points to the contemporaneous intensification of maize agriculture. The Caddo societies living during the time of the occupation of the Oak Hill Village were setting themselves apart from the societies that came before, not just in terms of settlement and subsistence strategies, but also in social organization and religious activities. The human and spiritual lived together at Caddo places like Oak Hill Village, as they consisted of "matrilineally organized communities of humans and spiritual beings" (Sabo 1998: 172–3).

The Keith (41TT11) multiple mound site may have served a similar organizational function in the Big Cypress Creek basin, as did such sites as the Sam Kaufman (41RR16), Wright Plantation (41RR7), Fasken (41RR14) and Sanders (41LR2) sites in the middle reaches of the Red River basin. Only a few possible Caddo mounds are known in the lower Sulphur River basin of East Texas, and they appear to consist of single mounds rather than large mound centers that had both earthen platforms and burial mounds.

The Keith site is located on a terrace remnant and the floodplain of Hart Creek, a southward-flowing tributary to Big Cypress Creek. The one mound at the site, 4.6 m in height and 48.7 × 73 m in width and length, was trenched by UT in 1934, led by archaeologist (then later cultural anthropologist) Walter R. Goldschmidt. That work exposed a series of sub-mound and mound platform structures, several

Fig. 60. Plans of the different kinds of structures at Oak Hill Village: a. large rectangular household structure; b. circular household structure; c. circular structure with extended entranceway; d. small structure, probably a granary

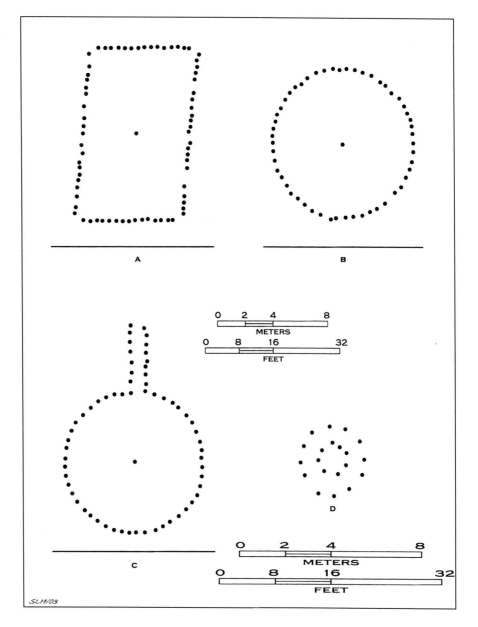

small associated midden deposits, as well as an outdoor activity area marked by post-holes, pits and concentrations of ash and charcoal.

There was a black (*hadikuh*) midden deposit beneath the mound itself, followed by layers of sandy and clayey loam mound fill intermixed with midden debris, perhaps in two or more stages. Excavations into the sub-mound midden deposit identified post-holes and other features at *c.* 3.6 m below the surface. They were exposed underneath thin layers of black carbonaceous material (1–5 mm thick), ash, yellow (*hakaykuh*) clay (5 cm thick) and sand (6.3–9.0 cm thick), with the top

of the post-holes in a second underlying black layer. These deposits indicate that
the Caddo structure that was built in the midden deposits was burned down,
probably deliberately, before it was capped with clay, structural debris and the
beginning mound fill zones. Other features include several sets of post-holes,
including portions of a circular structure post-hole pattern (Feature 1) as well as
associated internal posts and small midden areas, two north–south rows of posts
a few meters east and west of Feature 1, that are between 2.5–6.7 m long, that
may mark a wooden post enclosure around the structure that limited access to
this important structure, midden deposits (Features 3 and 6) and several 0.6 m
diameter pit features (Features 4 and 5) that originated in sub-mound contexts
in the western portion of the trench. The circular structure is estimated to be
approximately 9 m in diameter. There was also a concentration of daub about 0.9
m bs in the central portion of the mound that indicates that a structure stood on
the mound platform, and then was burned and capped with additional mound fill
sediments (Perttula 2014c).

The ceramic sherds from the Keith site are primarily from grog-tempered utility
ware vessels. The remainder are from fine ware (i.e., engraved, red-slipped and
red-slipped-punctated vessels). Among the utility ware sherds, the most common
decorative methods include incised, punctated (fingernail and tool punctated jar
rims), brushed and incised-punctated elements. Identified types that are associated
with the principal Caddo occupation are Canton Incised, Crockett Curvilinear
Incised, Davis Incised, Dunkin Incised, East Incised, Pease Brushed-Incised and
Weches Fingernail Impressed, *var. Alto*. The engraved sherds in the primary Middle
Caddo component are from carinated bowls, compound bowls and bowls, as well as
a few bottle sherds with curvilinear lines, diagonal lines, hatched triangle elements
and a hatched circle element. Many are from either Sanders Engraved or Hickory
Engraved vessels, and there are also a number of sherds with hatched or cross-
hatched zones, including curvilinear, triangular and diagonal or ladder-shaped
zones. The use of hatched or cross-hatched engraved lines to fill zones is a common
characteristic of East Texas ceramic assemblages beginning in Middle Caddo period
times. The common red-slipped sherds are from Sanders Slipped bowls or carinated
bowls, and there are two possible Maxey Noded Redware rim and body sherds.

Other material culture remains in the assemblage from the Keith site include
ceramic spindle whorls, a long-stemmed Red River pipe sherd, bone tools from
the sub-mound midden deposits, and polished pebbles. The chipped stone tools
include a few biface fragments and preforms, a Catahoula arrow point and a
petrified wood adze or gouge. Also recovered in the sub-mound midden deposits
are four celts or celt fragments.

The probability densities for two of the radiocarbon dates from the Keith site
peak from cal. AD 1380–1440. Since these dates are from both top layer and sub-
mound midden zones in the mound excavations, they imply that the mound was
built in the very latest years of the Middle Caddo period, and very rapidly indeed.
There is one earlier calibrated radiocarbon date from the site from charcoal in the
mound fill that has a 2 sigma age range of AD 1297–1495, suggesting major mound
construction at the Keith site anytime after AD 1297, but more likely instead after
c. AD 1383, based on the calibrated age range with the highest probability.

The Harling site (41FN1) is a little-known ancestral Caddo mound site located on the first alluvial terrace of the Red River in the northeastern corner of Fannin County in East Texas. The mound at the site appears to be the westernmost known of the Caddo mounds that have been reported in East Texas. According to Davis (1996: 463), the site is on the western frontier of Caddo communities in the Red River valley, and Caddo settlements are found at most only a few miles to the west of the site along the river, but are common to the east of the Harling mound. Based on the 1960 excavations of the mound and an examination at that time of the surrounding alluvial landforms – which were plowed – there was no substantial Caddo settlement at the Harling site, or any associated settlement cluster within c. 2.5 km of the mound, although there were scattered artifacts from the surface dispersed both east and west of the mound.

The single mound at the site was approximately 70 × 52 × 2.1 m in length, width, and height. There was a borrow pit area at the southern end of the mound. The 1960 excavations indicated that the site was likely constructed in Middle Caddo period times in one stage of different sand and clay deposits on top of the ground surface/A-horizon. There was no evidence of structures or burial features in or on the mound, but beneath the mound in the A-horizon were baked and charcoal-stained areas that likely represent the remnants of burned Caddo structures or other constructed facilities; grog-tempered and red-slipped Middle Caddo period grog-tempered sherds (i.e., Sanders Slipped) were present in the buried A-horizon deposits. The dated sample of deer teeth from a Middle Caddo period context at the Harling site has a 2 sigma calibrated age range of AD 1396–1437. In the top of the mound were several pit features excavated into the existing mound; post-AD 1500 shell-tempered ceramic sherds were found in these pits and in the top 30 cm of the mound itself.

The T. M. Sanders site (41LR2) on the Red River is one of the more important ancestral Caddo sites known in East Texas, primarily because of its two earthen mounds and the well-preserved mortuary features of Caddo elite persons buried in Mound No. 1 (the East Mound). The Sanders site is located on a broad alluvial terrace just south of the confluence of Bois d'Arc Creek and the Red River. Archaeological work began at the site in 1931 by The University of Texas at Austin (UT), with sporadic work by members of the Dallas Archeological Society in the 1940s and 1950s. Archaeological and bioarchaeological interpretations of the findings from this work at the Sanders site began with Krieger's analyses (1946; 2000; 2009) of the burial features (with single and multiple interments) and associated funerary objects (including marine shell gorgets, shell beads, arrow points and ceramic vessels). Although the Sanders site has not been dated by radiocarbon analyses, the general consensus is that the main Caddo occupation took place either around c. AD 1100–1300 (see Bruseth 1998), or c. AD 1200–1400 (Perttula et al. 2016c), contemporaneous with related Sanders phase sites downstream along the Red River near its confluence with the Kiamichi River, and other sites in the upper Sabine River basin (see Krieger 1946; 2009).

Archaeological survey investigations conducted in 2014 and 2015 at the T. M. Sanders site (Perttula et al. 2014a; 2015; Perttula and Nelson 2016) indicate that there are archaeological deposits on the alluvial terrace of the Red River that

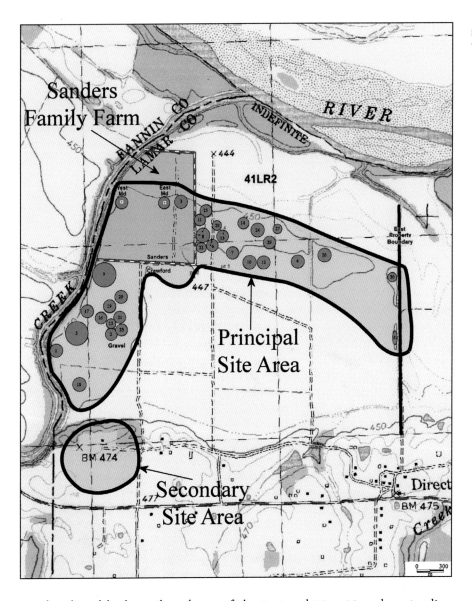

Fig. 61. Principal site area of the T. M. Sanders site

are distributed both south and east of the East and West Mounds, extending approximately 1260 m east from the East Mound and approximately 960 m south of the West Mound, an area of approximately 200 acres (*c.* 81 ha), with 34 distinctive clusters of surface collected artifacts beginning close to both mounds (Fig. 61). This extensive distribution of artifacts indicates that there is a large ancestral Caddo settlement at the site, not just two earthen mounds and a midden area between them (see Krieger 1946: fig. 9).

Geophysical investigations were conducted in 2014 on a 20 acre (*c.* 8.1 ha) area in the eastern part of the site, east of Mound No. 1. This remote sensing work was done to both assess the potential for such work to identify geophysical anomalies of ancestral Caddo origin, as well as assess the relationship between defined artifact

Fig. 62. Remote sensing-defined possible house clusters and artifact clusters at the Sanders site (41LR2) (image provided courtesy of Chester P. Walker)

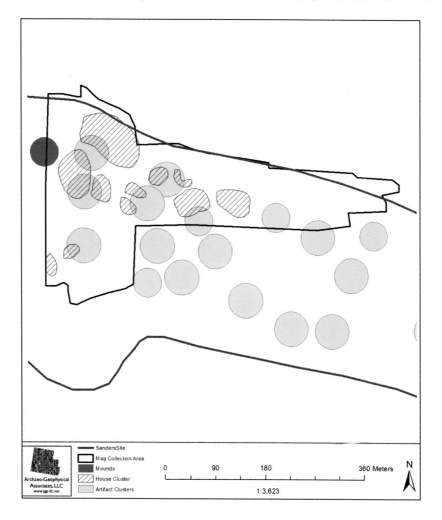

clusters in the eastern part of the site and the distribution of defined geophysical anomalies. During the course of the remote sensing, 11 possible ancestral Caddo house clusters were identified in areas east and southeast of Mound No. 1 (Fig. 62). Some correspond closely to the defined artifact clusters from surface collections and several shovel tests, while others are in proximity, suggesting that these artifact clusters represent both Caddo household deposits as well as extramural midden and activity area deposits.

The Middle Caddo period component at the Sanders site represents the type site of the Sanders phase (or focus) as first defined by Krieger (1946: 201–18). In formulating the character of the Sanders phase, Krieger focused on the burials and funerary offerings excavated in Mound No. 1 (East Mound) by UT in 1931, as well as artifacts recovered in the midden deposits in Mound No. 1 and the saddle between Mounds No. 1 and No. 2 (West Mound). Mound No. 2 was a platform mound with at least four levels of structures (Jackson et al. 2000). Krieger (1946: 201) noted that "the surface collections are almost wholly distinct from the grave and midden artifacts, and represent other known culture complexes"; these materials Krieger

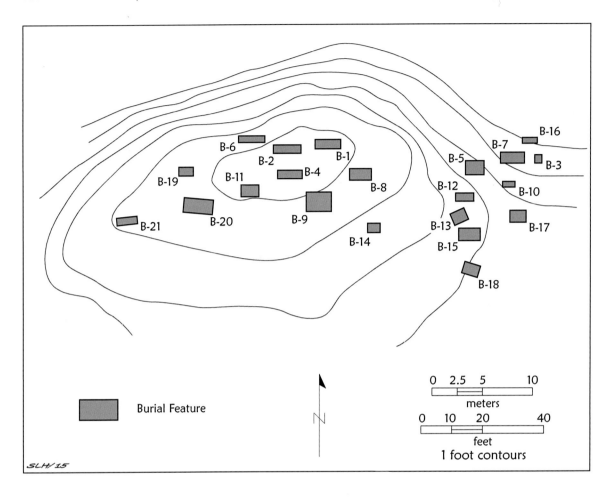

Fig. 63. Map of Mound No. 1 at the T. M. Sanders site, showing burials B-1 to B-21 (after Krieger 1946: fig. 10)

referred to are part of a late 17th–early 18th century Womack phase component.

The ceramic assemblage that can be associated with this component includes Sanders Plain or Bois d'Arc Plain, the utility wares Canton Incised, Sanders Incised and Monkstown Fingernail Impressed and the fine wares Sanders Engraved, Sanders Slipped (red-slipped) and Maxey Noded Redware. The one Haley Engraved vessel in the assemblage is likely a trade vessel made by a Haley phase Caddo potter in the Great Bend area of the Red River basin, well downstream from the T. M. Sanders site (see Fig. 48). Single examples of East Incised and Hickory Engraved vessels in burials at the site may also be trade vessels whose source is elsewhere in the southern Caddo area. A unique red-painted conjoined bottle-jar in Burial 15 is likely a trade vessel of Angel Negative Painted that originated in the Angel Mounds area in the lower Ohio River valley (Baumann et al. 2013: fig. 1). The Angel Mound site was occupied from cal. AD 1050–1420 (Monaghan *et al.* 2013), generally contemporaneous with the T. M. Sanders site. There are also long-stemmed Red River clay pipes, and Alba, Bonham and Hayes arrow points in the mortuary and domestic assemblages.

Excavations in Mound No. 1 or the East Mound at the T. M. Sanders site

Table 3. Burial features at the T. M. Sanders site (based on Jackson *et al.* 2000)

Burial no.	No. of individuals	No. of ceramic vessels	Other funerary offerings
1	1	2	Shell gorget; stone pipe; stone drills; shell beads
2	1	1	Ceramic pipe; shell gorget; shell beads; arrow point; shell pendant
3	1	1	Shell gorget
4	1	2	Ceramic pipe; arrow points; shell gorget; shell beads; shell discs
5	7	5	Shell gorget; stone pipe; arrow points
6	1	3	Ceramic pipe; shell pendants; shell beads; conch shell beads; bone awls
7	5	—	conch shell beads
8	1	1	Ceramic pipe; shell gorgets; conch shell dipper; shell beads
9	1	7	Bone awls; conch shell; shell gorget
10	1	—	—
11	1	4	Conch shell beads
12	5	6	Celt; arrow point; shell gorgets; conch beads; shell beads
13	6	4	Shell beads; shell gorget
14	1	—	arrow points; shell discs
15	6	6	Conch shell beads; bone needle
16	1	2	—
17	8	8	Shell gorget; stone scraper; ceramic pipe; conch shell beads; bone needle
18	4	—	Paint stone
19	1	—	Shell gorgets; arrow point; shell beads
20	4	7	Shell gorget; stone ear plugs; scapula hoe; conch shell beads; conch shell discs; shell pendants
21	3	2	conch shell beads
Totals	60	61	

uncovered 21 burial features, 12 graves with a single individual and the other nine burials with multiple individuals (a total of 48 individuals), from three to eight people in these burial features (Fig. 63 and Table 3). About 76% of the burials had ceramic vessel funerary offerings, with a range of 1–8 vessels per burial feature.

The burials with multiple individuals contain more ceramic vessels (a mean of 4.2 vessels per burial feature) than do the burials with single individuals (a mean of 1.9 vessels per burial feature) (Table 3). The burial features with the greatest number of ceramic vessels are situated either on the crest of the mound (Burials

B-9 and B-20) or along the eastern edge of the mound (Burials B-5, B-12, B-15 and B-17). Krieger (1946: 185) noted that the ceramics from the T. M. Sanders site burial features (and midden excavations) are "remarkably uniform in shape, decoration, paste and finish." The burials in the Mound No. 1 excavations at the T. M. Sanders site that have the very largest vessels (Burials 4, 9, 11 and 20) are each situated in features at the crest of the mound (see Fig. 63); these features also include numbers of marine shell gorgets, beads, discs and pendants. Three of the burial features have only a single interment, but Burial 20 has four individuals (see Jackson *et al.* 2000: 31), and the largest number of vessels, numerous marine shell artifacts and stone ear plugs. It is likely that these burials represent religious and/or political leaders in the Sanders site Caddo community.

Another Middle Caddo period mound center is the Fasken site (41RR14) in the Mound Prairie area of the mid-Red River basin. The Fasken site was occupied primarily during the Mound Prairie phase, the local equivalent to Sanders phase sites found to the west and southwest (Prikryl 2008). During this occupation three different mounds were constructed there: Mound A, 90 × 55 × 4.3 m in height, almost certainly a platform mound; Mound B, 60 × 40 × 1.6 m, a smaller platform mound; and Mound C, only 0.25 m in height and of unknown dimensions; this mound was built over a special purpose structure.

Mound A has not been excavated, but work by Prikryl (2008) in Mound B indicates that it was built in three construction episodes and with two platforms (marked by clay caps) that had important Caddo structures on them. According to Skinner *et al.* (1969: 10), a number of Caddo burials had been plowed from the mound when it was under cultivation. A single OCR date of AD 1118–1166 came from sediments just above Feature 3, a structure with an extended entranceway. A second platform may have had twin lobes for two different structures marked by clay floors (Prikryl 2008: 135). In Mound C, a sub-rectangular structure (Structure 1, Prikryl 2008: fig. 15) was covered with mound fill, then capped with a 7–10 cm thick clay zone. Calibrated 2 sigma radiocarbon age ranges of cal AD 1040–1257 and cal AD 1019–1226 were obtained either in a mound fill zone (Zone 4) or associated with a series of post-holes from another structure.

Recovered material culture remains in the mound excavations at the Fasken site, and in a non-mound area (Area A) marked by a daub concentration/house location, included many ceramic sherds, mostly from plain wares. Decorated sherds are from Sanders Engraved, Sanders Slipped and Canton Incised vessels. Chipped stone tools mainly include Alba and Bonham arrow points.

Key non-mound sites

The Paul Mitchell site (41BW4) is an ancestral Caddo habitation site and cemetery in a larger Upper Nasoni village on the Red River in Bowie County, in the northeastern corner of the present state of Texas (Fig. 64). Extensive excavations were conducted at the site in the 1930s by both professional and avocational archaeologists, as part of a UT-WPA relief project in 1938–1939, and in the 1940s by an avocational archaeologist (Perttula 2014b). The site is located in the McKinney Bayou floodplain

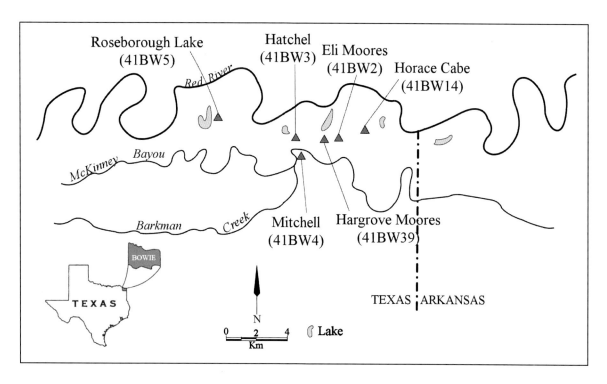

Fig. 64. The Paul Mitchell site and other Nasoni Caddo sites on the Red River in Bowie County, Texas

about 3.2 km from the current channel of the Red River to the north. The large platform mound at the Hatchel site (see Chapter 6) is about 1.6 km north of the Paul Mitchell site.

Although many of the burials (n=25) excavated by the WPA at the Paul Mitchell site had been previously disturbed and funerary offerings (including ceramic vessels) removed (Perttula 2014b: fig. 30), there is sufficient information available from the remaining burial features to construct an occurrence seriation (see O'Brien and Lyman 1999: 119–21) of vessel sets. This provides a view of the 200–300+ year temporal history of the use of the cemetery as well as the stylistic character of the ceramic vessels placed as funerary offerings in ancestral Caddo burial features at the Paul Mitchell site.

Middle Caddo period burials in the Paul Mitchell site cemetery occur primarily in the northern part of the cemetery. This definitely includes Burial K-2 (Jackson 1932; 2003), Burial MV-1 (Martin 1936), M-B2 and M-B3 excavated by Pete Miroir in 1946, Mathews (1935) burials 1–2, 5–6, 9–10, 13 and 21, and three WPA burials (Burials 44, 54 and 63). The one radiocarbon date from the site is on charred organic residue scraped from the exterior surface of a Dunkin Incised ceramic body sherd from the eastern part of the midden deposits. At 2 sigma, the calibrated age range of the charred residue is cal AD 1158–1262. Since the radiocarbon date is a good indication of when Caddo peoples were living at the Paul Mitchell site, and it overlaps with the estimated age range of a number of burials in the cemetery, then the most logical conclusion is that the people buried in the cemetery lived at the site. Ceramic vessels placed in these earlier burials (Set 1) include the fine wares Haley Engraved, Hickory Engraved, Hempstead Engraved, Friendship Engraved

Type or unidentified to type	No.	Percentage
Dunkin Incised	1	3.1
East Incised	1	3.1
Haley Complicated Incised	1	3.1
Haley Engraved	4	12.5
Hickory Engraved	4	12.5
Pease Brushed-Incised	2	6.3
Unidentified appliqued-punctated	1	3.1
Unidentified engraved	10	31.3
Unidentified incised	2	6.3
Unidentified incised-punctated	1	3.1
Unidentified incised-punctated-appliqued	1	3.1
Unidentified fingernail-punctated	1	3.1
Plain bottle	1	3.1
Plain carinated bowl	1	3.1
Plain jar	1	3.1
Totals	32	100.0

Table 4. Middle Caddo period ceramic vessels (Set 1) from the Paul Mitchell site: plain vessels, and vessels defined to types and unidentified to type

and Means Engraved, along with untyped engraved fine wares with rectangular, curvilinear and horizontal elements on carinated bowls as well as vertical engraved elements and horizontal-curvilinear-and triangular elements on bottles. Utility wares include Dunkin Incised jars as well as incised-punctated vessels, East Incised bowls, a Haley Complicated-Incised jar, a few Pease Brushed-Incised jars, incised, incised-punctated-appliqued and punctated-appliqued vessels. A few jars have handles. There are also plain ware carinated bowls, bottles and jars included as funerary offerings in these burial features (Table 4). More than 56% of the vessels in the Set 1 assemblage are fine wares; another 34% are utility ware vessels and 9.4% are plain ware vessels.

The Middle Caddo period component at the Paul Mitchell site is affiliated with the Haley phase, dating to c. AD 1200–1400 based on radiocarbon dates (see Samuelsen 2014) and the seriation of typologically and chronologically distinctive ceramic decorative styles. Because of a number of excavations over the last 100 years or so, this is a fairly well understood ancestral Caddo archaeological phase marked by mound centers (such as the Battle, Crenshaw and Haley sites) – both platform and burial mounds – large off-mound cemeteries, and large dispersed communities comprised of villages, hamlets and farmsteads along the Red River both upstream from, and in, the Great Bend area of the Red River in Southwest Arkansas and the northeastern-most part of East Texas. The nearby Hatchel and Cabe sites have Haley phase village deposits and/or burials, but the mounds at both sites were constructed after c. AD 1400 in the later Texarkana phase (see Chapter 6).

The Hurricane Hill site (41HP106) sits on a high upland landform overlooking the floodplain of the South Sulphur River. This landform was used repeatedly from early Woodland (*c.* 380 BC– AD 210 and AD 60–450 in two different parts of the site), Early Caddo (*c.* AD 1000–1200) and Middle Caddo period times (Perttula 1999). The South rise at the site has a Middle Caddo domestic compound marked by post-hole patterns from three structures with internal hearth and pit features, daub and burned clay concentrations, four discrete midden deposits, extramural pits, a dog (*diitsi?*) burial and burials of Caddo peoples (Fig. 65a). Although the post-hole patterns are not complete, structures A and B are circular to sub-rectangular in shape, between 6.0 × 7.6 m in length and width, and they have four center support posts. In the case of Structure B, there are two short parallel trenches that may mark a covered entranceway (Fig. 65b). Radiocarbon and archaeomagnetic dates from various features in this component suggest that Caddo peoples occupied this part of the site between *c.* AD 1250–1375.

The material culture remains from this occupation includes a diversity of arrow point forms, including Bonham and Perdiz, as well as chipped stone scrapers and expedient flake tools. Tools made from non-local lithic raw materials (most likely obtained from Red River gravels) are relatively abundant, and almost all are made on novaculite (Perttula 1999: 229). There are also celts and metates, as well as a large chunk of red ochre pigment stone.

The decorated ceramics in the occupation includes red-slipped punctated and punctated-noded Maxey Noded Redware sherds comparable to vessels in Sanders phase contexts on the Red River, and fine ware sherds with engraved ladder and engraved pendant triangle decorative elements. Chemical analysis of sherds from the South rise indicate that about 20% were from vessels that were not made locally in the upper Sulphur River basin. Most of these sherds appear to be from vessels made by Caddo potters living in the middle reaches of the Red River (Perttula 1999: 274). There are also several bowl and stem sherds from long-stemmed Red River pipes in the Middle Caddo component at the site, likely from Haley Variety pipes (Perttula 1999: 299 and fig. 9-29; see also Hoffman 1967).

Wild and cultivated plant foods were consumed by Caddo peoples at the Hurricane Hill site during the Middle Caddo period. However, the proportion of cultivated foods is dwarfed in flotation samples by charred nutshells of hickory and acorn. Nevertheless, the flotation samples do document an increased ubiquity of maize, but the ubiquity is much lower than is the case in contemporaneous contexts in the Sabine River and Big Cypress Creek basins.

In the Big Cypress drainage a *c.* AD 1200–1400 component at 41TT372 seems to be a small family-based agricultural farmstead. A large cemetery, however, with at least 12–18 burials, has been documented at the Vasturtium site (41UR209) in the Little Cypress Creek basin. At the Unionville site (Area C), 41CS150, 41CS155/156, Area B, 41BW553 and 41TT670 along White Oak Creek, the Middle Caddo period components had well-preserved middens, hearths, post-holes and other features.

The Tigert site (41TT36) on Hart Creek in the Little Cypress Creek valley had a small midden and an associated burial with grave goods, while the contemporaneous component at the Griffin Mound site (41UR142) in the Little Cypress Creek drainage contained a dense midden and a large (+2 m in diameter

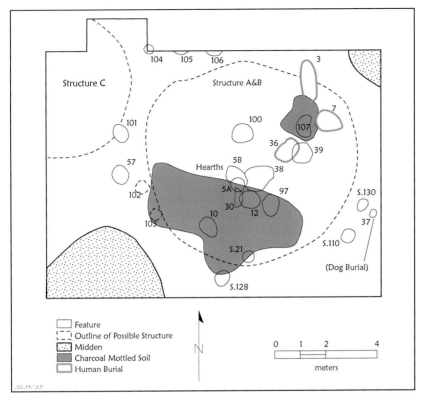

Fig. 65. Excavations on the South rise at the Hurricane Hill site: a. plan of structures, features, and middens; b. post-hole pattern of Structures A and B

a

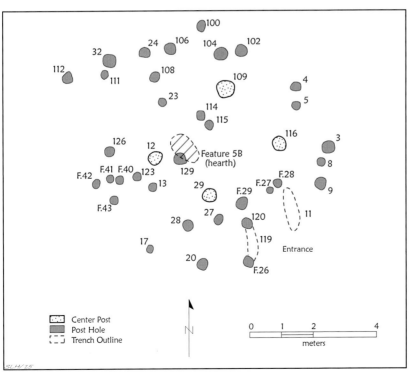

b

and 1 m in depth) storage pit feature, probably associated with a Caddo structure. At the Benson's Crossing site (41TT110) on an alluvial terrace along Big Cypress Creek, occupied perhaps *c.* AD 1300–1400, the Caddo occupation/midden there was the product of at least two extended families living in a farmstead or small hamlet for more than 20–30 years.

The cal. AD 1280–1400 component at the Rookery Ridge site (41UR133) represents a more substantial occupation on Kelsey Creek in the Little Cypress Creek basin, evidenced primarily by a burned structure and a ceramic assemblage with distinctly different decorative styles. According to Parsons (2015), the ceramic assemblage is not readily comparable to other Middle Caddo ceramic assemblages in the Big Cypress Creek basin, although it has recognizable ceramic styles that can be traced between various communities.

Recent excavations at the Hickory Hill site (41CP408) in the Little Cypress Creek basin exposed cal. AD 1340–1440 habitation deposits from an ancestral Caddo farmstead (Perttula and Ellis 2012). There are a total of four habitation areas on the site (Fig. 66), six pit features, 25 post-holes, two large occupational deposits, and two burial features well north of the western block. Each intra-site area may have been the locus of at least one Caddo house structure, and the eastern area appears to represent an associated outdoor work area with pits, hearths and other features to a habitation area. These habitation areas appear to have flanked an open area or courtyard (*c.* 20 × 10 m in size) that is characterized by a very low density of habitation debris.

Fig. 66. Schematic map of the Intrasite organization of the Hickory Hill site (41CP408)

Two adult burials from a small cemetery were located along the peripheries of the site. They had likely been buried in an extended supine position with their head facing west toward the Caddo House of Death. The Caddo House of Death is where the souls of the deceased travel to the afterlife (Hatcher 1927: 162), typically they traveled west. Each individual was buried with ceramic vessels (n=10) to accompany them on their journey to the House of Death; the vessels clustered near what would have been the head area of the deceased, and along the sides of the body (primarily the right side). These mortuary practices are similar to other Middle Caddo period burials that have been documented in the Big Cypress Creek basin.

The plain and decorated ceramic rim sherds from the Hickory Hill site are from small to medium-sized (10–19 cm orifice diameters) vessels designed for individual or individual family use, and not for communal use. Ceramic stylistic and technological

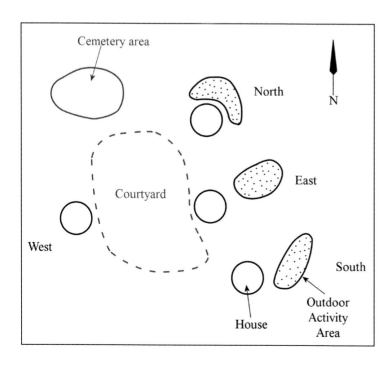

features of the Hickory Hill assemblages are shared with contemporaneous Middle Caddo societies that lived in the eastern headwaters of Little Cypress Creek and Caddo peoples and groups on the middle part of the Big Cypress Creek basin (see Fig. 48). Instrumental neutron activation analysis and petrographic analysis determined that 13.9–22.2% of the analyzed sherds from the Hickory Hill site may plausibly be from non-local sources, but that the remainder were from vessels made with local clays.

The analysis of the charred plant remains from the Hickory Hill site indicate that wood charcoal (representing fuel and burned structural remains) was abundant, as were plant foods such as maize, small starchy-seeded annuals (maygrass and chenopodium), nutshell (hickory and likely remnants of hickory nut oil production, walnut and acorn), as well as other wild food plants (e.g., bulbs and lotus seeds). The relative abundance of maize remains in the analyzed flotation samples (38%) is consistent with the Caddo occupants of the site having a maize-based diet supplemented by wild plant foods that is typical of East Texas Caddo sites dating after c. AD 1300. The cultivated plants and wild plant foods in the diet of these Caddo people were further supplemented by animal protein obtained in the successful hunting of deer, turkey, rabbit, turtle and fish.

The Leaning Rock site (41SM325) is a well-preserved 14th to early 15th century habitation site on a northward-flowing tributary to the Sabine River, in the upper Sabine River basin (Walters 2008). The site, which covers a c. 45 × 40 m area, is marked by two 10–12 m diameter midden deposits that may represent the habitation remains from two circular structures, as well as pit features and a hearth. Several radiocarbon dates on maize and hickory nutshells have established that the site was occupied around cal. AD 1350.

The material remains found at the site in one of the midden deposits included Perdiz arrow points, a series of flake tools and hand-held ground stone tools. The large assemblage of ceramic vessel sherds include sherds from both utility ware (83% of the decorated sherds) and fine ware (17%) vessels. Chemical analysis of the paste (instrumental neutron activation analysis) of a sample of the sherds indicate that they are mainly from locally made vessels (Walters 2008: 49, 61). Several ceramic spindle whorls in the assemblage indicate that Caddo women were weaving fibers for textiles at the Leaning Rock site.

The utility ware sherds are from vessels with incised, punctated and brushed decorative elements, while the fine wares are almost all from engraved or Washington Square Paneled vessels. The most distinctive of the engraved sherds are those with engraved rattlesnake elements (see Walters 2006: figs 30b and 31).

The diversity in vessel decoration and manufacture at this and other mid-Sabine River basin sites suggests the existence of several different Caddo communities living in the area around and after c. AD 1250. At that time, the cultural landscape of the Caddo peoples along the middle Sabine was changing dramatically, as the land was filling up with people, but locally and socially independent communities were developing their own ethnic and stylistic expressions (Perttula and Rogers 2007: 90–1). Even within these distinct and local ceramic complexes, there are stylistic and technological differences, hinting at social and/or temporal variations in ceramic traditions. These differences include the way vessels were tempered, the relative use of bone temper, how vessels were fired, the proportion of plain wares in assemblages, and the relative use of engraved fine wares versus incised or brushed-punctated vessels. These differences can be readily traced to specific technological, functional and stylistic decisions made by the Caddo potters in the region, and those Caddo that lived at the Leaning Rock site, on how to make, finish and decorate ceramic vessels that were used in domestic contexts.

The Caddo group that lived at the Leaning Rock site were farmers that cultivated maize (10- and 14-row) and squash. They also gathered wild plant foods, particularly hickory nuts and acorns. According to Dering (2008a: 75), the Caddo living at the Leaning Rock site were practicing maize-based agriculture, and also likely grew squash and beans. These Caddo also went to a "considerable effort to harvesting and processing forest mast, including acorns, hickory nuts and walnuts." Dering (2008a: 75) notes that this strategy of plant production and wild plant harvesting was typical of the Caddo economy in historic times (see Solis 1931; Tous 1930). Wild animal resources procured by the Caddo that lived at the Leaning Rock site included freshwater fish, toad/frog, turtle, turkey, opossum, cottontail rabbit, squirrel, raccoon and deer, as well as mussels.

41GG5 and the Joe Smith site (41GG50) are Middle Caddo period habitation sites and small cemeteries (Fig. 67a–b) on southward-flowing tributaries to the Sabine River (Grace Creek and Hawkins Creek) in the East Texas Pineywoods. They have distinctive assemblages of decorated fine ware and utility ware mortuary vessels, along with associated Bonham arrow points and plain elbow pipes. These sites are part of another community of ancestral Caddo peoples that lived along the Sabine River and its tributaries, and they were contemporaneous with better known Middle Caddo sites in the Pine Tree Mound community defined by Fields and Gadus (2012a: fig. 9–10) some 25–40 km downstream in the Sabine River basin – which was established in the 1300s – but the differences in the ceramics between the two areas suggest that 41GG5 and the Joe Smith site were not part of that particular community.

The burial features at the sites were those of adults that were laid in an extended, supine position on the floor of shallowly dug graves. One burial feature (Burial 1) at the Joe Smith site had two individuals laid out side-by-side in the grave, while the other burials had only a single individual. The burial pits were oriented northwest-southeast, with the head of the deceased at the southeastern end of the grave, and facing to the northwest. Burials with the same orientation have been identified in Middle and Late Caddo period cemeteries in the middle Sabine River basin (Heartfield, Price and Greene, Inc. 1988; Fields and Gadus 2012a). However, in Late Caddo Titus phase burials at several sites on Hawkins Creek north of the Joe Smith site, including 41GG51 and 41GG53-56, the burials were oriented east-west, as in Titus phase cemeteries to the north in the Little and Big Cypress basins (see Chapter 6).

Funerary offerings were placed with the deceased for their use on their journey to the Caddo's House of Death, and these included ceramic vessels (n=18 at 41GG5 and n=27 at the Joe Smith site). Bonham arrow points (n=21, in one burial at 41GG5 and two burials at the Joe Smith site), and a ceramic elbow pipe from the Joe Smith site. Clay pigment and a clay mass were also placed in the graves of two burials.

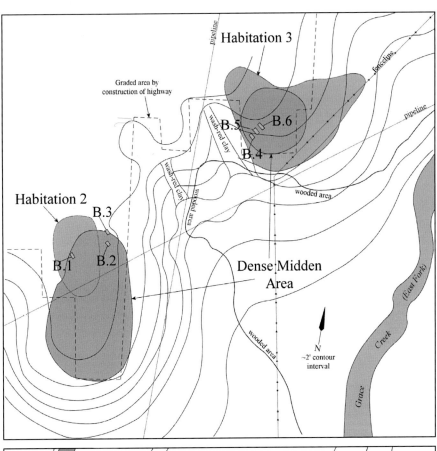

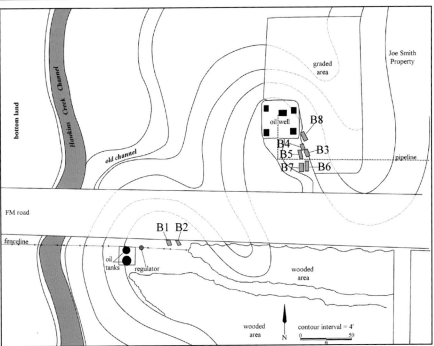

Fig. 67. Maps of 41GG5 and the Joe Smith site: a. 41GG5; b. Joe Smith

Fig. 68. Close-up of the engraved motifs on Vessel 1 from Burial 1 at the Joe Smith site

One unique bottle from the Joe Smith site has engraved panels divided by vertical appliqued ridges; the panels have different combinations of concentric ovals, pendant triangles, a hooked arm element and diagonal engraved zones, and one panel has a snake head and body (Fig. 68). Washington Square Paneled and/or Haley Engraved sherds were also identified from sherds found in burial fill at both sites. Based on associations of similar vessels and sherds from other East Texas sites in the Sabine and Angelina River basins (i.e., Corbin and Hart 1998; Dockall *et al.* 2008; Gadus *et al.* 2006; Hart and Perttula 2010; Rogers and Perttula 2004; Walters 2008), the ceramic assemblages from the Joe Smith site and 41GG5 can be clearly associated with Middle Caddo settlements and burial interments.

Engraved snake head and body motifs have been identified in a number of sites in the Big Cypress, Sabine, and Angelina River basins (Hart and Perttula 2010: fig. 2; Walters 2006). The two bottles from the Joe Smith site extend the distribution of engraved rattlesnake vessels and vessel sherds farther east, and now include a site on the north side of the Sabine River in addition to those from the Lake Clear (41SM243), Langford (41SM197) and Oak Hill Village (41RK214) on streams on the south side of the river (Hart and Perttula 2010: fig. 2). An engraved snake motif has also been identified from a Middle Caddo cemetery at 41HS74 on Hatley Creek (Heartfield, Price and Greene, Inc. 1988: fig. 6-16), some 25 km east of the Joe Smith site.

Utility wares from 41GG5 and the Joe Smith site include jars with vertical incised panels filled with tool punctations; brushed-incised lines; a jar with circular punctations in two rows and another with a tool punctated row at the rim-body juncture and vertical brushing on the body; and a jar with concentric incised ovals filled with punctations on the rim and vertical brushing on the vessel body. Another jar has vertical brushing marks on the body, while the rim is plain. Finally, there are four utility ware jars from the Joe Smith site that feature pinching decorations. These include one with horizontal brushing on the rim and vertical pinched rows on the body; two other jars with plain rims and vertical pinched rows on the body; and a jar with tool punctated rows on the rim and pinched circles on the body, centered around a large appliqued node.

Plain vessels are also common in the mortuary vessel assemblages, 22% of the vessels from 41GG5 and 30% of the vessels from the Joe Smith site. These are bowls, carinated bowls and jars. Altogether, the vessels represented from the burials at the two sites are carinated bowls (31%), bowls (20%), compound bowls (2%), jars (31%), beakers (2%) and bottles (13%).

Other distinctive features of the vessels include rim and lip treatments on two vessels from 41GG5 that have been generally associated with Middle Caddo ceramic vessels in the Sabine and Angelina River basins. These are sprocket rims (see Walters 2010: 115 and fig. 5) and the Redwine rim mode (Walters 2010: 81 and fig. 4). One of the Washington Square Paneled carinated bowls from one burial at 41HS718 on a Sabine River tributary has a Redwine mode rim (Gadus *et al.* 2006: fig. 4-40).

Site 41HS144 is a Middle Caddo period settlement and cemetery on a southward-flowing tributary to the Sabine River in the East Texas Pineywoods. It is about 15 km west of the Pine Tree Mound site (41HS15) (Fields and Gadus 2012a fig. 9.9; 2012b), and is in the territory of the Pine Tree Mound community (Fields and Gadus 2012a fig. 9.10). The site had a complex intra-site organization. Apparently three circular Caddo house structures and one rectangular structure were identified and excavated at the southern and western parts of the settlement (Fig. 69), along with three extensive areas of habitation/midden deposits (with ceramic sherds and lithic artifacts) between two structures as well as north and east of the two northernmost Caddo structures. Finally, there is a Caddo cemetery in the southeastern part of the settlement.

The Caddo cemetery at 41HS144 is in an area measuring *c.* 13.1 m northeast-southwest and 12.2 m northwest-southeast. The 18 grave pits are oriented northwest-southeast, like other Caddo burials in the Pine Tree Mound community (Fields and Gadus 2012a: fig. 5.35), with at least two rows of burials with between 6–8 individuals per row. The beginnings of two other rows at the northern end of the cemetery had two individuals per row. The burials ranged widely in size, suggesting that perhaps both adults and children/adolescents were buried in the cemetery. It is possible that the larger burial pits in the southern row had two individuals buried in these graves. The larger burial pits (n=6) were also deeper, ranging from 1.2–1.8 m in depth, while the 12 smaller burial pits were only *c.* 46–61 cm in depth.

Grog-tempered and bone-tempered sherds from utility ware vessels dominate the 41HS144 ceramic assemblage from habitation deposits, in particular high proportions of sherds from brushed, brushed-punctated, brushed-appliqued and brushed-incised Bullard Brushed and Pease Brushed-Incised vessels. A few sherds are from Maydelle Incised and Killough Pinched jars. The sherds from fine ware vessels are also distinctive, as they are from Washington Square Paneled, Haley Engraved and Tyson Engraved vessels, all ceramic types characteristic of the

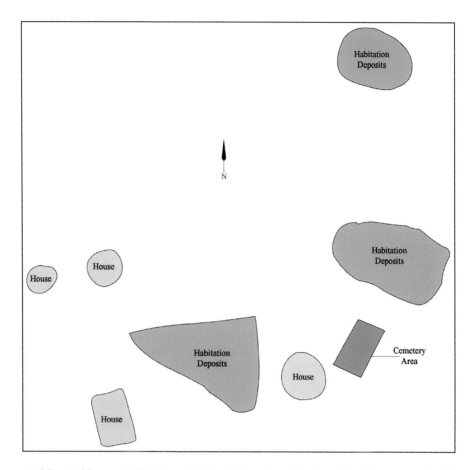

Fig. 69. Plan of the cultural features at 41HS144

Middle Caddo period in the middle Sabine River basin. Other fine ware sherds have decorative elements commonly recognized in Middle Caddo period sites in the region (cf. Hart and Perttula 2010), such as concentric circles and scroll fill zones; curvilinear lines and curvilinear hatched zones; open and excised pendant triangles on bottles; large open triangles, excised triangles and negative ovals on rim panels; horizontal, vertical and oval lines and a hatched zone; horizontal lines and a hatched zone; and a horizontal hatched zone.

These ceramic stylistic elements indicate that the ancestral Caddo settlement at 41HS144 took place sometime during the Middle Caddo period, probably during the late 14th–early 15th century AD. This is based on calibrated radiocarbon dates from the Musgano site (41RK19), another Caddo site in the burgeoning Pine Tree Mound community in the middle Sabine River basin.

The Musgano site (41RK19) is a well-preserved 14th to mid-15th century ancestral Caddo habitation site (with one to several inhabited house structures) in the Martin Creek valley in the mid-Sabine River basin (Perttula 2014d). The Caddo peoples that lived there were farmers that interacted widely with neighboring communities in the mid-Sabine and upper Neches River basins in East Texas, as surmised through similarities in decorative and technological styles of their locally produced ceramic wares.

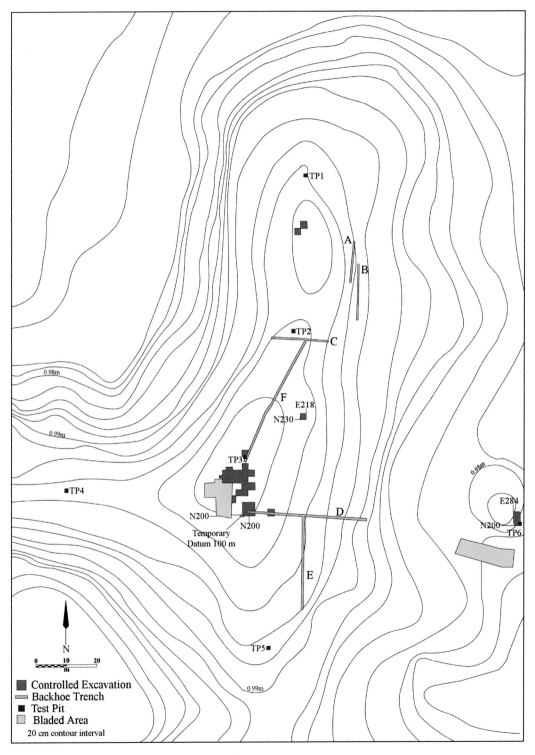

Fig. 70. 1972–1973 Excavations at the Musgano site

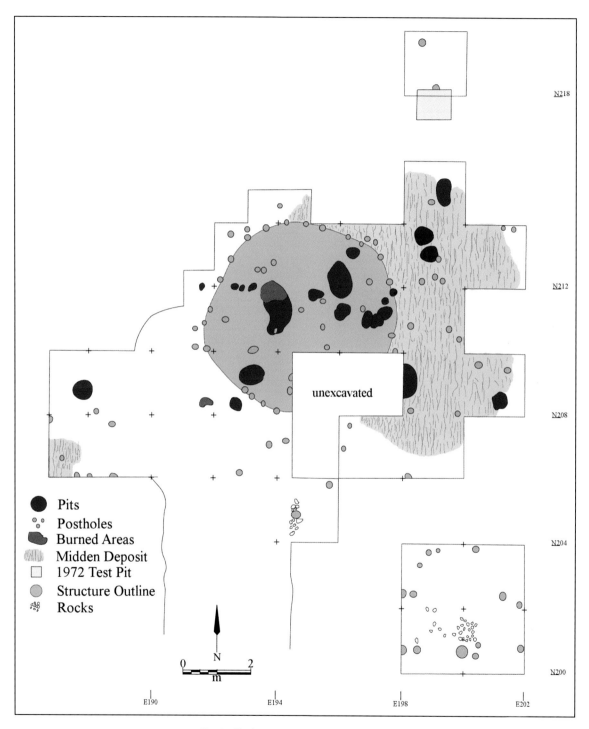

Fig. 71. Block excavations at the Musgano site

The site is located on several knolls across an eastward-projecting alluvial terrace between Martin Creek and Wasson Branch, overlooking a spring-fed slough in the Martin Creek floodplain (Fig. 70). The site is estimated to cover approximately 4 acres.

Numerous cultural features were identified in the block excavations and stripped areas at the site, in addition to midden deposits, including 90 post-holes, many associated with a circular Caddo house and several post-holes that may be part of a granary (Fig. 71). This feature is marked by a roughly circular pattern of posts about 3.5 m in diameter, a size consistent with other granaries identified and documented in East Texas Caddo sites. Other post-holes occur in several areas outside of the structure, in outdoor work and midden areas, and these likely represent elevated work platforms, racks and screens.

The one defined Caddo house is circular, c. 6 m in diameter. One 1.5 m gap in the structure wall post-holes suggests that the entrance to the house was on its southwest side. Within the house is a 40 cm diameter burned area with charcoal and ash that is the central hearth.

The main midden deposits at the Musgano site occur immediately outside portions of the east, north and south walls of the house (see Fig. 71). They are about 9 m north-south and 7.75 m east-west. The identification of a second midden deposit suggests there may be a second house and midden compound on the western part of the knoll.

Other features include pits (n=28) of various sizes and contents; 14 of the pits are inside the house; five pits are in the midden along the east side of the house; and the others are a few meters away from the west side of the house. The larger pits are probably storage pits that eventually were disused and trash was thrown into them for disposal. The smaller pits (n=13) had lesser quantities of charcoal and other trash than the larger pits, but their functions are not known.

The radiocarbon dating of six samples of organic remains from the archaeological deposits at the Musgano site indicate that the primary Caddo occupation took place between cal AD 1250–1440. The principal peaks in probability density occur at cal AD 1260–1280 and cal AD 1400–1440, and the calibrated median ages range from cal AD 1278–1431 (Perttula 2014d). The calibrated age ranges with the highest probabilities at 2 sigma are: cal AD 1244–1302, cal AD 1344–1395, cal AD 1394–1443, cal AD 1405–1455 and cal AD 1389–1437. Four of these age ranges fall between cal AD 1344–1455. It is likely that this period represents the principal Caddo occupation period of the Musgano site during the latter years of the Middle Caddo period in the mid-Sabine River basin.

The archaeological investigations at the Musgano site resulted in the collection of a large assemblage of decorated utility ware and fine ware rim and body sherds from habitation deposits on three different knolls. The stylistic character of these sherds is useful in outlining the historical relationships evidenced in the decorative elements and motifs that speak of cultural transmission and stylistic change and continuity in the decoration of Caddo vessels in the mid-Sabine River basin. The engraved fine wares are not stylistically similar to the post-AD 1450 fine wares documented from the Pine Tree Mound community (see Fields and Gadus 2012a; 2012b) a few miles to the north on another tributary of the Sabine River. Instead they are more like ceramic assemblages on Middle Caddo period sites in the mid-Sabine and Angelina River basins (cf. Gadus *et al.* 2006; Hart 1982: 2014; Hart and Perttula 2010; Perttula and Nelson 2013; Walters 2008: 2010), and it is likely that various Caddo communities in these areas had close social and cultural ties and established networks of contact and cultural transmission of ideas and practices.

The ceramic sherd assemblage is predominantly from grog-tempered vessels (88.7%), with the remainder from bone-tempered vessels. The rim sherds from plain wares represent 15.4% of all the rim sherds in the collection, indicating that plain ware vessels are common at the site; more than 70% of the rims are from utility wares.

Among the decorated rim sherds, 87% are from utility ware vessels, particularly vessels with punctated (primarily rows of tool punctations), incised-punctated (from Maydelle Incised jars), incised (most from Maydelle Incised vessels), brushed (probably from Bullard Brushed jars) and brushed-punctated (also probably from Bullard Brushed jars) decorative elements. Other utility wares include sherds from Pease Brushed-Incised vessels and Killough Pinched jar sherds. Several of the incised-punctated sherds from the Musgano site are from Washington Square Paneled vessels (Hart 1982; 2014).

Among the fine ware sherds, the rims from engraved carinated bowls and bowls in the Musgano assemblage feature circular and curvilinear elements, sets of diagonal lines and rims with horizontal lines and various associated elements. None of the rims have scroll elements, which feature so prominently in post-*c.* AD 1450 assemblages in the mid-Sabine River basin (e.g., Fields and Gadus 2012a). Many of the same engraved elements are present in the nearby and generally contemporaneous Oak Hill Village ceramic assemblage (Rogers and Perttula 2004: 217–22) as well as other mid-Sabine River basin sites.

Engraved sherds from bottles comprise almost 24% of the engraved fine wares from the Musgano site. There is one engraved rim sherd from a Hickory Engraved bottle. The decorative elements on the bottle bodies are diverse (Fig. 72), with circles, hatched and cross-hatched ovals and narrow panels and zones, as well as possible canebrake rattlesnake elements from Nacogdoches Engraved vessels (Fig. 72l). As previously mentioned, engraved canebrake rattlesnake motifs on bottles has been found in ceramic assemblages in at least 17 Caddo sites in the Big and Little Cypress Creek, mid-Sabine, Red River and Angelina River basins in East Texas.

Ceramic pipe sherds are from long-stemmed Red River pipes, probably *var. Haley* (Hoffman 1967), bowl and stem sherds from distinctive L-shaped elbow pipes, and portions of two squat L-shaped elbow pipes. The L-shaped elbow pipes have been found at a number of other East Texas (i.e., Sabine, Neches and Angelina River basins) Caddo sites with Middle Caddo period occupations.

The chipped stone tools from the occupation include two arrow point preforms and eight arrow points. Including the arrow point preforms, 40% of the arrow points at the Musgano site are made from non-local lithic raw materials. These materials have likely source areas in Red River gravels (novaculite and black chert) and Central Texas gravel sources (dark brown and dark grayish-brown chert).

Corn cob parts (cupules, glumes and fragments) are abundant in the charred plant remains from the Musgano site. Mean cupule width is 4.8 mm, and cupule

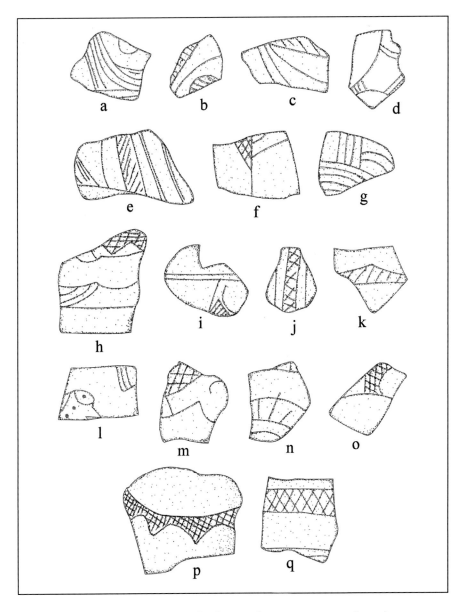

Fig. 72. Engraved bottle sherds from the Musgano site

height (thickness) is 2.2 mm overall. The cupule measurements from the Musgano site are consistent with those from other East Texas Caddo sites. Other charred plant foods include thick-shelled hickory and acorn. Wood charcoal is dominated by oak, with lesser amounts of hop hornbeam, hickory and pine. Fragments of river cane were also recovered from a feature; cane may have been used for mats, baskets, screens, arrow shafts, etc.

Identifiable animal remains at the Musgano site are comprised mainly of deer, and turkey; cottontail and squirrel are represented by at least two specimens each; there are many turtle shell fragments (probably box or musk/mud turtles). The deer elements recovered suggest that individuals (adults and young individuals) were butchered at or near the site. The presence of these animals in trash deposits and features at the site indicates the hunting of wetlands, bottomlands and wooded edges.

The Tyson site (41SY92) is a late 14th–mid-15th century Caddo habitation site located on a prominent hill about 25 m above the floodplain of the Attoyac River. This settlement contains evidence for structures and cooking and storage pit features, one large clay hearth and also has extensive midden deposits with an abundance of ceramic vessel and pipe sherds and well-preserved plant and animal remains. Lastly, there is a small cemetery of three children just outside of one structure (Middlebrook 1994; 2014).

One of the calibrated dates from the Tyson site was on a mussel shell included as a grave good with Feature 14 (Burial 1), the burial of a 1–2 year-old child, and a second even younger child, accompanied by many grave goods. Among the burial offerings were eight ceramic vessels near the head and feet of the child, two large paired deer antlers over the child's head (perhaps as part of a head dress), carved shell inlays near the head, two carved bone ear spools, 32 *Olivella* shell beads, three columnella beads from a necklace, a turtle rattle, a cache of mussel shell, smoothed stones, two pitted stones, a cache of six deer ulna awls and two beaver teeth, and a cache of lithic pebble cores, flakes, preforms and a notched shell point. The second child burial (Feature 15/Burial 2) was that of a "neonate and was either stillborn, or died within a few days of its birth" (Dockall 1994: 48). This child had funerary offerings of two ceramic jars, two marine shell columella beads, a mussel shell and a lump of potter's clay.

The Tyson site may represent the residence of a *caddi* or chiefly elite (Middlebrook 1994; 2014). This is primarily because of the diverse range of funerary offerings with one of the child burials, suggesting that child had an ascribed or inherited rank and that important and high ranking person(s) lived at the site:

> "Mortuary associated artifacts in juvenile Burial 1 are numerous, elaborate, and apparently of high status. Some of the artifacts are valuable jewelry or clothing that would have been traded from the coast (e.g., columella and *Olivella* beads). Other materials suggest that the very young child was in need of extensive (e.g., eight pottery vessels) and non-age appropriate provisions in the afterlife (e.g., a large lithic tool making kit) …The only reasonable interpretation of Burial 1 is that the individual was an offspring of a very important person or was a high ranking person in his own right …" (Middlebrook 1994: 30–1)

At the Tallow Grove site (41NA231) on Naconiche Creek in the Angelina River basin, a much different sort of Caddo occupation is apparent in Middle Caddo period times (Perttula 2008b). There is evidence for four different circular structures being constructed and used by family-sized groups (Fig. 73). Three of the structures or structure areas are north of a large midden, and one of these (probably the last of the three) actually extends a short distance across the existing midden area. The fourth structure/structure area is situated on and adjacent to a second midden deposit. A possible ramada was also constructed just to the southeast of one of the three northern structures. It is situated amidst an outdoor work area in the large midden, and is marked by many large and small basin-shaped pits. There does not appear to be any open plaza-like area at Tallow Grove, in contrast to what has been documented at the nearby Beech Ridge site (see below). There is a small cemetery, surely a marker of place for the commoner families that lived here, situated behind the area of the three northern structural deposits.

Conversely, the Middle Caddo period occupation at the Beech Ridge site (41NA242), probably lasting no longer than 20 years, had two occupational areas at the northern and southern parts of the landform, both with evidence of structures, indoor and outdoor pit features, and activity areas around the structures (Fig. 74). These activity areas were located both north, south and west of the area of structures, but did not encircle them. There was an open area – a plaza, common area, or courtyard – that separated the two occupational areas of domestic households, that had minimal occupational deposits. There are no midden deposits at the site, only six large basin-shaped storage pits, and no formal cemetery. The two burials were situated west of the structures.

Locally, stable carbon isotope values from three burials on Naconiche Creek (dating from the late 13th–early 15th centuries) range from –16.3‰ to –18.1‰ (see Wilson 2008). Following Schoeninger *et al.* (2000), these values indicate that maize comprised less than 30% of the diet of the Naconichi Caddo; maize ubiquity values from the paleobotanical analyses (see Dering 2008b) also suggest a relatively low consumption of maize. Thus, there is no evidence currently available that

Fig. 73. Schematic view of the character of the Middle Caddo period occupation at the Tallow Grove site.

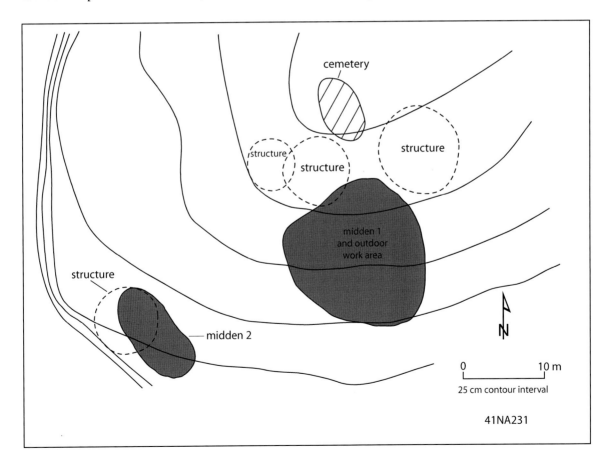

Fig. 74. Schematic plan of features and occupational areas at the Beech Ridge site during Middle Caddo period times

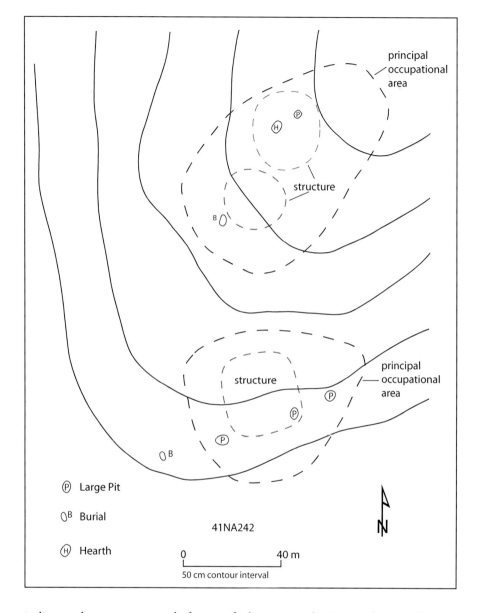

indicates there was a period of intensified maize production in this specific part of East Texas. It is possible that any intensification in maize production may have taken place after c. AD 1450 here, but there is actually minimal use of the Naconiche Creek valley by the Caddo after that time. Perhaps the movement of many Caddo peoples out of the valley after the mid-15th century is evidence of that intensification seen in other parts of East Texas by Caddo communities, with these Caddo moving to other parts of East Texas where more optimal agricultural pursuits could be undertaken.

6

The Full Flowering of Caddo Communities in East Texas, *c.* AD 1400–1680

Late Caddo period settlements across the East Texas landscape were distributed along both major and secondary streams, but in varying spatial densities, and were widely dispersed. They consisted primarily of functionally comparable small farmsteads and hamlets integrated with mound centers and sacred places on the landscape (i.e., community cemeteries and the residences of the *xinesi*). These settlements were part of a number of different communities, and most of these communities are associated with defined archaeological phases; these socio-political entities have long been recognized as phases in the regional archaeological record, a temporal-spatial taxonomic term (cf. Willey and Phillips 1958) in use since the 1950s in the Caddo area. This includes the McCurtain, Texarkana and Belcher phases from west to east on the Red River and its tributaries, the Titus phase in the Cypress Bayou and Sabine River basins, the Salt Lick phase on the lower Sabine, the Frankston phase in the Neches-Angelina River basins, and the Angelina phase in the lower Angelina River (Fig. 75).

Although rigorous regional settlement demographic studies (e.g., Drennan *et al.* 2015) have not been undertaken for any temporal period of the Caddo archaeological record, study of the settlements of Caddo peoples between *c.* AD 1400–1680 indicates that Caddo groups of varying size, complexity and local history were widely distributed across both major and minor streams in virtually all parts of East Texas. Milner's (2015: fig. 2.1) summary of the distribution of Native American population aggregates in eastern North America in the early 16th century depicts much of the southern Caddo area (of southwestern Arkansas, northwestern Louisiana, southeastern Oklahoma and East Texas) as being sparsely settled or uninhabited at that period. Rather, as attested to by many years of archaeological investigations of a variety of Caddo sites across the southern Caddo area, as well as the 1542 accounts of the de Soto-Moscoso entrada, the distribution and density of Caddo farming groups and communities reached its full and peak extent at around this time.

The distribution of Native American populations in eastern North America at the time of initial European contacts in the early to mid-16th century (see Jones 2014: fig. 2) has been important to establish in order to assess the place of Native American communities and groups across the landscape, the short-

and long-term effects of European contact, and the consequences of population change and decline following the introduction, timing and spread of Old World diseases after European contact. The research by George R. Milner (2015; see also Milner and Chaplin 2010) on depopulation, movement and warfare among Eastern North American Native American groups in the early 16th century has laid the foundation for a better understanding of their spatial distribution and their mean and absolute population sizes (Milner and Chaplin 2010: figs 4–5 and table 2). In turn, these findings have provided insights into the effects of European contact from the early 16th century onwards across eastern North America, and Milner (2015: 66) has concluded that:

> "much of the mid-continent was sparsely settled, surviving groups had spaced themselves as far apart as possible...When new diseases were introduced, isolation by distance likely impeded the spread of pathogens transmitted through direct person-to-person contact."

As part of Milner's research, he has compiled a map showing the distribution of "archaeologically identifiable early sixteenth-century population aggregates"

Fig. 75. Distribution of defined phases in the southern Caddo area at *c.* AD 1500 (prepared by Sandra Hannum)

(Milner 2015: 54 and fig. 2.1) that extend from the Atlantic Ocean on the east to the Caddo populations at the far western reaches of eastern North Americ. Figure 76 provides the locations of the population aggregates identified by Milner (2015: fig. 2.1) in the southern Caddo area (Perttula 2012a: figs 1–2). According to Milner (2015: 54), the unshaded areas on the map represent "tracts of unoccupied land," or land that was sparsely settled at that time by Native American groups, apparently including Caddo groups and communities.

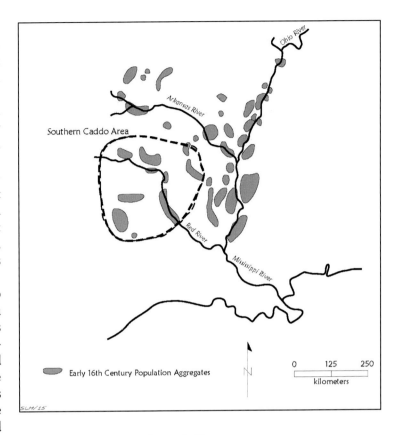

Milner's (2015: fig. 2.1; see also Milner and Chaplin 2010) contention that large swathes of East Texas (as well as other parts of the southern Caddo area in Louisiana and Arkansas) were unoccupied in the early 16th century, or are "places that are poorly known or those occupied by people who moved often" widely misses the mark. Contrary to some interpretations, the period between *c.* AD 1400 (the onset of the Late Caddo period), the mid-16th century, and then to the latter part of the 17th century, were periods of peak densities of Caddo settlements across the region. There is abundant evidence of Caddo settlements – ranging from small farmsteads, small hamlets, to larger villages and multiple mound community centers – in East Texas in the early 16th century (Girard *et al.* 2014: 68: 71–5 and fig. 3.1). The largest Late Caddo period mound in East Texas outside of the Red River, the Pine Tree Mound site (41HS15), was continuously occupied through the 16th and much of the 17th centuries (Fields and Gadus 2012a; 2012b), as was the multiple mound center and large village at the Hatchel site (41BW3) on the Red River (Fig. 77).

Fig. 76. Early 16th century population aggregates in the western part of eastern North America. This Figure is redrawn from Milner (2015: fig. 2.1) to focus on the southern Caddo area and immediately adjacent regions (prepared by Sandra Hannum)

The extent of Caddo settlement through this period also suggests that the adverse effects of European epidemic diseases, including depopulation, did not occur until after AD 1680 (Derrick and Wilson 2001: 101). When the de Soto-Moscoso entrada encountered Caddo groups along the Ouachita River in what is now southwestern Arkansas at the province of Chaguate in 1542 (Fig. 78), they noted a well-peopled province (Hudson 1993; 1997: 329); furthermore, Naguatex on the Red River (associated with the Belcher phase) was similarly described as a fertile and well-populated land. While there may have been buffers between Caddo provinces, particularly south of the Sabine River, there were well-populated Caddo communities along almost all the route taken by the entrada. The entrada accounts do not identify large areas that were uninhabited or sparsely settled by

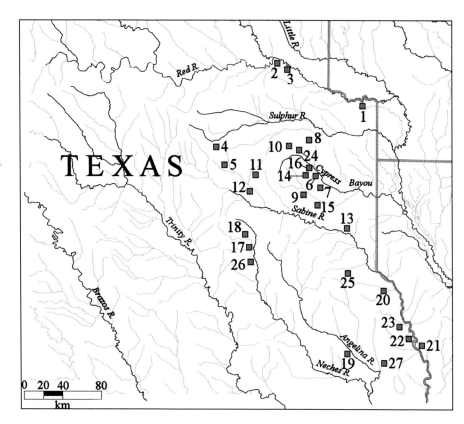

Caddo groups at that time (see Schambach 1989; 1993c; Bruseth and Kenmotsu 1991; 1993; Early 1993b; Hoffman 1993; Kenmotsu *et al.* 1993; Young and Hoffman 1993).

There were subtle population and territorial readjustments across the landscape during this period. Couple this with continued mound building in some major valleys (including the Sabine, Big Cypress and Red River basins), trade activities (in salt and bow wood) and other pursuits suggests that these areas were occupied by prosperous Caddo farmers with sustainable and well-developed social and political organizations.

With respect to the material culture of Caddo peoples, Late Caddo period ceramics retain their stylistic heterogeneity, but the fine ware, utility ware and plain wares are part of and associated with recognizable and relatively geographically coherent socio-political entities that arose out of the earlier and distinctive pre-AD 1400 archaeological traditions of the Caddo peoples (see Perttula 2000; 2013). In addition to these wares, there are also several stylistically and functionally distinctive vessels used for special purposes. Among these are horizontal engraved effigy bowls with modeled bird heads (Fig. 79a). The very common use of a bird's head appendage on effigy vessels, and a review of North American Indian maize myths by Lankford (2008: 37), may be linked to the fact that in these myths, maize is commonly described in a "maize-as-a-gift" tradition, as in a gift from a divinity or their emissary; this is the case among the Caddo, for instance (Lankford 2008: fig. 2.1). One of those emissaries is a bird. Perhaps, then, the bird on the effigy

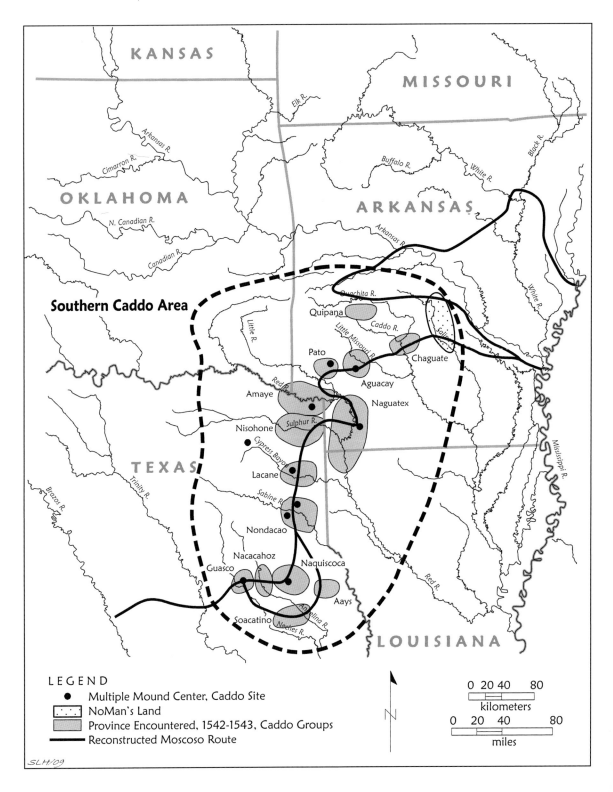

Southern Caddo Area

LEGEND
- ● Multiple Mound Center, Caddo Site
- ⬚ NoMan's Land
- ▨ Province Encountered, 1542-1543, Caddo Groups
- ▬ Reconstructed Moscoso Route

Fig. 78. Map of the postulated de Soto-Moscoso entrada across the southern Caddo area and selected Caddo provinces in southwest Arkansas and East Texas in 1542 (prepared by Sandra Hannum)

bowls made by East Texas Caddo potters is a unique symbolic representation of the bird emissary that brought maize in all its abundance to these Caddo people.

The incensario form (see Fig. 79b) has been suggested to have been a ritual vessel form "for tobacco usage among the Caddo in early historic times" (Lankford 2012: 55 and fig. 6b). Suhm and Jelks (1962: pl. 26a, c) label them rattle bowls, and examples are known from several Red River valley Caddo sites. Moore Noded vessels (see Fig. 79c) have small appliqued nodes that cover the entirety of the vessel surface. They are common at sites in the Great Bend area of the Red River valley. Similar knobby or noded vessels found in the American Southwest and Central Mississippi Valley have been suggested to have been ceramic *Datura* fruit effigies used for the storage and consumption of prepared datura (or jimson weed), a hallucinogenic plant (Huckell and Vanpool 2006: 152–3; Lankford 2012: 60). The Caddo were known to consume datura and peyote as part of shamanistic rituals (see Swanton 1942), and these noded vessels may be reflective of these rituals being used after *c.* AD 1450 by ancestral Caddo peoples living in East Texas. Other kinds of vessels may have been used for the serving of the Black Drink, used for ritual purification, made from holly leaves (*Ilex vomitoria*) available across parts of the southern Caddo area (Crown *et al.* 2012: fig. 2).

Fig. 79. Special purpose vessels made and used by Late and Historic Caddo groups in East Texas: a. Hood Engraved effigy bowl with a tail rider; b. incensario form; c. Moore Noded bowl

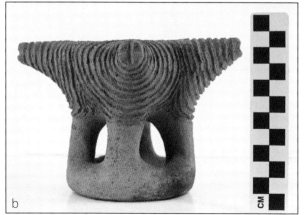

Peyoteism and the origins of Caddo religious thought
by Robert L. Cast

Peyote, or *Lophophora williamsii*, has long been a sacred medicinal plant to a number of tribes across the United States. The Caddo Indians have a distinguished and long history of using this important plant. John R. Swanton (1942: 121) noted:

> "It is interesting to remember that peyote was used by medicine men among the Hasinai at the beginning of the eighteenth century, and recalling the elaborate ritualism of the Caddo, as well as their various contacts with Christian missionaries, including the presence among them of established missions for three decades, one wonders whether such a background does not constitute part of the explanation of John Wilson. It may put the ancient fire cult of the Natchez and Caddo, Franciscan teachings, the Ghost dance religion, the peyote cult, and the North American churches founded on the last mentioned in one line of descent."

The Caddo Indians practiced a vibrant peyote religion long before John Wilson (Moonhead) or Quanah Parker re-ignited the Native American Church. Moreover, research has shown the importance of the peyote plant to the Caddo long before any European contact. The peyote religion at the time of the Spanish missions in Texas was full of songs and dances in honor of one known today as "*A?ah? hi-u kuu-i´-ha*" or "Father Above", translated to mean "*home where God lives*". Although Swanton proposes that the Hasinai medicine men used peyote "at the beginning of the eighteenth century" (a reference to Frey Hidalgo's Spanish account) how long had they been using this plant before any written records?

In Swanton's analysis of the Caddo Indians, he recognized that during the contact period with the Spanish and the establishment of Spanish missions in East Texas that the Caddo did not convert to Catholicism as hoped, because they had a long standing tradition of worshiping their God in their own way. Although the Caddo have long been referred to as being a part of a perpetual or eternal "fire" cult "*e´but ni-kuu*", literally grandfather fire, the fire was only a small part of the ritualism, the Peyote or "*sik'uh-ho*" (from the literal meaning "rock") has long been the central foundation for the religion.

Ethnohistorian Mariah F. Wade (n.d.) in her translation of a 4 November 1716 letter from Fray Hidalgo to the Viceroy of New Spain recognizes this as well and emphasizes several important points in her introduction to the translation: (1) the Caddo refused the religion of the Friars and the Catholic Church and, (2) that "researchers have not completely understood the essence of this refusal nor the strength of Caddo religious practices and convictions." Her translation goes on to describe Frey Hidalgo's biased but pertinent viewpoints regarding the Hasinai Caddo:

> "As far as we have determined all this Nation is Idolater, they have houses of Adoration and they have the perpetual fire, which they do not let be extinguished. They are very superstitious, and they will believe the visions related to them by the Indian male and female who gets drunk on the peyote, or the small bean, during the Dances that they hold. They prepare this drink specifically for the celebrations ... (Wade n.d.: 10)"

One interesting note is that Swanton refers to the use of peyote by "medicine men" when clearly by the earliest written accounts both men and women used peyote. If this is the case, then where did the Caddo Indians of East Texas gather peyote?

In recent years, the Caddo Nation of Oklahoma has had a number of consultation meetings with representatives of the El Camino Real de los Tejas National Historic Trails to discuss information related to the interpretation of the trail from a Native American perspective. At one meeting hosted at the Comanche Nation Museum in Lawton, Oklahoma, several tribes were represented including the Comanche, Kiowa and Wichita. During the meeting, each tribe voiced concerns with the trail as the National Historic Trails representatives showed them a large map explaining that the trail extended from Mexico to Nacogdoches, Texas. The Caddo voiced concerns that the route actually extended in the other direction, from Nacogdoches southward with branches of the trail ending up in Mexico. Several of the tribal representatives stated that they continued to use parts of this trail today to drive south to get peyote from the authorized dealers in Mexico. The irony is that the Caddo created the trail to gather their sacred plant hundreds of years earlier, with the Spanish later using it as a route from Mexico to explore and setup missions in Spanish Texas.

Anthropologists such as Weston LaBarre, Elsie Clews Parsons and John R. Swanton have only scantily referenced the Caddo's ancient use of peyote. More recently, however, Jay Miller (1996, 243–59) has described the connections with the Caddo use of peyote with some the ancient stories and names within the Caddo language such as *xinesi*, also known by the Spanish as "Mr Moon" or *Tsah Neeshi*, an important cultural figure in Caddo oral history. Cecile Carter (1995) also recognized this name as most likely a mishearing of the word by the Spanish for the name of the high priest of the fire temple mound.

Settlements and political communities

In the Great Bend area of the Red River, Late Caddo archaeological sites are included in the contemporaneous Belcher and Texarkana phases (see Fig. 75). Texarkana phase sites occur on the Red River northwest of Texarkana to the Arkansas/Oklahoma state lines, as well as on the lower Sulphur River, while Belcher phase sites are distributed from about Fulton, Arkansas, to below Shreveport, Louisiana. Upstream from communities of the Texarkana phase, the McCurtain phase represents another Late Caddo period archaeological complex in parts of East Texas and southeast Oklahoma.

In the Texarkana and Belcher phase areas, sites include large, permanent settlements with mounds and cemeteries, villages, as well as dispersed hamlets and farmsteads. The mound centers were marked by earthen mounds that were constructed for use as temples, burial mounds, or ceremonial fire mounds. These settlements were comprised of sedentary Caddo agricultural communities led by individuals with high religious and political status or rank who lived at the mound centers. Sites such as Belcher (16CD13) (Webb 1959), Battle Mound (3LA1) (McKinnon 2013), Hatchel (41BW3), Moore/Higginbotham (3MI3/30) and Cabe Mounds (41BW14) represent the larger villages or towns, with surrounding hamlets or farmsteads. These settlements – both the larger communities and the smaller hamlets/farmsteads – had pole and grass structures, outdoor ramadas or arbors, household cemeteries and midden deposits from household refuse. The 1691 Teran de los Rios map of the Nasoni village on the Red River documented the likely character of individual farmstead compounds and the layout of a dispersed village (see Chapter 7). In northwestern Louisiana, Belcher phase sites are distributed along recently abandoned Red River channels and its inactive meander belt. The Belcher phase is thought to date from c. AD 1500 to the late 17th century (Kelley 2012).

From stable isotope and bioarchaeological evidence, the McCurtain phase Caddo were also agricultural peoples, depending heavily on the cultivation of maize as the main staple of the diet. Bioarchaeological analyses of the burials from the Texarkana phase Hatchel-Mitchell-Moores complex on the Red River also indicates that the health of the Caddo people was good: well-healed fractures, the low to moderate severity of arthritis, mild anemia and periostitis, imply a fairly successful adaptation. The cranial modeling and enthesopathies suggest that the Caddo traveled long distances, perhaps for marriage and trade (Lee 1997). Mean stable carbon isotope values of –14.8±1.35‰ (n=28) from *c.* AD 1450–1650 Caddo sites, and –14.2±1.17‰ (n=18) in post-1650 Caddo sites in East Texas, southwestern Arkansas and northwestern Louisiana indicate the development and maintenance of an agricultural economy through the Late Caddo period (Wilson 2012; Wilson and Perttula 2013).

Mound construction in Texarkana phase sites seems to coincide with the main period of settlement at the Hatchel site. Both archaeological and historical information suggests that the main platform mound (with many levels of structures and features) at the Hatchel site may be the *templo* or temple mound shown on the 1691 Teran map. The Cabe mound site may also have been occupied at this time, and the Moore/Higginbotham mound center and community a few miles downstream from the Cabe site probably represents part of the upper Kadohadacho village that was eventually abandoned in 1788 after continued Osage depredations (Smith 2014: 190).

Like other Caddo groups on the Red River, the McCurtain phase settlement pattern includes numerous habitation sites (with household cemeteries and substantial midden deposits) and mound centers, though the mounds appear to have mainly been constructed in the early part of the phase (*c.* AD 1350–1500); the McCurtain phase is not well-dated through radiocarbon analysis, however. In some instances, mound centers were not directly associated with permanent settlements or middens. The McCurtain phase mounds were generally constructed in one or two stages over important public structures, with the structure abandoned, dismantled and/or burned, then capped with a ritually-charged zone of soil scraped from nearby deposits or clay sources. Simple and elaborate single and multiple burials were also placed in the mounds, as with the East Mound at the Sam Kaufman site (41RR16) on the Red River.

The density of McCurtain phase sites indicates that greater numbers of people are living in closer proximity than before. At the Sam Kaufman site, the mound in McCurtain phase times was used as a place for the burial of the social elite, as a shaft tomb with 11 individuals and many grave goods was located near the center of the mound. Special purpose salt-processing sites, such as the Salt Well Slough site (41RR204), are also common in the vicinity of the Roitsch site.

Radiocarbon dates from McCurtain phase contexts at the Sam Kaufman, Holdeman (41RR11) and Rowland Clark (41RR77) sites indicate that the McCurtain phase can be divided into early and late (*c.* AD 1500–1700) contexts, with corresponding changes in ceramic decorative styles and arrow point shapes. The early McCurtain phase residential and mortuary features at the Holdeman site date to cal AD 1392–1478 and cal AD 1332–1513 at Roitsch-Sam Kaufman, while 2 sigma calibrated dates from later burial features with slightly different ceramic assemblages at the Rowland Clark site range from cal AD 1447–1697. Calibrated radiocarbon dates from the Peerless Bottoms site (41HP175) in the upper Sulphur River basin, having virtually the same variety of Caddo ceramics as early McCurtain phase sites on the Red River, range between AD 1330–1524 (Fields *et al.* 1997).

Caddo salt-makers

The utilization of salt is a good measure of the relative contribution of domesticates to the Caddo economy. The physiological relationship between salt consumption and a diet based on domesticated plants is a major factor in the intensity with which salt exploitation is pursued. Regional differences in the archaeological evidence for salt production illustrate variations in the initiation and intensification of maize cultivation that support the plant and bioarchaeological data for an increased reliance on maize and other cultivated plants after c. AD 1300. The recent identification of a variety of salt-making sites in the Red, Little and Ouachita River drainages clearly indicates that the intensive use of salt-extraction sites by Caddo peoples occurred only after c. AD 1300–1400, but continued into the 18th century.

The synchronous pattern of salt production activities as an integral part of post-AD 1400 Caddo economies is analogous to that seen in the central Mississippi Valley, except that it took place there beginning in the 10th century AD compared to the 15th century in the southern Caddo area. For instance, it has been noted that there was a light usage of salt sites between AD 900–1200, but real salt production seems not to have begun until c. AD 1200–1400. Furthermore, we have yet to find any evidence of Fourche Maline or Woodland period usage of a salt site in the southern Caddo area. As long as these findings hold, they are strong evidence against any sort of major involvement in horticulture in Fourche Maline times.

The archaeological analysis of Caddo salt-making at the Hardman site in southwestern Arkansas indicates that salt was manufactured as one activity among a series of domestic compounds, but it was extensive enough to alter the local habitat through deforestation. Salt was made by boiling the briny waters, from a saline spring, in salt pan wares over large (mean area of 5.42 m²) outdoor hearths marked by lens of ash and charcoal (Early 1993a). Along Salt Well Slough in the Red River valley in East Texas, however, Caddo salt-makers relied on large jars for the boiling of salt-containing waters and the production of salt for the McCurtain phase Caddo inhabitants of the Mound Prairie area (Kenmotsu 2006; Perttula 2008b). These salt-making sites are marked by massive quantities of jar sherds found in association with large areas of burned soil and burned clay that are the residues of boiling the waters of the slough to make salt.

Key Texarkana and McCurtain Phase sites

The Sam Kaufman site (41RR16) is a large Early Caddo to Historic Caddo period village (paralleling the river for more than 1 km) on a natural levee of the Red River, situated not far downstream from the confluence of the Kiamichi River with the Red River. The site is on Mound Prairie, a natural tall grass prairie, in the Red River basin.

The first Caddo occupation at the site took place around and after c. AD 1100, during the Middle Caddo Mound Prairie phase. Excavations on the natural levee exposed several rectangular-shaped wood domestic structures and cemetery areas, but the extent of this occupation has not been well established. These remains are characterized by Maxey Noded Redware, Canton Incised, Sanders Engraved and Sanders Slipped vessels and long-stemmed Red River clay pipes.

Sometime after c. AD 1300–1350, the major occupation at Sam Kaufman began, and this village of maize farmers, marked by intensively occupied habitation areas and family cemeteries, as well as two earthen mounds constructed at the eastern end of the site, appears to have been more or less continually occupied until the late 17th–early 18th century (Bruseth 1998; Perttula 2008c; Skinner *et al.* 1969). The Caddo people in this area lived in both large villages as well as dispersed farmsteads and hamlets on both major and minor stream courses. The large villages have earthen mounds built over important structures and/or have had shaft tombs excavated into them, numerous house compounds with daub-covered houses, arbors or elevated work platforms, outdoor activity areas, storage pit features and household cemeteries. The population of these villages at any one time may have been as much as 100–200 adults and children, if not more. Farmsteads and hamlets may have had only one to a few houses, and been occupied by only a few families at a time. Another distinctive feature of the settlement and use of the Mound Prairie area by Caddo groups is the salt-making sites on Salt Well Slough, just southwest of the Sam Kaufman/Roitsch site (Kenmotsu 2006).

The Sam Kaufman site had two earthen mounds in the McCurtain phase village (Fig. 80). The West Mound, lost to river erosion in 1990, was comprised of a series of superimposed burned structural and mound fill layers from deliberately destroyed and burned structures that sat on a built-up platform that stood 2.2 m tall and 48 × 60 m in length and width when mound construction ceased. These structures may have been temples or the houses of the social and political elite in the village and surrounding community. The East Mound was a 1 m in height construction. The mound was built over a large rectangular structure (House 2) with a prepared clay floor – assuredly an important public and/or sacred building – that was burned sometime after *c.* AD 1275–1383, based on radiocarbon dates from Feature 101 in the northern part of the mound (Fig. 81).

Following the burning of the structure, the mound was built up with several different kinds of sediments, then a large shaft tomb measuring over 4 m in diameter and 1.8 m in depth was dug by the Caddo through the mound fill, the center of the burned structure floor (see Fig. 81), and deep into the natural clay subsoil. This pit was a shaft tomb dug between cal AD 1412–1511 for the burial of a prominent middle-aged adult male in the center of the tomb, an middle-aged adult female by his right side, and nine other individuals ranging from 13–14 years old to 36–50 years old at the time of their death, possibly retainers or slaves (Fig. 82). The two paramount individuals were placed in the tomb to lie over and upon three of the retainers or slaves, each a middle-aged male. The other deceased individuals were laid out on either side of the central area of the tomb. A diverse range of funerary offerings was placed in the tomb, including 32 whole vessels of both fine wares and utility wares and six clay pipes, 84 arrow points, a large biface of non-local raw material, four stone ear spools, marine shell (n=468) and turquoise (n=30) necklace and bracelet beads, pearl beads (n=28), plain and engraved marine shell gorgets (n=5), discs (n=4), pendants (n=1) and inlays (n=27), mussel shells, two drilled bear teeth and three ground stone celts. "The artifacts, representing the wealth of the deceased leader, and perhaps his lineage, were most likely used to provision himself and his entourage during their journey to the land of the deceased" (Perttula 2008c: 331).

Another tomb in the East Mound is Burial 17 (see Fig. 81). This burial had four individuals, and they were accompanied by 15 ceramic vessels, four marine shell beads and arrow points. There were other McCurtain phase burials (Burials 2–5) in the northeastern quadrant of the East Mound (see Skinner *et al.* 1969: fig. 5).

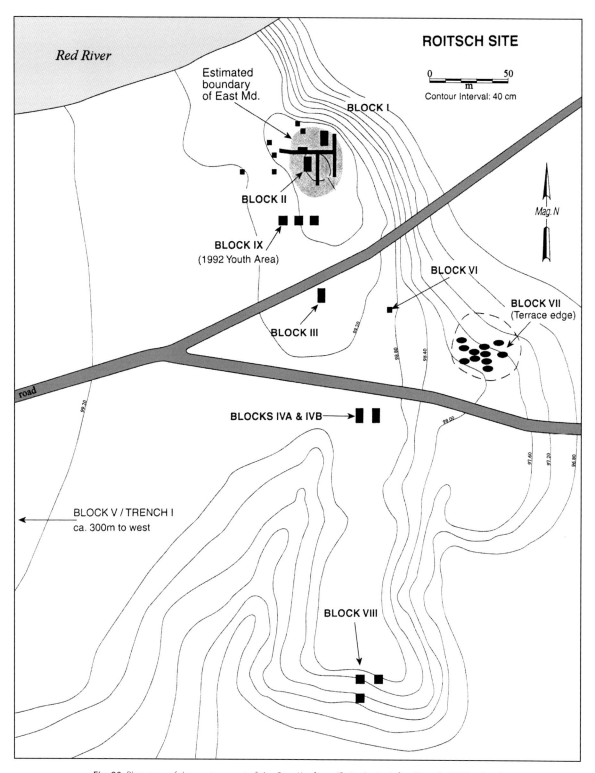

Fig. 80. Plan map of the eastern part of the Sam Kaufman/Roitsch site (after Perttula 2008 c: fig. 5)

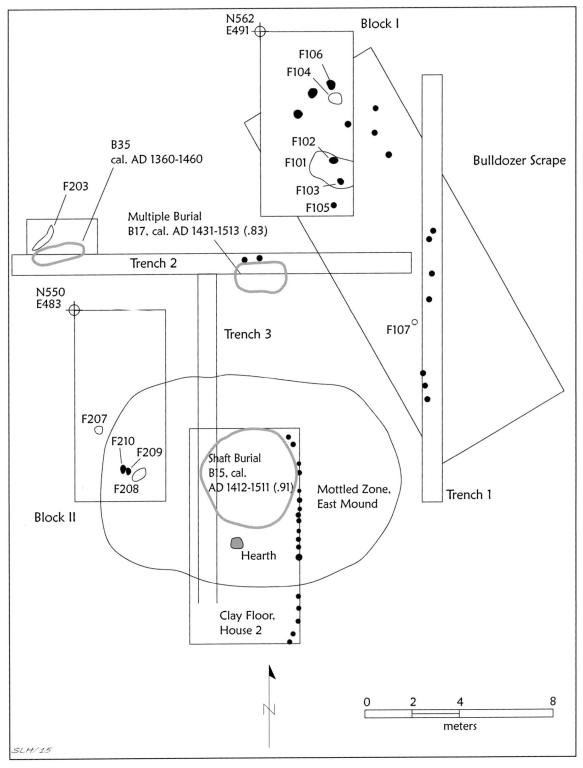

Fig. 81. Features and block excavations on the East Mound (after Perttula 2008 c: fig. 6)

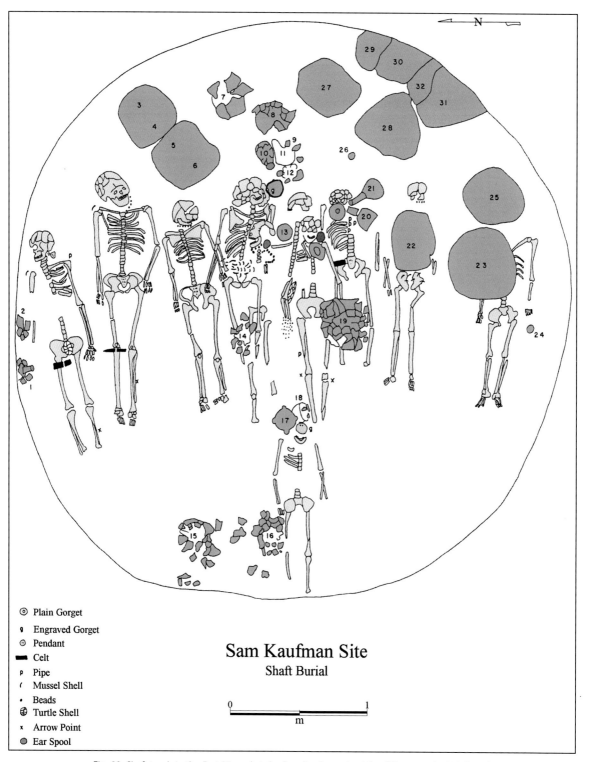

N

⊙ Plain Gorget
𝄞 Engraved Gorget
⊚ Pendant
▬ Celt
ρ Pipe
ʃ Mussel Shell
· Beads
🐢 Turtle Shell
ˣ Arrow Point
◉ Ear Spool

Sam Kaufman Site
Shaft Burial

0   1
          m

Fig. 82. Shaft tomb in the East Mound at the Sam Kaufman site (after Skinner *et al.* 1969, fig. 11)

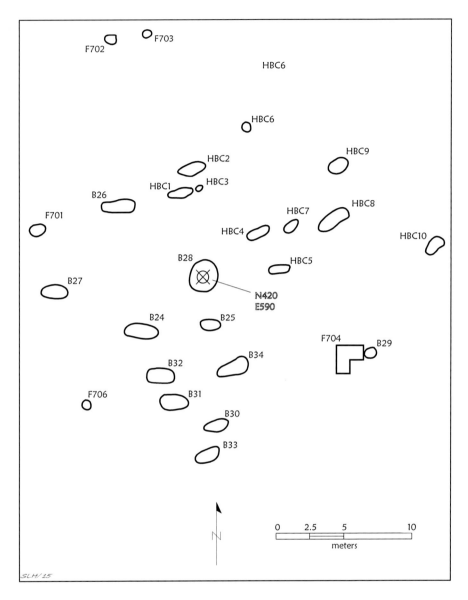

Fig. 83. Burials, human bone concentration, and features along the terrace edge southeast of the East Mound at the Sam Kaufman site

There are several cemeteries west of the West Mound at Sam Kaufman, and they have very late McCurtain phase to Historic Caddo burials, the latter with European glass beads (Skinner *et al.* 1969; Harris 1953a; 1953b). One such cemetery was excavated by Buddy Calvin Jones in the winter of 1961–1962 and consisted of eight burial features (Burials Nos 1–8) near the eroding bank of the Red River. These burials were oriented east-west, with the face of the deceased facing west; one burial was oriented northeast-southwest, with the head of the deceased pointing more towards the southwest. The majority of the burials from a terrace edge cemetery southeast of the East Mound were also oriented southwest-northeast (Fig. 83; see also Perttula 2008c: figs 5 and 37). In addition to 47 ceramic vessels included as funerary offerings, other offerings were a number of bone tools, bison bone, deer bone and a polished beaver tooth from Burial No. 4. The relatively quotidian and redundant character of the associated grave goods from these burials suggests they are the burials of typical village residents, and were not part of the elite (i.e., religious and political leaders and their retainers) population who lived at the site and were buried in the East Mound (Perttula 2008c: fig. 6; Skinner *et al.* 1969).

More mundane kinds of artifacts are found in the house structures, activity areas and trash deposits of the non-elite families living in the village. These primarily consist of thousands of sherds from broken shell-tempered vessels that were made at the Sam Kaufman site. The pottery is well-made and nicely fired and finished, and it is tempered with mussel shell, a distinctive middle Red River Caddo ceramic practice. Also found were large quantities of daub/burned clay from the clay covering of the houses, lithic debris, animal bones and a few chipped and ground stone tools; the latter include stemmed and triangular arrow points, flake tools and scrapers, drills and perforators, cores and tool fragments, as well as manos, grinding slabs, celts and hammerstones.

The Hatchel site (41BW3) was a large Nasoni Caddo mound center and village of the Texarkana phase on the Red River. The site contained at least five earthen mounds, including one primary platform mound, with many levels of important public or elite-occupied buildings, that stood 30 ft (9.1 m) high (Fig. 84). It had extensive domestic habitation and cemetery areas covering several hundred acres around the mounds and on natural levee deposits adjacent to an old channel of the Red River.

When the village was first visited by Europeans in 1687 by Henri Joutel, Henri de Tonti in 1690 and Don Domingo Teran de los Rios in 1691, it stretched for several miles along the river (Foster 1998; Hatcher 1999; Perttula *et al.* 2008). La Harpe built the Nassonite post in the near vicinity of the site in 1719 (Wedel 1978). Freeman and Custis described the principal Caddo village on the Red River, abandoned in 1788, as follows:

Fig. 84. Looking at the platform mound at the Hatchel site from the edge of the Red River floodplain (image 41BW3-9, Texas Archeological Research Laboratory, University of Texas at Austin)

"Around and near to this pond [on the Red River], are to be seen the vestiges of the Caddo habitations; it was the largest of their villages, and their cultivated fields extended for five or six miles from it in every direction" (Flores 1984:188)

The site was first occupied as early as *c.* AD 1100–1300. The platform mound and the main part of the associated village overlooks two channel lakes of the river; these likely were part of the channel of the river when the site was occupied by the Caddo. It was the premier Caddo civic and ceremonial center for a considerable part of the Red River valley. During excavations in the 1930s by the Works Progress Administration (Perttula 2005a) and then again 2003, several village areas with structures, post-holes, midden deposits and burials were identified east, southeast and southwest of the primary platform mound (Fig. 85a–b). A plaza was present south of the primary mound when it was visited by Teran de los Rios. The primary

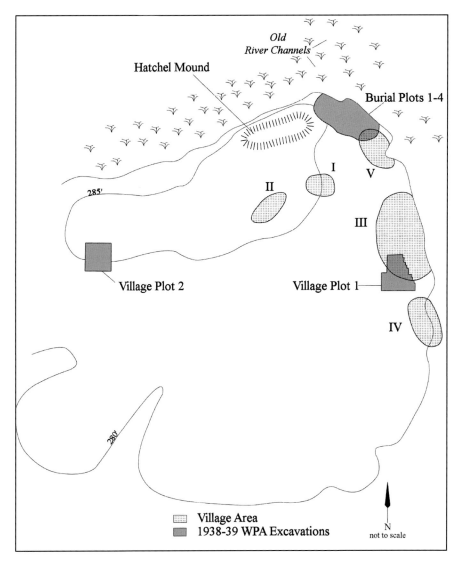

Fig. 85. Village areas near the primary platform mound:

a. Village Plot excavations and village areas;

mound itself was composed of several stages of mound construction fill, with most of the mound fill stages built to cover large (9–10 m in diameter) circular house structures that had stood on the mound and then been burned (Perttula 2014a). Many had extended entranceways, typically indicating an important Caddo public structure or one lived in by the political and social elite. The initial mound stage was built over an even larger circular structure (c. 13 m in diameter) that stood on the original ground surface and may have been built between c. AD 1100–1300. The remainder of the primary mound, and much of the village, was used by the Caddo between c. AD 1450–1690. Other mounds that are part of the Nasoni Caddo village at the Hatchel site are sub-structural mounds at the Hill Farm (Mound 2,

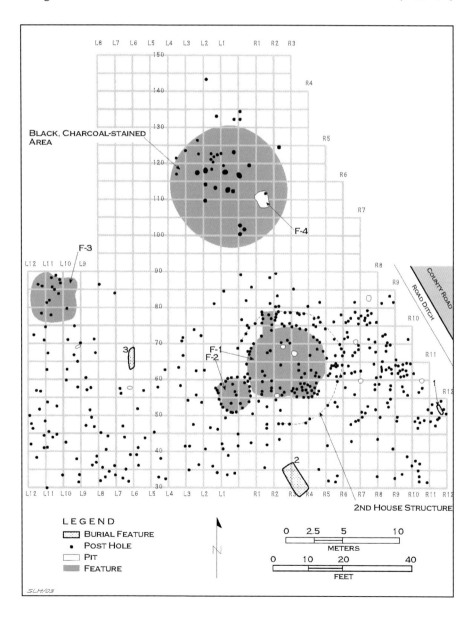

b. WPA Village Plot 1 excavations

41BW169) and Dogwood (41BW226) sites well southeast of the primary platform mound but near McKinney Bayou.

The platform mound at the Hatchel site was constructed over at least two specialized structures at what was the original ground surface (Zone K). These structures consisted of a very large circular structure (Feature 25) with an internal partition (Fig. 86a–b) and a structure of unknown size marked by an extensive ash deposit. The few artifacts that have been recovered from Zone K – as well as an artifact assemblage from nearby Village Area I (see Perttula and Nelson 2003) that is believed to be associated with Zone K – suggests that these structures were an important and central part of a pre-AD 1300 Caddo community at the Hatchel site, and remained so in the memories and ceremonies of later Nasoni Caddo peoples. By c. AD 1450, the first stages of the platform mound were constructed (Zone I–J) (Fig. 87) over the Zone K structures, and a ramp was built along the southern side of the mound, heading down into the Nasoni Caddo village that had grown up at Hatchel. These first stages of the platform mound did not have temple structures constructed on them.

The second stage in the construction of the platform mound at the Hatchel site was a stratified series of constructed structures on the northern part of the mound platform (Table 5). Most of this construction took place after c. AD 1550, and may have lasted until c. AD 1690, although no European artifacts have been recovered from any of these mound deposits. These structures were in eight

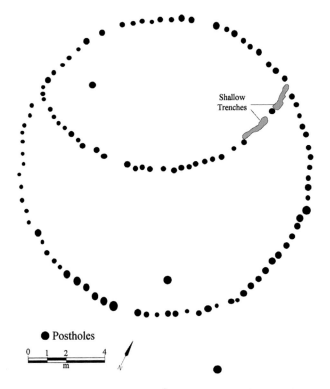

Shallow Trenches

● Postholes

0 1 2   4
m

a

b

Fig. 86. Feature 25: a. plan map; b. Feature 25 and its interior partition (image 41BW3-265, Texas Archeological Research Laboratory, University of Texas at Austin)

different mound zones (Zones A–H), in many cases with structures superimposed over one another, even though they were separated by mound fill. There were 16 circular structures in the mound structure zones, ranging from one (Zones F and G) (Fig. 88), two (Zones A–E) and three (Zone H) structures per zone (Fig. 89a–b); a third structure in Zone B appears to have been a granary, not a specialized structure associated with rituals and ceremonies on the platform mound. That most of the zones have two structures – situated at the eastern and western ends of the platform – may be an expression of the basic duality identified by Sabo (2012: 439, 441) in Caddo cosmology and social organization, and the fact that different rituals were performed in these simultaneously used Nasoni Caddo temple structures. In Zones F, G and H, other cosmological and social rituals and principles of the spirit realm expressed in deliberate spatial differences from later mound structures zones may have held sway.

Where entrances can be identified in these structures, they were facing to the south or southeast, in the same direction as the ramp that was attached to the principal platform mound, and thus facing in the direction of the central part of the Nasoni Caddo village and other mounds in the larger community. The plaza at the Hatchel site as suggested by the 1691 Teran map (see Sabo 2012: fig. 15-1) appears to be associated with only the latest mound zones, because post-AD 1600 village occupations occur near the platform mound in several village areas. Extended entranceway structures are present in six of the eight mound structure zones; two structures in Zones G (Feature 22) and H (Features 19/20) have double walls; and one structure (Features 16 and 17) in Zone H has an exterior post partition (see Fig. 89). All these features were likely designed to restrict access to the buildings, probably marking a tangible boundary "between the human and spirit realms" (Sabo 2012: 442).

Zone	Feature No.	Shape	Diameter (m)	Area (m^2)	Comments
A	1	circular	9.14	65.67	extended entrance
B	5	circular	3.66	10.51	probable granary
C	7	circular	9.14	65.61	extended entrance
D	12	circular	8.87	61.79	–
E	13	circular	9.06	64.47	–
	14	circular	8.84	61.36	extended entrance; possible prepared clay floor
F	15	circular	9.75	74.72	extended entrance
G	22 (outer)	circular	10.72	82.03	double-walled
	22 (inner)	circular	8.53	57.15	–
H	16	circular	7.32	42.03	extended entrance
	17	circular	6.40	32.18	partition to Structure 16?
	18	circular	8.60	58.03	extended entrance
	19/20	circular	12.00	113.10	double-walled

Table 5. Characteristics of the clearly defined structures on the platform mound at the Hatchel site (after Schultz 2010, table 20)

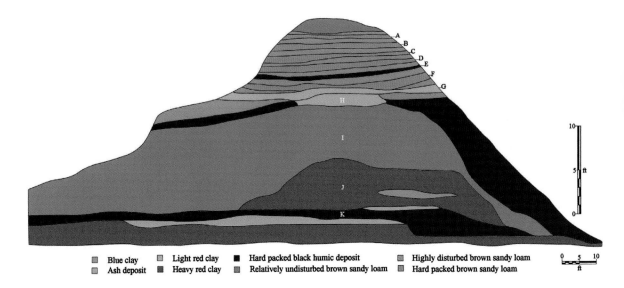

Blue clay   Light red clay   ■ Hard packed black humic deposit   Highly disturbed brown sandy loam
Ash deposit   ■ Heavy red clay   Relatively undisturbed brown sandy loam   Hard packed brown sandy loam

At regular intervals over more than 100 years, these mound structures were dismantled, destroyed and burned. The few masses of daub, ash and charred wood/charcoal found in association with the mound structures suggests that: (a) the structures were likely mainly thatch-covered, without wattle and daub walls, although at least one structure seems to have had a wattle and daub-covered extended entranceway (Feature 7 in Zone C) (Perttula 2014a: fig. 17), and (b) whatever burned and dismantled structural debris there was removed from the structures themselves, and became incorporated in the next mound fill zone that covered the structures.

Fig. 87. Cross-section of Zones A–K in the platform mound excavations at the Hatchel site

Fig. 88. Plan map of Zone F structure and other features

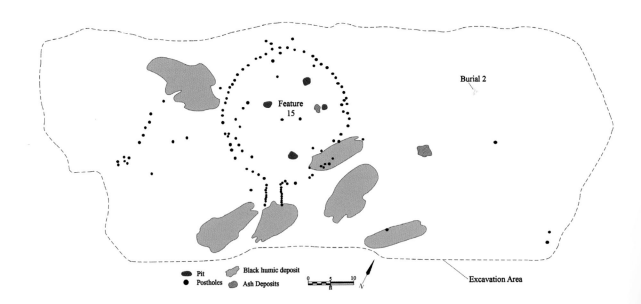

Pit   Black humic deposit
Postholes   Ash Deposits   Excavation Area

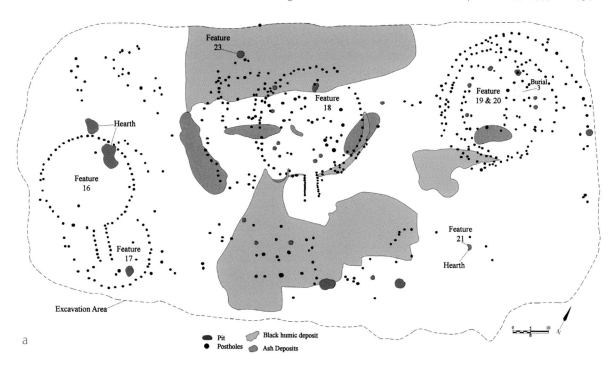

a

b

Fig. 89. Zone H structures and other features: a, plan map; b, looking east at Features 16 and 17 in Zone H (image 41BW3-163, Texas Archeological Research Laboratory, University of Texas at Austin)

Other investigated village areas in the Hatchel village include geophysical work at the Hill Farm site (41BW169), about 400 m east of the platform mound (see Walker and McKinnon 2012: fig. 7-6). A number of structures were identified in magnetometer surveys, and they are circular and circular with extended entranceways; the structures range from 8-12 m in diameter, except for Feature 4, which is 17.5 m in diameter. Ceramic vessel sherds in Areas A and B at the Hill Farm site indicate that the residential occupation by Caddo peoples took place after c. AD 1500, and probably as late as c. AD 1650 (Sundermeyer et al. 2008: 228,

235–6), contemporaneous with the principal construction and use of the platform mound at the Hatchel site.

The Eli Moores site (41BW2) is an important ancestral Caddo mound center (with two mounds) and living area on a natural levee of the Red River in the East Texas Pineywoods. The site was investigated by the University of Texas (UT) in 1932, and in one of the mounds and in associated midden deposits (Fig. 90), the remains of Caddo structures, midden deposits, features, eight burials (with nine individuals), and a large ceramic and lithic assemblage were recovered, along with well-preserved plant and faunal remains (Perttula 2014e). Other cemeteries were known to the north of the site (Fig. 91).

The UT 1932 excavations at the Eli Moores site concentrated on Mound #1. This mound was estimated to be c. 20 m in diameter and 1.5 m in height, and there was a borrow pit directly north of the mound. A blue glass bead had been previously found on the surface of the mound. Mound #2 is c. 12 m southwest of Mound 1, while an unexplored mounded midden deposit is c. 15 m south of Mound #1. Mound #2 had a small "test hole" excavated in it by the UT crew, but only midden deposits were encountered there; a small borrow pit was located just south of this mound. Jackson also noted that there were several midden deposits north and east of Mound #1, one of which had much daub, suggesting it was the location of a burned clay and thatch-covered structure. In another midden deposits (about 45 m east of Mound 1), a Caddo burial (J-1) and a flexed dog burial (Feature 1) were discovered lying about 1.8 m apart in the excavations; the small to medium-sized

Fig. 90. The Eli Moores site: plan of mounds, borrow pits, and midden areas

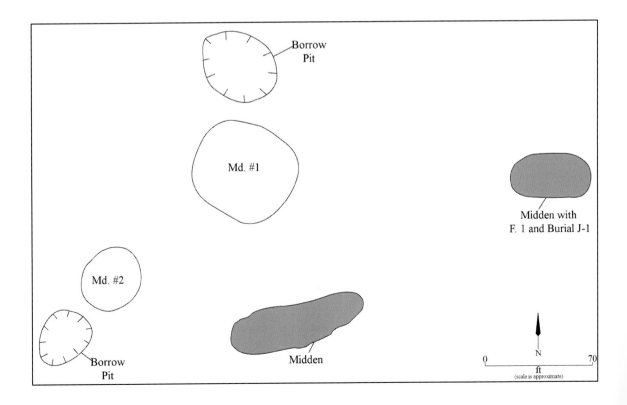

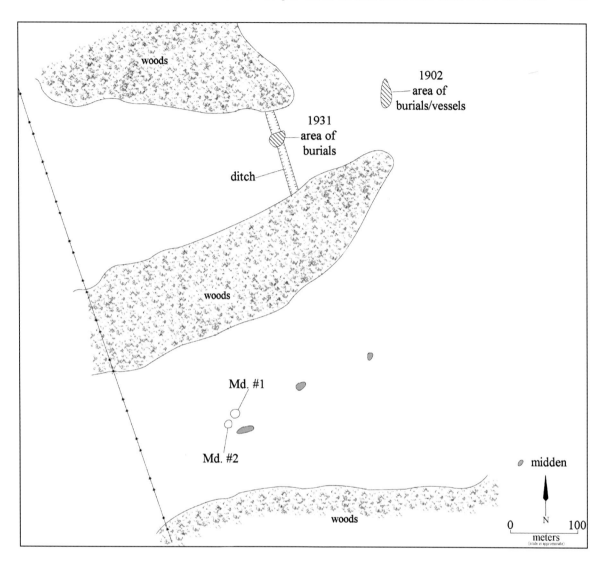

Fig. 91. The Eli Moores site: the mounds and middens, and 1902 and 1931 areas of burials and ceramic vessels

adult dog may have been associated with the Caddo individual as it lay near the feet of the deceased Caddo adult.

The excavations in Mound #1 encountered evidence of two wood structures (that may have been burned down), an ash pit and seven burials (J-2 to J-8) (Fig. 92). Six of the burials (and seven individuals) are children less than 6–7 years of age at their death, while Burial J-3 is that of an adult Caddo male; this burial may have been intrusive into the mound, while the others were likely buried during the accumulation of the mound midden deposits. Funerary offerings with the burials included ten ceramic vessels or broken vessel sections, four Maud arrow point and a Maud point preform, one Bassett point, a celt, a conch shell bead, three *Olivella* sp. shell beads, mussel shells, a drilled turtle shell, a deer mandible and several long bones, a smoothed raccoon bacculum bone, and a bone needle. Burial J-3 had two lead balls in its rib cage, probably the cause of death.

Profiles on the north and south sides of the north–south trench bisecting Mound #1 indicates that the mound deposits were comprised of stratified midden deposits and clay zones, the latter indicative of either structural zones or a clay cap in the mound fill. The mound fill comprised of midden deposits also contained evidence for the burning of structures as well as much wood, producing a 92 cm thick deposit with quantities of ash, burned clay and charcoal. The red clay zones were used to first create a mound platform (125–155 cm bs) and then also as a mound fill capping event (10–33 cm bs). One of the burned structures on the mound (Structure 1) had a concentration of cane matting and pecan nutshells (Fig. 93).

The ten vessels from the Texarkana phase burials at the Eli Moores site include plain bowls (n=2), an incised-punctated jar, an appliqued jar and a Karnack Brushed-Incised jar, as well as a Simms Engraved carinated bowl, an engraved bottle with a pendant triangle element on the body, a Belcher Engraved, *var. Belcher* compound bowl and two Barkman Engraved carinated bowls. Several different kinds of

Fig. 92. UT 1932 map of excavated areas in Mound #1, and locations of burials, structures, and various artifact find spots

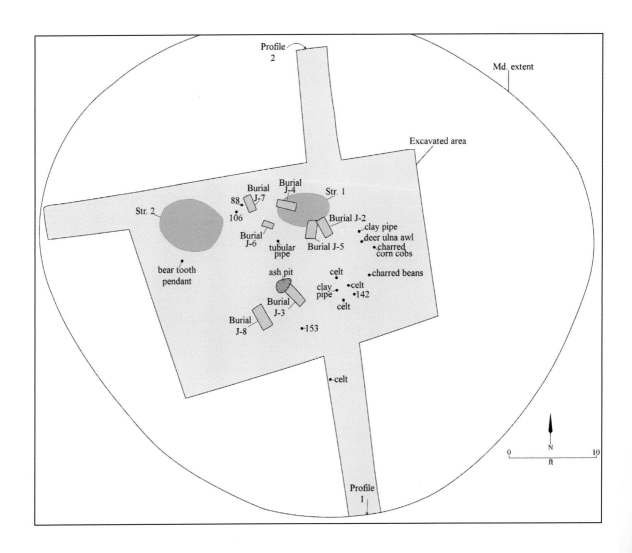

Fig. 93. Close-up of the cane matting and pecan nutshell cache in Structure 1 at the Eli Moores site (image courtesy of the Texas Archeological Research Laboratory, University of Texas at Austin)

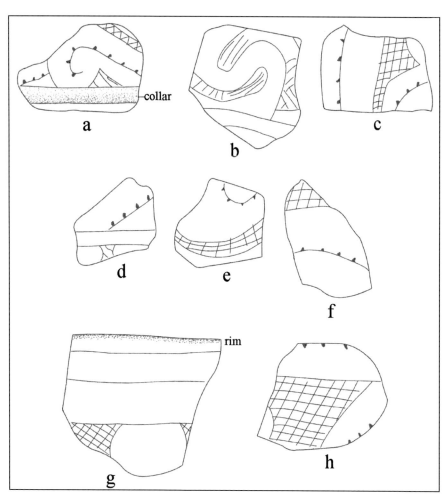

Fig. 94. Decorative elements on Natchitoches Engraved and Hodges Engraved fine ware sherds from the Eli Moores site

utility wares are represented in the sherds from the mound deposits, principal among them are sherds with incised, brushed, appliqued, punctated and trailed-incised decorative elements from Emory Punctated-Incised, Foster Trailed-Incised, Karnack Brushed-Incised and McKinney Plain vessels. There are also Cowhide Stamped, Moore Noded, Nash Neck Banded, Pease Brushed-Incised and Belcher Ridged, *var. Belcher* sherds in the utility wares.

The constellation of engraved and trailed fine ware types at sites such as Eli Moores and Hatchel suggest that the principal occupation at Eli Moores and other Nasoni Caddo sites is contemporaneous with the latest Belcher phase (Belcher IV) occupation at the Belcher site, and at the late 17th century to early 18th century component at the Chakanina phase Cedar Grove site (3LA97) in southwest Arkansas (Trubowitz 1984). Sherds from Barkman Engraved vessels and the stylistically later Simms Engraved type dominate the fine wares from the Eli Moores site. Other identified fine ware engraved ceramic types in the assemblage include Avery Engraved, Belcher Engraved, Natchitoches Engraved (Fig. 94a, c), Hodges Engraved (Fig. 94b, d–h), Hatchel Engraved, Taylor Engraved and Glassell Engraved. The trailed fine ware sherds are from Keno Trailed bowls and bottles. Only the Barkman Engraved, Hatchel Engraved and Simms Engraved fine wares were likely produced locally by Red River Caddo potters, but the other defined ceramic types were likely manufactured by contemporaneous Great Bend Belcher phase Caddo potters living downstream along the Red River.

There is an assortment of bone tools in the Eli Moores assemblage, which is notable because bone tools are not commonly preserved in Caddo archaeological deposits. This includes 12 deer antler tools and an unmodified antler stub fragment. The antler tools are polished, with either rounded or blunted ends. Other bone tools include one bird bowl awl with a rounded and worn tip, a polished and grooved bird bone with a spur and 12 deer ulna awls.

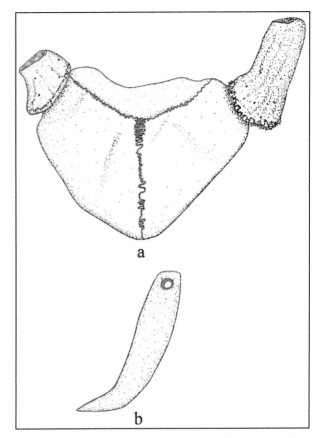

Fig. 95. Bone artifacts from the Eli Moores site: a, deer cranium with attached antler stubs; b, perforated bear tooth

Fig. 96. Split cane basketry fragment from the Eli Moores site (photograph courtesy of the Texas Archeological Research Laboratory, University of Texas at Austin)

In addition to the various bone tools, there is a large section of a deer cranium with attached antler stubs (Fig. 95a). There are also four bear teeth from the Eli Moores investigations, three that are unmodified. The one modified bear tooth is a pendant with a single perforation near the root of the tooth (Fig. 95b). There are two *Busycon perversum* conch shell artifacts in the Eli Moores collection from the 1932 UT excavations. The first is a small conch shell bead made from the columella. The other is an apical whorl fragment; it is otherwise unmodified.

Botanical remains were collected from the Eli Moores site by UT excavations in 1932 (Bush 2014). The collection includes pecan nuts (many in a cache associated with basketry), parts of other nuts (hickory and acorn), corn (cob fragments and cupules), cultivated beans (*Phaseolus vulgaris*), wood charcoal from common floodplain trees and two seeds (persimmon). It also includes five charred basketry fragments made from split river cane (*Arundinaria gigantea*) (Fig. 96), a rare find on open sites in the Caddo area. Most of these remains likely represent a single cache of food items that were burned when a Caddo structure was burned down and then covered with mound fill. Other remains came from a nearby midden that marks a non-mound habitation deposit.

Seven samples of pecan shell, cane matting, corn, charred beans and a carbonized persimmon seed from the Eli Moores excavations have been radiocarbon-dated. The summed probability distribution of the calibrated radiocarbon dates indicate that the likeliest temporal range at two sigma of the Caddo occupation was cal

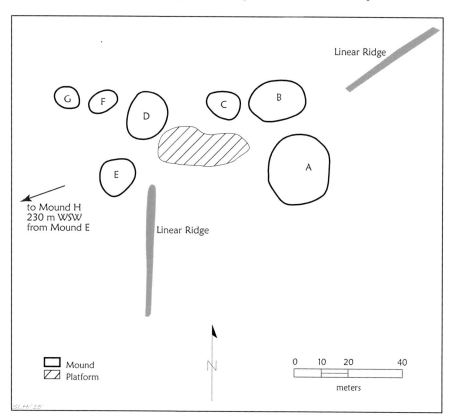

Fig. 97. The mounds and elevated platform, and linear ridges, at the Horace Cabe site on the Red River

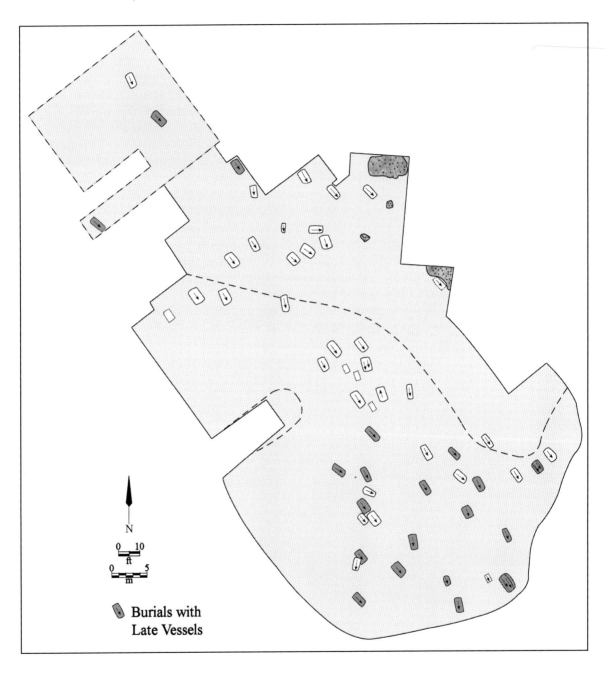

N

0 ___ 10
ft
0 ___ 5
m

🖌 Burials with
Late Vessels

AD 1400–1660. The major peaks in probability density are at *c.* AD 1460–1520 and AD 1580–1640. The calibrated age ranges with the highest probabilities from the charred matting/pecan deposit in the mound are cal AD 1448–1530, cal AD 1487–1651 and cal AD 1620–1670 (Perttula 2014e: 74–5). This indicates this deposit dates to the latter years of the Texarkana phase, but before the historic Nasoni Caddo occupation of the site.

Fig. 98. The distribution of Late Caddo burials in the cemetery at the Paul Mitchell site

As previously mentioned, the Hatchel site as well as the nearby Eli Moores and Horace Cabe sites are major components of the Texarkana phase, with both constructed mounds and extensive village habitation deposits. The Cabe mounds surround a platform that may have been used to elevate important structures; there are also north–south and northeast–southwest-oriented linear ridges (Fig. 97) that may have been aligned to both lunar and solar events.

The later ancestral Caddo occupation at the Paul Mitchell site – principally marked by its use as a large cemetery – is also a component of the Texarkana phase. There are a range of forms represented in the ceramic vessels from Late Caddo burials in the southeastern part of the cemetery at the Paul Mitchell site (Fig. 98). The most common forms are jars, carinated bowls and bottles. The majority of the interments date from the Early Texarkana phase (*c.* AD 1400–1550) and have vessels of the types Barkman Engraved, as well as Bowie Engraved and Hatchel Engraved vessels and Avery Engraved compound bowls with flaring rims. The utility wares include McKinney Appliqued, Moore Noded, Nash Neck Banded, Cass Appliqued and Pease Brushed-Incised types, as well as brushed-punctated jars and a punctated-appliqued jar with handles.

The 15th–17th century Caddo peoples that lived in a number of communities in the Big Cypress Creek basin in East Texas (Fig. 99) as well as parts of the mid-Sabine River basin (see Fields and Gadus 2012a; 2012b) were a strong and socially powerful group of peoples in their region. Archaeological evidence from these Caddo sites indicate that many of the components represent permanent, year-round, settlements of agricultural peoples. These Caddo sites belong to the Titus phase, first defined in the 1950s, which represents what archaeologists think of as a culturally and historically connected people living in the same area for about 250 years.

They were farmers that lived in dispersed communities comprised primarily of individual to multiple farmstead compounds, and they were active traders. These Caddo groups were amongst the most populous and socially complex of the many Caddo societies living at that time in the Caddo archaeological area (e.g., Early 2004: 573), as suggested by the earthen mounds they built within a number of political communities in the Big Cypress and Sabine River basins, and they were also the westernmost aboriginal group in Texas that was in any sense socio-politically akin to aboriginal polities living in the southeastern United States and the Midwest (Blitz 2010). These dynamic farming communities effected new means of holding their societies together, successfully forming several stronger communities that were centered around the establishment of a series of small mound centers, community cemeteries and villages at key landscape nexuses in the Big Cypress Creek and Sabine River basins (see Fields 2014: fig. 17).

The Titus phase archaeological record in the Big Cypress Creek basin "refers to a number of distinctive socio-cultural groups, not a single Caddo group; these groups or communities were surely related and/or affiliated by kinship, marriage and social interaction" (Perttula 2005b: 401). The social and cultural diversity that probably existed among Titus phase cultural groups is matched by the stylistic and functional diversity in Titus phase material culture, particularly in the manufacture and use of fine ware and utility ware ceramics, ceramic pipes and arrow points. A

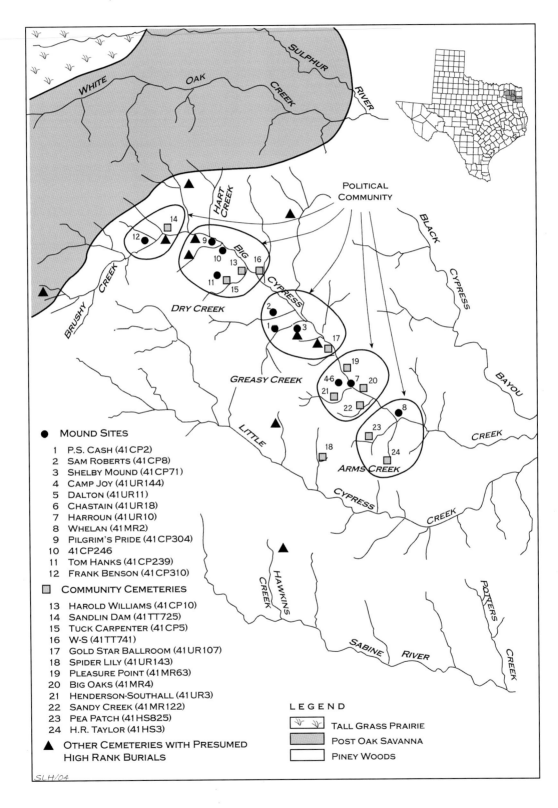

● **Mound Sites**

    1   P.S. Cash (41 CP2)
    2   Sam Roberts (41 CP8)
    3   Shelby Mound (41 CP71)
    4   Camp Joy (41 UR144)
    5   Dalton (41 UR11)
    6   Chastain (41 UR18)
    7   Harroun (41 UR10)
    8   Whelan (41 MR2)
    9   Pilgrim's Pride (41 CP304)
    10 41 CP246
    11 Tom Hanks (41 CP239)
    12 Frank Benson (41 CP310)

▢ **Community Cemeteries**

    13 Harold Williams (41 CP10)
    14 Sandlin Dam (41 TT725)
    15 Tuck Carpenter (41 CP5)
    16 W-S (41 TT741)
    17 Gold Star Ballroom (41 UR107)
    18 Spider Lily (41 UR143)
    19 Pleasure Point (41 MR63)
    20 Big Oaks (41 MR4)
    21 Henderson-Southall (41 UR3)
    22 Sandy Creek (41 MR122)
    23 Pea Patch (41 HS825)
    24 H.R. Taylor (41 HS3)

▲ **Other Cemeteries with Presumed**
    High Rank Burials

LEGEND

ψψ Tall Grass Prairie
▨ Post Oak Savanna
▢ Piney Woods

SLH/04

Fig. 99. Titus phase political communities in the Big Cypress Creek basin in East Texas, and various Titus phase mound sites and community cemeteries studied in recent years

Stouts Creek Titus phase community made and used hand-molded clay figurines. It is the character of their stylistically unique material culture (see Parsons 2015; Bruseth and Perttula 1981; Fields and Gadus 2012a; Fields *et al.* 2014; Perttula 2012b; Perttula and Sherman 2009; Thurmond 1990), coupled with the development of distinctive mortuary rituals and social and religious practices centered on the widespread use of community cemeteries and mound ceremonialism as means to mark social identities, that most readily sets these Caddo groups apart from their neighbors in East Texas and in the Red River basin to the north and east (Early 2004: 568).

Radiocarbon dates from Titus phase components consistently range from the early 15th century to the latter part of the 17th century (Perttula 2012b, table 13-1). The most reasonable of the numerous recent calibrated radiocarbon dates from a variety of Titus phase domestic, mortuary and mound contexts consistently span the period from cal AD 1430–1680, although in some parts of the Big Cypress and upper Sabine River basins, there are Titus phase sites that date at least one generation after *c.* AD 1680.

In Titus phase times, when the Caddo peoples had a diet that primarily consisted of cultivated plants like maize, beans and squash (see Perttula 2008a), agricultural pursuits were of particular importance in determining the location of individual farmsteads and hamlets. The overall settlement pattern was dispersed, and this dispersion occurred in conjunction with a heightened emphasis on situating sites across the land along the secondary streams and the spring-fed branches. These areas may have had more dependable water, or more accessible water, at least at that time, and it is also likely that fields would have been easier to clear along the more open upland forests than if fields had to be located in the more mesic and thickly wooded valleys.

This dispersed settlement arrangement would have helped lessen the competition for available plant, animal and mineral resources among Titus phase families and communities, and would not have allowed for any sort of large scale environmental degradation of those suitable habitats by a single large community. This dispersion of population would also have permitted the Caddo peoples to take advantage of the diversity in habitats to exploit a number of them from season to season and year to year – and the wide range of animal species exploited by Caddo peoples is a testimony to the diversity of animals used for meat, hides and furs – thus insuring that the overall community or communities of interacting farmsteads, households and individuals living in those farmsteads could survive if there were economic difficulties or failures (i.e., local droughts, flooding, fires) in some habitats but not in most of the others.

As was noted above, the population of Caddo peoples was quite a bit higher during the Late Caddo period than at other times during the Caddo era in much of the region, and there are a number of recognizable clusters of Titus phase settlements throughout the central part of East Texas (cf. Davis *et al.* 2010; Fields and Gadus 2012a; Fields *et al.* 2014; Perttula 2012b; Thurmond 1990) that apparently represent parts of contemporaneous small communities. These small communities are part of *political communities*, namely a cluster of inter-related settlements and associated cemeteries that are centered on a key site or group of sites distinguished by public architecture (i.e., earthen mounds) and large domestic village areas. A number of political communities are present along Big Cypress Creek and its tributaries (Perttula 2012b: fig. 13-2), in the Sabine River basin (Fields 2014: fig. 17), and Parsons (2015) has identified part of another such community in the Little Cypress Creek basin; surely there are others that await archaeological scrutiny.

The Shelby site (41CP71) on Greasy Creek in the Big Cypress Creek basin is the social and political center of one of these communities, and stretches for several hundred meters along the creek and a small tributary, with an earthen mound at the northern end of the village and a large cemetery at its southern end. Domestic village areas occur between the one mound and the cemetery and cover at least 10–15 acres (c. 4–6 ha) (Perttula and Nelson 2004). The earthen mound covered a burned structure at the base of the mound, and a second structure had been built that stood on the mound itself, and was then burned and capped with a final sandy fill. The arrangement of mound, domestic areas and planned cemetery here is essentially duplicated at the Pilgrim's Pride site (41CP304) (Perttula 2005b: fig. 11-2) farther upstream in the Big Cypress Creek basin, although the village areas and the size of the cemetery at the Shelby site are considerably larger.

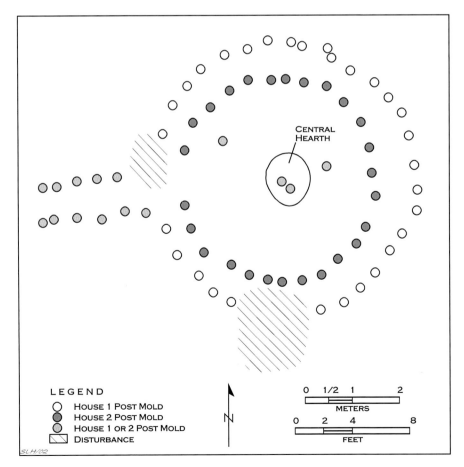

Fig. 100. Examples of extended entranceway structures in Titus phase sites:

a. under Mound C at the Harroun site;

Another community nexus is in the Meddlin Creek and Big Cypress Creek areas, midway between Greasy Creek and Arms Creek (see Fig. 99). It includes three or four mound sites, namely Harroun (41UR10), Dalton (41UR11), Chastain (41UR18) and Camp Joy (41UR144), various small domestic settlements in valley and upland settings, along with several large community cemeteries. As evidence of the integration of these mound centers, there are extended entranceway structures at the Harroun site that point towards each other (in the case of Mounds B and D), and another (on Mound C) is oriented to face an extended entranceway structure at the nearby Dalton site (Fig. 100a) (Davis et al. 2010). In turn, the extended entranceway structure at the Dalton site points southwest towards a mound platform (with burned structures and burials) (Fig. 100b) at the nearby Camp Joy Mound site (41UR144, Perttula and Nelson 2001). The Camp Joy, Dalton, Chastain and Harroun sites may comprise individual portions of a single multiple mound center used by a large Titus phase community. Each of these sites have mounds built over wooden structures that had a special religious and ritual purpose to the Caddo communities and/or with particular leaders, and the earthen mounds were

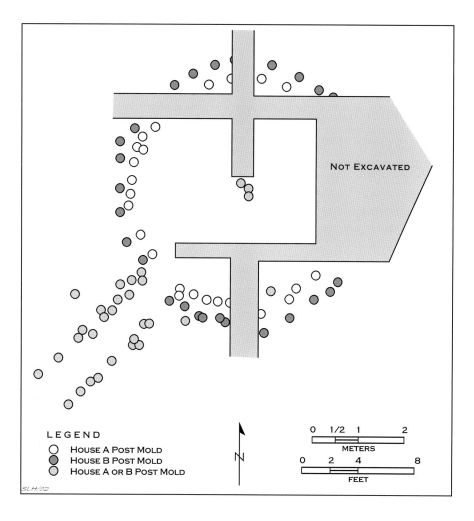

b. under the mound at the Dalton site

built up over the structures after they had been set afire. Here, the community cemeteries are not found in close association with the mound centers, as they are in the Greasy Creek Caddo community, but instead they are situated along Big Cypress Creek and its tributary streams, presumably in general proximity to the many farmsteads that must have been dispersed across the countryside at that time. This may also be the case in other communities where no large community cemeteries have been identified.

Other than the village centers, how were other Titus phase domestic settlements organized and laid out spatially across the landscape? Fortunately, recent excavations at four Titus phase settlements – two sites in the Tankersley Creek valley in the Big Cypress Creek basin, the Rookery Ridge site at Lake Gilmer in the Little Cypress Creek basin and the Ear Spool site (see Fields 2014; Fields *et al.* 2014; Parsons 2015; Perttula and Sherman 2009) – have provided solid archaeological evidence of their character. The settlements appear to have been composed of one to several family units that occupied the sites for one or two generations that are marked by house midden/daub concentrations and trash midden deposits; many activities occurred outside the house areas, resulting in trash-filled pits, hearths and posts in these work areas (Fig. 101). At the Ear Spool site (41TT653), there were four different circular structures (probably thatched and daub-covered), one with an extended entranceway that pointed towards the other three houses, that may have been from two temporally different and sequential Titus phase occupations (see Perttula and Sherman 2009: fig. 6-1). There was a broad, open area between the houses there, as there were at the George Richey (41TT851) and William Ford (41TT852) sites, that may have been a plaza or courtyard, as there are marker poles at the center of the Ear Spool site, and there were clusters of pits along its margins.

The Rookery Ridge site (41UR133) excavations exposed two early Titus phase circular structures and extensive midden deposits. The middens were about 15 m south of the one structure with an extended entranceway; the entranceway faced to the north, suggesting that other habitation features were present on the northern part of the alluvial landform along Kelsey Creek (Parsons 2015). Titus phase extended entranceway structures at other sites tended to point to the west or southwest, however. Child and adult burials were present either inside a structure or immediately outside, in an earthen embankment along the structure walls (Structure 1), but there was no larger family cemetery at the site. Using several lines of evidence, particularly the occurrence of well-preserved burned house debris and the placement of several child burials just outside the walls of the extended entranceway structure, Parsons (2015) has suggested that this structure had a soil berm around it, and when the structure was burned, it was covered with a very low mound of relatively clean sediments.

The distribution of Titus phase settlements, mounds and community cemeteries strongly suggests that the density of Caddo peoples was concentrated in several parts of the Big Cypress Creek basin, including its many southward-flowing and eastward-flowing tributaries. Nevertheless, other parts of the Caddo homeland occupied by Titus phase peoples were also well settled, such as the Dry Creek and Caney Creek valleys in the upper Lake Fork Creek valley (see Bruseth and Perttula 1981). Here, at sites like Burks (41WD52), Steck (41WD529), Spoonbill (41WD109)

Fig. 101. Plans of the
features at the George
Richey and William Ford
sites on Tankersley Creek
(image provided courtesy
of the Texas Archeological
Society)

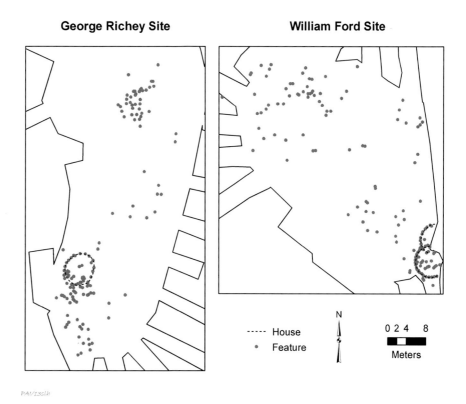

PAI/13slh

and Goldsmith (41WD208), as well as in the Stouts Creek valley to the north, the farmstead occupations have house and trash midden deposits, apparently from two to four structures each, and nearby family cemeteries with roughly 5–15 individual interments (Perttula 2004a: fig. 13.28). The density of Titus phase settlements along Caney Creek is impressive, with more than 50 components on a *c.* 7 km stretch of the creek and the adjacent upland landforms. The majority of the sites are in the uplands, rather than in the Caney Creek valley, situated along the upland edge or on smaller tributaries of Caney Creek. Habitation sites are well dispersed across the landscape, as are the habitation sites with reported cemeteries. The village-mound-large cemetery association noted for Titus phase communities in the Big Cypress Creek basin, however, seem to be absent in the Caney Creek cluster, and other settings, although overall population densities from one locale to another may have been comparable. The Kelsey Creek area, in the Little Cypress Creek basin, was also thickly settled by the Caddo in the early to mid-15th century AD, but not after.

There are currently 12 known Titus phase mound sites in the Big Cypress Creek basin (Fields 2014; Perttula 2004a: fig. 13-30). The Pine Tree Mound site (41HS15) on Potters Creek in the Sabine River basin is the most impressive Titus phase ceremonial center and village with at least three mounds, a plaza, five associated habitation areas, shaft tombs and at least one cemetery (Fields and Gadus 2012a; 2012b). There is also evidence of moderate mound buildings activities at the

Rookery Ridge site. As Early (2000a: 126) notes, the mounds and the community centers they were found on were the focus of mortuary and ritual activities for Caddo peoples. The mounds became permanent markers on the cultural landscape, because they were associated with specific rituals, events and peoples.

Titus phase mounds built by the Caddo were sub-structural mounds; no pyramidal platform or burial mounds are known for this time period (see Story 1990). Sub-structural mounds are restricted to mounds that cap a burned circular structure that was constructed on the ground surface or in a small, shallow pit. In at least two known instances, however, the mounds contained sequent structures, but the "structures originated at higher levels in the mound[s] due to occupational accumulations of soil and ash, and not the result of any deliberate capping" (Thurmond 1990: 168). At the Camp Joy Mound, the 2.3 m high mound apparently had two tiers or platforms, the latest tier capping a burned structure (marked by a 7 cm thick charcoal lens) dated to cal AD 1495–1605 (Perttula and Nelson 2001).

The structures that were capped by a mound deposit, or built at higher levels in the mound itself (as at the Harroun site), were circular, with extended entranceways generally facing west, and with central hearths. They were partially dismantled and burned, then capped with sediments. Again at the Harroun site, as well as one of the structures at Ear Spool (Perttula and Sherman 2009), the structures were built inside large circular pits, and there were obvious soil berms around the enclosing pit and the structure. A standing structures with berms around it would look like the structure was literally buried (or partially buried) in the mound itself (cf. Schambach 1996). At the Dalton site, two temporally sequent circular structures (with clay-lined floors) of slightly different sizes were both built and used within the same shallow pit; when the second one was burned and destroyed, it and the surrounding pit were buried by a sandy mound fill to a depth of 80 cm (Davis *et al.* 2010: 66–9). At the Whelan site (41MR2), one of the mounds buried four temporally sequent circular structures that ranged from 5.2–6.4 m in diameter (Thurmond 1990: 168).

Exactly what triggered the dismantling and burning of the structures, or their capping with mound sediments, at these community centers is not clear. Given the generally close association between the mound places and the community cemeteries (many of which held the burials of members of the political and social elite), it may be that the house destruction and mound building episodes occurred after the death and burial of a leader or a member of the elite. However, these elite individuals were buried in separate graves alongside their peers and kin-affiliated relations in the community cemetery, not in the mound itself, and thus in essence the mound-building rituals of the Titus phase Caddo consisted of "public building-oriented ceremonialism" (Schambach 1996: 41), such that the mounds "contain the remains of important buildings rather than important people."

There are several key differences in the Titus phase mound sites that hint at the socio-political diversity that was present in the various communities that existed at the time in the Big Cypress Creek basin. The first obvious difference is in the number of mounds on a site: the Harroun and Whelan sites each have four mounds, while the other sites have only one. The proximity of the Chastain, Dalton and Camp Joy Mound sites to each other on a prominent upland landform (the three mound sites are each within 250–500 m of each other) probably is evidence of a single large Titus phase mound and community center, not three disparate and unrelated sites.

It is especially notable that the only multiple mound centers in the Big Cypress Creek basin are situated in its lower reaches, while the other single mound sites are found some distance upstream, or in the Little Cypress basin, in different political communities. These differences in the complexity of the various mound sites are likely to be a reflection of differences in the power and authority that each political community had, as the construction of earthen mounds expressed that power and authority in visible and tangible ways. It may well also be the case that the area with the most important centers was also home to the highest densities of Titus phase Caddo peoples, as the size of each political community's population would also be evidence of their chiefly power.

Another difference between the mound centers is whether or not the mound center was a discrete part of a larger planned village. In the case of the Rookery Ridge site, the mound occurs amidst a moderately-sized settlement, but this was hardly a village. At the Pilgrim's Pride and Shelby mound sites, the one earthen mound at each site was situated at the northern end of a large (+10 acres/4 ha) village community. At the P. S. Cash site (41CP2), the one mound was 400 m north of a small associated cemetery; there are extensive Titus phase habitation deposits immediately across Greasy Creek at the E. S. Dooley Farm (41CP4) (see Thurmond 1990: 139 and fig. 17). The Sam Roberts site had a single 1.1 m tall mound that capped a burned circular structure (Tunnell 1959: 4–7). There was a *c.* 200 m^2 midden deposit on the northeastern side of the mound, but there were much more extensive habitation areas 200 m east of the mound itself. In the immediate area of the Dalton, Chastain and Camp Joy mound sites, there are extensive Titus phase habitation areas, as there are around the Pine Tree Mound in the Sabine River basin (see below). These occur either on the mound sites themselves, or in nearby and associated domestic settlements.

The only habitation area at the Whelan site was a *c.* 2000 m^2 archaeological deposit southeast of one of the mounds near Big Cypress Creek (Thurmond 1990: 16). The other three mound sites lay to the east and northwest. The small habitation area contained one 7.9 m diameter household structure and an elevated 3.1 m diameter granary structure, but other habitation features probably existed in the many areas not subjected to excavations (Davis *et al.* 2010). No habitation deposits were identified at the Harroun site, but rather only four small mounds spread out along Big Cypress Creek (Jelks and Tunnell 1959).

This dichotomy between mound and habitation associations on Titus phase mounds, with the main multi-mound centers at the Harroun and Whelan sites having little if no associated habitation debris, while most of the other mounds did, suggests that there were differences in the scale of complexity of these communities. For most of the communities, the ritual, power and authority of the elite leaders had not been divorced from the populations living in the communities, especially those living in and near the largest villages. This intimate relationship – as seen by the placement of mounds across the landscape – between the community and its leaders was not duplicated in Titus phase Caddo communities living along the lower Big Cypress Creek basin. Here, the community mound centers were basically kept separate from domestic affairs and were focused more exclusively on ritual activities and the control of ritual knowledge. Those leaders that lived at the Harroun and Whelan sites may have gained their prestige and authority through their control of ritual affairs important to the people living in their associated communities.

A series of repetitive rituals centered on communal feasting apparently took place at the Whelan site, with the end result being a large midden refuse deposit filled with broken ceramic vessels and animal bones. Such feasting activities would certainly have served to help establish and preserve inter-community alliances and integration of families, at least at this particular political community. Furthermore, the Caddo community that was hosting the public feasting activities could well have "gained a measure of prestige that could be translated as a source of political influence for individual village headmen" (Knight 2001: 327). Visualized in this matter, it would seem to be no coincidence that the scene of repeated public feasting activities by the Titus phase Caddo would be situated in the largest community mound centers.

Cemeteries represent distinctive and socially significant places on the Caddo landscape. They are places where past Caddo societies created and renewed a sense of place and developed a sense of social memory, leading to an appreciation of the social and spatial dimensions of mortuary practices. Burials, and cemeteries, whether small family cemeteries or the larger community examples, reflect a continuity of kin and community, ethnicity and identity, at their locations relative to the inhabited and habitable landscape and in their locations relative to other deceased Caddo peoples.

There are at least 140 known Titus phase cemeteries, and they fall readily into two groups: the community cemetery and the family cemetery (see Perttula *et al.* 1998; Perttula 2012b: fig. 13-8; Fields *et al.* 2014). The community cemeteries are large and well-planned, with more than 70–80 individuals, and oft times must have been the final resting place of individuals of higher social status or rank within various communities (cf. Burden *et al.* 2014: 431); in fact, their burials may have been the impetus for the creation of community cemeteries. These very large cemeteries appear to be the result of burials from a number of farmsteads and small village compounds within many of the political communities mentioned above, and their existence – and persistence in use for a number of generations – show that there was a broad community-wide participation in ceremonial and mortuary rituals. A detailed study of Titus phase mortuary practices indicate also that "family cemeteries have little indication of variable burial treatment based on status" (Burden *et al.* 2014: 431).

Mortuary practices of the Titus phase Caddo peoples are believed to be guided by the cultural and social beliefs, ideas and traditions of the living Caddo people concerning the afterlife as well as the relationship of the living with their ancestors (cf. Sullivan and Mainfort 2010: 7-12). These ideas and relationships – essentially social ties expressed in shared mortuary rituals – can endure for generations. Shared ritual mortuary practices among the Caddo living in the Big and Little Cypress Creek basins, and in parts of the middle and upper Sabine River basin, lasted as least 250 years (roughly ten generations). Because these mortuary practices were based on the active beliefs of the living Caddo who laid the deceased in graves in certain sacred areas, with specific burial pit forms and orientations, as well as certain kinds and quantities of grave furniture, mortuary practices provide insights into Caddo cosmology and ideology, particularly beliefs on the afterlife, the nature of the soul, and steps necessary to protect and save the souls of the deceased.

The setting of cemeteries across the Big Cypress Creek basin is not haphazard, but has a spatial and historical context that can be related to traditions and beliefs shared by Caddo peoples about universal orders and the structure of the cosmos. The demographic dispersion of agricultural Caddo peoples, and the apparent belief that the dead needed to be kept near to the living, led to the accompanying dispersion of cemetery sites, even family cemeteries, in proximity to habitation areas and settlements. These Caddo households, or groups of households comprising a community of kin-related groups, defined their own sense of place and who they were by the unique juxtaposition of the living and the dead in circumscribed areas within larger farming communities. Although these Caddo shared similar views on social memory and the place of the dead in their lives, it was their households and associated cemeteries (i.e., their ritual space) that were the center of their universe, in juxtaposition to the larger and socially more diverse communities that they shared cultural traditions with.

The average Titus phase cemetery contained about 26 individuals arranged in a number of rows, with little if any overlapping of graves (Fig. 102). These burials were interred in an extended supine position with the head of the deceased generally facing west (towards the House of Death) and usually they were accompanied by a variety of grave goods, including ceramic vessels to hold food and liquids on the six day journey to the House of Death, stone tools, as well as perishables such as baskets and wooden implements). In early 18th century observations of Hasinai Caddo mortuary practices by Fray Espinosa (Hatcher 1927: 162), he noted that:

> "as soon as the souls leave the body they travel towards the west and from there they rise once more into the air and go close to the presence of the great captain whom they call *caddi ayo*. From there they go to wait in a house located towards the south, called the House of Death."

For the Caddo, the soul's travel to the west is also associated with the setting of the sun (*sakuh*). An east–west body orientation was likely chosen primarily because of a near universal belief in the direction of the afterlife and the soul's journey to the afterlife.

The family cemeteries are generally found in the immediate proximity of a farmstead or hamlet, and they contain far few interments compared to the much larger community cemeteries. They seem to have had about 10–20 individuals in cemeteries along the western margins of the Titus phase area and between 20–40 individuals along Big Cypress Creek, suggesting that there were intra-areal differences in population densities and the social organization of extended families and lineages. Burials within the family cemeteries generally included single extended inhumations within a patterned arrangement of burials in rows, sometimes aligned east–west and other time in roughly north–south rows. Burial

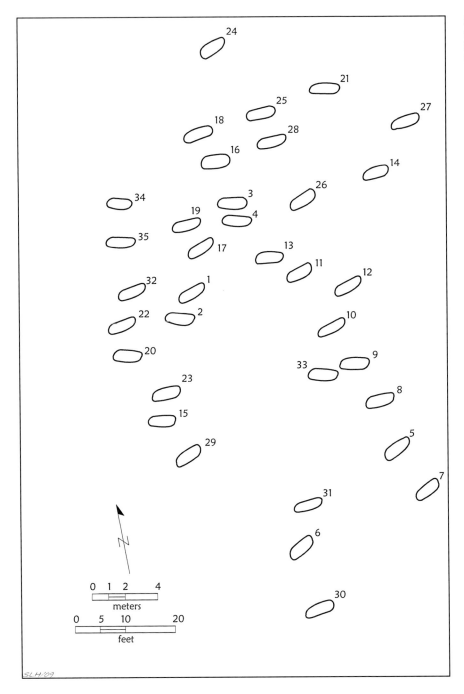

Fig. 102. The cemetery plan at the Johns site (41CP12) in the Big Cypress Creek basin

pit sizes, funerary offerings and preserved human remains suggest the majority of the burials in the family cemeteries are adult males and females.

The Johns site (41CP12) is one such larger family cemetery (see Fig. 102). The burials occurred in a number of east–west rows, with the head of the deceased oriented almost always to face to the west. The deceased were placed in long,

Burial No.	Head facing	Length (m)	Max. depth (m)	No. of vessels	Other offerings; comments
1	W	1.53	0.91	7	celt
2	NW	1.75	1.29	9	deer tooth under 1 vessel; large charcoal stain under several vessels
3	W	1.63	1.19	9	pipe; celt; arrow points; three Gary points
4	W	?	1.08	3	arrow points; child
5	W	2.01	1.02	9	smoothing stone; ear spool; pipe; 1 arrow point
6*	W	1.50	1.07	8	arrow points
7*	W	1.57	1.14	5	arrow points
8	W	?	0.81	4	
9	?	1.60	0.74	5	
10	WSW	1.83	0.81	5	pipe
11	W	1.90	1.50	11	
12	W	2.03	?	8**	
13	W	1.90	1.12	7	pipe; excavations here suggest the burial is in the vicinity of a Caddo house
14	W	2.16	0.97	7	arrow points; 1–2.5 cm layer of white sand placed on the floor of the burial pit
15	W	1.77	0.84	5	arrow points; ash layer on floor of burial pit
16	W	2.29	1.35	10	scraper; smoothing stone
17	W	?	1.07	8	blade; celt
18*	W	2.08	1.37	16	arrow points; kaolin clay mass
19	W	2.25	1.37	10	arrow points
20	?	?	0.87	4	quartz crystal; ochre; hammerstone; knife; pipe; flakes; arrow points
21	W	1.68	1.22	10	
22	?	1.93	1.00	10	celt; arrow points
23	SW	1.98	1.04	5	arrow point
24*	?	1.73	0.89	6	
25	W	2.13	1.37	5	7–10 cm thick layer of white sand on the floor of the burial pit; arrow points
26	W	1.19	1.12	9	a layer of white sand on the burial pit floor; 2 smoothing stones; adolescent
27*	W	1.58	1.05	10	white sand on the burial pit floor; arrow points
28	W	1.68	1.34	10	charcoal concentration on burial pit floor; celts; pipe; arrow points; drill; flakes
29	WNW	3.00	1.29	8	charcoal staining on burial pit floor; celt; pipe; smoothing stone; two quivers of arrow points
30*	W	2.03	1.14	10	white sand on burial pit floor; arrow points in two quivers
31	?	?	0.76	9	arrow points in a quiver; ear spool
32	WNW	1.60	1.62	14	black clay layer on floor of burial pit; quiver of arrow points by lower leg
33	W	2.23	1.30	10	two arrow point quivers; pipe
34	W	2.06	1.27	11	arrow points
35	W	2.03	1.65	11	two arrow point quivers; celt; pipe

*Burials identified by Turner (1978) as the late component at the Johns site.
**Determined during the documentation effort; the burial plan does not indicate the number or placement of funerary offerings

Table 6. Characteristics of the Titus phase burials at the Johns site (41CP12).

narrow and relatively deep burial pits in an extended supine position, with funerary offerings generally placed along both sides of the body and at the feet (Table 6). Funerary offerings consisted of ceramic vessels (3–16 vessels per burial), ceramic pipes, arrow points (usually in quivers), celts, smoothing stones, as well as scrapers and other chipped stone tools. All of the burials have ceramic vessel funerary offerings, but only a small proportion had either ceramic pipes (25.7% of the burials), arrow points (62.9% of the burials), celts (17.1% of the burials), or other stone tools (17.1% of the burials) placed in the burial pit.

In some instances, the floors of the burial pits at the Johns site were covered with a thin layer of clean white sand before the deceased was laid in the pit. Several others had concentrations of ash and/or charcoal, suggesting a fire had been set in the burial pit before the body was laid in it (see Table 6).

Grave good associations and burial treatment of Caddo peoples in the family cemeteries do not show much evidence among these individuals for differential status or social rank. Artifact associations in family cemeteries differ primarily by age and sex: adolescents tended to be buried with more funerary offerings than either children or infants, but would have had fewer funerary offerings than the adults, whether they were male or female. The graves of males often had clusters of arrow points in patterns suggesting they represented quivers of arrows, and females commonly had polishing stones or more numerous pottery vessels. Items of non-local origin (either ceramic vessels or stone tools) were extremely rare in burials of either sex. Finally, graves with very large numbers of funerary offerings were quite limited in these family cemeteries. This minimal diversity in burial treatment is part of the evidence preserved in the mortuary practices of these Caddo peoples that strongly points to minimal social differences between affiliated and kin-related farmsteads that created these cemeteries (cf. Carr 1995: 157 and tables xiii and xiv). Body treatment, body preparation and body orientation closely track beliefs about the soul and the afterlife more than they do the social position of the deceased (see Carr 1995, tables xi and xiv).

There are a number of burials found in Titus phase cemeteries that are clearly those of important people, either adult members of the political, religious and social elite, individual community leaders or even heads of paramount lineages. They received special treatment at death, including having unique and rare artifacts placed with them in the burial pits, just as they must have had during their lives. In the case of top-tier leaders (i.e., individuals with the highest political or religious authority in communities), they were buried in shaft tombs along Big Cypress Creek or at the Pine Tree site in the Sabine River basin (Burden *et al.* 2014: 432). These unique burials are for Caddo peoples in several different Titus phase political communities that must have had considerable power and authority, at least in their own community, and perhaps as also recognized in other Caddo communities outside the Big Cypress Creek basin. Such burials are rare, comprising less than 2% of the Titus phase population at any one time (Perttula 2012b).

In summary, the communities of Caddo peoples that lived in the Big and Little Cypress Creek basins in the 15th–17th century AD comprised a series of groups that were tied together by social, political and religious beliefs embodied in the creation and use of large community cemeteries as well as the construction of small earthen mounds at key locations within the basins. These sites appear to have been the ceremonial and political facilities of politically and socially integrated social groups of Caddo peoples. The development of these social institutions, unique to these agricultural Caddo societies in the East Texas Pineywoods, created the context for different forms of social life and interaction that were in turn sustained for ten or more generations among Titus phase groups.

These Caddo groups had leaders that apparently promoted social solidarity and the incorporation of diverse groups and communities into a number of linked polities, in part because:

> "power and political decision making [was] diffused across many elements of society and individual wealth and status [was] de-emphasized. These kinds of polities are united by ideologies that stress the corporate solidarity of society" (King 2006: 76).

Conflict or warfare was not part of the social equation that led to the establishment of relatively permanent political communities among Titus phase groups, probably because of the expansive territory that was available for settlement, as well as the absence of competing polities (e.g., Dye 2008: 12).

Each of these polities in the Big Cypress Creek basin had at its heart a newly created larger and community-centered Caddo mound and village settlement, places where the most important and life-giving ceremonies, rituals and decisions were made by the social and political elite that guided and organized the changing Titus phase societies living along Big Cypress Creek and its many tributaries; each had their own distinctive social identity. The Rookery Ridge site may have served these same functions for one such local community in the Little Cypress Creek basin before it was abandoned. Smaller farming households were apparently dispersed for several miles around the mound centers and community cemeteries. Life for these Caddo was organized around the rhythm of planting and harvesting the cultivated plants, men hunting large game, the rituals and ceremonies of the seasons and daily life in the households and village settlements.

At death, these Caddo peoples were laid to rest in sacred cemetery plots used by related families, or in large community cemeteries set up and maintained for several generations near the seat of political authority in each of the political communities. These larger cemeteries were usually established some distance, both symbolically and in life, from the domestic compounds. But family cemeteries were immediately adjacent to habitation areas. Caddo children that died at a young age were kept close to the living, as they were buried beneath and/or near the household they had probably been born and raised in. The deceased men, women and adolescents, as well as the social and political elite, were buried in ceremonies that lasted several days, and they were accompanied by various offerings placed in the graves that were meant to help them in their journey to the afterlife.

At a broader spatial scale, then, the distribution of Titus phase Caddo cemeteries across the Big and Little Cypress Creek basins represent tangible evidence of the Caddo's past in the landscape, as also do the abandoned farmsteads and farmstead compounds of different communities. The burials themselves, and the consecration of each cemetery as sacred ground, gave each place a long-lasting meaning and cultural significance in everyday life.

Key Titus phase sites and constructed mounds

with contributions by Ross C. Fields

The Ear Spool site (41TT653) is a small (0.5 acres/0.2 ha) Titus phase settlement on a sandy ridge, along an intermittent tributary to East Piney Creek, in the East Texas Pineywoods. This creek flows north into White Oak Creek, a major tributary stream in the larger Sulphur River basin. Excavations were conducted here in 1997–1998 (Perttula and Sherman 2009).

The site was occupied on two different occasions by Caddo groups, first from *c.* AD 1400–1480 (Component I) and then again from *c.* AD 1480 to the early 17th century (Component II). Each component had a distinctive assemblage of decorated ceramic fine and utility wares, and lithic assemblages in each seem to have been geared to the production and use of triangular Maud arrow points.

Four circular structures were identified and excavated at the Ear Spool site, two in the earlier component (Structures 1 and 3) and two in the later (Structures 2

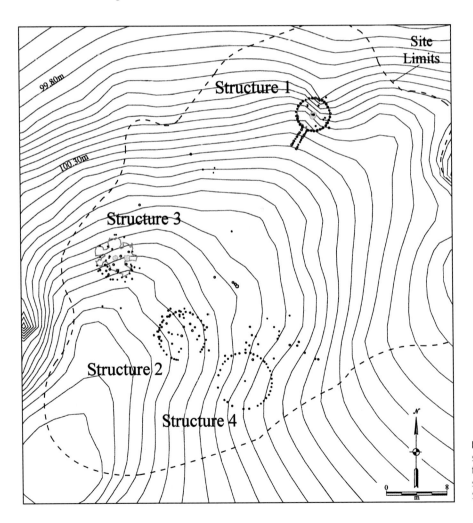

Fig. 103. Plan of the structures and outdoor features from the Ear Spool site (from Perttula and Sherman 2009, fig. 1–2)

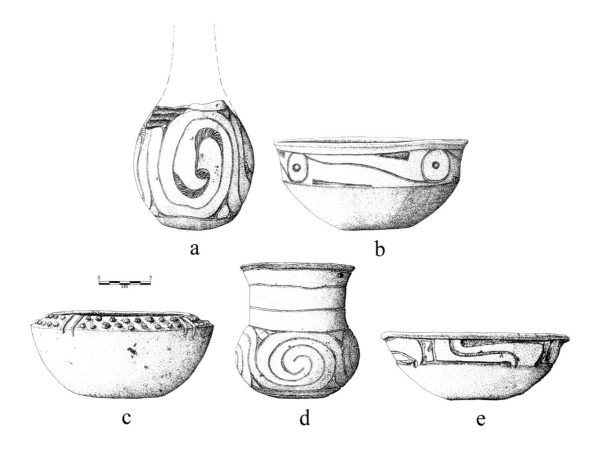

a   b

c   d   e

Fig. 104. Engraved and appliqué noded vessels from the Ear Spool site

and 4) (Fig. 103); a small mound was constructed over Structure 1 after it had been burned. In outdoor areas were two burials, ten pit features and several activity areas marked by post-holes from ramadas, arbors, or racks, along with three marker posts in the courtyard area that were "sequential center posts (set or reset three times) for a courtyard or open area where outdoor work activities took place" (Perttula and Sherman 2009: 85) and had relatively high densities of ceramic sherds, lithic artifacts and animal bones. The four circular structures ranged in size from approximately 4.65 m to 7.52 m in diameter with interior floor areas of 16.27 –44.41 m^2.

The Component I structures were both constructed within shallow (25–45 cm bs) circular pits and had reddish-brown prepared clay floors and central hearths. Structure 1 also had an extended entrance that was oriented southwest, towards Structure 3, about 30 m away across a relatively open courtyard. Both Component I structures were apparently intentionally burned down, and the structure pits filled with different kinds of fill and burned structural materials (including much daub/burned clay in Structure 1), as well as discarded trash, leading to the creation of a small mound over Structure 1. A single marker post was then excavated by the Caddo through the burned structural deposits, terminating in the central hearth. The marker was likely intended to mark the burned Component I structure and its central hearth for later residents of the Ear Spool site, and it was probably erected during Component II times (Perttula and Sherman 2009). These characteristics of the structures suggest that they may not have been strictly for domestic habitation, but were used for important public, ritual and spiritual activities at the site and in the surrounding community.

The Component II structures were also circular structures, placed next to each other, and less than 10 m southeast of Structure 3 from Component I (see Fig. 103). These structures were not in pits and did not have prepared clay floors, and they apparently represent domestic constructions. Structure 2 was also burned upon its abandonment, but was not intentionally covered with fill.

The material culture recovered from the Ear Spool site provides insights concerning the range of activities that took place there by several Caddo families. The manufacture of arrow points and other tools indicate that the production of hunting, scraping and cutting tools was important, especially during Component II times. A Caddo stone tool knapper may have lived in Structure 2. The abundance of stone tools and debris suggests that the hunting and processing of large game was a particular focus of the adult men and women living at Ear Spool. There also was a large assortment of ground stone tools used to pound, grind and chop plant and animal foods, including manos, grinding slabs, abraders, as well as celts to chop and work wood.

The more than 1950 decorated sherds and 14 vessels (Fig. 104) from the two Titus phase components at Ear Spool site constitute a diverse set of engraved and slipped fine ware serving vessels and bottles as well as incised, punctated, incised, incised-punctated, brushed and appliqued utility ware cooking and storage jars. The principal fine ware is Ripley Engraved in both components (Fig. 104b, e), along with Wilder Engraved bottles and compound bowls (Fig. 104a, d), and the utility wares are from Maydelle Incised, Pease Brushed-Incised, La Rue Neck Banded, Moore Noded (Fig. 104c) and McKinney Plain jars. Vessels are medium to large in size, with mean orifice diameters ranging from 19.8–24.1 cm.

The Mockingbird or *Kahbakayammaahin* (the Caddo word for mockingbird) site (41TT550) is a 15th and 16th century Titus phase Caddo cemetery that was partially excavated in 1990 and 1994 prior to proposed lignite mining (Perttula *et al.* 1998). The cemetery is situated on a sandy landform overlooking the Hart Creek floodplain; the creek is a southward-flowing and stream-fed tributary to Big Cypress Creek.

Eleven Caddo burials were excavated here before it was decided to halt the excavations and that further excavations of the cemetery were not necessary. It was deemed more appropriate that the site be preserved and protected in the long-term; the cemetery area (estimated to have 20–25 individual burials) was capped with a thick layer of concrete to protect it long-term.

Based on the size of the burial pits, and the kinds and range of funerary offerings placed with the deceased, the burials from the Mockingbird site are primarily adults (both male and female), and two adolescents; human remains were not preserved in the acidic sandy sediments. The burials were arranged in rows, with funerary offerings of different sorts usually placed in rows on either one side or another of the body, or near the feet. The deceased's head would have faced to the west, towards the House of Death. Adult males, adult females, and adolescents received different amounts of kinds of funerary offerings to accompany them on their death journey, and to be of use in the afterlife: celts, clay pipes, chipped stone tools (arrow points), along with ceramic vessels, characterize the adult male burials; adult females primarily had ceramic vessels of different kinds and sizes; adolescents and children also had ceramic vessels placed with them in the grave, and these tended to be smaller in size than those placed in the adult graves.

The mortuary assemblage from the Mockingbird site includes 89 ceramic vessels ranging from 0.5 liters to more than 4 liters in volume; the majority are Ripley Engraved carinated bowls and bottles. Ripley Engraved, with its diverse decorative motifs, is the principal fine ware type on all Titus phase Caddo sites (Perttula 2000). The utility wares are cooking and storage jars of the following types: Maydelle Incised, Pease Brushed-Incised, La Rue Neck Banded and Bullard Brushed. There are also small dishes and miniature jars that were used to hold clay pigments.

Stone tools are also among the funerary offerings, but they are not common in any individual burial. One burial, that of an assumed adult male, had an arrow point-making kit or cache placed in the grave. Among the tools from the cemetery are eight arrow points; seven bifaces (probably unfinished tools); two flake tools; small piles of lithic debris; five ground stone celts made from raw materials found in the Ouachita Mountains in southeast Oklahoma; quartz crystals; one petrified wood chunk with crystal inclusions; and a grinding slab that would have been used in life to grind plant foods and seeds.

The Tuck Carpenter site (41CP5), on Dry Creek several miles from its confluence with Big Cypress Creek (see Fig. 99), is a well known Titus phase community cemetery in the Big Cypress Creek basin (Turner 1978; 1992). More than 95% of the 45+ graves had the bodies of single individuals laid in an extended supine position on the floor of the pit, but two burial features had two individuals placed side by side in the burial pit. The cemetery was apparently used for the interment of Caddo peoples for a considerable span of time from the 15th to the 17th century AD.

The burials were laid out in an east–west direction in a number of rows (Turner 1978: fig. 3), amidst an existing midden deposit. A wide assortment of funerary offerings was placed in the graves, including 402 ceramic vessels; eight ceramic pipes; four ceramic ear spools; two wood ear ornaments; one sandstone ear spool with a copper plate covering; one unadorned sandstone ear spool; 57 Talco arrow points; 19 Maud points; 55 Bassett points; 57 Perdiz point; one arrow point of unidentified type; one large chipped biface or Galt biface (Thurmond 1990, table 23) of non-local chert (Thurmond 1990: 144); one biface fragment; seven celts; one metate; four manos; four abrading stones; two polishing stones; one chipped gouge; deer mandibles; deer beamers; clay pigment masses; one marine shell columella bead; turtle carapaces, and mussel shells (Turner 1978: 12–49).

The large community cemetery, with more than 40 burials, at the Henry Spencer site (41UR315) on Gum Creek in the Little Cypress Creek basin (Fig. 105) may have been in use for as much as 200 years, from c. AD 1450–1650, but was primarily used as a place of burial from cal. AD 1450–1530 based on the radiocarbon dating of organic residues preserved on two vessels. The recovery of a single European glass bead in a vessel in one of the latest burials at the site (Perttula et al. 2012c) suggests it was also used after c. AD 1680.

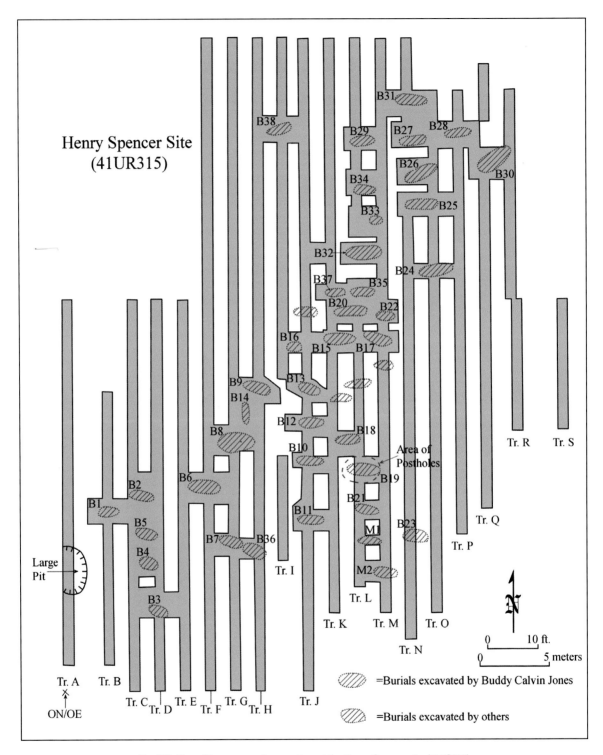

Fig. 105. Plan of the community cemetery at the Henry Spencer site (41UR315)

The Gum Creek and Little Cypress Creek basins were well populated during the time the Henry Spencer cemetery was in use. There are several distinctive burials in the Henry Spencer site cemetery burial groups that may represent the burials of important people, either adult members of the social elite, individual community leaders, or even heads of paramount lineages. They received special treatment at death, including having unique and rare artifacts placed with them in the burial pits. These individuals may represent those with a higher social position, likely the heads of different lineages or extended kin groups that resided in farmsteads comprising an established community, and ended up being interred in associated cemeteries amidst their kin relations.

The Shelby Mound site (41CP71) on Greasy Creek is one of the more important known Titus phase archaeological sites because of its large and well-preserved settlement with abundant habitation features as well as preserved plant and animal remains, evidence of mound building activities and a large community cemetery with at least 119 burial pits (Fig. 106) and perhaps as many as 200 (Perttula and Nelson 2004); the burials were laid out on a northeast–southwest axis. The Shelby Mound site is the nexus of one Titus phase political community in the Big Cypress Creek stream basin.

One Caddo individual (Burial 117) in the cemetery was buried with two 9 ft (c. 2.75 m) long cedar poles, and this person appears to have been politically and socially important, since the cedar poles were part of a wood litter upon which the deceased would have rested; the poles were found along each side of the individual placed in this burial. No other such Caddo litter burials are known from East Texas mortuary contexts, which certainly points to the social significance of this Caddo individual, although a number of cedar pole litter burials from individuals with a "superior social standing" (accompanied by a truly unique assortment of grave goods) have been documented in 14th century AD burials in the Special Mortuary of the Craig Mound at the Spiro site in the Arkansas River valley in eastern Oklahoma (see Brown 2012).

At death, this individual at the Shelby Mound site, probably an adult male, was accompanied by a number of decorated pottery vessels – two large brushed ollas; a Bailey Engraved bottle; a probable Wilder Engraved bottle; one red, yellow and tan bowl (possibly a Hatinu Engraved vessel, see Perttula et al. 2010c); and sherds from an unknown number of crushed vessels – as well as more than 20 expertly knapped Talco arrow points. This person appears to have then been buried on the cedar pole litter in a tomb placed below the floor of a structure, after which the structure was burned, capping the tomb, and leaving a large deposit of daub overlying the burial. The calibrated radiocarbon age range of the Burial 117 cedar pole (AD 1430–1640 at 2 sigma and with a calibrated radiocarbon intercept of AD 1470) is apparently contemporaneous with the construction of the earthen mound at the Shelby Mound site (and the use and then burning of at least one structure in the mound between cal AD 1420–1490) as well as village deposits on a natural levee about 50 m south of the mound itself. Considered in context with the radiocarbon dates from mound and habitation features, Burial 117 burial litter at the Shelby Mound site may well have been interred in the large community cemetery in the latter part of the 15th to the first part of the 16th century, perhaps

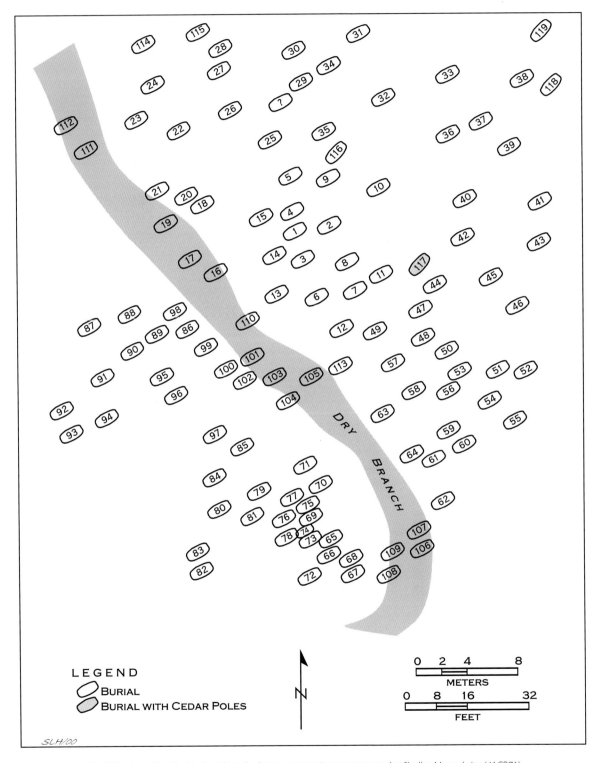

Fig. 106. Map of the Caddo burials in the large community cemetery at the Shelby Mound site (41CP71)

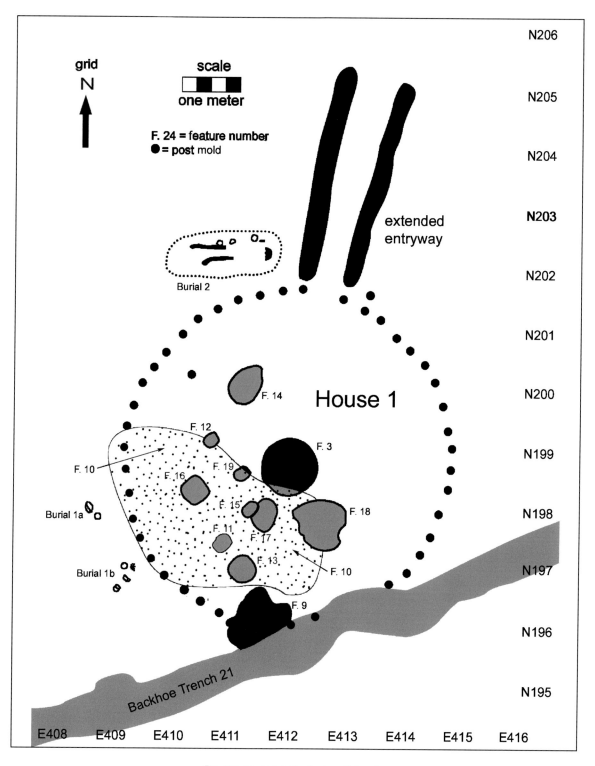

Fig. 107. House 1 at the Rookery Ridge site

during the cemetery's early use. The 2 sigma calibrated age range of the Burial 117 cedar pole and the associated Talco arrow points also indicates (or does not rule out the possibility) that the burial litter may date as late as the early 17th century. Seriation analysis of ceramic vessels and arrow point styles from Titus phase burials and cemetery sites in the Big Cypress Creek basin suggests that the large community cemeteries date after the early 16th century and were in use until at least the early to mid-17th century. The preponderance of archaeological evidence from the Shelby Mound site and 13 known community cemeteries in the Big Cypress Creek basin, in conjunction with the 2 sigma calibrated radiocarbon age range from the Feature 117 litter burial itself, point to the unique burial on a cedar pole litter of a socially superior Caddo individual in a Titus phase political community sometime after the early part of the 16th century AD

At Lake Gilmer in the Little Cypress Creek basin, the Late Caddo sites apparently date only to the 15th century AD, based on a series of calibrated radiocarbon dates from the Kelsey Creek Dam site (41UR118), the Verado site (41UR129) and the Rookery Ridge site (41UR133) (Parsons 2015). These sites have Titus phase components marked by distinctive batches of Ripley Engraved bowls and bottles, Wilder Engraved bottles, as well as utility ware jars of Bullard Brushed, Maydelle Incised, Killough Pinched, Harleton Appliqued, La Rue Neck Banded and Pease Brushed-Incised, and features: houses, including daub concentrations that mark house locations, pits, burials in domestic contexts and a family cemetery of 20–30 burials at another. Parsons (2015) views these as components as part of a dispersed Caddo village comprised of domestic farmsteads and a specialized structure that were the focus of ritual activities by the social and political elite. In the case of Lake Gilmer, House 1 (and the mound that covered it after it was burned) at the Rookery Ridge site, with its extended entranceway (Fig. 107), appears to have been the focus of local ritual and social activities.

The Pine Tree Mound site, by Ross C. Fields

The Pine Tree Mound site (41HS15), in south-central Harrison County, Texas, is on a prominent upland surface between Potters and Starkey creeks, c. 7.3 km north of where Potters Creek flows onto the floodplain of the Sabine River (Fig. 108). It is a large (800 × 720 m) ceremonial and civic complex that the Caddo occupied from sometime in the AD 1300s to the 1700s, with the most intensive use between AD 1400–1525. The site lies at the heart of a community documented first in July 1542 as the Nondacao province by the remnants of the Hernando de Soto expedition. According to Chafe (1993: 223), Nondacao comes from the Caddo word *Nadaakuh*, meaning "the place of the bumblebee" or the people of that place. These people were known as the Nadaco Caddo by the 18th century. Test excavations in 2004 examined the entire site, and more-intensive excavations in 2006–2007 focused on several possible village areas (Fields and Gadus 2012a; 2012b). All told, the excavations covered almost 15,000 m^2 and exposed about 3300 cultural features relating to at least 38 Caddo houses and their associated ancillary structures and activity areas in multiple village areas arranged around a ceremonial precinct. The work also identified four cemeteries.

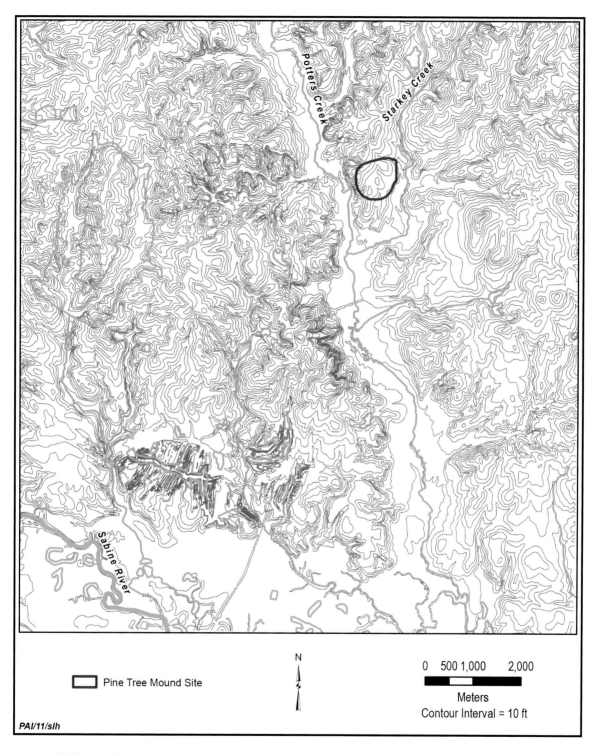

PAI/11/slh

Pine Tree Mound Site

N

0   500 1,000   2,000

Meters
Contour Interval = 10 ft

Fig. 108. Topographic map showing the location of the Pine Tree Mound site relative to the Potters and Starkey Creek valleys

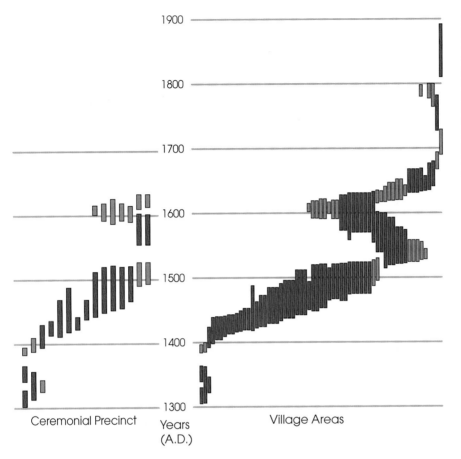

Fig. 109. Graphs of one-sigma calibrated ranges of radiocarbon dates from 76 contexts in the ceremonial precinct and village areas at the Pine Tree Mound site; only intervals with high (dark gray; p > .38 at the one-sigma level) and moderate (light gray; p = .17–.35 at the one-sigma level) probabilities are shown

Ceremonial Precinct

Years (A.D.)

Village Areas

The 102 useful radiocarbon dates obtained as a result of the excavations indicate that the history of Native American occupation evolved through five stages, covering a span of as much as 400 years (Fig. 109). The first stage, in the AD 1300s, involved a slow start to both residential and ceremonial activities. It is not certain where the people who settled there came from, but one possibility is that they were descendants of people who lived at and around the Hudnall-Pirtle site (see Chapter 4). This Early Caddo ceremonial and civic center, which is on the south side of the Sabine River *c.* 14 km southwest of Pine Tree Mound, was apparently abandoned after the mid-1200s (Bruseth and Perttula 2006: 147–8). One piece of evidence that could tie these two sites together is the poorly known Lane Mitchell site (41HS4/41HS233), which lies 9.3 km southwest of Pine Tree Mound and 3.8 km northeast of Hudnall-Pirtle. Lane Mitchell contains four or five small mounds and a borrow pit. There is no obvious plaza, although too little work has been done there to say much about the overall site layout, and the mounds seem not to be associated with numerous surrounding village areas like Pine Tree Mound. Limited excavations indicate that most or all of the mounds contain burned structures, presumably ceremonial in nature, and the ceramics recovered indicate that the site dates to the Late Caddo period, making it contemporaneous with the Pine Tree

Mound site. Just how Pine Tree Mound and Lane Mitchell are related is unknown, but the fact that the latter sits astride a straight northeast-southwest line between Pine Tree and Hudnall-Pirtle, on a high spot with the Sabine floodplain beyond, suggests that it may have served as a geographic marker connecting the old center of power and authority (Hudnall-Pirtle) with the new (Pine Tree Mound).

By the early 1400s and continuing through the early 1500s, residential activities were both widespread across the Pine Tree Mound site and intensive, as was use of the ceremonial precinct. These patterns continued through the 1500s, but in a less intensive fashion than before. At least one part of the site continued to be used for residential activities into the mid-1600s, but it appears that ritual-associated construction was no longer taking place in the ceremonial precinct. The focus of such activities had shifted elsewhere by then. The final stage, in the 1700s, may have little to do with what came before. One area saw residential use, but it was not intensive and may have been by people whose main villages were elsewhere. At least four Historic Caddo sites, probably dating to the 18th century, are known downstream on Potters Creek, and others have been documented both north and south of the Sabine River in the vicinity. One branch of the Nadaco apparently had moved south into the Angelina River basin to be near the Hasinai Caddo by 1717, but the account of Pedro Vial's journey indicates that a northern branch was still living in this part of the Sabine River basin in 1788, occupying a village with 13–15 houses scattered over a distance of 3 leagues, or about 13 km (Perttula 1992: 175–7). The ancestors of these villagers most likely participated in building the mounds at Pine Tree and were involved in ritual ceremonies performed there.

The ceremonial precinct was the core of the community that the Nadaco Caddo established on Potters Creek in the AD 1300s. This area, encompassing 5.7 ha, is a well-defined ceremonial landscape that undoubtedly served as the center for higher-level religious and political activities for the larger community (Fig. 110). An open central plaza covered most of the area, with the largest mound, Mound A measuring 55 × 45 m in size and 2.4 m high at its south end. This was a platform mound that was built rapidly, probably to support one or more important buildings on its summit, although other such buildings likely stood here before the mound was erected. Mound C is a similar but much smaller (27 × 33 m and 0.4 m high) platform mound about 60 m northeast of Mound A. About 90 m northwest of Mound A, on the western side of the plaza, is Mound B, which measures 33 × 37 m and is 1.2 m high. It accumulated through the construction, destruction and capping of a sequence of important buildings, reflecting a more complex and probably slower construction history than Mounds A and C (Fig. 111).

Post-holes and other features indicate that various structures bordered the plaza between Mounds A and B, north of Mound B, east of Mound A and south and north of Mound C; these probably were buildings with ritual functions or houses for people critical to those functions. The plaza's northwest corner was marked by a large cemetery where important members of the community were buried. Above-ground poles probably marked some of the graves in this cemetery. The limited excavations here indicate that the cemetery probably had more than 200 graves, some containing multiple individuals. Of the six graves that were documented, the largest measured 4.4 × 2.4 m horizontally, and the deepest one extended to 4 m

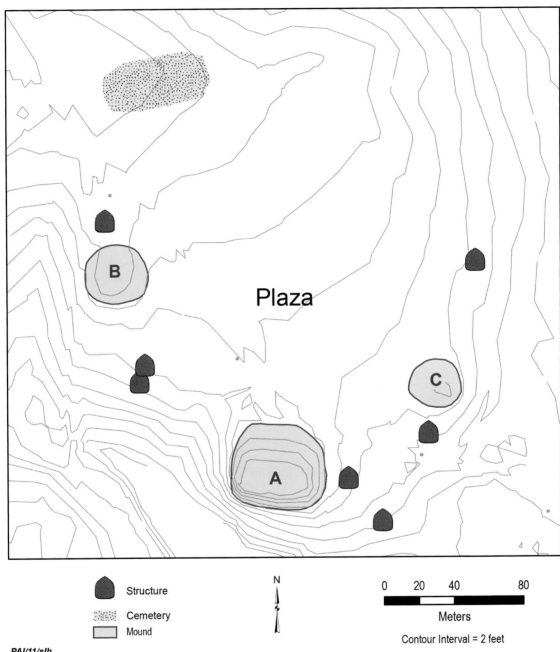

Structure

Cemetery

Mound

N

0   20   40   80

Meters

Contour Interval = 2 feet

PAI/11/slh

below the surface. Together with the three earthen mounds, these shaft graves represent an enormous amount of effort invested in creating a landscape designed to serve the ceremonial needs of the people who lived at and near the site.

Combining the data from Pine Tree Mound with that from two other adjacent tested sites, it appears that there may have been about 15 residential areas on the same landform within 100–370 m of the ceremonial precinct (Fig. 112). At

Fig. 110. Layout of the ceremonial precinct at the Pine Tree Mound site

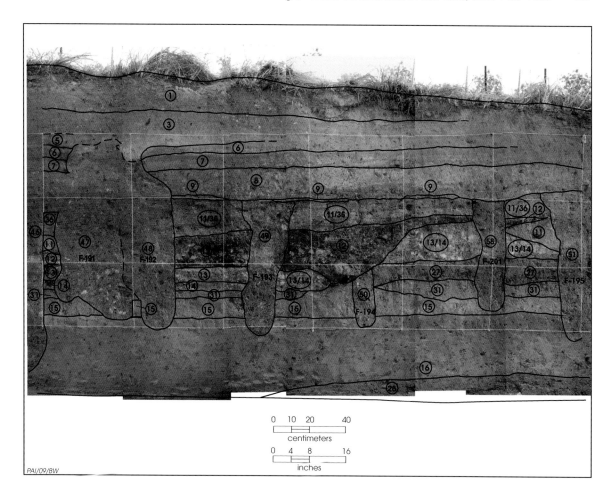

0   10   20   40
centimeters

0   4   8   16
inches

PAI/09/BW

Fig. 111. Composite photograph of part of the wall of a backhoe trench cut into Mound B. Circled numbers are sediment zones. Everything above Zone 16 is mound fill, representing multiple superimposed surfaces on which buildings were constructed. Most of the vertically oriented features (F-192, 193, 194, 195, and 201) are post-holes for these buildings

its height, the nucleus of this village may have been home to about 125 people, including its elite members living in the ceremonial precinct. It seems that each non-elite residential area usually consisted of a single circular pole-and-thatch house averaging 6.3 m in diameter where a single nuclear or extended family lived. Two houses may have stood simultaneously in some areas at certain times, but this appears to have been the exception. These houses likely had central hearths and benches or alcoves along the walls flanking and opposite the entryways. Auxiliary structures such as ramadas and granaries were likely present around the houses but are not well-defined. Outside activity areas relating to various mundane activities are present, and these likely were associated with less-substantial structures such as drying racks and wind screens (Fig. 113).

The residential areas also contain small family cemeteries set off at varying distances from the house compounds, as well as single graves and pairs of graves closer to the houses. One of the excavated cemeteries contained a single row of five graves. The other had 13 graves arranged in multiple, less-systematic rows. These cemeteries could have been marked by poles or other visible elements, like the cemetery in the ceremonial precinct.

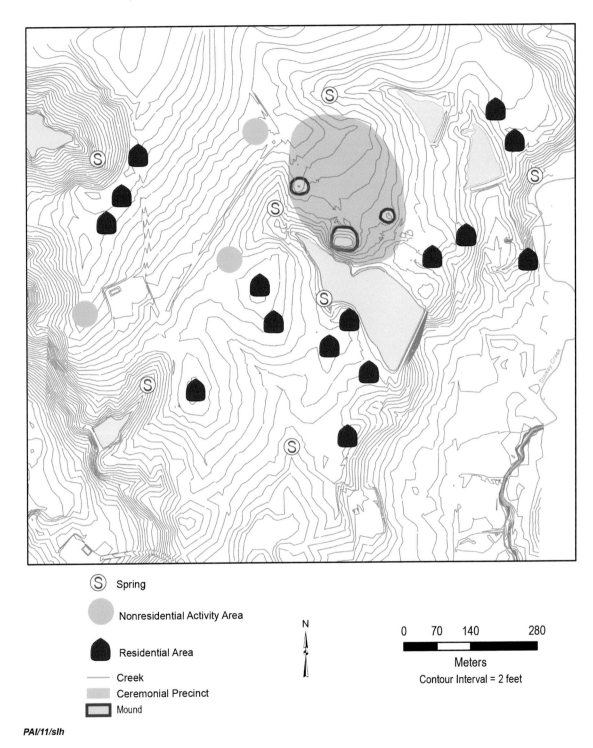

S   Spring

⬤   Nonresidential Activity Area

⬤   Residential Area

—   Creek

    Ceremonial Precinct

▭   Mound

N

0   70   140   280

Meters
Contour Interval = 2 feet

PAI/11/slh

Fig. 112. Map showing components of the Pine Tree Mound community around the ceremonial precinct

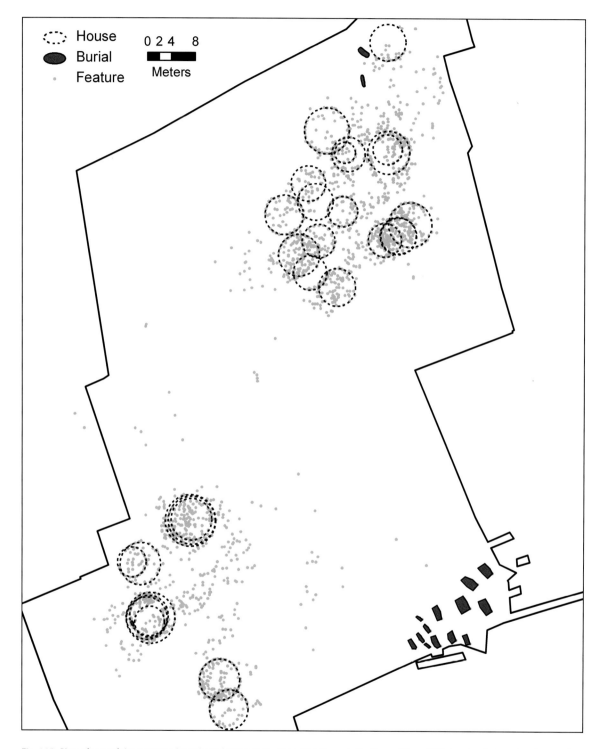

Fig. 113. Plan of two of the excavated residential areas at the Pine Tree Mound site (Areas 2N and 2S) showing feature locations and identified houses

These residential areas were not occupied continuously throughout the site's history. A house was built and then rebuilt once, twice, or three times, spanning perhaps no more than 40 years, and then that area was abandoned for a period of time before being reoccupied and a new house built. These are multi-generational family house compounds, but not ones that had simple use histories of genesis followed by continuous use and then abandonment. The ebb and flow of occupation may have been related to events such as the death of a lineage head, for example.

Aside from the house compounds and ceremonial precinct, other landscape components that contributed to the character of the site included non-residential activity areas, cultivated fields, freshwater springs and drainages, borrow areas where the more than 5000 m^3 of fill used for mound construction was obtained, and pathways or lines of sight. There are three known concentrations of cultural materials outside the ceremonial precinct that are interpreted as something other than residential areas. Only one saw much excavation. It contains no houses and likely represents a large activity area, but there is little indication in the artifacts that those activities were much different than those performed in the residential areas, with the possible exception of an emphasis on plant food processing.

Cultivated fields likely occupied much of the ridge where houses and other features the Caddo built were not present, with fields shifting around as house compounds were created, expanded and abandoned. There is no direct archaeological evidence for fields near the house compounds, but the presence of sumac wood and seeds in some village area features may be indicative of this, as sumac grows best on disturbed land such as abandoned agricultural fields. Most of the ridge between Potters and Starkey creeks contains well-drained fine sandy loam soils that today are classed as prime farmland and that would have been better suited to cultivation by the Caddo than the floodplain soils along Potters and Starkey creeks. Prime farmland soils also are extensive both north and south of the site and in upland areas to the east across Starkey Creek and west across Potters Creek, and the Pine Tree Mound Caddo had ample room to raise crops.

Seven freshwater springs are on and adjacent to the site, and these probably were the main sources of water when the site was occupied. If these sources, and perhaps others undiscovered in the drainages on the site, did not fill the residents' water needs, Potters and Starkey creeks were short walks away. These water sources likely had cosmological significance as portals to the underworld of the multi-level cosmos represented by Mississippian and Caddo iconography (see Gadus 2013), and it is probably no coincidence that Mounds A and B are close to springs, with the springs linking the mounds to that watery realm.

Some of the sandy fill composing the mounds could be sediments scraped from the surface almost anywhere on the site. If fill was obtained in this way, borrow pits that would still be recognizable today may not have been created. The clayey mound fill units likely came from elsewhere, though, in areas where deeper parts of the solum were exposed naturally. A potential source area for these is along the now-dammed drainage that borders the south side of the ceremonial precinct. A 1935 aerial photograph shows what appears to be a steep northern bank of the drainage east of Mound A, and it is possible that this was a borrow area for fill for the mounds. One other possibility for on-site fill procurement is at the head of this drainage and southwestward from there. No pits are evident, but this often marshy expanse contains sediments similar to some of the white and light gray mound fills, and it is possible that the Caddo obtained fill here by scraping it from the surface. Fill for mound building also could have been brought in from off site.

The final landscape element mentioned above, pathways, left no archaeological signatures. They surely were present, though. Further, it is likely that clear lines of sight were maintained between the family compounds and the ceremonial precinct, preserving visual communication with the village center. Given the number of residential areas, as well as the likelihood of cultivated fields surrounding them, the site probably was mostly open with stands of trees only along the few larger drainages when the Nadaco Caddo lived there.

With almost 16,000 ha of land north of the Sabine River near the Pine Tree Mound site having been surveyed, about 400 Native American sites having been documented, and 35 sites having seen some amount of excavation, it is possible to look beyond the immediate vicinity of Pine Tree Mound and identify other places where Caddo people who were members of this community lived. Based on radiocarbon dates and, more commonly, the kinds of pottery found, it appears that 40 of the known sites are directly associated with Pine Tree Mound. They are heavily concentrated in the Potters Creek valley, with much smaller numbers on other creeks to the west and along the valley wall overlooking the Sabine River floodplain. This suggests that the principal Pine Tree Mound community village extended for a distance of about 5.5 km along Potters Creek, with the ceremonial precinct at its northern, upstream end. Although part of the Potters Creek valley above Pine Tree Mound has not been surveyed systematically, sufficient acreage has been examined to indicate that associated sites there are scattered rather than clustered as they are downstream.

The associated sites include the previously mentioned Lane Mitchell mound site that may have been a subsidiary nexus of ceremonial activities for the community. At the other end are sites that apparently were used as short-term campsites during procurement or processing forays, by members of the Pine Tree Mound community. In between these extremes are small Late Caddo residential sites or outlying hamlets.

There are no other sites like Pine Tree, with its conspicuous ceremonial landscape, anywhere nearby in the Sabine River basin, and it is certain that the religious and political leaders who lived there exerted influence over an expansive territory (Fig. 114). The Pine Tree Mound territory is estimated to have extended across an area roughly 50 km north–south by 60 km east–west, encompassing some 2400 km^2 with the Sabine River running through the middle, and the Hasinai Trace bisecting it from north to south. People were not distributed evenly throughout this area, as the main village was north of the river, stretching for 5.5 km along the Potters Creek valley and anchored by the Pine Tree Mound site at its north end. The rest of the community appears to have been more rural, although at two different scales. Other north-side tributary valleys may have supported moderately scattered settlements. The entire territory south of the river, accounting for well over half of it, appears to have been sparsely settled during the Titus phase.

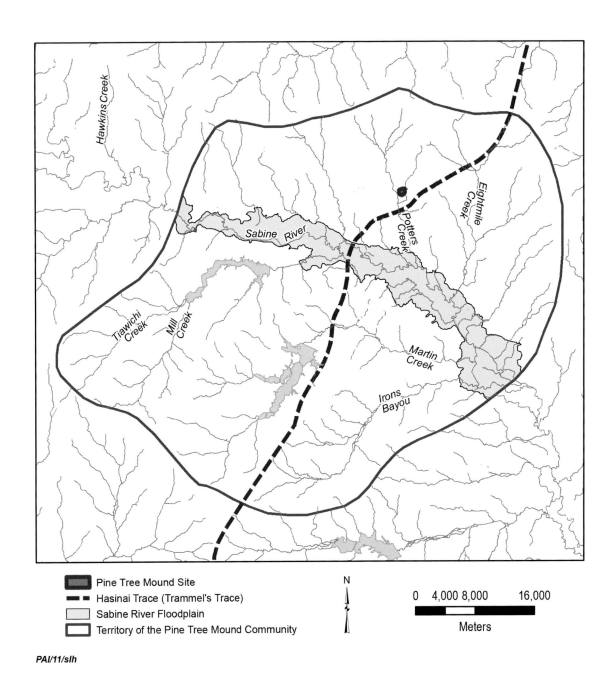

Pine Tree Mound Site
Hasinai Trace (Trammel's Trace)
Sabine River Floodplain
Territory of the Pine Tree Mound Community

N

0   4,000 8,000   16,000

Meters

PAI/11/slh

Fig. 114. Map showing the hypothesized extent of the territory of the Pine Tree Mound community

Key Frankston, Angelina and Salt Lick phase sites

The Frankston phase is comprised of farmsteads, hamlets and small villages in the Neches and parts of the Angelina river basins (see Fig. 75) that date from *c.* AD 1400–1680. Only a single Frankston phase mound is known, the A. C. Saunders site (41AN19). This small mound had thick ash beds and fill zones, and probably represents a Caddo fire temple used by the social and political elite of one Frankston phase community (Jackson 1936; Kleinschmidt 1982; Story and Creel 1982: 36 and fig. 8). Other Frankston phase sites are represented by small residential settlements in dispersed agricultural communities, with small family and/or community cemeteries not used for long periods of time, such as at the Lang Pasture site (41AN38) (Perttula *et al.* 2011). Concentrations of Frankston phase sites in one section of the upper Neches River basin seem to comprise base settlement clusters with middens, burials and house structures, likely representing permanent settlements on streamside flats with fertile soils in the uplands. Other site types have sherd scatters, that perhaps are gathering stations in which pitted stones are found with a few sherds, and small campsites. The Omer and Otis Hood cemetery (41CE14) with 20 burials is one of the larger known Frankston phase cemeteries. Many others have fewer than ten individuals, laid out individually in extended supine position, with a variety of grave goods (principally ceramic vessels). In at least one instance, a Frankston phase cemetery in the upper Neches River basin at the Joe Meyers Estate #1 site (41SM73) in Smith County, Texas (see also Chapter 4), contained the burial of socially elite individuals in a family and/or village cemetery context. This particular burial was in a 3.6 m wide pit, and three individuals had been placed in the grave. Among the funerary objects placed with the multiple burial were 21 pottery vessels, a ground stone celt and a large chipped biface (Jowell knife); baskets or matting were apparently also present in the grave.

The A. C. Saunders mound center is on an upland landform near, but on the west side of the Neches River, in the upper part of the river basin. The small mound (2.2 m in height and 26 × 33 m in length and width) found there, and excavated in the 1930s by The University of Texas (Jackson 1936; Kleinschmidt 1982), had a thick and virtually culturally sterile ash bed (1.06 m) and fill. The site may have been the nexus of ritual and feasting activities for a Caddo community living in this part of the upper Neches River basin.

South of the mound about 40 m away was a large and thick (up to 79 cm thick) midden deposit (and a second mound?) that covered an important circular structure with a possible entrance on its eastern side, based on its impressive size (14 × 13.2 m) and several large interior hearths and interior support posts (Fig. 115). The structure was built and dismantled in the 16th century, based on a seriation of Frankston phase ceramic assemblages from other upper Neches Caddo sites, then overlain by likely redeposited midden deposits. There were also two hearths excavated just outside the eastern walls of the structure, suggesting some outdoor cooking activities may have taken place there during the occupation.

The midden deposits contained an abundance of Caddo artifacts from apparent residential or domestic settlements in the area, including fragments from an

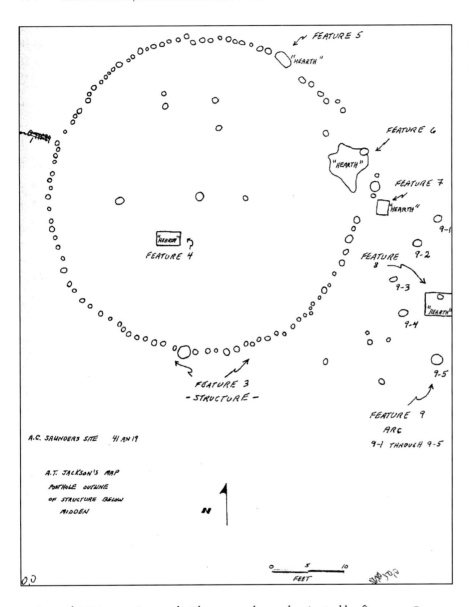

Fig. 115. The large circular structure under the midden deposit at the A. C. Saunders site

estimated 1291 ceramic vessels. These vessels are dominated by fine ware Poynor Engraved bowls, engraved effigy bowls and utility ware jars of the Bullard Brushed, Maydelle Incised and La Rue Neck Banded jars. The remainder of the material culture assemblage included numerous decorated elbow pipes, Perdiz arrow points, stone drills, mussel shell digging tools, an assortment of bone tools (awls, needles and beamers) and shell columnella beads.

The Pipe site (41AN67) was a Late Caddo period, Frankston phase habitation and cemetery occupied between c. AD 1480–1560 on a low terrace or lower toe slope near the Neches River. The cemetery of 21 individuals was in and around a midden area (Fig. 116). Stable isotope analysis of collagen and apatite in a right femur from Burial 11 indicates that the ancestral Caddo group that lived in this

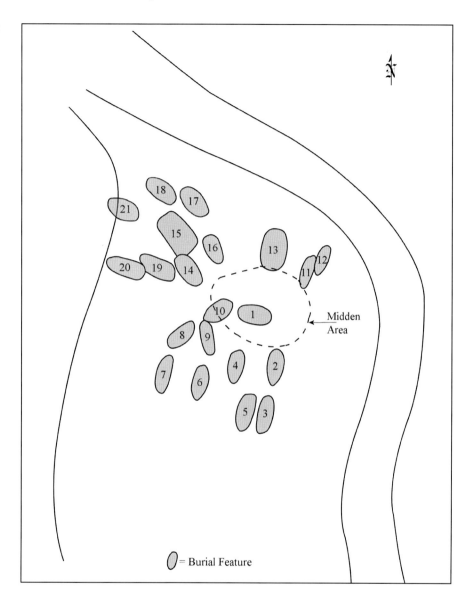

Fig. 116. Plan of features at the Pipe site

part of the upper Neches River basin had a diet with a high contribution of maize (Wilson *et al.* 2012: 83).

The burial that was centrally placed in the cemetery and midden was notable. This burial was oriented east–west, with the head at the east end of the burial pit, facing to the west (Fig. 117), and likely laid out in an extended supine position in the burial pit. A number of items had been placed as funerary objects with the deceased, including a marine shell gorget at the neck, four ceramic vessels on the right side of the body, and a fifth vessel along the area of the left leg (*kasuh*) on the left side of the body. The vessels on the right side of the body included a carinated bowl by the shoulder, along with a bottle and two jars from the right arm to what would have been the right leg of the individual.

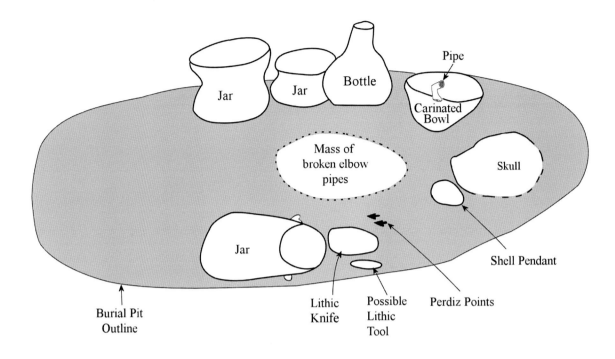

Fig. 117. Burial 1 and associated funerary offerings at the Pipe site

Several stone tools had been placed along the left side of the body. This included two Perdiz arrow points with their tips facing away from the head of the deceased, a large chipped stone knife and a possible bi-pointed lithic tool (perhaps a Jowell knife). Jowell knives are bifacially chipped to shape, have areas of use wear along the edges and/or tips of the tools and have rounded or bi-pointed proximal and distal ends (see Cole 1975: 183); the blades are often resharpened, probably after the tool became dulled. Finally, there was an elbow pipe placed within the carinated bowl by the right shoulder, along with a mass of broken bowls and stems from many elbow pipes that had been placed on the chest area of the deceased.

There were 105 ceramic elbow pipe sherds from the mass of broken pipes that was resting on the chest of the deceased Caddo individual. This included 46 plain bowl rim sherds, four decorated bowl rim sherds, 39 plain stem sherds and 16 decorated stem sherds. No attempt was made at pipe reconstruction, but based on the distinctive decorations on the bowl and stem sherds of a number of these broken pipes (Fig. 118), there were at least parts of more than 30 individual pipes in the mass of broken pipes. The burial of a single Caddo person with this many pipes, even in pieces, is unprecedented in the southern Caddo archaeological area.

Ceramic pipes and pipe sherds are common artifacts found in upper Neches River basin Caddo sites, especially those sites occupied after c. AD 1400 (Jackson 1933; 1936; Kleinschmidt 1982; Perttula et al. 2011). Ceramic pipes and pipe sherds seem to be relatively abundant in both domestic and mortuary archaeological deposits, with individuals perhaps having one or two pipes placed in grave pits as burial offerings for the deceased Caddo on their journey to the House of Death. The abundance of clay pipes in midden and habitation contexts on Frankston phase

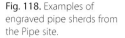

Fig. 118. Examples of engraved pipe sherds from the Pipe site.

Caddo sites clearly stands in contrast to the assertion by Schambach *et al.* (1982: 121) regarding Caddo pipe use that "normal farmsteads exhibit an absence of pipes or pipe fragments," and that "pipes denote religious ceremonial activity." Rather, the prevalence of clay pipes in both domestic and mortuary contexts throughout the upper Neches River basin indicate that the ritual activities associated with pipe smoking – and the smoking of tobacco (see Rafferty and Mann 2004; Winter 2000a; 2000b) – were actually part of daily life and the everyday ceremonies that the Caddo carried out in interacting with the spirits and souls around them. Pipes were likely made in many individual farmsteads and hamlets in various communities, and the different pipe styles and decorative elements on them, as well as their local use, may represent one of the more distinctive material culture remains of these various communities.

Pipes were probably smoked on a daily basis by adult members of farmsteads and communities – mainly adult males, but not always – and when the pipes broke during their ordinary use, they were discarded in nearby middens. Pipes were certainly made locally for daily use, but may have "conferred prestige on the person or household possessing them" (Dancey 2005: 118). Others must have been made for use in Caddo rituals and ceremonies involving smoking and tobacco, and finally, others were also made for, or contributed to use in mortuary rituals, as clearly exemplified by the very distinctive mortuary rituals (i.e., the apparent intentional breakage of more than 30 pipes) that were carried out as part of the interment of one adult Caddo individual at the Pipe site.

The archaeological evidence from the Pipe site suggests that a large number of plain and decorated elbow pipes were deliberately broken and placed together in a mass on the chest of the deceased. At the suggestion of Dr Frank Schambach (2010 personal communication), I looked especially to the archaeological record of the Hopewell culture for analogs to the behavior represented by the mass of broken pipes in the one burial at the Pipe site. According to Romain (2009: 125), in a study of the prehistoric religion of the Hopewell:

> "... a considerable number of Hopewell artifacts appear to have been intentionally damaged or destroyed before being buried. Among the best known are the Hopewell effigy pipes. At Tremper, 145 pipes were found in two caches ... The large cache contained 136 pipes; the smaller cache contained 9 pipes. All the pipes in the large cache had been broken. At Mound City, a cache of approximately two hundred pipes were discovered in Mound 8 ... All of these pipes were broken."

Romain (2009: 125) went on to suggest a number of reasons why objects such as pipes would be intentionally destroyed by Hopewell peoples or "killed" prior to discard or at the time of their burial. Such possibilities could include that they were broken as part of a social display of disposable wealth, or to negate their value. They might be broken to signify that their spiritual power could be dissipated and not to be used again (see Rafferty 2004: 19–20). Objects may be broken because the breaking of the object would cause it to become intact again in the spirit world. Objects might be broken to release their souls, and such "killed" objects placed with the dead also journey to the House of Death with the deceased, and once there would be of use to the deceased. If the Caddo living at the Pipe site and the local community had such beliefs, then the breaking of these elbow pipes could have had two intended consequences: (a) the pipes would be dispatched to the House of Death when their use in this world ended; and (b) once broken and their spirits released in this world, the pieces of the pipes would appear whole again in a reversed Otherworld (Romain 2009: 125).

In examining the context and meaning of the many broken pipes placed on a chest of a deceased Caddo individual at the Pipe site, it is important to reiterate how important pipe smoking was as a form of communication by Native American peoples, presumably including the Caddo, with the spirit world (Rafferty and Mann 2004, xiii–xv; Winter 2000a: 305). "The smoke was believed to carry the thoughts and prayers of the smoker to the upperworld ... pipes created and reinforced the link between this world and the Otherworld" (Romain 2009: 87). That being said, the possibility that this Caddo individual might have been a pipe maker in a upper Neches River basin community, and these pipes mark the importance of his craft, goes against the incontrovertible and unique evidence of the offering of so many pipes (pipes used in life, based on the sooting in bowls and stems), pipes broken apparently deliberately, in the burial of this Caddo adult. Since there were undoubtedly other pipe makers in many Caddo communities across the upper Neches River basin, it seems likely that there would be other burials found and documented that would represent the commemoration of a pipe maker and their special craft, but this is not what the archaeological record of the Caddo people tells us.

In this particular case, then, the mass of broken pipes associated with this one individual at the Pipe site suggests they had a connection with this person because the individual was likely spiritually or politically powerful and was intimately familiar with the rites and ceremonies of pipe smoking and/or was associated with a spiritually or politically powerful group or lineage (cf. Drooker 2004: 76) within this local Caddo community. Pipes, and rituals associated with their use, were a conduit to spiritual interactions by certain religious practitioners, and the deceased individual at the Pipe site may well have been such a practitioner. The mass of broken pipes also suggests that this individual may also have been responsible for developing alliances with other groups through the powerful venue of ritual tobacco smoking.

The Lang Pasture site (41AN38) is on a tributary in the upper Neches River basin. It was the location of a permanent settlement of Caddo peoples during the early years of the Frankston phase. Associated with the domestic settlement was a small family cemetery of Caddo peoples that likely resided there (Perttula *et al.* 2011). The stylistic character of the recovered ceramic vessels, particularly the engraved fine wares, from the burial features indicate that the Lang Pasture burials share stylistic features with both pre-AD 1400 and early (c. AD 1400–1450) Frankston phase mortuary ceramics in the upper Neches River basin.

The principal Caddo component in the investigated portion of the Lang Pasture site included two circular domestic structures (Structures 1 and 2) that were inhabited by at least one family of Caddo adults and children. The 6.8–9 m diameter structures were built of wood, grass and thatch; they were marked by arcs of post-holes and were less than 5 m apart. The two structures are considered, based on spatial proximity and a broad similarity in the ceramic material culture found in the excavations, to be part of a household compound, probably one of at least several such compounds that may be preserved at the Lang Pasture site.

Such a compound at Caddo sites in the upper Neches River basin of East Texas would have consisted of a series of domestic structures set around an open courtyard, with outdoor activity areas and ancillary facilities. At Lang Pasture, these outdoor activity areas were marked by pits, smudge pits and hearths not far removed to either the north and east of the domestic structures; these were also trash disposal areas, based on the broad scatter of broken ceramic vessels and pipe sherds in these same areas. Outdoor storage pits were also found in these areas. Ancillary facilities include at least one small (2 × 4 m) arbor or ramada (i.e., elevated work platform, Structure 3) east of Structure 1.

There was an associated Caddo family household cemetery north and northeast of Structure 1 at the Lang Pasture site, but physically distant from it. Seven burial features (including one with three individuals interred in it) were identified and excavated and they were found in two distinct groups. Based on the size of the cemetery, it is unlikely that it was in use for any substantial period of time by any one household compound or related group of households, perhaps no longer than 10–30 years.

One group of burials was composed of adults (Features 8, 88 and 91–4) and the other, not far removed from Structure 1, of children (Features 76A–D). The deceased Caddo adults and children were laid out in extended supine positions, with their heads either facing west (adults) or northwest (children) towards the House of Death and the setting sun, and they were accompanied by a modicum of funerary offerings (ceramic vessels and elbow pipes) that would have served as provisioning on the deceased's journey. The mortuary practices evidenced with the Lang Pasture burials are clearly comparable to those employed by other Caddo populations that lived in the upper Neches River basin from the 15th to the early 18th centuries (Perttula *et al.* 2011: 403–33).

Among the funerary offerings placed with the Caddo burials at the Lang Pasture site are ten carinated bowls, 11 bowls, three compound bowls (apparently a rare vessel form in the upper Neches), three jars and four bottles. These are the same vessel forms used in domestic contexts, but with significantly higher numbers of serving bowls in mortuary contexts; this is a practice shared with later upper Neches Caddo groups. The particular shape and form of these vessels is a hallmark of the technology and style of Caddo pottery vessels in the upper Neches River basin ceramic tradition, and these shapes and forms would have been immediately recognizable (e.g., Stark 2003: 212) to other Caddo as belonging to those of a particular social group. Sadie Bedoka, a Caddo-Delaware woman, noted some years ago that potters from one group could tell those of another simply by different pottery shapes (e.g., La Vere 1998: 92).

The Caddo ceramics found in domestic, household contexts at the Lang Pasture site include fine wares, utility wares and plain wares, including bowls and bottles; they are dominated by decorated utility ware jars. There are technological and stylistic differences between the wares and the Caddo potters that made these vessels clearly had a considerable range in choices and practices in how they were made and decorated. The ubiquity of these wares in every part of the site indicates that they were available to all the Caddo that lived there, and that there was no restricted access to the use of fine wares. These same wares are also found in the mortuary vessel assemblage at the Lang Pasture site but in very different proportions, with an increased emphasis on fine wares as one of the principal funerary offerings.

Charred plant remains were relatively abundant in habitation contexts at the Lang Pasture site. A total of 45 flotation samples and five macrobotanical samples (of maize cob segments) indicate that oak, pine, willow/cottonwood and hickory wood likely formed the tree canopy around the site during the 15th century AD ancestral Caddo occupation. Plant foods included acorn and hickory nuts, squash and maize. Hickory nuts were ubiquitous, occurring in 84.4% of the flotation samples, and maize (including cob segments, cupules, kernels and glume fragments) was present in 42% of the flotation samples with squash rind in 6.7% of them.

The analysis of the human remains recovered in the burial features at the Lang Pasture site indicated that the ancestral Caddo peoples were generally in good health with a high adaptive efficiency, based on low infection rates detected in these remains as well as those studied from other upper Neches River basin sites (Wilson 2011). Stable isotope and caries data point to a significant use of maize in the diet after the 14th century AD in the region (Wilson and Perttula 2013), as well as at the Lang Pasture site.

In the Angelina phase in the Angelina River basin (see Fig. 75), dating after c. AD 1450, the Walter Bell and the Etoile (41NA11) sites have small midden deposits, evidence for circular structures, pit features and/or burials (Jelks 1965). The three circular structures at Walter Bell range from 6.4–12 m in diameter. This site also had a small cemetery with six burial features with extended and flexed burials of children and adults. Four of the burials (Burials 1–3 and 6) were in close association (either inside the house and underneath the house floor) with House 1, one (Burial

Fig. 119. Map of the
cultural features at the
Walter Bell site (41SB50)

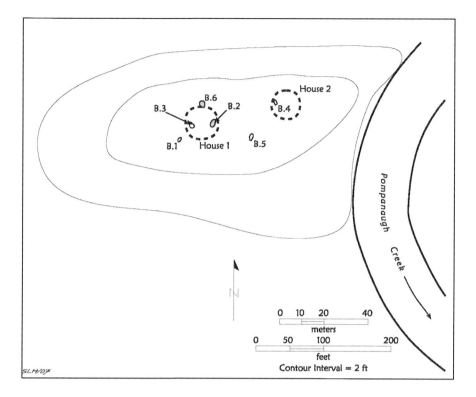

Fig. 119. Map of the cultural features at the Walter Bell site (41SB50)

4) was inside House 2, and Burial 5 was in an open area, possibly a courtyard or work area between the two Caddo houses (Fig. 119). Funerary objects placed with the deceased included 1–6 vessels per individual, Perdiz arrowpoints, conch shell beads, deer ulna tools and deer food offerings, mussel shells and engraved bird bone flageolets. The engraved designs on the vessels included small and large rows of triangle elements. Based on the kinds of artifacts found at the site (i.e., clay elbow pipes, a high proportion of brushed utility ware sherds from Broaddus Brushed vessels and lower proportions of Pineland Punctated-Incised vessel sherds), the Walter Bell site was apparently occupied after c. AD 1500, during the late Angelina phase (see Middlebrook 1994: 26–9 and fig. 4; 1997; Perttula et al. 2009: 22).

Post-AD 1400 communities are present in the Toledo Bend area along the Sabine River and tributaries in northwestern Louisiana and extreme eastern Sabine and Shelby counties in East Texas, particularly along Palo Gaucho Creek near the La Nana and Camino Arriba crossings of El Camino de los Tejas, an ancestral Caddo trace. These sites – such as Goode (16SA1), Bison, Area B (16SA4) and Salt Lick (16SA37a) – have extensive midden deposits (0.3–1.5 acres/0.1–0.6 ha) with evidence of residential features (post-holes, hearths and trash pits) and small cemeteries. At Bison, Area B, excavations encountered two large trash/storage pits, five possible charcoal-filled smudge pits and a number of post-holes from a possible rectilinear structure or an arbor near a family residence. Ceramic assemblages from the Bison, Area B, Salt Lick and Goode sites indicate the Caddo settlements along this stretch of the Sabine River were contemporaneous with Angelina phase Caddo communities in the Angelina-Attoyac drainage basins some 40–50 km to the west.

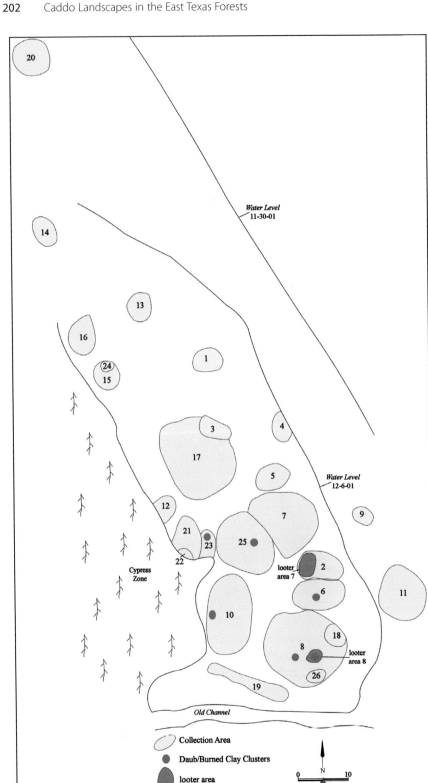

Fig. 120. Plan map of 41SY280 along the shoreline of Toledo Bend Reservoir, depicting the daub/burned clay clusters and collection areas

Post-AD 1430 Caddo archaeological sites at Toledo Bend Reservoir are included in a Salt Lick phase. Recognized decorated types in these sites include Belcher Ridged, Glassell Engraved, Keno Trailed, Mound Tract Incised and Brushed, Pease Brushed-Incised, Pineland Punctated-Incised, Ripley Engraved and Taylor Engraved, but many ceramic vessels and sherds cannot be identified to a defined type. The majority of the vessels are bone-tempered, while most of the sherds from domestic assemblages are from grog-tempered vessels. Only at the Salt Works Lake site (16SA47) are sherds from bone-tempered vessels more common in domestic contexts than grog-tempered vessels.

Well-known Late Caddo period sites at Toledo Bend Reservoir that have both ceramic vessels and decorated sherd assemblages include Salt Lick and Bison, Area B (McClurkan *et al.* 1966; Woodall 1969). On the basis of the whole vessels from these sites, their cultural affiliations may be said to exist with the middle Sabine River Caddo peoples at the Pine Tree Mound site community (see Fields and Gadus 2012a; 2012b), given the popularity of Ripley Engraved, Taylor Engraved, Karnack Brushed-Incised and Wilder Engraved vessels in the burials; Belcher Ridged vessels from Belcher phase sites are also funerary object inclusions in burials. However, it remains to be determined if any of these engraved vessels were locally manufactured, or were traded to a distinct and local Caddo community that lived in this part of the Sabine River basin (see Kelley 2006; Kelley *et al.* 2010).

The sherds from domestic contexts at these sites, as well as at the nearby Burnitt site (16SA204; Kelley 2006; Kelley *et al.* 2010), are dominated by typologically unidentifiable fine ware and utility ware sherds as well as Belcher Ridged, incised, brushed and Pineland Punctated-Incised sherds. The proportion of ridged utility wares is suggestive of cultural connections with Belcher phase Caddo groups on the Red River to the east and northeast (cf. Webb 1959).

Site 41SY280 is along the shoreline of Toledo Bend Reservoir, and covers a maximum area of *c.* 130 m north–south and 50 m east–west (Fig. 120). The density of ceramic sherds by collection area suggests that the main ancestral Caddo occupation is concentrated in a *c.* 40 × 40 m area at the southern end of the site and landform.

The site had been looted in the past, and exposed to shoreline fluctuations, and large quantities of archaeological material remains were also exposed on the site surface. The combination of looting and surface exposure led to the identification of 26 surface collection areas, as well as a circular area with six different clusters of daub and burned clay in the southern part of the site (see Fig. 120). These daub and burned clay clusters likely represent the locations of burned Caddo house structures. The distribution of high sherd density collection areas and the plotted locations of daub/burned clay clusters suggests that there is an ancestral Caddo occupation here that may represent a hamlet with a number of occupied houses; the high sherd density areas represent the accumulation of discarded broken ceramic vessels in outdoor work areas and trash disposal locations.

The ceramic assemblage contains a wide variety of utility and fine ware sherds, including sherds from brushed vessels, as well as Spradley Brushed-Incised, Karnack Brushed-Incised, Belcher Ridged, Cowhide Stamped, Glassell Engraved, Hodges Engraved, Belcher Engraved and Keno Trailed. The occurrence of Belcher

Ridged *var. Belcher* in the utility wares suggests that the main ancestral Caddo occupation of the site began after *c.* AD 1500, and was contemporaneous with the Belcher phase in the Red River valley in Northwestern Louisiana. The very considerable use of burned bone for temper (81.7%) at the site is consistent with other ancestral Caddo sites in the Toledo Bend Reservoir area. Finally, a thin (0.7 mm) cut and shaped piece of cupreous metal was recovered in Area 10 (see Fig. 120). This may be a fragment of an unidentified European trade good, suggesting a Caddo occupation occurred here that postdated *c.* AD 1680.

Caddo habitation sites on tributaries to the Sabine River, including Patroon Bayou, Palo Gaucho Bayou and Housen Bayou have ceramic assemblages comparable to those recognized in Salt Lick phase sites along the Sabine River at Toledo Bend Reservoir, particularly in the proportions of brushed sherds (see Kelley 2006, table 6-3). These sites were likely occupied between *c.* AD 1400–1500. This period may represent the peak period of Caddo settlement in these three eastward-flowing tributaries of the Sabine River in the East Texas Pineywoods.

This group of Late Caddo sites can be subdivided into: (a) sites on Palo Gaucho Bayou with high proportions of sherds from bone-tempered vessels, and (b) sites on Patroon Bayou, Housen Bayou and Palo Gaucho Bayou that have high proportions of sherds from grog-tempered vessels. There are also differences in these ceramic assemblages in the use of tempers to manufacture utility ware and fine ware vessels. Only one site, in the Palo Gaucho Bayou basin, has any sherds from shell-tempered vessels (see Perttula 2015b, table 9). This is not surprising given the rarity of shell temper use in Caddo pottery in this part of the Sabine River basin (Kelley 2006: 50).

Cemeteries of comparable size and character to those of the Frankston and Angelina phase groups are also present in post-AD 1400 Caddo archaeological sites in the Toledo Bend Reservoir area. At Salt Lick, there were four extended burials and five flexed burials, while the Bison site, Area B cemetery had 15 extended burials and a single flexed burial (Woodall 1969). Common mortuary goods included ceramic vessels, Perdiz and Bassett arrow points, ceramic elbow pipes, mussel shells, deer bones and clay pigments; one burial at the Bison site had sandstone pulley-shaped ear spools. In terms of their ceramics, these Caddo groups have affiliations with Titus phase groups to the north and with contemporaneous Caddo groups living to the west in the Neches-Angelina river basins and groups to the east in the Red River basin. Using the same mortuary treatment criteria employed in identifying elite burials in Titus phase cemeteries (i.e., burial in shaft tomb, burial in mound, burials with large chipped bifaces, burials with large quantities of grave goods and multiple burials with quantities of grave goods), Burial 4 at the Bison site, Area B may be an adult male of presumed high rank, and comparable (based on quantities of grave goods) to elite adult male burials among his Titus phase neighbors.

One of the few ancestral Late Caddo period mound sites in the middle reaches of the Sabine River basin is the Morse Mound site (41SY27), situated along an eastward-flowing tributary of the Sabine River. The site has two small mounds and a midden deposit just west of one of the mounds (Middlebrook 2014). Mean calibrated radiocarbon ages from two wood charcoal samples from the site are AD 1478 and AD 1527 (Middlebrook 2014: 100).

Fig. 121. Block excavations in Mound A, Morse Mound, showing the post-holes for the burned structure, and the outline of the shaft tomb in the center of the structure (image courtesy of the Texas Archeological Society)

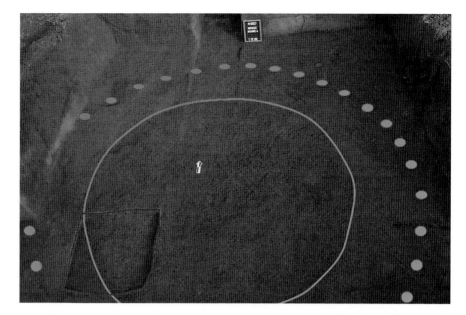

Fig. 122. The shaft tomb in Mound A, Morse Mound, showing the outline of the coffin and the placement of funerary offerings in the tomb (image courtesy of the Texas Archeological Society)

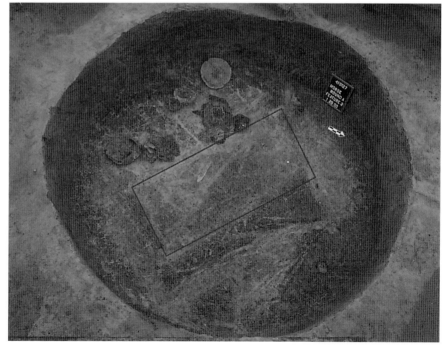

Mound A stood 1 m high and is 15 m in diameter. A 5.6 m diameter circular structure had been built first at this location, followed by the excavation of a 3.6 m diameter shaft tomb inside the structure while it was still standing (Fig. 121). The shaft tomb was partially filled in, the house then burned, and these features were capped with mound sediments (Middlebrook 2014: 100). The preservation

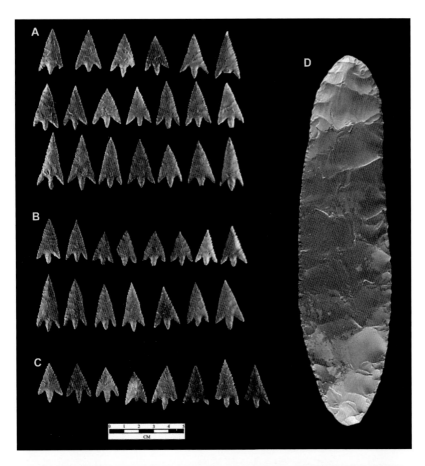

Fig. 123. Selected funerary offerings from the Mound A shaft tomb at the Morse Mound site: lithic artifacts in and around the coffin, including arrow point quivers (A–C) and large Edwards chert biface (D)

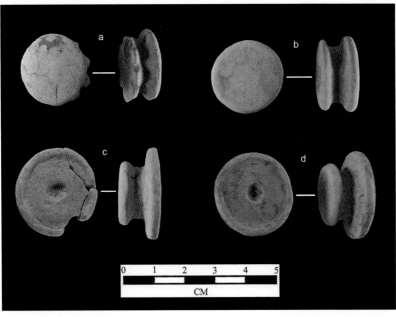

Fig 124. Selected funerary offerings from the Mound A shaft tomb at the Morse Mound site: ear spools, including those found in the coffin (a–b), and those found just north of the coffin (c–d) (images courtesy of the Texas Archeological Society)

of the shaft tomb preserved evidence of wood boxes or containers as well as a rectangular wood coffin (Fig. 122).

An impressive range of funerary offerings were placed either in the coffin or alongside the tomb. Among them were 11 ceramic vessels, a clay pipe, a large Edwards chert biface, three quivers of Bassett arrow points and two sets of two ear spools (Figs 123–4). Possible sacred bundles may have been placed in boxes and baskets. Based on the character of the tomb and its various offerings, Middlebrook (2014: 103) suggests that the individual buried in the coffin in the shaft tomb may have been the community's religious leader, the *xinesi*.

Mound B at the Morse Mound site was built over a 5 m diameter structure with a prepared red clay floor. This structure was likely used for special ritual purposes in the community.

Finally, recent excavations at the Murvaul Creek site (41PN175) in the Sabine River basin Pineywoods investigated a *c.* AD 1450–1510 Caddo domestic component (McKee *et al.* 2015). The work, confined to a proposed expansion to a highway right-of-way, sampled several outdoor work areas with pit features and post-holes from drying racks and ramadas as well as a refuse midden. The analyses of features and recovered artifacts suggests that the "bulk of the feature and artifact collection represents a farmstead that was occupied for a single generation" (McKee *et al.* 2015: 488).

The Caddo peoples that lived at the Murvaul Creek site were farmers that cultivated maize and squash; wild plant foods, including hickory, oak and walnut as well as tubers, were also collected to supplement the diet. The chipped stone tool kit was comprised of Perdiz and Perdiz/Bassett arrow points, flake tools and scrapers. The ceramic assemblage had a high incidence of brushed vessels and other utility wares, and few fine ware vessels, most made with bone temper added to the vessel paste. The decorative styles in the ceramic vessel sherds at the site, as well as the chemical analysis of a sample of sherds (McKee *et al.* 2015: fig. 170), suggest that the closest affiliations of the Caddo group that lived at the Murvaul Creek site were with other Caddo communities living not far to the south and southwest in the Angelina and Attoyac river basins, as well as with Caddo groups living in parts of the Sabine River basin to the northwest. This same broad area of East Texas was occupied in historic times by numerous Caddo groups that were affiliated with the Hasinai Caddo, including the Nasoni, Nadaco, Hainai and Nacogdoche (see Chapter 7, Bolton 1987; Swanton 1942).

7

Caddo Peoples and Communities in East Texas at the Time of European Colonization, *c.* AD 1680–1838

Sustained contact between the Caddo peoples and the Spanish, French, Mexican, Texan and American governments brought European trade materials and technology to Caddo peoples in tandem with the social objectives and policies of these foreign polities. In addition to efforts aimed at replacing Caddo cultural identity under the guise of religious conversion and testimonies of Indian "barbarism", European colonization relied on trade, and participation of Indian nations as consumers in a burgeoning market economy, albeit one of relatively small scale at the time. This chapter considers the archaeological character of communities in East Texas at the time of European colonization, between *c.* 1680–1838, when contact between Caddo peoples and Europeans, Americans and Texans led to massive depopulation of Caddo peoples and dispossession of Caddo lands.

When the Caddo Indian peoples living in East Texas were first encountered by Europeans in 1542, the remnants of the de Soto-Moscoso entrada (Bruseth and Kenmotsu 1993) described to chroniclers that the Caddo in East Texas lived in numerous but dispersed settlements and communities with abundant food reserves of corn. Barr (in press) has convincingly argued that the Caddo peoples "had a singular 'encounter' with the Spaniards at that time when compared to aboriginal tribes in the rest of the Southeast". She attributes this to the dispersed settlements of the Caddos, their system of border control and the ability of Caddo polities to monitor and control Spanish movements within their lands.

The entrada moved along pre-existing east–west and north–south Caddo trails through East Texas, and from Hasinai Caddo groups in the Neches-Angelina River basins to Naguatex/Kadohadacho groups on the Red River (Fig. 125). The east–west aboriginal trail in most particulars became subsumed within the later East Texas portions of El Camino Real de los Tejas first established by the Spanish in the late 17th century (Weddle 2012: 1–28; Williams 2007: fig. 8) atop a "well beaten" Caddo road (Barr 2011: 11), while the north–south trail became known as the Caddo Trace.

Archaeological investigations carried out in East Texas since the early 20th century confirm that Caddo communities were widely dispersed in ancestral times throughout all of the major and minor river valleys of the region. The most intensive settlement of the region may have been after *c.* AD 1400, especially in

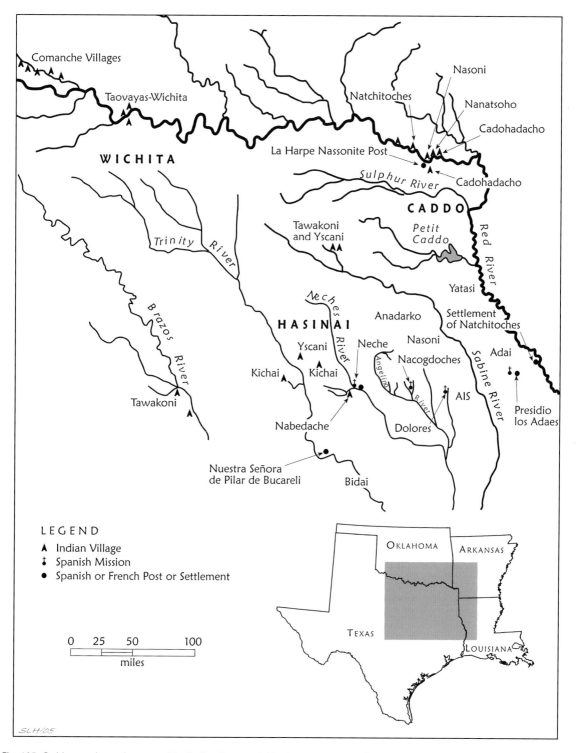

Fig. 125. Caddo peoples and communities in East Texas, neighboring nations, as well as 17th and 18th century French and Spanish missions and settlements

The Wild Indians of Texas
by Robert L. Cast

From the papers of Mirabeau Buonaparte Lamar the underlying attitudes toward the Caddo Indians from the Texans serving in the Republic of Texas can be easily ascertained and help us gain insight into why the Texas military, Texas settlers and Texas legislature performed horrendous acts towards all Indians in support of the Republic's anti-Indian policies.

One perception crafted by the Texans to make the Caddo Indians appear to be more dangerous and unpredictable than they really were, and as such, further garner support for why they needed to be removed, was to simply refer to them as "wild". History, though, tells quite another story in that the Caddo Indians played a crucial role in mediating for peace between the Texas tribes such as the Comanche, Kiowa and Apache that plundered and killed both Indians and pioneering Texans. During Lamar's administration however, the Indian, no matter of what tribal affiliation, was considered to be sub-human, and needed to be exterminated. By lumping together all the Indians as "wild", the Texas Republic immediately struck fear in the minds of pioneers everywhere, thereby justifying the government's actions against the Indians.

In a letter dated 1 December 1838 from H. McLeod giving a report to the "General" from Port Caddo "detailing the intended movements of Genl Rusk against the Caddoes of Louisiana" (Gullick and Elliott 1922: 308), McLeod stated that after General Rusk surrounded a group of Caddo he basically made them an offer they could not refuse. They would either go back into Shreveport, until after the war was over, or fight on the spot.

The Chief of the Caddo replied that, "if deprived of his arms, he would have no means of subsisting his people & they would starve" (Gullick and Elliott 1922: 308). General Rusk agreed to furnish the Caddo provisions with a few stipulations. McLeod stated that they:

> "then departed to meet in Shreveport the next day & deposit the arms – his horses being in the Swamp he could not start with us but left his next chief as a hostage, and I went with him & his tribe – he did all that he had stipulated, treated me kindly, and agreed if required to go, with his four principle [*sic*] men to Nacogdoches & remain there until the end of the war – This, Genl Rusk declined as it might appear *like a recognition of them as Texas Indians*". (Gullick and Elliott 1922: 308) (emphasis added)

McLeod went on to explain:

> "So stands the matter, but you must understand that these are not all the Caddoes by far the larger portion of the tribe, under *Tarshar*, or the *Wolf*, are among the wild Indians of Texas, at the three forks of the Trinity – This Cheif [*sic*] Cissany, says, he has no connexion [*sic*] with them, and often, [as] in the present instance, is suspected of *their rascalities*". (Gullick and Elliott 1922: 308)

After readily admitting that some of the Caddo under the leader Tarshar could be perceived as "Texas" Indians, McLeod then gives Lamar some advice:

> "Let us drive these wild Indians off, and establish a line of block houses, and we have done all we can *now* – If the U States *will not remove their own Indians*, to wit, Cherokees, Shawnees, Delawares, Kickapoos, Choctaws, Alabamas, & Coushattes, to say nothing of these Caddoes who they have literally ordered & driven into our territory – I say if the U.S. is faithless enough to refuse to remove them We must await a more auspicious moment than the present, to exterminate them". (Gullick and Elliott 1922: 309) (emphasis in original)

Since the original land cession treaty of 1835 between the Caddo and the United States never addressed a place for them to actually go to, or a homeland to be set aside for them by the U.S. government, this statement by McLeod is pertinent to any historical discussion of the abuses the U.S. government levied against the Caddo as well. Given nowhere else to go, many of the Louisiana Caddo crossed into the Republic of Texas. This was a death sentence for the people for whom the state of Texas was named!

Perceptions of the Caddo and Indians in general were much different with the French, who had lived with the Indians of both Spanish Texas and French Louisiana. Bossu, a naval officer with the French, recounts a memoir of one of the first French officers to encounter the Indians of the Gulf coast. Monsieur de Belle-Isle served as a Major General on the French Navy and later Major of New Orleans. His captivity among the "Attakapas" is recounted by Bossu (1777: 340), who stated:

> "about two years after his captivity, some deputies arrived at the *Attakapas*, from a nation who sent them the calumet of peace. A kind providential care! This nation lived in *New Mexico*, and were the neighbours of the *Natchitoches*, where M. *de Hucheros de Saint Denis* commanded, who was beloved and respected by the deputies of this nation, though they lived on Spanish ground."

Bossu explained that upon this meeting, that Belle-Isle took one of the Indians aside and turned over to him his military commission and scrolled a note with a crow-quill and some ink made from soot, the following:

> "*To the first chief of the white men*. I am such and such a person, abandoned at the bay of *St. Bernard*; my comrades died of hunger and wretchedness before my face, and I am a captive of the *Attakapas*". (Bossu 1777: 341)

When this Indian arrived back in Natchitoches and presented St Denis the letter, St Denis begins began to cry explaining to the Indian that:

> "he wept for his brother who was captive among the *Attakapas*. The Indian who brought the letter promised to fetch M. de Belle-Isle, and some other Indians joined him". (Bossu 1777: 342)

The Caddo Indians set out, ten on horseback, armed with guns, promising to M. de Saint Denis to return in two moons time with his brother upon a horse, which they led with them. In short, these "wild" Indians rescued a French Naval officer from the Attakapas whom the "American" nations referred to as the "men-eaters," according to Bossu.

The Texans never learned the lesson that the French had long before understood. Not all of the tribes living in the Republic of Texas were "wild" or "bad" or intended harm to the settlers. Bossu makes a profound statement in regard to the humanity of the Indians and Belle-Isle's previous plight throughout the last half of the 18th century:

> "As I know the goodness of your heart, I am sure you will pity the unhappy fate of this poor officer; great souls are not ashamed to show that they are touched by the misfortunes of others: even the Indians say, that he who is not sensible to the sufferings of his brothers, is unworthy of bearing the name of a man, and that he ought to be avoided as a pest of society". (Bossu 1777: 334)

the Neches-Angelina River basin (Story 1995) as well as along the Red River, Big Cypress Creek and the Sabine River. By the mid-1600s, the Hasinai Caddo peoples of East Texas were referred to by the Spanish as the "Great Kingdom of the Tejas" because they were considered to be a populous and well-governed people. The area of the Tejas nations was described by a French priest in 1686 as:

> "one of the largest and most populous that I have seen in Americ. It is at least twenty leagues long, not that it is constantly inhabited, but in hamlets of ten or twelve cabins, forming cantons, each with a different name. Their cabins are fine, forty or fifty feet high, of the shape of beehives". (Cox 1905: 231)

To travel within the domain of the East Texas Caddo, Europeans had to rely on "passport systems" devised by the Caddo to identify friends or allies (Barr 2011: 28).

When Europeans began to actually venture into East Texas in the 1680s and 1690s, the territory of the various Hasinai Caddo tribes became well understood (see Barr 2011: fig. iv; Ewers 1969; J. Jackson 1999; R. H. Jackson 2004). The area known to have been occupied by the Hasinai Caddo in the late 17th century was called "Tejas" by the Spanish (from the Caddo word *taysha*), while the French called the Caddo in this area the "Cenis." The Nabedache Caddo villages on San Pedro Creek in the Neches River basin were the principal western entranceway to the lands of the Hasinai Caddo tribes that lived in the Neches and Angelina River basins, and one of the routes of El Camino Real de los Tejas came to and through this place from the late 17th to the early 19th century (Corbin 1991; Cunningham 2006). According to Weddle (2012: 2):

> "The Spanish first focused their interest on the Nabedaches with a short-lived mission in 1690, for it was among the Nabedaches that La Salle's remnant had appeared, just a few years previously, as it sought a path to the Mississippi. Thus, the amorphous Camino Real first directed itself toward the Nabedache village, situated between the Trinity and Neches Rivers. Beginning in 1716, missionary endeavors would be directed at other tribes of the Caddoan [*sic*] confederacies as well."

The Spanish sought effective control of the East Texas lands to minimize the French influence, and bring missions to the Caddo peoples (Corbin 1989b; R. H. Jackson 2005: 22–3, 26; Wade 2008: 107–13). Between 1690 and 1719, the Spanish established a number of missions among the Hasinai Caddo in East Texas, with most of them situated in the middle of Caddo communities and along what became the Camino Real de los Tejas. Despite the efforts of the missionaries, the Caddo refused to congregate in the vicinity of the missions (Marceaux and Wade 2014; Barr in press), and no Caddo peoples were ever converted to Christianity; instead, baptisms "were administered to [Caddo] people who had died or were dying, half of whom were children" (Wade 2008: 112).

As a result of ever increasing contact and conflict in the early historic period, the Caddo peoples experienced devastating population losses from epidemic diseases, amounting to an estimated 75% loss in population between 1687 and 1790, as well as group amalgamations, increased hostilities from slave-raiding Osage warriors, territorial abandonments and group movements, fundamental changes in trading prerogatives, and the eventual forced removal from their ancestral homelands. During this era, Caddo groups moved their villages, or coalesced into one village for protection. The Hasinai Caddo groups – including the Nacogdoche, Hainai, Nasoni, the Nadaco, Neche and the Nabedache – remained in their East Texas homelands, living in the early 1800s outside of the Spanish settlement of Nacogdoches, and on aboriginal lands west to the Neches River, and apparently north of the El Camino Real (see Fig. 125). Between about 1836 and 1839, the Hasinai tribes had all been forcibly pushed out of East Texas by the Republic of Texas government, and they either moved to Indian Territory (now the state of Oklahoma), or farther west in Texas and even into Mexico. Nevertheless, the Caddo peoples have survived, with a powerful influence over other Native Americans in Texas during much of that time. Their survival called on all their religious faith, their political strength, influence and leadership and their continued traditions and beliefs.

Table 7. Caddo populations through the Colonial era

Year	Source	Warriors*	Estimated population
Hasinai			
1699	Pierre Talon	600–700	2400–2800
1716	Ramon		4000–5000
1721	Aguayo		c. 1378
1779	De Mezieres	135	540
1783	Morfi	380 (?)	1520
1805	Sibley	200	800
1818–20	Cincinnati Gazette	150	650
1820	Padilla		1450
1828	Terán	23	92
1828	Berlandier	30–40	120–160
1834	Almonte		400
1836	Republic of Texas		200#
1847	Burnet	200	800
1851	Stem	c. 100	c. 315
Hainai			
1783	Morfi	80	320
1798	Davenport	60	240
1809	Salcedo	60	240
1828	Berlandier	10	40
Nabedache			
1779	De Mezieres	40	160
1783	Morfi	40	160
1798	Davenport	80	320
1819	Padilla		500
1828	Terán	15	60
1828	Berlandier	80	400
Nacogdoche			
1783	Morfi	300	1200
1798	Davenport	50**	200
1809	Salcedo	50	200
1828	Berlandier	50	200
Nadaco			
1798	Davenport	100	400
1809	Salcedo	100	400
1828	Terán/Sanchez	29	116
1828	Berlandier	30	150
1856	Neighbors	38	190
1859	Neighbors	235	
Ais			
1716	French traders		320
1779	De Mezieres	20	80
1805	Sibley		25

Year	Source	Warriors*	Estimated population
1818–20	Cincinnati Gazette		50
1820	Padilla		300
1828	Muckleroy/Terán		640
1828	Berlandier		300
Kadohadacho			
1700	Bienville	500–600	2000–2400
1709	La Harpe		2500
1718	Bienville	200	800
1719	La Harpe		400
1773	De Mezieres	160	640
1798	Davenport	200	800
1809	Salcedo	200	800
1805	Sibley	100	400
1818–20	Cincinnati Gazette	120	500–600
1820	Miller	300	1200
1820	Padilla		2000
1825	Schoolcraft		450
1828	Berlandier	300	1200
1829	Porter		450
1834	Almonte	500	
1836	Morfit	250	1000
1838	Riley	120–130	480–520
1838	Office of Indian Affairs	156+	
1849	Neighbors	280	1400##
1851	Stem		161++
1851	Upshaw		167+++
1854	Hill		500^
1856	Neighbors	35	175
1857	Neighbors		235
1859	Neighbors		244
Natchitoches			
1700	Bienville	450	1800
1718	Bienville	80	320
1719	La Harpe		200
1805	Sibley	12	48
1825	Gray	10	40
1825	Schoolcraft		61
Yatasi			
1773	De Mezieres	3	12
1798	Davenport	40***	160
1805	Sibley	8	32
1809	Salcedo	30	120
1825	Gray	12	48

*one warrior is assumed to equate to four members of a family, but it is likely that this underestimates population sizes; some sources estimated five members to a family or five people per warrior. This table is based in part on the work of Swanton (1942: 22–3) and Jelks (2002: 5–6).
**Nacogdoche and Ais groups; ***Yatasi and Adaes groups; +Shreveport Kadohadacho; ++Texas Kadohadacho only; +++Oklahoma Kadohadacho only;

^ Kadohadacho, Hainai and Nadaco; #Hasinai and Nacogdoche; ## Kadohadacho, Hainai and Nadaco

Ultimately, the aim of dispossession of Caddo lands was achieved by Texans and Americans by the mid-1830s, who sought these rich lands in what became Arkansas, Louisiana, Oklahoma and Texas (Marceaux and Perttula 2010). However, under the strong leadership by various *caddices*, who relied on long-standing commonalities and alliances between kin-related Caddo groups and families, and an appreciation for trade and exchange that had before then been solidly based on kin and gender relationships and reciprocity, these Caddo groups and families had to coalesce to maintain their cultural identity and assure their survival in a chaotic world. Although the population of Caddo groups continued to decrease because of the continued introduction of European epidemic diseases as time passed – from *c.* 28,000 in the late 17th century to about 500 people when they left the Brazos Reserve in the summer of 1859 (Table 7) – they continued to be important participants in the Texas and Louisiana market economies through the 1830s. For example, upon a request from the United States to allow other tribes to enter their lands, in effect asking that they share their limited resources, the Caddo demanded compensation. Dehahuit, the Caddo's leader or *caddi* at the time, stipulated that an annuity be paid in return for allowing other tribes to reside alongside the Caddo. Cultural identity was built on the strength of Caddo relationships to their land, and they insisted upon fair treatment in the frontier market economy, as long as they were able to hold onto those lands in the Caddo's homeland. Everything changed for the Caddo peoples after 1835.

The Caddo stood no chance of living in peace in Texas when the United States and Texas governments began land expropriations of the rich farmlands and woodlands that were where the Caddo's homes stood. This was disastrous to the Caddo, and led to their eventual harried and forced removal from their homelands. Within a generation of settling land boundaries with the United States in 1835, and after attempting to cling to lands within the new Republic of Texas, the Caddo were gone from all of Texas.

With the permanent Anglo-American settlement of the region in waves of immigration after about 1815, it was the Caddos' misfortune to have been living on choice and fertile farmlands desired by Anglo-Americans. In a few short years, they were dispossessed of their traditional homelands, their lands and goods swindled from them by U.S. Federal Indian agents in the Caddo Treaty of 1835, and eventually they were forced, in 1859, to relocate from the Brazos Reserve in Texas to the Wichita Agency in western Oklahoma (then Indian Territory). Shortly thereafter, they were caught up in the Union and Confederate struggle for the Indian Territory during the Civil War, and with little trust for either the rebel or federal governments, the Caddo tribe abandoned their lands in Indian Territory for lands in Kansas. To date, there is a virtual absence of archaeological data from these post-1835 Caddo Indian settlements, or on the 1860s' and later Caddo settlements in western Oklahoma and Kansas. This is one of the great archaeological challenges in the years ahead: to actually identify these Caddo settlements, which should contain significant and unique information on Caddo lifeways during a period of heightened acculturation and culture changes.

Between about 1836 and 1842, as the Hasinai, Nadaco and Kadohadacho tribes had all been forcibly pushed out of East Texas, some moved into Indian Territory, while others moved west into the upper Brazos River drainage. This was the final and bitter end to the Caddo settlement of their traditional homelands in East Texas. Though the Caddo groups made a successful agricultural living for a few short years in the hard but seemingly fertile lands of their reserve in the upper Brazos River valley, they were never secure from Anglo-American encroachments, even when settled on the Brazos Reserve. They were compelled in 1859, according to John R. Swanton, noted ethnologist at the Smithsonian Institution, "to abandon their homes, the fruit of their labors, and the graves of their kindred," and were removed to the Washita River valley in Indian Territory (Neighbours 1973; 1975).

Settlements and communities

Using the distinctive Caddo ceramics of the era (see Chapter 2; see also Tomka *et al.* 2013: 250–4) and the presence of European trade goods, including glass beads, guns (*da?chah*), gun parts and gunflints, and metal of various forms in archaeological contexts, over 100 historic Caddo sites are currently known in East Texas; this is a far cry from the number of *c.* AD 1400–1680 sites known in the region. Most of these have been found in either the Allen phase (*c.* 1680–1830), Kinsloe and Womack phase areas of East Texas, in the Natchitoches, Louisiana, area, or along the Red River in the Great Bend area visited by the Freeman-Custis expedition in 1806 (Fig. 126).

Some of these Caddo villages were large, and would have been impressive to behold. Freeman and Custis described the principal Caddo village on the Red River, abandoned in 1788, as follows:

> "Around and near to this pond [on the Red River], are to be seen the vestiges of the Caddo habitations; it was the largest of their villages, and their cultivated fields extended for five or six miles from it in every direction" (Flores 1984: 188)

While a single farmstead may have only included one or two structures, an Allen phase Caddo community was apparently composed of many farmsteads spread out over a considerable distance. In 1687, in the community of Nabedache Caddo on San Pedro Creek in the Neches River basin, Henri Joutel noted:

> "we took the path to the village where the Indians conducted us to the chief's hut which was a long league's distance from the entrance to the village. On the way, we passed several huts that were grouped in hamlets; there were seven or eight of them, each with twelve to fifteen huts together with space between each other and fields around the huts". (Foster 1998: 206)

Individual Hasinai Caddo families lived in farmsteads, and a number of farmsteads were organized into rancherias spread out over about 15–30 leagues (about 39–78 miles/*c.* 63–126 km). Each rancheria was separated from the others by unoccupied lands (see Foster 1998: 208) and hunting territory (see also Barr 2011).

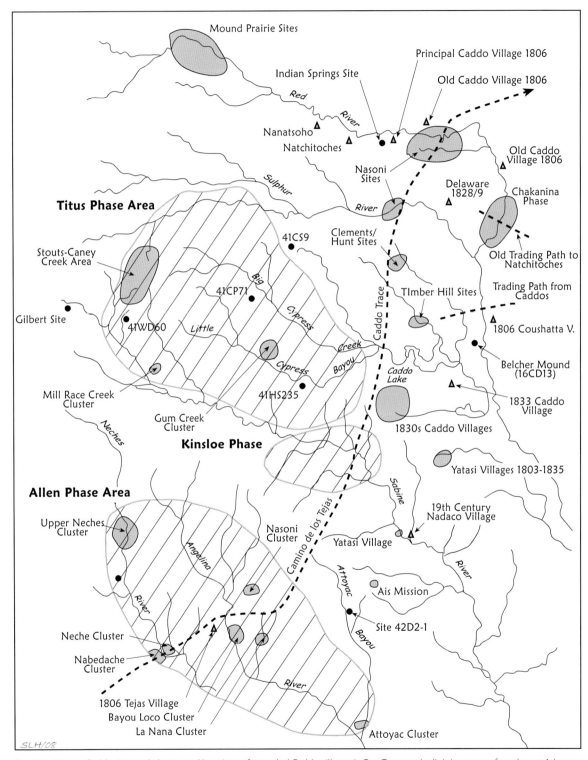

Fig. 126. Historic Caddo sites and phases, and locations of recorded Caddo villages in East Texas and adjoining parts of southwest Arkansas and northwest Louisiana

Key sites

The Womack site (41LR1) lies on an alluvial landform south of the Red River (Fig. 127) and was occupied by Caddo peoples between *c.* AD 1700–1730. This occupation was characterized by midden deposits, probable house features and several cemeteries, along with a robust chipped stone assemblage focused on the hunting and processing of large game animals for their hides and meat, and a diverse ceramic tradition with plain, fine and utility ware vessels and sherds; Womack Engraved vessels and sherds from the site are the iconic archaeological symbol of the Womack phase in East Texas (see Harris *et al.* 1965).

Four ancestral Caddo burials were excavated by Harris *et al.* (1965: 289–91) at the Womack site. These burials (Burials 1–4) had been interred in midden deposits. The deceased individuals had been buried in an extended supine position with their heads to the north or northeast, and facing south or southwest. There were associated funerary offerings with Burials 1–3, and they included 12 ceramic vessels of the following types: Emory Punctated-Incised, Hudson Engraved, Natchitoches Engraved, Simms Engraved and Womack Engraved (Harris *et al.* 1965: figs 4 and 5a–e).

A large assemblage of artifacts was recovered in the Harris *et al.* (1965) investigations beyond the ceramic vessels associated with Burials 1–3. This included 2570 ceramic sherds from "grit-tempered" and shell-tempered vessels, a clay figurine fragment and ceramic elbow pipes; there were also fragments of three stone pipes. There were also conch-shell beads, seven stone beads, a quartz crystal, two marine shell ornaments and native-made brass beads and tinklers. The substantial

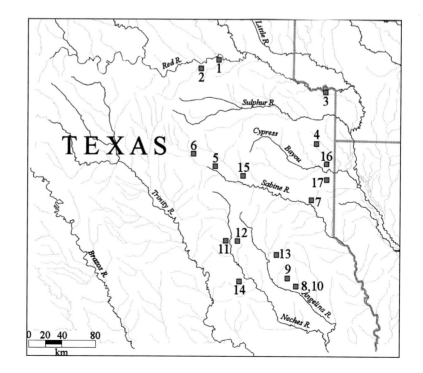

Fig. 127. Historic Caddo sites mentioned in the text:

1. Womack
2. Sanders
3. Hatchel, Eli Moores, and Roseborough Lake
4. Clements
5. Gilbert
6. Pearson
7. Susie Slade
8. Deshazo, Henry M. and 41NA344
9. J. T. King
10. Mayhew
11. Richard Patton
12. 41CE354
13. Mission Nasoni
14. George Moore 1b, 1c, 41HO211, and 41HO214
15. Woldert and 41WD331
16. Timber Hill
17. 41HS840

lithic assemblage from the Womack site was comprised of more than 900 arrow points, mostly of the triangular Fresno type, knives, 872 scrapers, gravers, native-made gunflints, celts, manos, abraders and hammerstones.

The European trade goods recovered at the Womack site by Harris *et al.* (1965: 307–57) included glass beads (n=2123); a variety of gun parts from French flintlocks; gunflints (n=8); lead bullets (n=6); lead shot (n=2); a possible sword guard; iron axes and wedges (n=7); iron knives (n=7); an iron awl; horse trappings, a strike-a-light; a possible piece of armor; many brass kettle fragments; hawk bells; brass and lead discs; a disc-shaped medal; brass buttons (n=10); and mirror glass sherds. Also recovered was a single wheel-made vessel (Harris *et al.* 1965: fig. 23), possibly of faience or majolica from French or Spanish sources.

Key aspects of the material culture record for Womack phase components are a variety of European trade goods, likely obtained from French traders, and Fresno arrow points, scraping tools and beveled knives. The abundance of these hunting tools and scrapers at Womack phase sites strongly suggests that the Caddo inhabitants were heavily invested in the procurement and processing of hides (deer and bison) for the burgeoning fur trade, and the exchange of hides with French traders were what led to their adoption and acquisition of French guns, tools and ornaments.

Also comprising diagnostic attributes of Womack phase components are the manufacture and use of engraved elbow pipes and shell-tempered ceramics (both fine wares and utility wares), along with the continued making of grog- and bone-tempered plain, fine and utility wares. Womack Engraved ceramic vessels are the principal fine ware in Womack phase sites, and Emory Punctated-Incised jars are the principal utility ware. The stylistic character of the engraved motifs known to occur on Womack Engraved vessels, and the stylistic relationships between certain distinctive engraved motifs and inverted rim carinated bowls in other East Texas Caddo assemblages, indicates that the Womack phase groups and communities were ancestral Caddo groups and communities, and not Norteno (Wichita [*Witsitah*]/ Kichai [*Kiitsaysh*]) peoples.

A late 17th–mid-18th century Caddo occupation is also present at the Sanders site (41LR2) (e.g., Harris *et al.* 1965: 288; Harris and Harris 1967: 131). Harris and Harris (1967: 131) commented that European "trade material is exceptionally scarce" at the Sanders site, but they do note that 478 glass beads had been found at the site. Harris (1953a: 20) noted that several Caddo burials with European trade goods had been found along Bois d'Arc Creek south of Mound No. 2, the larger or West Mound at the site.

European trade goods found at the Sanders site include gunflints, glass beads (from the surface and from one burial), metal kettle pieces, white ball clay trade pipe sherds, brass tinklers, a 1774 Spanish coin (obviously from what may have been the latest ancestral Caddo occupation of the site) and iron spikes. Aboriginal materials associated with these European trade goods include many triangular arrow points in the collections, as well as probably most of the scraping tools (Fig. 128). The abundance of hunting tools and scrapers at the Sanders site at this time also strongly suggests that the Caddo inhabitants there were heavily involved in the procurement and processing of hides (deer and bison) for the fur trade.

Fig. 128. Historic Caddo arrow points from the Sanders site

The material culture assemblage for this component are plain and decorated elbow pipes, a catlinite pipe sherd, along with plain and decorated shell-tempered pottery – including the utility wares Nash Neck Banded and Emory Punctated-Incised and the fine wares Avery Engraved, Hudson Engraved and Simms Engraved, as well as Clement Redware – and the grog- and bone-tempered Womack Engraved vessel sherds; Womack Engraved is the principal fine ware type. The two vessels in the T. M. Sanders site vessel assemblage from the Historic Caddo period component include a hubcap-style (cf. Story *et al.* 1967: fig. 53a) Simms Engraved carinated bowl with grog temper and an Emory Punctated-Incised (see Story *et al.* 1967: 136–9 and fig. 57g–i) bone-tempered jar. Both vessels were recovered in the midden excavations between the two mounds (Perttula *et al.* 2016c).

When the Teran entrada reached the Nasoni Caddo village on the Red River near what is now Texarkana in 1691, on the border between the present-day states of Arkansas and Texas, a detailed map was produced of the village (Fig. 129). It depicted a *templo* or temple mound at the western end (Fig. 130); this is believed to be the primary platform mound at the Hatchel site, and the residence of the religious leader or *xinesi*. The *caddi* or political leader lived a few miles away at either the Eli Moores (41BW2) or Horace Cabe (41BW4) mound sites. As documented

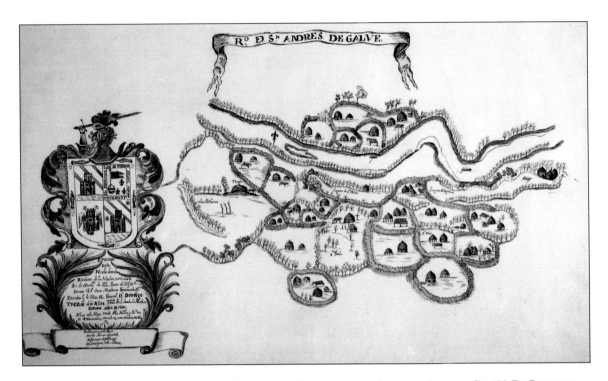

on this map, individual farm compounds in the village contained one to three structures, an above-ground granary and an outdoor ramada or arbor (Fig. 129). At least 36 structures, including family and chiefly residences, were arranged within the numerous compounds. The residence of the *caddi* near the center of the village was marked by a large cross, possibly erected by Father Damian Massanet, who accompanied the expedition.

Fig. 129. The Teran map: overall view of the 1691 Nasoni Caddo village (original in the Archivo General de Indias. map collection, CN 00920, The Center for American History, University of Texas at Austin)

If the platform mound at the Hatchel site is the temple mound and *templo* structure shown on the 1691 Teran map, then it seems likely that one of the structures in the latest mound zone, Zone A (see Chapter 6), is the 1691 *templo*. Feature 1 at the eastern end of the platform mound in this zone is a circular structure with extensive ash deposits on the floor (Fig. 131). Both Schambach

Fig. 130. *Templo* or temple atop the mound at the Nasoni Caddo village as shown on the 1691 Teran map

(1996: 41) and Sabo (2012: 435) suggest that the *templo* was partially buried within the mound, likely because there were soil berms placed around it. The WPA excavations in Zone A – as well as in the other mound structure zones – did not identify evidence of any such soil berms associated with Feature 1; Zone A was covered with only a thin mound fill before use of the platform mound was discontinued.

The Nasoni Caddo village itself extended several miles along the Red River, likely encompassing contemporaneous sites such as Eli Moores (41BW2), Paul Mitchell (41BW4), Hargrove Moores (41BW39) and Horace Cabe (41BW14). The Roseborough Lake site

(41BW5) is a later Nasoni Caddo settlement that postdates the community shown on the Teran map by a generation or more.

The Eli Moores site may have been the residence of the *caddi* of the Nasoni Caddo when it was visited by the French and Spanish. Excavations at the site in 1932 concentrated on what turned out to be Texarkana phase archaeological deposits in Mound 1 (see Chapter 6). However, one of the burials in the mound (a 30–40 year old male) had two lead balls (9.5 mm in diameter) in its rib cage. This individual, argued by Gilmore and Gill-King (1991) as being a murdered Frenchman, is most likely a Caddo male, based on dental evidence and cranial/postcranial metrics (Lee 1997: 163). Mound #2 was dug into by the landowner, Eli Moores, after the UT work at the site. Moores wrote a letter to A. T. Jackson in 1933, indicating that he had excavated five burials at that time, and recovered 18 associated ceramic vessels and several hundred glass beads; a small sample of donated beads are in the Texas Archeological Research Laboratory collections from the site. The glass beads are small (2.2 mm in diameter), rounded and drawn beads with simple or monochrome bodies, either an opaque blue (n=15) or an opaque white (n=1). The Caddo preferred the color blue for fabrics as well as for the beads they used for ornamentation of their clothes and in necklaces. Glass beads are rare on Caddo sites before the first quarter of the 18th century, and trends in glass bead use on Caddo sites in the region suggest these beads from Mound #2 at the Eli Moores site likely date to the early part of the *c.* 1700–1767 era. During this time period, beads tended to be small drawn beads, likely "garment" or "embroidery" beads.

Moores also found nine metal artifacts in his digging, made either from brass, copper, or bronze, with these burials. Moores continued to dig at the site, and by 1935 had discovered ten or 11 burials and additional ceramic vessels. Based on these finds, it seems likely that the Mound #2 deposits at the Eli Moores site are associated with the *caddi's* residence occupied in 1691 and for several years thereafter.

The Roseborough Lake site (41BW5) is a large historic Caddo village occupied from the 17th century until the late 18th century, with habitation features and cemeteries (Miroir *et al.* 1973: Gilmore 1986); the principal occupation was between 1719–1778. It also is the location of a Nassonite post established by the French in the 1720s, known by the Spanish as San Luis de Cadohadacho.

Investigations at the Roseborough Lake site by Miroir *et al.* (1973) and Gilmore (1986) recovered Historic Caddo ceramics, mainly shell-tempered, of the types Emory Punctated-Incised, McKinney Plain, Keno Trailed, Simms Engraved, Natchitoches Engraved, Womack Engraved and Avery Engraved, along with brushed, incised, punctated and red-slipped body sherds and clay figurines and pipes. The chipped stone tool assemblage included Fresno and Maud arrow points, drills, large knives, many end/side scrapers as well as a diorite celt. European trade goods are particularly abundant at the site, and they include: iron axes and scrapers; iron bridle bits and knives; iron strike-a-lights; scissors; iron kettle pieces; pendants; many flintlock gun parts; gunflints; lead balls; brass rings; tinklers; bells; and rivets; brass and iron arrow points; metal buttons; green wine bottle glass; mirror glass; faience; majolica; and Delft ceramics, along with many glass beads (n=2958) and marine shell beads (n=18). Substantial samples of animal bones are

Fig. 131. Plan map of
Zone A structures and
other features on the
Hatchel site platform
mound

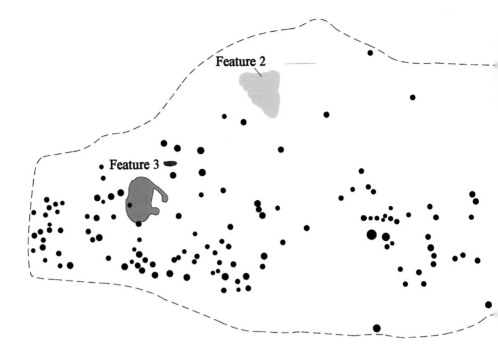

also present in the archaeological deposits at the site, along with carbonized maize cob fragments (Gilmore 1986: 105–34).

The Clements site (41CS25) is a late 17th to early 18th century Nasoni Caddo settlement and cemetery in the Black Bayou basin in the Pineywoods, not far from the Caddo Trace. The Caddo Trace was an aboriginal trail that led from the Hasinai Caddo settlements in East Texas to the Kadohadacho settlements on the Red River, and its route is fairly well-known because the historic 19th century Trammel's Trace (see Pinkerton 2016) followed its route through East Texas. The Nasoni Caddo that lived at the Clements site and other sites in the area were not apparently heavily involved in the hide trade, unlike the Caddo peoples living on the Red River to their northwest.

The site was first explored in 1898 by a W. T. Scott, then by the University of Texas in 1932, and this work led to the excavation of 22 Nasoni Caddo graves as well as a small midden or trash deposit. As best as can be determined from the distribution of the different kinds of funerary objects in the 22 burials, the Clements site was used as a place for the Caddo to bury their dead during at least two different episodes that may have lasted a generation or more (Gonzalez *et al.* 2005; Perttula *et al.* 2010b). The earlier cemetery use includes burials in several north–south rows at the western end of the site, including burials 8–13, 16–20 and 21 (Fig. 132). The eastern half of the cemetery was used sometime around the beginning of the 18th

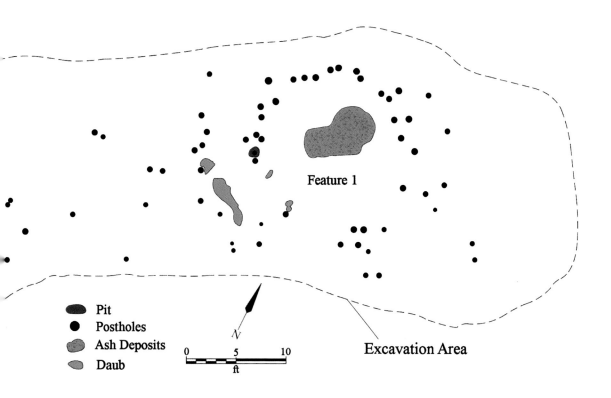

Feature 1

Pit
Postholes
Ash Deposits
Daub

N

0   5   10
ft

Excavation Area

century (Burials 1–7, 14 and 15); these burials had among their various offerings a few strands of European glass beads traded to the Nasoni Caddo. One of the western burials (Burial 21) also was part of this later cemetery, as this individual had a Keno Trailed, *var. Phillips* bowl among its funerary offerings and this form is thought to be an excellent ceramic marker for the period *c.* 1700–1730.

A relatively diverse assemblage of funerary objects was recovered from the site. Conch shell ornaments made from Gulf Coast marine shells were the most common item placed with the deceased, including probable bead necklaces from at least three burials (Burials 2, 8 and 15), bracelets (Burial 15), ear discs and portions of pendant necklaces (Fig. 133). The zoomorphic style of the conch shell pendants from the Clements site is very similar to ones recovered at both the Belcher and Cedar Grove sites, as well as from Belcher phase components at the Foster, Friday and Battle sites, along the Red River in southwestern Arkansas (McKinnon 2015: fig. 1).

Half of the Clements burials had conch shell ornaments, indicative of a ready access to this material of exotic origin (i.e., the conch shell would have been found along the Gulf Coast of Texas); a similar relationship was noted in the Historic Caddo Chakanina phase burials at the Cedar Grove site (Trubowitz 1984). Along with the shell ornaments were European glass beads (1–26 beads per burial) from five separate interments at Clements. In two instances, shell beads or other shell

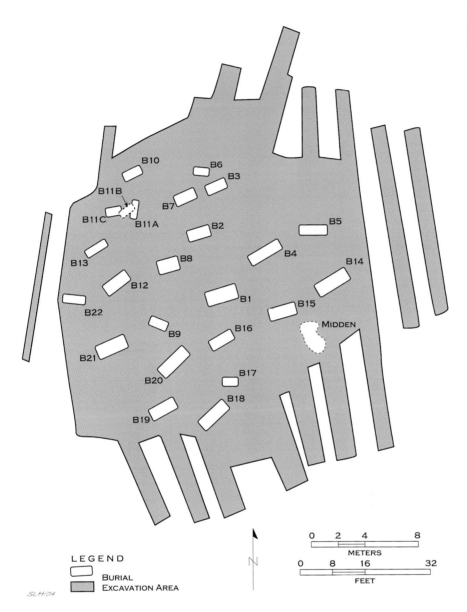

Fig. 132. Map of the arrangement of the Clements site burials

ornaments were found together in the same burial with the European glass beads.

Pottery vessels were also commonly placed as funerary objects in the burials, with as many as nine vessels placed in one burial feature. Others had 1–6 vessels per burial. Fifteen of the burials at the Clements site had clay pigment (green, brown, red and gray colors) and/or mussel shell offerings. Four of the five burials with European trade goods had pigments, particularly a green pigment from a local glauconitic clay.

The Gilbert site (41RA13) is a mid-18th century site on a large alluvial terrace of Lake Fork Creek, near its headwaters, in the far western reaches of the Post

Fig. 133. Marine shell pendants from the Clements site

Oak Savannah. The site is marked by 20 small midden mounds that appear to represent trash heaps spread out across about 14 acres (c. 5.7 ha) of the landform (Fig. 134); there were trash-filled storage pits in a few of the midden mounds; structures likely stood adjacent to these trash middens. The site was excavated by the Texas Archeological Society (TAS) in 1962, and there have been subsequent intensive metal detecting work done by Jay C. Blaine, a noted expert on European metal trade goods.

Based on the kinds and range of both aboriginal and European artifacts at the Gilbert site in the TAS excavations and later work, the site most likely is a hunting camp occupied by a horse-bound Caddo group engaged in the French-Caddo fur trade. Distinctive Historic Caddo pottery (from at least 47 vessels), including sherds from Womack Engraved vessels, Simms Engraved, Natchitoches Engraved, Emory Punctated-Incised and Womack Plain types (see Story et al. 1967), is relatively abundant in the middens. So too are chipped stone tools, among them about 200 triangular-shaped arrow points (as well as about 20 metal arrow points fashioned by the Caddo from recycled European iron and brass), more than 500 side and end scrapers and more than 50 knives, drills and graving tools. The frequency of scrapers is indicative of the intensive processing of white-tailed deer for their hides and meat.

Certainly the most distinct aspect of the Gilbert site artifact assemblage is the quantity and diversity of European trade goods found in the midden mounds. Pieces from French flintlock trade guns are particularly common, including elaborately decorated butt plates, as well as lock plates, frizzens, iron gun cocks, gunlocks, ramrod guides, trigger guards and gun barrel fragments (Blaine and Harris 1967). Both aboriginal and French-made gunflints are present, and about 60% of the gunflints were probably made by Caddo stone tool knappers.

These Caddo hunters also had ready access to many other kinds of European trade goods beyond the flintlock guns; they were likely obtained from French traders for deer hides, bear grease and other products of the hunt. It has been estimated that at least 20 French guns at the site had been discarded and reduced to parts and fragments for other uses. There are metal French clasp and case knives; axes; wedges; hoes; hatchets; awls; and scissors; possible Spanish sword fragments; and possible ornaments attached to clothing or worn on the body, such as hawk bells; tinklers; pendants; finger rings; bracelets; and 3400+ glass beads. There were also pieces of brass kettles, horse trappings and gear (bridles), glass mirrors and bottle glass.

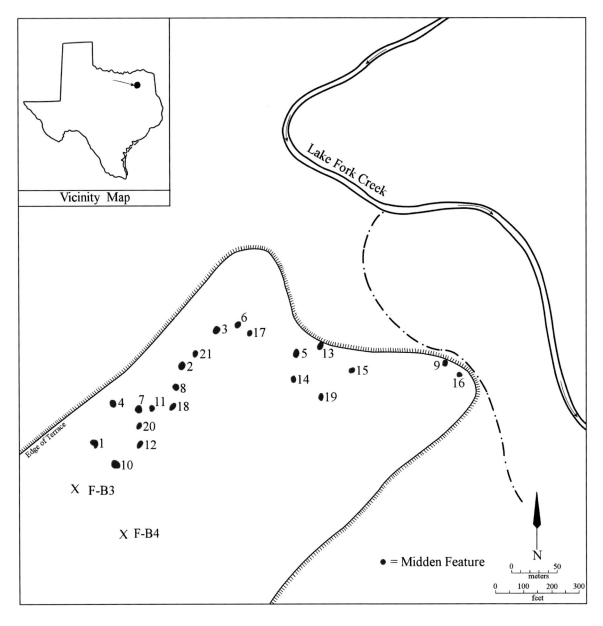

Fig. 134. Map of the middens at the Gilbert site

The Pearson site (41RA5) is a later (c. AD 1775–1830) Historic Caddo settlement in the upper Sabine River basin, at the eastern edge of the Blackland Prairie (Duffield and Jelks 1961). The site covers c. 25 acres (11.2 ha) on a series of sandy rises, one of which had a 4.5 m concentration of glass beads, an iron hatchet, a religious medal and end scrapers; this concentration is likely from at least 1–2 burial features (Duffield and Jelks 1961: 12).

The material culture assemblage made and used by Caddo peoples included numerous triangular arrow points, chipped stone scrapers and ceramic sherds from at least eight vessels. The principal fine ware at the Pearson site was Womack

Engraved (Duffield and Jelks 1961: fig. 4o–t). European trade goods are abundant, and include 1848 glass beads as well as six bead clusters that may represent remnants of clothing with beads sewn on them (Duffield and Jelks 1961: 51); a lead bead and a copper bead; brass tinklers and a brass kettle bail ear; many fire arms parts – gun barrels, gun locks, a frizzen, trigger guard bows, side plates, a forestock plate and musket balls – and 11 gunflints; iron axes; cast iron pot fragments; a pair of scissors; knive fragments; fork/spoon handles (*kiyuh*); a file blade; buttons; and iron scraping and chisel tools. There were also horse parts (harness gear and brass buckles), and a *c.* 1800-1830 religious medal (Duffield and Jelks 1961: 63).

The Susie Slade site (41HS13) is an ancestral Nadaco Caddo and Kinsloe phase settlement and cemetery on a sandy knoll in the Potters Creek valley in the Sabine River basin. The site is known to have had a large cemetery (>90 burials) that was excavated by a number of East Texas collectors and amateur archaeologists in 1962 (see Webb *et al.* 1969: 8), University of Texas (UT) archaeologists (Scurlock 1962) and Buddy Calvin Jones (1968: 98–125). One burial reportedly had 36 stacked Simms Engraved vessels as funerary offerings, and glass beads and other 18th century European trade goods were common funerary offerings in the Nadaco Caddo cemetery.

The burials at the Susie Slade site were reportedly spaced 1.8–4 m apart, and they were oriented in extended supine position in east–west pits, with the head of the deceased facing to the west or southwest (Jones 1968: 102). The UT investigations in 1962 excavated two burials at the site: Burial 4 and Burial 5 (Scurlock 1962). Burial 4 did not have any ceramic vessel funerary offerings, but did have 15 marine shell beads, seven blue glass beads and one Fresno arrow point. Funerary offerings in Burial 5 included nine blue glass beads, ten marine shell beads and one marine shell disk bead (Scurlock 1962).

Three radiocarbon dates have been obtained from the Susie Slade site, dating organic residue on a La Rue Neck Banded jar and an incised-punctated jar in two different Caddo burials excavated by Jones (Perttula and Selden 2014; 2015). The three calibrated age ranges are cal AD 1652–1880, cal AD 1662–1811 and cal AD 1661–1815 and the likeliest probabilities of the three dates overlap between cal AD 1720–1811 (Perttula and Selden 2015: 40). The calibrated dates clearly support the notion that the occupation of the Susie Slade site by the Nadaco Caddo took place during much of the Historic Caddo period.

In historic times, the archaeology of the Hasinai Caddo groups in the Neches and Angelina river basins is associated with the Allen phase, dated from *c.* AD 1680–1800 or later (Fig. 135). "The Allen phase is believed to have developed out of the Frankston phase, and more importantly, to have shared the same form of organization, kinds of inter-group interaction, and settlement patterns" (Story and Creel 1982: 34). The Allen phase Caddo groups who occupied the Neches and Angelina river basins were direct ancestors of the Hasinai tribes who were living in or near the Spanish missions that had been periodically established and maintained in the region between *c.* 1690–1731, and they continued to live there until the 1830s (see Jackson 1999: pl. 98).

Story and Creel (1982: 32) suggest that the Frankston and Allen phase populations were organized in a "weakly hierarchical structure" analogous to

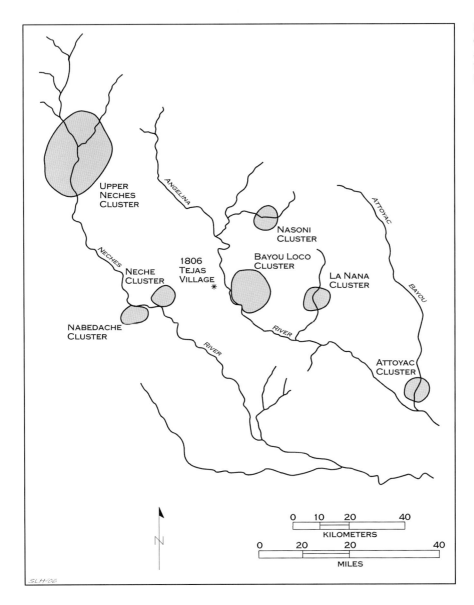

Neches

Angelina

Upper
Neches
Cluster

Nasoni
Cluster

Bayou Loco
Cluster

Attoyac

Neche
Cluster

1806
Tejas
Village

La Nana
Cluster

Bayou

Nabedache
Cluster

River

River

Attoyac
Cluster

N

| 0 | 10 | 20 | | 40 |

KILOMETERS

| 0 | 20 | 20 | | 40 |

MILES

SLH/06

Fig. 135. The boundaries of seven clusters of historic Allen phase Caddo sites in the Neches-Angelina river basins

that of the Hasinai confederacy (see Swanton 1942). Allen phase components and clusters of sites are found in the Neches and Angelina river basins in Cherokee, Anderson, Smith, Houston, Rusk and Nacogdoches counties (see Cole 1975; Erickson and Corbin 1996; Kenmotsu 1992; Marceaux 2011; Perttula 2004b; Perttula and Nelson 2006; 2007; Story 1982; 1995), and they usually contain small amounts of European trade goods, including glass beads, metal knives, gun parts, lead balls and other goods found in village and burial contexts. Caddo domestic remains at these settlements and farmstead compounds included household structures and features as well as a variety of decorated and plain ceramic fine wares (principally Patton Engraved) and utility wares, usually bone- or grog-tempered (depending upon the area) and with brushed vessel bodies, triangular and stemmed arrow points (including the Cuney and Perdiz types), distinctive plain and decorated elbow pipes, ground stone tools and bone tools.

There is a temporally and spatially coherent Caddo ceramic tradition in the upper Neches River basin in East Texas. The ceramic tradition probably lasted through the 18th century. The spatial context for this Late Caddo to Historic Caddo ceramic tradition is a c. 6600 km² area of the upper Neches River basin. Ancestral Caddo mortuary ceramics in the upper Neches River basin are dominated by fine wares: 73.3% of the ceramic vessel database from the basin are fine wares (Perttula et al. 2011, table 6-35). Mortuary vessels in upper Neches River Caddo sites were made in a wide variety of sizes. Surely these vessels held liquids and foodstuffs for the deceased to use on the journey to the House of Death. In most cases, the vessels included with the deceased by his living relatives easily would have held multiple servings of food and liquids (perhaps enough to last for the 6-day journey).

Excavations at the Deshazo site (41NA13), the best studied Allen phase settlement (Story 1982; 1995), indicates it was a small centralized hamlet of an affiliated group with a series of circular structures and an associated household or family cemetery. Most sites of the Allen phase were apparently occupied for only short periods of time, perhaps an average of 20–40 years, based on an analysis of structure rebuilding episodes at the Deshazo site (Good 1982: 67–9).

The Deshazo site is situated just north of El Camino Real de los Tejas, on an alluvial fan near Bayou Loco. Archaeological investigations indicate it had a series of nine circular structures along with an associated household or family cemetery. The site was apparently occupied for only a short period of time between the late 17th and early 18th century, based on an analysis of structure rebuilding episodes, archaeomagnetic dates and the size of the family cemetery.

The structures occurred in three different clusters, with evidence of structure rebuilding in northern (Structures 4–6) and southern clusters (Structures 1–3, 7 and 9), with an open courtyard or small plaza between them (Fig. 136); Structure 8 was on the opposite side of the creek from the main settlement area. A communal trash midden accumulated immediately to the south of the southern cluster of house structures. The structures ranged between 9 and 12.2 m in diameter, each had a center post, and there were large clay-lined hearths inside as well as immediately outside several of the structures. Three children were buried in pits dug through the floor of two of the structures in the village. Each of these vessels had a single ceramic vessel left as a funerary offering.

The site had small amounts of European trade goods found to only a limited extent in the village but they are much more common in burial contexts. The family cemetery had ten adult individuals, each buried in an extended position, with the deceased's heads facing uniformly towards the northwest. The majority of the European goods used as funerary objects were glass beads (n=4600+) worn as necklaces that accompanied the deceased on the journey to the House of Death. Other funerary offerings included 13 ceramic vessels, several stone tools, a clay pipe, pigments, metal trade goods (iron knives and a bell) and a possible rattle.

Caddo domestic remains at this settlement included an abundance of a variety of plain and decorated ceramic fine wares (principally Patton Engraved) and

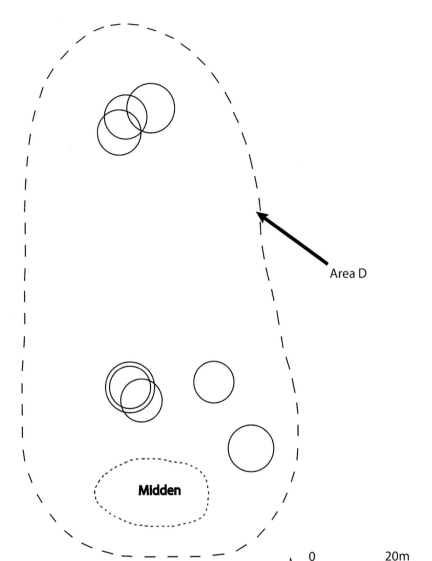

Fig. 136. Settlement
plan at the Deshazo site,
Nacogdoches County, Texas
(after Story 1982: fig. 11)

Area D

Midden

0   20m

utility wares, the latter usually bone-tempered and with brushed vessel bodies,
triangular and stemmed arrow points (including Turney and Perdiz types), elbow
pipes (plain and decorated), ground stone tools and bone tools. These Caddo groups
were successful agriculturists and hunters of wild game (see Henderson 1982).

The J. T. King site (41NA15) is another early 18th century Caddo or Hasinai Caddo
habitation site in East Texas. It is located directly on the northern route of El Camino
Real de los Tejas in western Nacogdoches County, Texas, and is on an alluvial terrace
along the west side of King Creek, about 5 km east of the Camino Real's northern
crossing of the Angelina River.

Archaeogeophysical work covering 2.5 ha was done at the site in 2008 and 2010. That research obtained significant data on the spatial organization of a Caddo settlement that was occupied at the time of the Spanish colonization of East Texas, particularly information on the layout of buildings, courtyards, granaries and other domestic features, as well as their spatial inter-relationships (Walker and Perttula 2011).

The interpretation of the magnetometer data is that there are ten possible Caddo structures in the archaeogeophysical survey area, and they are round to sub-round in shape and range from 3.7 to 12.5 m in diameter. Seven of the possible structures have anomalies situated in or close to their center that may mark central hearths or large center posts inside the domestic structures. None of the possible structures have complete geophysical signatures and it is not possible to make out an entranceway or easily discern the orientation of the structures. An area with a drop in background magnetic activity in the central part of the eastern collection area is interpreted as a possible courtyard flanked by structures of different shapes and sizes (Fig. 137).

Excavations at the J. T. King site have documented that it has well-preserved archaeological deposits and domestic features in several areas west and south-southwest of a possible courtyard (Fig. 138) and between the various geophysical anomalies that have been interpreted as possible Caddo structures. The overall character of the collected material culture assemblage from the site compares well with other Allen phase sites in western Nacogdoches County along Bayou Loco, Legg Creek, and the Angelina River.

These excavations recovered thousands of ceramic sherds, including sherds from bowls and carinated bowls from the principal fine ware type, Patton Engraved; ceramic elbow pipe sherds; pieces of burned clay; lithic debris and chipped stone flake tools and arrow points (mostly made from non-local raw materials); chipped stone Jowell knives; copper or brass tinkler cone fragments made from kettle fragments; glass beads; and lead balls for use in a flintlock musket; and animal bone, as well as charred plant remains. The plant remains reflect the Caddo exploitation of the local forests for fuel wood and nut resources, the cultivation of corn and the collection of cane or other grass stems for construction or craft projects.

The J. T. King chipped stone tools are dominated by those made of chert, much of it of non-local origin; the Caddo that lived at the site had ready access to Central Texas chert raw materials. The Caddo either had trade partners that lived in the Central Texas and east central Texas prairies from whom they obtained lithic raw materials and/or completed tools, or they had direct access to those raw material sources and/or tool makers, probably by horse travel. The Caddo in East Texas already had considerable numbers of horses by the mid-1680s.

Excavations at the Henry M. site (41NA60) on Bayou Loco in the Angelina River basin exposed a well-preserved Historic Caddo midden deposit that partially overlapped a c. 8.8 m circular Caddo structure (apparently rebuilt to some extent) marked by a variety of cultural features and stains, including two central posts from sequent structure use (Fig. 139). There is a probable storage platform or arbor just outside the north wall of the structure. The Patton Engraved sherds, the two gunflints and one European glass bead found there suggests that the Henry M.

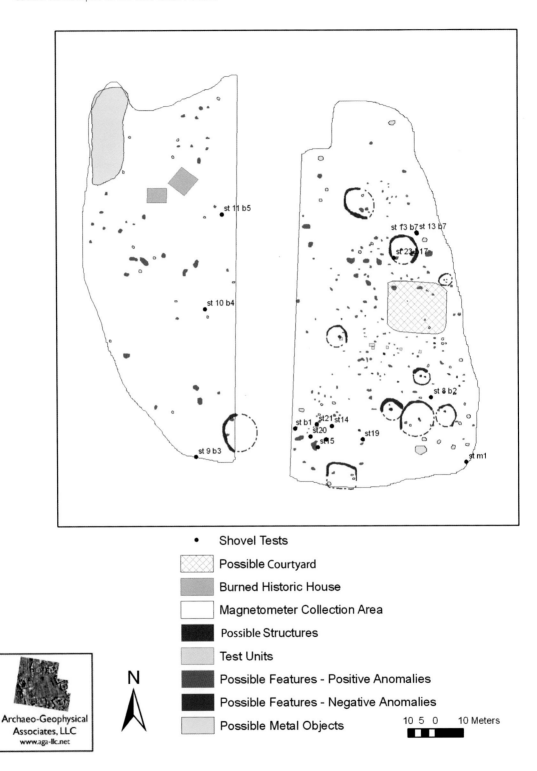

Fig. 137. Interpretive map of the J. T. King site based on the magnetometer findings

site was occupied by a Caddo group in the late 17th–early 18th century (Perttula *et al.* 2010a). Given that Caddo wood structures would probably only last at most 20 years before they begin to deteriorate (see Good 1982: 69), available feature evidence suggests that the houses and midden deposit were created over a *c.* 20–40 year period, at most, by one or two Caddo families that lived at the site year-round.

Recovered archaeological materials represent domestic activities, including food processing, cooking and serving foods, hunting and animal procurement and trash disposal. Maize and other plant foods were grown at the site during the occupation and a variety of wild plant foods were also gathered, particularly hickory nuts. With respect to the animal species that were exploited by the Caddo during the occupation, white-tailed deer was most important, both for meat as well as for its pelts. Other key animal food sources include a variety of fish (including freshwater drum, gar and catfish), turtles (notably the box turtle), turkey and several mammals, among them opossum, rabbit and raccoon. Several other animals may have been gathered for their pelts.

Fig. 138. Features and geophysical anomalies identified at the J. T. King site

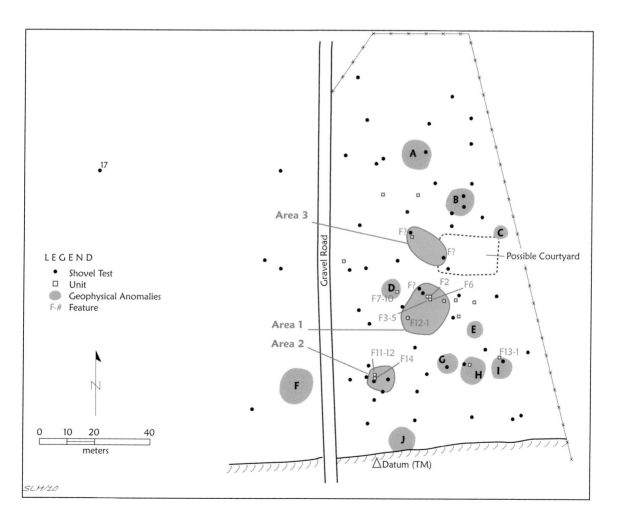

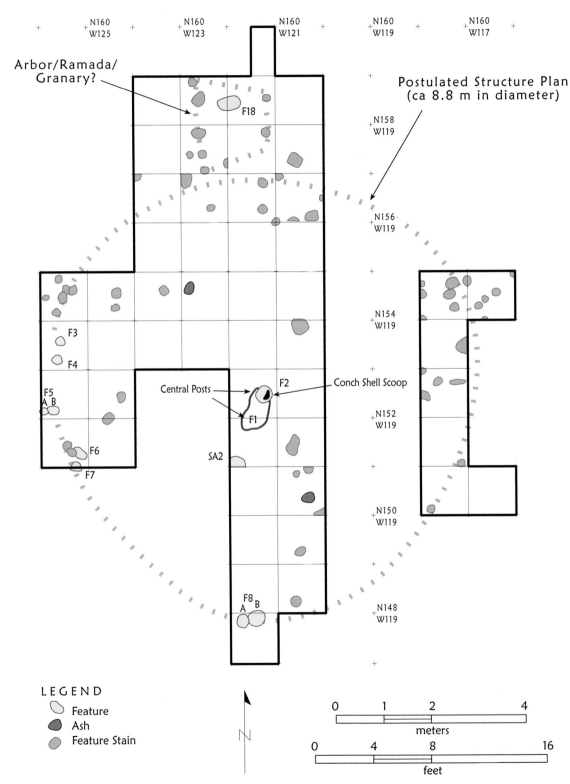

Arbor/Ramada/
Granary?

Postulated Structure Plan
(ca 8.8 m in diameter)

F18

Central Posts
Conch Shell Scoop
F2
F1

F3

F4

F5
A B

F6

F7

SA2

F8
A B

N160 W125
N160 W123
N160 W121
N160 W119
N160 W117
N158 W119
N156 W119
N154 W119
N152 W119
N150 W119
N148 W119

LEGEND
Feature
Ash
Feature Stain

N

0   1   2   4
meters

0   4   8   16
feet

SLH/08

Fig. 139. Cultural features and likely feature stains in the block excavations at the Henry M. site

Technological and stylistic comparisons of the ceramic assemblages between the Henry M., Deshazo and Spradley (41NA206) sites (see Perttula *et al.* 2010a, tables 12–13), and then with other Historic Caddo sites in Nacogdoches County (see Perttula *et al.* 2010a, tables 14–15) indicated that: (a) the closest ceramic comparisons between the Henry M. site and the other known Nacogdoches County historic Caddo sites is with the Deshazo site; (b) Bayou Loco and Angelina River sites are dominated by brushed utility wares; and (c) the La Nana Creek Caddo, Legg Creek and Attoyac Bayou sites are part of a different local ceramic tradition, where brushed pottery is much less important. The Henry M. site appears to be part of a temporally and culturally related community of Caddo peoples within a small part of the Angelina River basin, although at present it is not known which of the many related tribes in the Hasinai Confederacy they are affiliated with.

Other Nacogdoches County sites

by Tom Middlebrook

Research conducted during the past decade in western Nacogdoches County, Texas, has helped to clarify early 18th century Caddo interactions with Europeans. A number of Allen phase sites along Bayou Loco, Legg Creek and King Creek may represent communities of Hainai Caddo, the lead tribe of the Hasinai Caddo confederacy.

Work done since 2010 has identified the location of Mission Nuestra Señora de la Purísima Concepción de los Hainais within a complex of four closely-related sites: the mission proper (41NA344), the likely village of the Hainai *caddi* (41NA345), and mission-associated sites (41NA338 and 41NA346) (Fig. 140). Mission Concepción is on the southern end of a terrace (or "mesa" as noted by the Spanish) above the eastern floodplain of the Angelina River (M. Jackson *et al.* 2012). Its topographic location as well as its proximity to two flowing springs and a "little marsh" match the description in the 1716 Possession document written by Domingo Ramon, whose expedition founded six missions in the "Kingdom of the Tejas" that represented the first permanent European presence in Spanish Texas. Except for a brief abandonment during 1719–1721, Mission Concepción was occupied until 1730.

During the field work conducted at the mission site, 532 colonial metal artifacts, seven beads and three dark green wine glass sherds were recovered. The metal included 329 nails, two hinges, 37 French and Spanish gun parts, 29 lead objects (mostly lead balls), five fragments of horse gear, 32 cut cupreous bucket fragments and 100 other forged iron objects. The clustering of nails and other

Fig. 140. Mission Concepcion and related mission-associated Caddo sites (image provided courtesy of Tom Middlebrook)

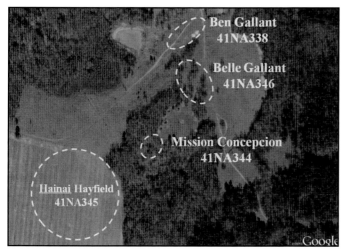

Ben Gallant
41NA338

Belle Gallant
41NA346

Mission Concepcion
41NA344

Hainai Hayfield
41NA345

artifacts suggested the presence of at least two specific buildings, the church and the priests' domicile.

As in the case of other known Spanish mission sites in East Texas, the dominant artifacts at Mission Concepción are of native manufacture. The lithic artifacts from the mission site include three Historic Caddo style arrow points, one gunflint and two possible strike-a-lights. Ceramic sherds (n=842) are primarily from brushed Caddo vessels (78% of the decorated sherds). Utility ware ceramic metrics (ratios of various decorative styles, see Middlebrook 1994; 2007; Marceaux 2011; Perttula 2016) are generally consistent with either the Bayou Loco/Legg Creek/King Creek clusters (Marceaux 2011) or the Middle Angelina I/Bayou Loco I clusters (Perttula 2016b). Patton Engraved sherds dominates the fine wares at the site. With the almost total absence of European ceramics at the site, it appears that the local Hainai tribe provided the Spanish Franciscan padres with all the ceramic vessels they needed for storage, cooking of food and meal presentation.

Just to the west of Mission Concepción on the margin of the Angelina River floodplain is the Hainai Hayfield site (41NA345), probably the main village of the Hainai *caddi*. The archaeological information about the site derives from surface collections and 36 shovels tests; one shovel test yielded the outline of a deep post-hole from a possible Caddo structure. The recovered assemblage is typical of other Allen phase sites in the area, and no European artifacts have been recovered there.

Approximately 300 m from Mission Concepción are two adjacent mission-related sites (see Fig. 140). In addition to several thousand Caddo ceramic sherds from the Ben Gallant site (41NA338), there are a number of pipe fragments. The 15 glass seed beads from the site are white and blue; the ten glass beads found at the mission are blue. Spanish colonial era metal objects recovered include a few forged nails, lead balls and a gun part. A magnetometer survey identified a 12 m circular Caddo-style house with a center post. The Ben Gallant site may have been a portion of the Hainai village and/or the location of Mission Concepción activities such as the residence of Spanish soldiers.

Magnetometer anomalies at the nearby Belle Gallant site (41NA346) also suggest the locations of at least two circular structures. Ground-truthing excavation identified a 30 cm round diameter post-hole with two forged nails and a small robin-blue glass bead in the matrix. Another strong magnetometer anomaly 18 m away was that of a clay hearth; six stone arrow points were associated with the hearth. While several European artifacts have been found at the site including three blue glass beads, two lead balls and two gun parts, the majority of all analyzed artifacts are Caddo ceramic vessel sherds (n=610). Just as at the mission site, brushed sherds from utility ware vessels are most common (76% of the decorated sherds). Belle Gallant may have been part of the Hainai village or represent instead a military residential area.

The Mayhew site (41NA21) is about 8 km east of Mission Concepción in the Bayou Loco basin. Earlier investigations suggested either that the site may have been a French trading post occupied by a native trader or simply a small Hasinai farmstead. Morris Jackson, Tom Middlebrook and George Avery returned to the Mayhew site in 2010 to conduct a metal detector survey and obtain a surface collection in another part of the site that contains significant archaeological deposits with

Fig. 141. French Type C and D trade gun parts at the Mayhew site: a–b. butt plates; c–d. butt plate finials; e. trigger guard bow; f–g. side plate finials; h. cock; i. lock plate; j. mainspring (image provided courtesy of Tom Middlebrook)

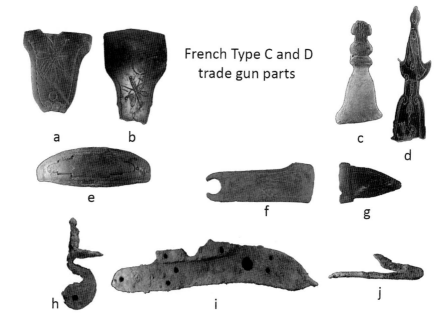

French Type C and D trade gun parts

both Caddo and French artifacts. Eight forged nails found here suggest that at least one structure stood on the site. This recent work indicates that it is significantly larger than was previously known, and French trade items found are abundant. Louis Juchereau de St. Denis, the founder of the Natchitoches post, was known to trade with the Hasinai groups in Eastern Texas prior to 1714. Mayhew may well have been his trading post with the Hainai and many other native groups as well as with the four Spanish missions and one presidio in the area.

Caddo ceramics from this new area at Mayhew do not differ significantly from other apparent Hainai sites in western Nacogdoches County, with a high proportion of brushed utility ware sherds (62% of the analyzed sherds). Patton Engraved was the most common fine ware (6%), while the only European colonial ceramic found at the site was a Puebla Blue on White majolica gaming piece fragment.

The recent research at Mayhew also recovered 258 metal artifacts, including a remarkable number of gun parts (n=29), all consistent with French Type C and Type D trade guns (Fig. 141), along with 57 lead balls. Other metal trade items found were three sword handle fragments; 13 knife blades; one cupreous clasp knife side plate; two scissors; seven cuprous tinklers; one chocolate drinking vessel handle; one chain; two large ferrous spikes; and three cupreous pail bail ears and numerous pail fragments. Five fragments of horse bridle were present, as well as 16 glass beads.

In the upper Neches River basin, the Richard Patton site (41AN26) has ancestral Caddo habitation deposits as well as a small cemetery that dates to the Historic Caddo period, probably from *c.* AD 1690–1720, before more extensive contacts between Caddo populations and European traders (see Marceaux and Perttula 2010; Marceaux 2011; Marceaux and Wade 2014). The landowner, Mr Patton, located and excavated 12 burials there that were in two north–south rows, and recovered 29 ceramic vessels (Cole 1975: 129). Two blue glass beads were found in one of the burials (N1-N3) re-investigated by the University of Texas in August 1933 (Cole 1975, table 8).

The vessel forms represented in the vessels from the Richard Patton site include bowls (n=4), carinated bowls (n=6), globular bowls (n=18) and one bottle with a collared neck. Fine ware types include several varieties of Patton Engraved and Poynor Engraved.

The Kah-hah-ko-wha[1] site (41CE354) is a very well-preserved Caddo habitation or small residential site that is located on an upland rise and saddle in the Flat Creek valley (Perttula and Nelson 2007), a westward-flowing tributary of the Neches River. The Caddo archaeological component at the site covers approximately 1 acre (0.4 ha), and there are at least three distinct concentrations of archaeological materials (particularly ceramic sherds, animal bones, charred plant remains and various lithic artifacts) within the site's known boundaries. These three areas likely represent the locations of Caddo house structures, features and related trash deposits.

These three areas appear to date to the early part of the Allen phase, likely from c. AD 1680–1700. The site was apparently occupied during the momentous times when Caddo peoples began to have contact and interaction with European groups that were exploring and trading with them in East Texas. The Kah-hah-ko-wha site is part of the Upper Neches Cluster of the Allen phase (see Fig. 135). No Caddo groups were living in this area after the time of sustained contact with Europeans (after c. AD 1720), and the tribal and ethnographic identity of the Upper Neches Cluster Caddo groups is not known.

In each of the three areas of the Kah-hah-ko-wha site there are discrete archaeological deposits. The remains are tightly clustered within them, and are habitation deposits (i.e., structural remains and trash deposits) left by Caddo families or extended families. Based on the size of the intensively used areas, and estimated annual accumulation rates of utility ware pottery sherds, each of the Caddo occupations appear to have lasted less than 5–10 years. The occupations are probably contemporaneous parts of a Caddo settlement.

The plant assemblage includes various charred plant remains from cultivated plants (maize, beans, goosefoot seed and legume seeds) and hardwood nutshells (from forest mast collection). The wood charcoal indicates the site area was forested with oaks, hickory and willow/cottonwood; pine charcoal was notably absent, suggesting the site area was situated within the oak-hickory savannah. Recovered animal bones include fish, various turtle species, deer, turkey, opossum and rabbit, as well as unidentified small to large-sized mammals. The subsistence data from the Allen phase component at the Kah-hah-ko-wha site point to a maize-based diet by the Caddo peoples that lived there, supplemented with the hunting of a diverse range of mammal and aquatic species and the collecting of wild plant foods from the surrounding forest. These data are comparable in species diversity to the plant and animal remains at the Deshazo site in the Angelina River basin (e.g., Ford 1982; Henderson 1982), and other Allen phase components, but they are better preserved at the slightly older Kah-hah-ko-wha site.

The Allen phase component at the Kah-hah-ko-wha site displays distinctive

[1] This is the Caddo name for the site and refers to the four hawks that visited the site while we were working there (Perttula and Nelson 2007: 130).

material culture assemblages that indicate the Caddo families had their own and different ways to make, fire and decorate ceramic vessels. There is a heavy emphasis on the manufacture of medium-sized brushed utility ware cooking jars and storage vessels in each area of the site, and the use of Patton Engraved fine ware bowls and carinated bowls for serving containers. The ceramic assemblages in different areas of the site had subtle stylistic and technological differences in: (1) the kinds of utility ware decorations, (2) the frequency of fine ware vessels from one area to another, (3) the occurrence of plain ware vessels, and (4) technological choices and manufacturing strategies with respect to temper-paste composition, firing conditions, surface treatment and vessel wall thickness.

The lithic assemblages are characterized by few formal chipped or ground stone tools (i.e., a few arrow points and a hematite celt), but many expedient flake tools, including several small scraping tools. Hunting was apparently only an occasional pursuit geared primarily to deer and various small mammals, and included some deer hide processing. There is no evidence of intensive hunting activities or the participation of the Caddo inhabitants in any incipient deer hide trade with Europeans. The recovery of two gunflints from the site does indicate, however, that the Caddo living here had access to, and the use of, French muskets. The only other European good was a poorly preserved piece of iron that may be part of an iron kettle bail or handle.

European goods from the Kah-hah-ko-wha site are believed to have been obtained from French sources by its Caddo inhabitants. The scarcity of European goods indicates that it was occupied early in the Allen phase, most likely before AD 1700. While there were very sporadic contacts between East Texas Caddo groups and Europeans (particularly the Spanish) before the late 17th century (see Foster 1995), it is doubtful that this sporadic interaction resulted in many, if any, European goods being given or traded to the Caddo at that time. Rather, the beginning of the introduction of European goods from Spanish and French sources in any quantity among the Caddo, except for the horse, which the Caddo were obtaining from native middlemen on the southern Plains after 1675 (Fenn 2014, map 6.1), dates from c. 1687, when the La Salle expedition traversed parts of East Texas and met a number of Caddo groups.

Glass beads and metal artifacts were among the items the Frenchmen brought to trade with the Caddo. However, it was not until the establishment of French trading posts on the Red and Sabine rivers, and Spanish missions and presidios in East Texas and Louisiana, in the first quarter of the 18th century that more dependable sources of European goods became available to the East Texas Caddo (Rogers and Sabo 2004: 19). The earlier Allen phase Caddo sites (those pre-dating c. AD 1720) tend to produce very few European artifacts (see Cole 1975; Story 1982; 1995; Perttula and Nelson 2006), while European goods (beads and various metal artifacts, particularly gun parts and knives) are much more common on later Allen phase sites such as Mayhew (41NA21) and the Nabedache Azul site (41HO214) that were apparently occupied as late as AD 1750–1760 (Kenmotsu 1992; Perttula and Nelson 2006; and see above).

Mission San José de los Nasonis (41RK200) and two contemporaneous Nasoni Caddo sites (41RK191 and 41RK197) were located on an upland ridge along a small

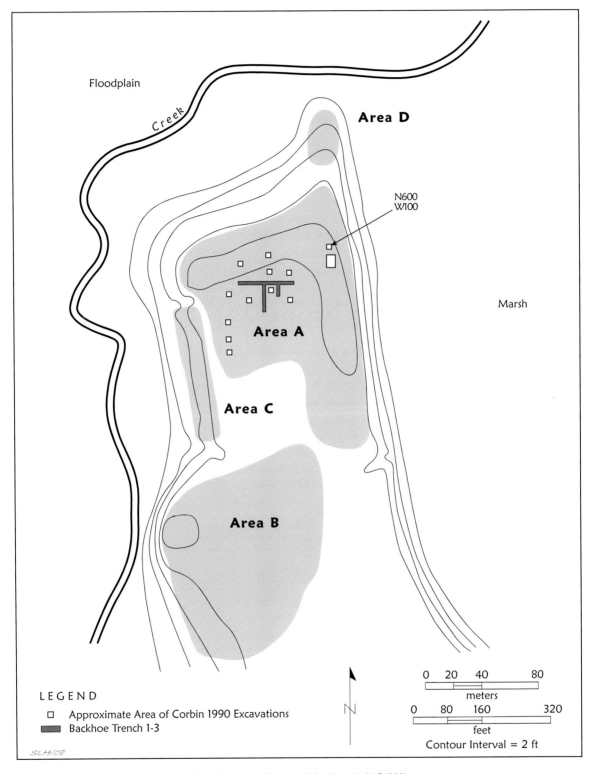

Fig. 142. Mission San Jose de los Nasonis (41RK200)

tributary to the Angelina River (Fig. 142). The topographic setting of Mission San Jose conforms in all particulars to the settings of other known mission sites established among the Caddo (Corbin 1989b: 273): small hills adjacent to a floodplain, next to a stream, with the hills "lower extensions of more extensive upland areas." Corbin (1989b: 273) also noted that these missions "were located within the area of the local dispersed Caddoan [*sic*] village, none of the locations are places suited to support the Indian-based community that the Spanish hoped to entice to the location."

This mission was established as one of six different missions by the Spanish in 1716 during their second attempt (the first being in 1690–1691) to establish a religious and political presence among the Caddo peoples (Corbin 1989b: 269–270) in East Texas, specifically to minister to the Nasoni Caddo living in the area. Mission San Jose de los Nasonis was formally established on July 10, 1716 (Tous 1930). Father Espinosa and Captain Don Domingo Ramon, the leader of the expedition, had noted that there were many Hasinai Caddo ranchos in the general area along with arroyos of water and good places for settlement (Foik 1999: 147). Both Nasoni and Nacono Caddo were then living in this area of the Angelina river.

An expedition to bring supplies to the East Texas missions was led by Governor Martin de Alarcon in 1718, and the expedition visited Mission San Jose de los Nasonis in November of that year (see Celiz 1935; Foster 1995: 139; 2008: 209). Celebrations were held by the missionaries and the local Caddo when the governor arrived. According to the diary of Father Celiz (1935), 31 Caddo had been baptized at Mission San Jose de los Nasonis. Shortly thereafter, in 1719, Mission San Jose was abandoned due to conflicts between the colonial Spanish and French governments (Castaneda 1936: 115), and the Spanish withdrew from the region.

The mission was re-established in August 1721 by the Governor of Texas, Marques de San Miguel de Aguayo (Forrestal 1999; Foster 1995; 2008), along with the five other missions and two presidios that had first been established a few years before. When Aguayo reached Nasoni on 12 August, according to Father Pena, "The Indians of this mission ... welcomed him with great demonstration of joy" (Forrestal 1999: 198). After restoration of the mission, 300 Nasoni Caddo assembled before the governor as he invested the local Caddo leader (or captain, otherwise known as *caddi* in the Caddo language) with his insignia of office (a silver-headed baton). Aguayo then:

> "clothed the captain in a complete suit of Spanish cloth and of the Spanish style, clothed all the rest in the same kind of garments as he had distributed at the other missions, and, as he had done at other pueblos, gave to the missionary Fray Benito Sanchez clothing for the Indians who at the time were absent guarding their cornfields and houses. The natives, 300 of whom were clothed here, were happy, and all day long they brought pumpkins, watermelons, ears of corn and pinole." (Forrestal 1999: 198–199).

Along with the gifts of clothing, Aguayo likely also distributed other gifts to the Nasoni, as he had done at Mission Concepcion the day before to the Tejas Caddo as well as some visiting Kadohadacho from the Red River. These would have included "knives, combs, awls, scissors, mirrors, *belduques* [large knives], chain-links, *chocomites*, belts, necklaces, earrings [*nahkiitsuunih*], glass beads and finger rings" (Forrestal 1999: 98). Mission San Jose de los Nasonis was finally and permanently abandoned in 1730.

A metal detector survey defined four specific concentrations of European metal goods over a 3.8 acre (*c.* 1.5 ha) part of Area A and C at the site, and these concentrations (likely marking mission structures), along with 8500+ Nasoni Caddo ceramic vessel sherds, occur around an open area (mission courtyard or plaza) (see Fig. 142). The most recognizable ceramic sherds are from Patton Engraved vessels; later forms of Poynor Engraved (*var. Cook* and *var. Blackburn*, see Perttula *et al.* 2011: fig. 6-64) also appear to be present in the mission assemblage. The particular significance of the Mission San Jose de los Nasonis ceramic assemblage is the abundance of Nasoni Caddo ceramics, constituting strong evidence that the missionaries and soldiers interacted with the nearby Nasoni Caddo, who clearly must have supplied the Europeans with hand-made pottery for their use, and probably also supplied them with food stuffs, hides, pelts and bear grease, among other local and familiar resources.

The Nabedache Caddo that lived on San Pedro Creek in Houston County in the East Texas Pineywoods were a prominent nation during the early years of European contact, from *c.* AD 1687–1730. Their villages, hamlets and farmsteads sat astride an aboriginal Caddo trail that came to be known as El Camino Real de los Tejas, and thus their community was a principal gateway to Europeans and other Native American tribes who came from the west in Spanish Texas to meet with the Tejas or Hasinai Caddo peoples. The first Spanish mission in East Texas was established amidst the Nabedache Caddo community in 1690 (Weddle 2012: 2).

One of the better known Nabedache sites is the George Moore 1b site (41HO64), situated on an alluvial terrace or alluvial fan of San Pedro Creek. Burials dating from *c.* AD 1690–1730 had been plowed up there from a cemetery in the 1930s, and then looted in the 1970s. Funerary offerings with these burials include more than 7600 glass beads in 22 varieties, mainly aqua blue or opaque white (Perttula 2004b). Beads were mentioned by Joutel on numerous occasions in his 1684–1687 journal, and these "trinkets" were apparently traded frequently to the Nabedache Caddo by the La Salle expedition members, including Joutel (Foster 1998: 197, 204, 205, 208–9, 213, 220). The Nabedache Caddo apparently preferred the color blue (see Bolton 1987: 133–4) for fabrics, and apparently also for the beads they used for ornamentation of their clothes and in necklaces. Glass beads in general are, however, rare in habitation contexts on Neches River Caddo sites and include only a few large blue beads from Allen phase sites (Cole 1975, table 19), including one site (41HO91) on San Pedro Creek in the specific vicinity of the Nabedache Caddo village visited by the La Salle Expedition, and at the Nabedache Azul (41HO214) and Nabedache Blanco (41HO211) sites (see Perttula and Nelson 2006).

Other material remains at this Nabedache site were Caddo ceramic vessel and pipe sherds and other French trade goods, among them gun parts and ammunition, a possible iron knive blade and a native-made gunflint. A catlinite pipe came from the George Moore #1c site (41HO65), about 160 m to the west of the George Moore #1b site. The pipe, made from catlinite from the Pipestone National Monument area of southwestern Minnesota (Perttula 2004b: fig. 11), has a short, but square

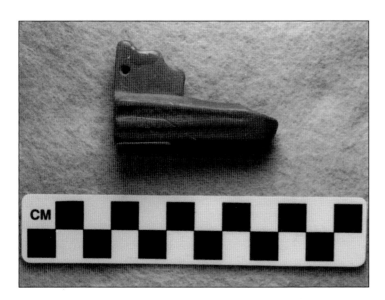

Fig. 143. Side-view of the Catlinite pipe from the George Moore 1c site

stem in cross-section, with a prow protruding from the front of the stem (Fig. 143). The prow also has notched projections along its ridge crest, as well as a 2.5 mm drilled hole near one end; the drilled hole may have been used to hold white feathers, as these stood for peace. There are two broad incised lines etched into the stem, extending from the stem opening to near where the cylindrical bowl would have been attached.

The catlinite pipe is a calumet or peace pipe, and would have been used in greeting ceremonies and other rituals by the Caddo, as well as many other tribes living in the eastern United States; the Caddo must have obtained it from the French, as the French widely distributed these pipes to Native American groups in the late 17th and early 18th centuries. Specifically, the pipe from the George Moore #1c site is the smokestack type of catlinite pipe (see Brain 1979: 248).

Henri Joutel witnessed a calumet ceremony in 1687 among the Cahinnio Caddo (Foster 1998: 254–5), who lived on the Ouachita River in southwestern Arkansas:

> "In the evening, we attended a ceremony that we had not seen before. A group of elders followed by a few young men and some women came as a group singing at the top of their voices near our hut. The first one carried a calumet [or pipe] decorated with various feathers. Having sung for some time before our hut, they entered the hut and continued their songs [*kahkinay?aw*] for about a quarter of an hour."

The singing and ceremonies with Joutel and other members of his party continued throughout the night (*napba*). Then, in the early morning, while the singing continued:

> "the master of ceremonies took the calumet which he refilled with tobacco, lit, and presented to the Abbe. He drew back and advanced, without giving it to the Abbe, until this was repeated ten times. When he finally put it in the Abbe's hands, he pretended to smoke it and returned it to them. Next, the Indians made us all smoke, and they also all smoked in return, the music always continuing". (Foster 1998: 254)

The singing and ceremonial activities finally wound down around 9 A.M., according to Joutel, and the Caddo wrapped the calumet in a deer skin sack with "two forked sticks and a crosspiece of red wood," and then they offered the calumet to the Abbe. When they did, they told the French that with the calumet, the French "could go to all the tribes who were their allies with this token of peace and that we would be well received everywhere" (Foster 1998: 255).

When Joutel's party came through East Texas in 1687, including the Nabedache Caddo villages along San Pedro Creek, they made no mention of the calumet (Foster 1998: 255, fn 8). However, later journeys to these Caddo villages in 1716 and 1718 by

Spanish soldiers and missionaries mention the performance of the calumet. Captain Diego Ramon wrote in the diary of his expedition that the calumet pipe was "adorned with many white feathers as a sign of peace among them" (Espinosa 1927: 152).

The Woldert site (41WD333) and nearby 41WD331 are likely mid-18th century Nadaco Caddo settlements in the upper Sabine River basin (Perttula and Skiles 1989), associated with *Le Dout*, a French trading establishment. The Woldert site contains abundant numbers of French trade muskets as well as other French trade goods, while 41WD331 has glass beads and gun barrel fragments as well as artifacts of Caddo manufacture. In the mid-18th century, French traders were very active among East Texas Caddo peoples. In 1740 testimony, French voyageur Pierre Mallet noted that "though these French do not have fixed habitations, but only come and go to sell muskets and other things needed by the Indians, from who they obtain annually about 100,000 pounds of furs, as well as tallow and the oil of bears, buffaloes and deer" (Hackett 1931–1946, vol. iii: 417). As late as 1788, the Nadaco also had a widely dispersed village scattered over 3 leagues (*c.* 7.8 miles or 12 km) somewhere downstream on tributaries to the Sabine River (Loomis and Nasatir 1965: 346).

One site from the pueblo of Nacogdoches, re-occupied in 1779 by Gil Ybarbo and settlers at the site of the former Mission Nuestra Señora de los Nacogdoches (abandoned in 1772), contains both Caddo and European ceramics and other European goods (most notably glass beads and the bones of domestic animals) in contexts suggesting considerable interaction between Caddo groups living around Nacogdoches and the Spanish and Mexican settlers and ranchers throughout much of the market economy period (M. Jackson *et al.* 2012). This is not surprising since Nacogdoches was at that time a local center of European commerce and trade. European ceramics found at this site included creamware and pearlware vessel sherds in abundance, as well as faience brune and Mexican majolica and Caddo ceramic vessel sherds; these vessels probably held items such as bear fat and corn traded and bartered with the citizens of Nacogdoches.

The Bernardo D'Ortolan ranch (1796–1813) was an outpost west of the pueblo, and one of the many large ranchos established by the Spanish government around Nacogdoches (M. Jackson *et al.* 2012). The floor of the main structure at the ranch contained plain and brushed Caddo ceramics along with European-made artifacts typical of those found elsewhere in colonial New Spain and Texas. D'Ortolan, like other Europeans living in this frontier economy, was probably heavily involved in the trade with the local Native Americans, including the Caddo. In 1828, skins from more than 40,000 deer, 1500 bear, 1200 otter and 600 beaver were traded by Native Americans in Nacogdoches, although the trade in livestock was probably a more important part of the frontier market economy at that time. Even General Terán, the Mexican envoy on an inspection tour, considered the trade to be important to the commerce of the Province of Texas (Ewers 1969: 47, fn 27).

The Caddo archaeological record in East Texas from *c.* 1775 to 1850 is virtually invisible in modern considerations of Caddo history, which is remarkable considering the relatively wide-spread distribution of Historic Caddo peoples during much of that era. Archaeology, however, is a poor attendant to this period of Caddo strife and turmoil. It may be that Kadohadacho sites such as Timber Hill

(41MR211, see Parsons *et al.* 2002) are the prototype for this period; we simply do not know. It may also be the case that archaeologists have been reluctant to search for sites of this period, focusing instead on the many ancestral Caddo sites with impressive mounds and burial grounds. Regardless, from 1835 to the present the U.S. government has done little to acknowledge the Caddo presence in East Texas and surrounding areas. For the most part, disregard has followed displacement.

One of the more important sites of the *c.* 1775–1838 period is the Timber Hill site, or *Sha'chahdínnih*. It has been characterized by some as the "last village of the Kadohadacho Caddo in the Caddo homeland region" (Parsons *et al.* 2002, iii), although there were at least four other Kadohadacho villages in East Texas up to the fall of 1838 (see Tiller 2007; 2008). The principal Kadohadacho village in the early 19th century, and probably occupied until the early 1830s (Tiller 2007; 2008), Timber Hill was named after the first village founded after the Caddo emerged from the earth and left *Cha'kani'na*, the place of crying (Carter 1995: 217; Dorsey 1905: 7–13; Swanton 1942: 27–8). The site was established on Caddo Lake in 1800 (Parsons *et al.* 2002: 5), likely covered several hundred acres, and had at least 300 families living there during much of its existence.

The ancestral Caddo ceramic tradition continued in full-force at the Timber Hill site, even at this late date (Parsons *et al.* 2002: 35). It appears that the ceramics at Timber Hill were made and used for cooking, re-heating, serving and storage of food stuffs. Even after extensive contact with Europeans, presumably more than a century after the introduction of metal cookware (i.e., iron kettles), the Caddo continued to use their own ceramics. This strongly implies that traditional means of food processing and culinary practices were maintained by the Caddo living at Timber Hill and that they held fast to their cultural and social traditions.

The Caddo ceramics found at the Timber Hill site are an apparent amalgamation of the traditions of different but ethnically related Kadohadacho groups because they are diverse in terms of tempers used in the vessel paste (i.e., shell temper favored by some Caddo groups, and grog and bone by others), and in the range of decorations seen on the fine wares and utility wares. In another example of Caddo ceramic manufacture and use/culinary continuity, several mid-1830s Caddo vessels apparently collected from Caddo peoples living in northwestern Louisiana are similar in vessel shape to late 18th century vessel forms and they have recognizable Historic Caddo engraved motifs (Perttula 2001).

The corn grown and eaten at Timber Hill consisted of traditional varieties, as well as a larger variety of Eastern Complex corn, but "both kinds of corn described by 18th-century Spanish missionaries were simultaneously cultivated into the 19th century" (Parsons *et al.* 2002: 86). Features found on the site suggest that deer hides were carefully smoked over smudge pits to produce high-quality deer skins.

European goods, including ceramic cups, bowls and plates, glass bottles, metal containers such as kettles (an important item offered by trading factories, and employed by the Caddo to render bear fat) and Dutch ovens, as well as various domestic tools, had become part of the material culture of the Caddo living at Timber Hill, and many began to supplement or even replace goods of Caddo manufacture by this time (Parsons *et al.* 2002). In addition to common European goods obtained in trade from U.S. factories, there were glass beads, military buttons from traded greatcoats, thimbles, tinklers, hawk bells, gun parts, horse trappings (harness buckles and rings as well as a bridle bit), as well as nails from crates or wagons. Clearly throughout the first quarter of the 19th century, the Caddo participated in the frontier market economy, and benefited materially from it.

Another important – but still little known – Caddo site occupied in the first years of the 19th century is the Middle Caddo village in East Texas. This is one of the Caddo villages probably established along the loose boundary between American Louisiana and Texas after the 1835 U.S. Treaty with the Caddo (Tiller 2007; 2008). As an 1837 petition from the Caddo to the U.S. government indicates, the Caddo purposefully established their villages outside the domain of the U.S.:

> "We have established our villages near the head of Lake Sodo [Caddo Lake] which we believe to be without the boundary of the United States, but on running the line between Mexico and the U.S. should it be found to be within the jurisdiction of the latter, we will instantly remove further to the west [into Texas]. Hope you will inform the President of our great wish to have this line run out as we can make no permanent settlement until this is done." (National Archives and Records Administration, Letters Received by the Office of Indian Affairs, 1824–1881. Roll 31, Caddo Agency, 1824–1842. *Letters, Caddo Agency.* Petition, Caddo Chiefs to Joel Poinsett, 9 January 1837).

The Middle Caddo village was still in existence in early 1838 (Oates 1963: 26). This village (41HS840) appears to have covered about 40 acres (16.2 ha), based on very limited investigations (primarily shovel testing and metal detecting). Items obtained in the market economy abound here, and include such trade goods obtained from nearby U.S. trade factories as gun parts and rifle balls (of several calibers) from muskets, gunflints, axe blades, iron kettles, case knives, horse gear, pearlware cups and plates and wine bottle glass. There is evidence of both blacksmithing and the on-site manufacture of rifle balls, and there are pieces or cut-outs of silver ornaments and copper sheet fragments that suggest the Caddo were manufacturing ornamental items from available trade metal sources. They also made sheet copper and iron arrow points. One of the square cut nails had evidence of use as a tool, as did pieces of chipped glass; chipped glass and ceramics were probably used as scrapers on deer hides, and such implements have been recovered from other *c.* 1790–1835 Caddo sites. Caddo ceramic vessel sherds are also present at the site, along with clay pipe sherds.

The wide range of metal artifacts from both Timber Hill and the Middle Caddo Village indicates that the Caddo living there had ready access to European and American metal tools and goods. In some cases the metal goods were used and reworked by the Caddo to suit their own purposes. When the metal goods no longer served a useful purpose or were broken, they were readily discarded as trash by the Caddo, seemingly because they could be easily replaced.

8

The Future of Caddo Archaeology

"…introspective wandering into the past" (Michael Ondaatje, 1999)

Archaeological research on the native history of the Caddo peoples has made many impressive findings since the 1880s, and there is every reason to think that this will continue well into the 21st century and beyond. Caddo archaeology entered the modern world of Eastern Woodlands and North American archaeology in 1941, with the foundational work of Alex D. Krieger (1946; 2009). Krieger developed "an encompassing cultural-historical framework for the interpretation of southern Caddoan prehistory by the early 1940s. Although it has been considerably modified over the years, this scheme greatly advanced Caddoan archaeology" (Story 1993:615).

Krieger worked to organize and understand the culture history of the Caddo Indian peoples that lived in East Texas, southwest Arkansas, northwest Louisiana and eastern Oklahoma. He also examined cultural connections between the Caddo and aboriginal populations in the Southeast, the Great Plains, the Southwest and Mexico (see especially Krieger 1946). This culture-historical work, although hampered by the foreshortened chronologies in use in the Southeast in the absence of radiocarbon dating, has served Caddo archaeology and archaeologists well, but Caddo archaeology today is so much more than culture-historical analysis. If nothing else, the more than 70 years of archaeological and bioarchaeological studies that have been completed in the Caddo area since Krieger's groundbreaking research have shown the complex cultural and biological intertwining of both early–middle (*c*. AD 800–1400), late (*c*. AD 1400–1680) and historic (*c*. AD 1680–1840) Caddo sites, assemblages, cultural traditions and social networks, populations, communities and societies in East Texas.

Over more than a millennium, Caddo families, groups and communities established and maintained social, political, religious and cosmically-charged settlements in the East Texas forests. These settlements were organized diachronically and spatially around a number of mound and/or civic-ceremonial centers in the major river valleys – including the Red, Sulphur, Big Cypress, Sabine and the Neches-Angelina (Fig. 144) – and their dispersion across the landscape surely reflect both short and long-term changes in social and political relationships, broad and intensive networks of interaction, information flow and cultural transmission, as well as changes in settlement systems.

Our understanding of Caddo landscapes in East Texas is facilitated by a number of detailed studies of Caddo settlements and communities, including households

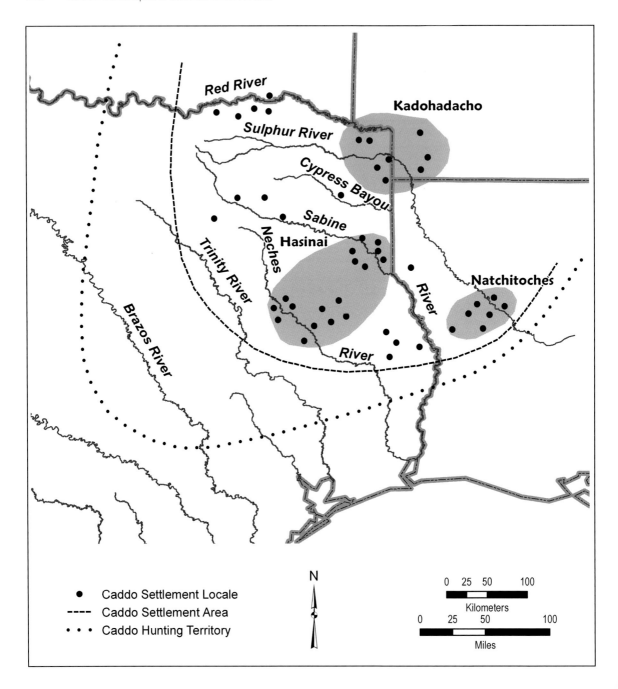

Fig. 144. Settlement locales, areas, and hunting territories in the post-AD 1680 East Texas Caddo world (after Barr 2011)

and farmsteads, hamlets, villages, mound centers and cemeteries and the interlinking of these places with the study of the rich material culture heritage of Caddo peoples (in particular their plain and decorated ceramic wares), combined with more intensive radiocarbon dating of Caddo settlements to establish refined estimates of occupation spans. Such investigations have shed light on the character

Fig. 145. Will Soule's
c. 1869–1875 photograph
of Long Hat's Camp in
western Oklahoma

of the East Texas Caddo archaeological record since the 9th century AD, but more importantly have not only led to a better appreciation of the native history of the Caddo peoples, but to a broader and fuller understanding of Caddo cultural and social landscapes.

Several of the enduring images of Caddo native history that resonate across time are the late 19th century photographs of a Caddo settlement in western Oklahoma that have been called Long Hat's Camp (Fig. 145). The Long Hat's were Hasinai Caddo, and a prominent family in early 20th century Caddo society (Parsons 1941: 10). The various structures shown on the photographs include at least two oval to rectangular-shaped dwellings, a collapsed dwelling, at least one ramada or open work area and a dome-shaped structure that may be a storage facility (Early 2014: 55).

What is significant about these late 19th century Caddo structures at the camp is not just that they resemble structures that were drawn on the 1691 Teran map of the Nasoni Caddo village (see Fig. 129), but that these kinds of structures have been documented on Caddo archaeological sites in East Texas dating from the very beginnings of the southern Caddo area tradition, from as long as 1000 years before Soule's photographs, and they still had resonance in those traditions in the late 19th century. Early (2014: 58) suggests that:

> "the architectural style exhibited in the Longhat camp photographs was a very old Caddo architectural model that retained powerful associations with core Caddo traditions and leadership roles. Whether by choice or obligation, the Longhat family employed this building style at a time when the Caddo had been uprooted from their ancestral lands and were facing monumental challenges in adapting to a new social, economic and religious landscape."

Final thoughts

The pursuit of Caddo archaeological research over the last 100+ years has led to considerable gains during that time in the understanding of such research issues as settlement patterning, subsistence change and diet, health and adaptive efficiency, socio-political organization, ceremony and ritual, iconography and exchange networks among the Caddo peoples and their past communities (see Girard *et al.* 2014). Much of this has been the result of intensive cultural resource management investigations over the last 40 years in southwestern Arkansas, northwestern Louisiana, eastern Oklahoma and East Texas, along with focused archaeological research projects conducted by university archaeological programs and state and regional archaeological societies. The years ahead promise to continue to shed new light on the character and understanding of the *c.* AD 850–1850s Caddo archaeological record in East Texas, as well as in the other parts of the Caddo area.

Despite these hard-won gains in our understanding and explanation of the Caddo archaeological record and Caddo native history, Caddo archaeological research investigations remain much too parochial and state-bound (i.e., based on the detailed analyses of particular sites or groups of sites in a regional locality). Large scale diachronic and geographic syntheses (i.e., macro-regional in scope and crossing state lines) and grand challenges (e.g., Kintigh *et al.* 2014) of the Caddo archaeological data are needed if we are to ever fully appreciate, detail and refine the character of the native histories of Caddo peoples. No one part of the Caddo area was isolated from other contemporaneous Caddo communities, locales and regions. As in the Southwestern United States and the study of ancestral Pueblo communities through successful large scale and multi-year synthetic research efforts and the accompanying creation of useful databases – as in the Chaco Research Archive, the Southwest Social Networks databases and the Village Ecodynamics Project – the "ability of scholars to pursue synthetic research depends on the commitment of the ... archaeological community to make project data available in state archaeological record files, museums, and burgeoning digital repositories" (Schachner 2015: 56, 84).

While considerable steps have been made by the Caddo archaeological community in creating useful databases of archaeological data, more efforts along these lines are still needed for analytical study and research purposes. There are large and specialized digital Caddo databases being cumulatively developed concerning such things as radiocarbon dating of features and archaeological deposits, vessel documentation and digitization, ceramic sherd databases, databases of the instrumental neutron activation analysis and petrographic analysis of Caddo ceramic vessels and sherds, as well as the distribution of novaculite artifacts – and there are surely others – but these efforts ought to be expanded to reach across state lines and individual researchers to extend their full use and capabilities for Caddo archaeologists and those that are interested in the history of Caddo peoples and their ancestral communities. Just as importantly, we also need the collaboration of scholars working in all parts of the Caddo archaeological area on large-scale and major research questions, so as to be able to actively engage in the comparison of the variable regional character of the Caddo archaeological record in material culture expressions, social and political practices, use of landscapes, subsistence strategies and use of cultivated plants, interaction with neighbors and the tempo of cultural changes. For example, the synthesis of the stylistically diverse Caddo ceramic wares in different recognized ancestral communities across the Caddo area would seem to be tailor-made for studies of ancestral Caddo social networks and social identities that rely on large regional ceramic datasets (see Collar *et al.* 2015; Mills *et al.* 2015; Hart 2016), but such social network syntheses wait to be done.

Such a next step would be to more formally and statistically assess the regional variation in Caddo ceramic assemblages in a Geographic Information System. This should be based on a further delineation of temporal and spatial divisions in the character of Caddo ceramics (i.e., principally data on decorative methods and the use of different tempers) across East Texas sites and other parts of the Caddo area, and then constructing networks of similarities between ceramic assemblages from these sites (cf. Peeples and Roberts 2013: 3003–4) that can be used to assess the strength of cultural and social relationships among Caddo communities in the region through time and across space. These postulated relationships could then be explored to determine the underlying reasons for the existence of such relationships, including factors such as the frequency of interaction and direct contact between communities, the trade and exchange of ceramic vessels, population movement and similarities in the organization of ceramic vessel production. The results of past and current instrumental neutron activation analysis (INAA) and petrographic analysis of Caddo Area ceramics, including East Texas (where there is a robust INAA database) should also be explored as a means to corroborate production locales (cf. Selden and Perttula 2014; Selden *et al.* 2014), establish the chemical and paste characteristics of local fine ware and utility ware ceramics in assemblages of different ages, and evaluate the possible movement of ceramic vessels between different Caddo communities in East Texas and the broader Caddo world.

Finally, in conjunction with a database on 2D/3D-scanned Caddo ceramic vessels from East Texas sites, the East Texas Caddo ceramic sherd database can be made part of a digital database where comprehensive mathematical and quantitative analyses of morphological attributes and decorative elements on sherds and vessels can be conducted (e.g., Smith *et al.* 2014). Queries to such a combined database of vessels and sherds should lead to better understandings of regional Caddo ceramic stylistic and technological attributes and their spatial and temporal underpinnings.

If large-scale syntheses of the Caddo archaeological record are important to undertake, how can the collaboration of Caddo archaeologists be encouraged? How can databases of specific sets of information be created, designed and shared between Caddo archaeologists working on common research problems? A research climate needs to be fostered where "big" syntheses can be developed through both short-term and long-term project collaborations and database (spatial and analytical) compilations. Research projects of varying scopes ought to be developed that would rely on the collaboration of Caddo archaeologists working in different regions on research questions and problems of mutual interest and making such information and datasets accessible on their websites or other platforms.

Who knows what the future of Caddo archaeology will hold, or what kinds of new and improved understandings of the Caddo archaeological record will come in the years ahead. Without expending effort in large-scale syntheses of ancestral Caddo archaeology, and continuing to work with the Caddo peoples themselves, we will not be taking full advantage of the richness of our knowledge of Caddo native history.

Appendix 1. Key Caddo sites to visit in the East Texas forests

George C. Davis Site (Caddo Mounds State Historic Site)

1649 State Hwy 21, West Alto, TX 75925 caddo-mounds@thc.texas.gov

The George C. Davis site (41CE19) in Cherokee County in East Texas was in private ownership until 1940 when the Texas Forest Service purchased 75 acres (*c.* 30.4 ha) east and south of Highway 21 and established the Indian Mound Nursery to raise forest tree seedlings. Their holdings were later expanded to over 300 acres (121+ ha). The portion of the site north and west of Highway 21 continued in private ownership and was used as a peach orchard until 1975 when the State of Texas acquired 70.1 acres (28.4 ha) of the site. In 1981, the Texas Parks and Wildlife Department (TPWD) purchased an additional 23.7 acres (9.5 ha) from the Texas Forest Service.

 The Caddo Mounds State Historic Site opened to the public in 1982 under the management of the TPWD; one of its major attractions was an experimental Caddo house reconstruction built by students from The University of Texas; this structure

Fig. 146. Caddo Mounds State Historic Site in East Texas (image provided courtesy of Anthony Souther, Texas Historical Commission)

was burned down in 1995 before it collapsed (Perttula and Skiles 2014). As of this writing, another reconstructed Caddo house has just recently been built at the site by Phil Cross, an Oklahoma Caddo. In 2007, the Texas legislature transferred management of the site to the Texas Historical Commission (THC), and in 2010 the THC purchased the 303.9 acres (123 ha) of the adjacent Texas Forest Service property in order to preserve and manage the entire site. Today, the 397.7 acre (161 ha) Caddo Mounds State Historic Site contains a visitor center, maintenance compound, site manager residence, and more than a mile of trails with wayside interpretive panels that are open to the public (Fig. 146).

The park is open Tuesday–Sunday 8:30 a.m.–4:30 p.m. Closed Thanksgiving, Christmas Eve, Christmas Day, New Year's Eve, and New Year's Day. There is a small admission fee.

The Archaeological Conservancy Preserves

Although the Caddo preserves owned or controlled by The Archaeological Conservancy (TAC) in East Texas are not open to the public, it should be possible to arrange a tour at selected sites under the direction of a local preserve steward/ monitor and the cooperation of The Archaeological Conservancy. These preserves include: Horace Cabe (41BW14), Hale (41TT12), Hudnall-Pirtle (41RK4), Redwine (41SM193), A. C. Saunders (41AN19), Fasken (41RR14), portions of the Pine Tree Mound site (41HS15), and Jamestown (41SM54). These sites are in the Southwest Region of the TAC network (headquartered in Albuquerque, New Mexico), and, at the time of writing (2016) the Regional Director is Mr Jim Walker (505-266-1540). The Southwest Field Representative for The Archaeological Conservancy is Mr Chaz Evans (chaztac@gmail.com).

Bibliography

Anderson, D. G. (2012) Monumentality in eastern North America during the Mississippian Period. In *Early New World Monumentality*, ed. R. L. Burger and R. M. Rosenwig: 78–108. University Press of Florida, Gainesville FL.

Anderson, D. G. and Sassaman, K. E. (2012) *Recent Developments in Southeastern Archaeology: From Colonization to Complexity*. SAA Press, Washington DC.

Babcock, M. (2015) Rethinking the Balance of Power in Southwestern America: Apache, Caddo, and Comanche Political Organization and Territoriality, 1700–1800. MS on file with the author.

Banks, L. D. (1990) *From Mountain Peaks to Alligator Stomachs: A Review of Lithic Sources in the Trans-Mississippi South, the Southern Plains, and Adjacent Southwest*. Memoir 4. Oklahoma Anthropological Society, Norman OK.

Banks, L. D. and Winters, J. (1975) *The Bentsen-Clark Site, Red River County, Texas: A Preliminary Report*. Special Publication 2. Texas Archeological Society, San Antonio TX.

Barr, J. (2011) Geographies of power: mapping Indian borders in the "borderlands" of the early Southwest. *William and Mary Quarterly* 68 (1): 5–46.

Barr, J. (2015) Borders and borderlands. In *Why You Can't Teach United States History Without American Indians*, eds S. Sleeper-Smith, J. Barr, J. M. O'Brien, N. Shoemaker and S. M. Stevens: 9–25. University of North Carolina Press, Chapel Hill NC.

Barr, J. (in press) There's no such thing as "pre"-history: what the *longue durée* of Caddo and Pueblo history can tell us about Colonial America. *William and Mary Quarterly* 74 (2).

Barr, J. and Countryman, E. (2014) Maps and spaces, paths to connect, and lines to divide. In *Contested Spaces of Early America*, eds J. Barr and E. Countryman: 1–28. University of Pennsylvania Press, Philadelphia PA.

Baumann, T. E., Gerke, T. L. and Reber, E. A. (2013) Sun circles and science: negative painted pottery from Angel Mounds (12Vg1). *Midcontinental Journal of Archaeology* 38 (2): 219–44.

Beck, R. A., Jr. (2007) The durable house: material, metaphor, and structure. In *The Durable House: House Society Models in Archaeology*, ed. R. A. Beck, Jr.: 3–24. Occasional Paper 35. Center for Archaeological Investigations, Southern Illinois University, Carbondale IL.

Blaine, J. C. and Harris, R. K. (1967) Guns. In "The Gilbert Site: A Norteno Focus Site in Northeastern Texas," ed. E. B. Jelks. *Bulletin of the Texas Archeological Society* 37: 33–86.

Blake, L. W. (1981) Early acceptance of watermelon by Indians of the United States. *Journal of Ethnobiology* 1 (2): 19–29.

Blake, L. W. and Cutler, H. C. (1979) Plant remains from the Upper Nodena Site (3MS4). *Arkansas Archeologist* 20: 53–8.

Blitz, J. H. (2010) New perspectives in Mississippian archaeology. *Journal of Archaeological Research* 18 (1): 1–39.

Bolton, H. E. (1987) *The Hasinai: Southern Caddoans as Seen by the Earliest Europeans*. University of Oklahoma Press, Norman OK.

Bossu, M. (1777) *Nouveaux Voyages Dans L'Amerique Septentrionale, contenant Une collections de Lettres escrites fur les lieux, par l'Auteur, a son ami, M. Douin, Chevalier, Capitaine dans les troupes du Roi, ci-devant son comarade dans le nouveau Monde*. Chez Changuion, à la Bourse, Amsterdam.

Brain, J. P. (1979) *Tunica Treasure*. Papers of the Peabody Museum of Archaeology and Ethnology 71. Peabody Museum of Archaeology and Ethnology, Harvard University, Cambridge MA.

Briggs, R. V. (2016) The civil cooking pot: hominy and the Mississippian standard jar in the Black Warrior Valley, Alabama. *American Antiquity* 81 (2): 316–32.

Brown, J. A. (1996) *The Spiro Ceremonial Center: The Archaeology of Arkansas Valley Caddoan Culture in Eastern Oklahoma* (2 vols). Memoir 29. Museum of Anthropology, University of Michigan, Ann Arbor MI.

Brown, J. A. (2010) Cosmological layouts of secondary burials as political instruments. In *Mississippian Mortuary Practices: Beyond Hierarchy and the Representationist Perspective*, eds L. P. Sullivan and R. C. Mainfort Jr.: 30–53. University Press of Florida, Gainesville FL.

Brown, J. A. (2012) Spiro reconsidered: sacred economy at the western frontier of the eastern woodlands. In *The Archaeology of the Caddo*, edited by T. K. Perttula and C. P. Walker: 117–138. University of Nebraska Press, Lincoln NE.

Brown, K. M. (1976) Fused volcanic glass from the Manning Formation. *Bulletin of the Texas Archeological Society* 47: 189–207.

Bruseth, J. E. (1998) The development of Caddoan polities

along the middle Red River Valley of eastern Texas and Oklahoma. In *The Native History of the Caddo: Their Place in Southeastern Archeology and Ethnohistory*, eds T. K. Perttula and J. E. Bruseth: 47–68. Studies in Archeology 30. Texas Archeological Research Laboratory, University of Texas at Austin, Austin TX.

Bruseth, J. E. and Kenmotsu, N. A. (1991) Soldiers of misfortune: The de Soto Expedition through Texas. *Heritage* 9: 12–18. Texas Historical Foundation, Austin TX.

Bruseth, J. E. and Kenmotsu, N. A. (1993) From Naguatex to the River Daycao: the Route of the Hernando de Soto Expedition through Texas. *North American Archaeologist* 14(2): 99–125.

Bruseth, J. E. and Perttula, T. K. (1981) *Prehistoric Settlement Patterns at Lake Fork Reservoir*. Texas Antiquities Permit Series 2, Archaeology Research Program, Southern Methodist University, Dallas and Texas Antiquities Committee, Austin TX.

Bruseth, J. E. and Perttula, T. K. (2006) Archeological investigations at the Hudnall-Pirtle Site (41RK4): an Early Caddo mound center in northeast Texas. *Caddo Archeological Journal* 15: 57–158.

Bruseth, J. E., Banks, L. and Smith J. (2001) The Ray Site (41LR135). *Bulletin of the Texas Archeological Society* 72: 197–213.

Burden, D., Fields, R. C., Gadus, E. F. and Hatfield, V. L. (2014) The Thomas B. Caldwell and A. P. Williams cemeteries and Titus Phase mortuary behavior. In Fields *et al.* (eds) 2014: 335–433.

Bush, L. L. (2011) Plant remains from the Boxed Springs Site (41UR30). In Perttula 2011a: 138–146.

Bush, L. L. (2014) Eli Moores Site (41BW2) plant remains. In Perttula 2014e: 63–73.

Butler, B. M. and Welch, P. D. (eds) (2006) *Leadership and Polity in Mississippian Society*. Occasional Paper 33. Center for Archaeological Investigations, Southern Illinois University, Carbondale IL.

Carr, C. (1995) Mortuary practices: their social, philosophical-religious, circumstantial, and physical determinants. *Journal of Archaeological Method and Theory* 2 (2): 105–200.

Carter, C. E. (1995) *Caddo Indians: Where We Come From.* University of Oklahoma Press, Norman OK.

Castaneda, C. E. (1936) *Our Catholic Heritage in Texas, 1519-1936, Volume 2: The Mission Era: The Winning of Texas, 1693-1731.* Von Boeckmann-Jones, Austin TX.

Celiz, F. (1935) *Diary of the Alarcon Expedition into Texas, 1718-1719.* Ed. and trans. F. L. Hoffman. Quivira Society, Los Angeles CA.

Chafe, W. (1993) Caddo names in the de Soto documents. In Young and Hoffman (eds) 1993: 222–6.

Cole, N. M. (1975) Early Historic Caddoan Mortuary Practices in the Upper Neches Drainage, East Texas.

Master's thesis, Department of Anthropology, University of Texas at Austin.

Collar, A., Coward, F., Brughmans, T. and Mills, B. J. (2015) Networks in archaeology: phenomena, abstraction, representation. *Journal of Archaeological Method and Theory* 22: 1–32.

Cook, B. I., Cook, E. R., Smerdon, J. E., Seager, R., Williams, A. P., Coats, S., Stahle, D. W. and Villanueva Diaz, J. (2016) North American megadroughts in the Common Era: reconstructions and simulations. *Climate Change*, doi: 10.1002/wcc.394.

Cook, E. R. and Krusic, P. J. (2004) *The North American Drought Atlas.* Lamont-Doherty Earth Observatory and the National Science Foundation. Electronic document, http://iridl.ldeo.columbia.edu/SOURCES/.LEDO/.TRL/.NADA2004/.pdsi-atlas.htm, accessed October 1, 2015.

Corbin, J. E. (1989a) The Woodland/Caddo Transition in the southern Caddo area. In *Festschrift in Honor of Jack Hughes,* ed. D. Roper: 117–24. Special Publication 5. Panhandle Archeological Society, Amarillo TX.

Corbin, J. E. (1989b) Spanish-Indian interaction on the Eastern Frontier of Texas. In *Columbian Consequences, Volume 1: Archaeological and Historical Perspectives on the Spanish Borderlands West*, ed. D. H. Thomas: 269–76. Smithsonian Institution Press, Washington DC.

Corbin, J. E. (1991) Retracing the Camino de los Tejas from the Trinity River to Los Adaes: new insights into east Texas history. In *A Texas Legacy: The Old San Antonio Road and the Caminos Reales, a Tricentennial History, 1691–1991,* eds A. J. McGraw, J. W. Clark, and E. A. Robbins: 191–219. Texas State Department of Highways and Public Transportation, Austin TX.

Corbin, J. E. (1998) Reflections on the Early Ceramic Period and the Terminal Archaic in south central east Texas. *Journal of Northeast Texas Archaeology* 11: 108–16.

Corbin, J. E. and Hart, J. P. (1998) The Washington Square Mound Site: a Middle Caddo mound complex in south central east Texas. *Bulletin of the Texas Archeological Society* 69: 47–78.

Cox, I. J. (1905) *The Early Exploration of Louisiana.* University Studies Series 2, Vol. 11, 1. University of Cincinnati, Cincinnati OH.

Creel, D. G. (1996) Hatchel-Mitchell Site. In *The New Handbook of Texas*, Vol. 3, ed. R. Tyler: 504–5. Texas State Historical Association, Austin TX.

Creel, D., Hudler, D., Wilson, S., Schultz, C. and Walker, C. (2005) *A magnetometer survey of Caddoan Mounds State Historic Site.* Technical Report 51. Texas Archeological Research Laboratory, University of Texas at Austin TX.

Creel, D., Hudler, D., Wilson, S., Walker, C. and Schultz, T. C. (2008) Geophysical survey of the Mound B area at the George C. Davis Site. *Bulletin of the Texas Archeological Society* 79: 177–90.

Crown, P. L., Emerson, T. E., Gu, J., Hurst, W. J., Pauketat, T. R. and Ward, T. (2012) Ritual Black Drink consumption at Cahokia. *Proceedings of the National Academy of Sciences* 109 (35): 13944–9.

Cunningham, D. S. (ed.) (2006) The Domingo Ramon Diary of the 1716 expedition into the Province of the Tejas Indians: an annotated translation. *Southwestern Historical Quarterly* 110 (1): 39–67.

Cutler, H. C. and Blake, L. W. (1977) Corn from Cahokia sites. In *Explorations into Cahokia Archaeology*, ed. M. L. Fowler: 122–37. Bulletin 7. Illinois Archaeological Survey, Urbana IL.

Cutler, H. C. and Blake, L. W. (2001) Plants from archaeological sites east of the Rockies. In *Plants from the Past*, by L. W. Blake and H. C. Cutler: 93–147. University of Alabama Press, Tuscaloosa AL.

Dancey, W. S. (2005) The enigmatic Hopewell of the eastern woodlands. In *North American Archaeology*, eds T. R. Pauketat and D. D. Loren: 108–137. Blackwell Publishing, Malden MA.

Davis, E. M. (1996) Harling Site. In *The New Handbook of Texas*, Vol. 3, ed. R. Tyler: 462–3. Texas State Historical Association, Austin TX.

Davis, E. M., Davis, W. A., Gipson, J. R. and Golden, B. (2010) *Archeological Investigations at Lake O' The Pines, Marion and Upshur Counties, Texas, 1957–1959.* Archival Series 4. Texas Archeological Research Laboratory, University of Texas at Austin TX.

Dering, J. P. (2004) Archaeobotanical evidence for agriculture and wild plant use at 41RK214. In Rogers and Perttula 2004: 329–36.

Dering, J. P. (2008a) Plant remains from the Leaning Rock Site (41SM325). *Caddo Archeology Journal* 17: 68–75.

Dering, J. P. (2008b) Plant remains from five prehistoric archeological sites in the Lake Naconiche area, Nacogdoches County, Texas. In Perttula 2008b: 611–44.

Derrick, S. M. and Wilson, D. (1997) Cranial modeling as an ethnic marker among the prehistoric Caddo. *Bulletin of the Texas Archeological Society* 68: 139–46.

Derrick, S. M. and Wilson, D. (2001) The effects of epidemic disease on Caddo demographic structure. *Bulletin of the Texas Archeological Society* 72: 91–103.

Diehl, M. W. (2005) Morphological observations on recently recovered early agricultural period maize cob fragments from southern Arizona. *American Antiquity* 70 (2): 361–75.

Diggs Jr., G. M., Lipscomb, B. L., Reed, M. D. and O'Kennon, R. J. (2006) *Illustrated Flora of East Texas, Volume One: Introduction, Pteridophytes, Gymnosperms, and Monocotyledons* Sida, Botanical Miscellany 26. Botanical Research Institute of Texas, Fort Worth TX.

Dockall, H. D. (1994) Human skeletal remains from the Tyson Site (41SY92). *Journal of Northeast Texas Archaeology* 3: 37–50.

Dockall, J., Katauskas, S. and Fields, R. (2008) *National Register Testing of Four Sites in the Sabine Mine's Area M, Harrison County, Texas.* Reports of Investigations 157, Prewitt and Associates, Inc., Austin TX.

Dorsey, G. A. (1905) *Traditions of the Caddo.* Publication 41, Carnegie Institution of Washington, Washington, DC. Reprinted 1997 by University of Nebraska Press, Lincoln NE.

Drennan, R. D., Berrey, C. A. and Peterson, C. E. (2015) *Regional Settlement Demography in Archaeology.* Eliot Werner, Clinton Corners NY.

Drooker, P. B. (2004) Pipes, leadership, and interregional interaction in protohistoric midwestern and northeastern North America. In In *Smoking and Culture: The Archaeology of Tobacco Pipes in Eastern North America*, eds S. Rafferty and R. Mann: 73–123. University of Tennessee Press, Knoxville TN.

Duffield, L. F. and Jelks, E. B. (1961) *The Pearson Site: a historic Indian Site at Iron Bridge Reservoir, Rains County, Texas.* Archaeology Series 4. Department of Anthropology, University of Texas, Austin TX.

Dye, D. H. (2008) *War Paths, Peace Paths: An Archaeology of Cooperation and Conflict in Native Eastern North America.* AltaMira Press, Lanham MA.

Dye, D. H. and King, A. (2007) Desecrating the Sacred Ancestor Temples: chiefly conflict and violence in the American Southeast. In *North American Indigenous Warfare and Ritual Violence*, eds R. J. Chacon and R. G. Mendoza: 160–81. University of Arizona Press, Tucson AZ.

Early, A. M. (1988) *Standridge: Caddoan Settlement in a Mountain Environment.* Research Series 29, Arkansas Archeological Survey, Fayetteville AR.

Early, A. M. (1993a) Hardman and Caddoan saltmaking. In *Caddoan Saltmakers in the Ouachita Valley: the Hardman Site*, ed. A. M. Early: 223–34. Research Series 43. Arkansas Archeological Survey, Fayetteville AR.

Early, A. M. (1993b) Finding the middle passage: the Spanish journey from the Swamplands to Caddo Country. In Young and Hoffman (eds) 1993: 68–77.

Early, A. M. (2000a) The Caddos of the trans-Mississippi south. In *Indians of the Greater Southeast*, ed. B. G. McEwan: 122–41. University Press of Florida, Gainesville FL.

Early, A. M. (ed.) (2000b) *Forest Farmsteads: A Millennium of Human Occupation at Winding Stair in the Ouachita Mountains.* Research Series 57. Arkansas Archeological Survey, Fayetteville AR.

Early, A. M. (2004) Prehistory of the Western Interior after 500 B.C. In *Handbook of North American Indians, Southeast*, Vol. 14, ed. R. B. Fogelson: 560–73. Smithsonian Institution, Washington DC.

Early, A. M. (2014) What does "Long Hat's Camp" really tell us? A consideration of the meaning of two popular photographs to Caddo studies. *Bulletin of the Texas Archeological Society* 85: 49–59.

Eckert, S. L., Schleher, K. L. and James, W. D. (2015) Communities of identity, communities of practice: understanding Santa Fe black-on-white pottery in the Espanola Basin of New Mexico. *Journal of Archaeological Science* 63: 1–12.

Eerkens, J. W. (2003) Residential mobility and pottery use in the western Great Basin. *Current Anthropology* 44 (5): 728–38.

Ellis, L. W. (2013) Woodland ceramics in East Texas and a case study of Mill Creek Culture ceramics. *Bulletin of the Texas Archeological Society* 84: 137–80.

Ellis, L. W., Rogers, R., Wallace, C., Burden, D., Burden, A,. Kalter, A., Smith, M. and Heiligenstein, C. (2013) *Data Recovery at the Hawkwind Site (41HS915), Harrison County, Texas*. Report 138, Archeological Studies Program, Texas Department of Transportation, Austin TX.

Elson, K. M., Smith, C. and Perttula, T. K. (2004) Additional maize studies. In Rogers and Perttula 2004: 337–344.

Emerson, T. E. (1989) Water, serpents, and the underworld: an exploration into Cahokian symbolism. In *The Southeastern Ceremonial Complex: Artifacts and Analysis, The Cottonlandia Conference*, ed. P. Galloway: 45–92. University of Nebraska Press, Lincoln NE.

Emerson, T. E. (2007) Cahokia and the evidence for late Pre-Columbian war in the North American midcontinent. In *North American Indigenous Warfare and Ritual Violence*, eds R. J. Chacon and R. G. Mendoza: 129–48. University of Arizona Press, Tucson AZ.

Emerson, T. E. (2015) The Earth Goddess cult at Cahokia. In *Medieval Mississippians: The Cahokian World*, eds T. R. Pauketat and S. M. Alt: 54–61. School for Advanced Research Press, Santa Fe NM.

Emerson, T. E., Hedman, K. M., Hargrave, E. A., Cobb, D. E. and Thompson A. R. (2016) Paradigms lost: reconfiguring Cahokia's Mound 72 beaded burial. *American Antiquity* 81 (3): 405–25.

Erickson, E. C. and Corbin, J. E. (1996) *Archaeological Survey and Cultural Resource Assessment of Mission Tejas State Historical Park, Houston County, Texas*. Texas Parks and Wildlife Department, Public Lands Division, Cultural Resources Program, Austin TX.

Espinosa, F. I. F. de (1927) Descriptions of the Tejas or Asinai Indians, 1691–1722, Trans M. A. Hatcher. *Southwestern Historical Quarterly* 31: 150–80.

Ewers, J. C. (ed.) (1969) *The Indians of Texas in 1830*. Smithsonian Institution Press, Washington DC.

Fenn, E. A. (2014) *Encounters at the Heart of the World: A History of the Mandan People*. Hill and Wang, New York.

Fields, R. C. (2014) The Titus Phase from the top and bottom: looking at sociopolitical organization through the Pine Tree Mound and U.S. Highway 271 Mount Pleasant Relief Route Projects. *Bulletin of the Texas Archeological Society* 85: 111–46.

Fields, R. C. and Gadus, E. F. (2012a) *Archeology of the Nadaco Caddo: The View from the Pine Tree Mound Site (41HS15), Harrison County, Texas* (2 vols). Reports of Investigations 164, Prewitt and Associates Inc., Austin TX.

Fields, R. C. and Gadus, E. F. (2012b) The Pine Tree Mound Site and the archeology of the Nadaco Caddo. *Bulletin of the Texas Archeological Society* 83: 23–80.

Fields, R. C., Blake, M. E. and Kibler, K. W. (1997) *Synthesis of the Prehistoric and Historic Archeology of Cooper Lake, Delta and Hopkins Counties, Texas*. Reports of Investigations 104, Prewitt and Associates Inc., Austin TX.

Fields, R. C., Hatfield, V. L., Burden, D, Gadus, E. F., Wilder, M. C. and Kibler K. W. (2014) *Testing and Data Recovery Excavations at 11 Native American Archeological Sites along the U.S. Highway 271 Mount Pleasant Relief Route, Titus County, Texas* (2 vols). Reports of Investigations 168. Prewitt and Associates Inc., Austin TX.

Flores, D. L. (ed.) (1984) *Jefferson & Southwestern Exploration: The Freeman & Custis Accounts of the Red River Expedition of 1806*. University of Oklahoma Press, Norman OK.

Foik, P. J. (1999) Captain Don Domingo Ramon's Diary of his expedition into Texas in 1716. In *Wilderness Mission: Preliminary Studies of the Texas Catholic Historical Society II*, ed. J. F. de la Teja: 129–48. Studies in Southwestern Catholic History 2. Texas Catholic Historical Society, Austin TX.

Ford, R. I. (1982) The Archeobotany of the Deshazo Site. In *The Deshazo Site, Nacogdoches County, Texas, Volume 1: The Site, Its Setting, Investigation, Cultural Features, Artifacts of Non-Native Manufacture, and Subsistence Remains*, ed. D. A. Story: 158–63. Texas Antiquities Permit Series 7. Texas Antiquities Committee, Austin TX.

Forrestal, P. P. (1999) Pena's Diary of the Aguayo Expedition. In *Wilderness Mission: Preliminary Studies of the Texas Catholic Historical Society II*, ed. J. F. de la Teja: 161–214. Studies in Southwestern Catholic History 2. Texas Catholic Historical Society, Austin TX.

Foster, W. C. (1995) *Spanish Expeditions into Texas, 1689–1768*. University of Texas Press, Austin TX.

Foster, W. C. (ed.) (1998) *The La Salle Expedition to Texas: The Journal of Henri Joutel, 1684–1687*. Texas State Historical Association, Austin TX.

Foster, W. C. (2008) *Historic Native Peoples of Texas*. University of Texas Press, Austin TX.

Fowles, S. M. (2013) *An Archaeology of Doings: Secularism and the Study of Pueblo Religion*. School for Advanced Research Press, Santa Fe NM.

Fritz, G. J. (1986) Prehistoric Ozark Agriculture: The University of Arkansas Rockshelter Collections. Ph.D. dissertation, Department of Anthropology, University of North Carolina-Chapel Hill.

Fritz, G. J. (1990) Multiple pathways to farming in Precontact North America. *Journal of World Prehistory* 4: 387–435.

Fritz, G. J. (1993) Archaeobotanical analysis. In *Caddoan Saltmakers in the Ouachita Valley: The Hardman Site*, ed. A. M. Early: 159–68. Research Series 43. Arkansas Archeological Survey, Fayetteville AR.

Fritz, G. J. (2006) Archeobotanical remains from the Hudnall-Pirtle Site (41RK4), Rusk County, Texas. *Caddoan Archeology Journal* 15: 133–7.

Fritz, G. J. (2011) The role of "tropical" crops in early North America. In *The Subsistence Economies of Indigenous North American Societies*, ed. B. D. Smith: 503–16. Smithsonian Institution Scholarly Press, Washington DC.

Gadus, E. F. (2013) Twisted serpents and fierce birds: structural variation in Caddo engraved ceramic bottle motifs. *Bulletin of the Texas Archeological Society* 84: 213–45.

Gadus, E. F., Fields, R. C., McWilliams, J. K., Dockall, J. and Wilder, M. C. (2006) *National Register Testing of Seven Prehistoric Sites in the Sabine Mine's Area Q, Harrison County, Texas*. Reports of Investigations 147. Prewitt and Associates Inc., Austin TX.

Gautney, J. R. and Holliday, T. W. (2015) New estimations of habitable land area and human population size at the Last Glacial Maximum. *Journal of Archaeological Science* 58: 103–12.

Gilmore, K. (1986) *French-Indian Interaction at an Early Eighteenth Century Post: The Roseborough Lake Site, Bowie County, Texas*. Contributions in Archaeology 3. Institute of Applied Sciences, North Texas State University, Denton TX.

Gilmore, K. and Gill-King, H. (1991) An archeological footnote to history. *Bulletin of the Texas Archeological Society* 60: 303–24.

Girard, J. S. (1997) Caddoan settlement in the Red River floodplain: perspectives from the Willow Chute Bayou Area, Bossier Parish, Louisiana. *Louisiana Archaeology* 22: 143–62.

Girard, J. S. (2010) Caddo communities of northwest Louisiana. In *Archaeology of Louisiana*, ed. M. A. Rees: 195–210. Louisiana State University Press, Baton Rouge LA.

Girard, J. S. (2014) The James Pace Site (16DS268) and Early Caddo developments along the upper Sabine River. *Bulletin of the Texas Archeological Society* 85: 61–81.

Girard, J. S. and Perttula, T. K. (2016) Copper artifacts from Caddo Sites in the southern Caddo area. *Caddo Archeology Journal* 26: 19–28.

Girard, J. S., Perttula, T. K. and Trubitt, M. B. (2014) *Caddo Connections: Cultural Interactions Within and Beyond the Caddo World*. Rowan & Littlefield, Lanham MD.

Glowacki, D. M. (2015) *Living and Leaving: A Social History of Regional Depopulation in Thirteenth-Century Mesa Verde*. University of Arizona Press, Tucson AZ.

Goldborer, S. E. (2002) Macrobotanical evidence of subsistence at Timber Hill. In Parsons *et al.* 2002: 81–6.

Gonzalez, B. (2005) Caddo tribal religious burial ceremonies beyond archeology. In Gonzalez *et al.* 2005: 55–59.

Gonzalez, B., Cast, R., Perttula, T. K. and Nelson, B. (2005) *A Rediscovering of Caddo Heritage: The W. T. Scott Collection at the American Museum of Natural History and Other Caddo Collections from Arkansas and Louisiana*. Historic Preservation Program, Caddo Nation of Oklahoma, Binger OK.

Good, C. E. (1982) Analysis of structures, burials, and other cultural features. In D. A. Story (ed.) 1982: 51–110.

Goode, G. T., Perttula, T. K., Bush, L. L., Marceaux, S., Schniebs, L. and Todd, J. (2015) *Excavations at the Early Caddo Period Mound Pond Site (41HS12) in Harrison County, Texas*. Special Publication 38. Friends of Northeast Texas Archeology, Austin and Pittsburg TX.

Gremillion, K. J. (2007) Southeast plants. In *Environment, Origins, and Population*, ed. D. H. Ubelaker: 388–95. Handbook of North American Indians vol. 3. Smithsonian Institution, Washington DC.

Griffith, W. J. (1954) *The Hasinai Indians of East Texas as Seen by Europeans, 1687–1772*. Philological and Documentary Studies 2 (3). Middle American Research Institute, Tulane University, New Orleans LA.

Gulick, C. A. and Elliot, K. (eds) (1922) *The Papers of Mirabeau Buonaparte Lamar, Volume II*. Texas State Library, Austin TX.

Hackett, C. W. (ed. and trans.) (1931–1946) *Pichardo's Treatise on the Limits of Louisiana and Texas* (4 vols). University of Texas Press, Austin TX.

Hally, D. J. (2008) *King: The Social Archaeology of a Late Mississippian Town in Northwestern Georgia*. University of Alabama Press, Tuscaloosa AL.

Hamilton, D. L. (1997) Observations on Caddoan burial practices at the Sanders Site (41LR2). *Bulletin of the Texas Archeological Society* 68: 115–34.

Harris, R. K. (1953a) Two recent trips to sites in Fannin and Lamar Counties. *The Record* 11 (5): 19–20. Dallas Archeological Society, Dallas TX.

Harris, R. K. (1953b) The Sam Kaufman Site, Red River County, Texas. *Bulletin of the Texas Archeological Society* 24: 43–68.

Harris, R. K. and Harris, I. M. (1967) Trade beads, projectile points, and knives. In *A Pilot Study of Wichita Indian Archeology and Ethnohistory*, assem. R. E. Bell, E. B. Jelks and W. W. Newcomb: 129–62. Final report for Grant GS-964, National Science Foundation, Washington DC.

Harris, R. K., Harris, I. M., Blaine, J. C. and Blaine, J. (1965) A preliminary archeological and documentary study of the Womack Site, Lamar County, Texas. *Bulletin of the Texas Archeological Society* 36: 287–365.

Hart, J. P. (1982) An Analysis of the Aboriginal Ceramics

from the Washington Square Mound Site, Nacogdoches County, Texas. Master's thesis, Department of Anthropology, Northeast Louisiana University, Monroe.

Hart, J. P. (2014) *An Analysis of the Aboriginal Ceramics from the Washington Square Mound Site, Nacogdoches County, Texas*. Stephen F. Austin State University Press, Nacogdoches TX.

Hart, J. P. (2016) Networking the Past. Paper presented at the 58th Caddo Conference, Nacogdoches, Texas.

Hart, J. P. and Perttula, T. K. (2010) The Washington Square Mound Site and a southeastern ceremonial complex style zone among the Caddo of northeastern Texas. *Midcontinental Journal of Archaeology*: 199–228.

Hatcher, M. A. (1927) Descriptions of the Tejas or Asinai Indians, 1691–1722, Parts I–IV. *Southwestern Historical Quarterly* 30-1.

Hatcher, M. A. (1999) The expedition of Don Domingo Teran de los Rios into Texas. In *Wilderness Mission: Preliminary Studies of the Texas Catholic Historical Society II*, ed. J. F. de la Teja: 1–66. Studies in Southwestern Catholic History 2. Texas Catholic Historical Society, Austin TX.

Hawkins, M. G. and Hicks, T. J. (2010) Glasco, Jesse Martin. Handbook of Texas Online (http://www.rshaonline.org/handbook/online/articles/fg103, accessed November 9, 2015). Published by the Texas State Historical Association.

Heartfield, Price and Greene, Inc. (1988) *Data Recovery at 41HS74, Harrison County, Texas*. Heartfield, Price, and Greene, Inc., Monroe LA.

Henderson, J. (1982) Faunal analysis. In Story (ed.) 1982: 131–57.

Hodder, I. (2014) Temporal trends: the shapes and narratives of cultural change at Catalhoyuk. In *Integrating Catalhoyuk: Themes from the 2000–2008 seasons*, ed. I. Hodder. Catalhoyuk Research Project 10, British Institute at Ankara Monograph 49/Monumenta Archaeological 32. Cotsen Institute of Archaeology Press, University of California at Los Angeles CA.

Hoffman, M. P. (1967) Ceramic pipe style chronology along the Red River drainage in southwestern Arkansas. *Arkansas Archeologist* 8 (1): 4–14.

Hoffman, M. P. (1993) Identification of ethnic groups contacted by the de Soto Expedition in Arkansas. In Young and Hoffman (eds) 1993: 132–42.

Huckell, L. W. and VanPool, C. S. (2006) *Toloatzin* and Shamanic journeys: exploring the ritual role of sacred Datura in the prehistoric southwest. In *Religion of the Prehispanic Southwest*, ed. T. VanPool, C. S. VanPool and D. Phillips: 147–63. AltaMira Press, Lanham MD.

Hudson, C. (1976) *The Southeastern Indians*. University of Tennessee Press, Knoxville TN.

Hudson, C. (1993) Reconstructing the de Soto Expedition Route west of the Mississippi River: Summary and Contents. In Young and Hoffman (eds) 1993: 143–54.

Hudson, C. (1997) *Knights of Spain, Warriors of the Sun*. University of Georgia Press, Athens GA.

Jackson, A. T. (1930) Exploration of a burial site on R. L. Jaggers Farm, Franklin County, Texas. MS on file, Texas Archeological Research Laboratory, University of Texas at Austin.

Jackson, A. T. (1932) Exploration of a Cemetery on Paul Mitchell Farm in Bowie County, Texas. MS on file, Texas Archeological Research Laboratory, University of Texas at Austin.

Jackson, A. T. (1933) Some pipes of east Texas. *Bulletin of the Texas Archeological and Paleontological Society* 5: 69–86.

Jackson, A. T. (1936) A perpetual fire site. *Bulletin of the Texas Archeological and Paleontological Society* 8: 134–74.

Jackson, A. T. (2003) Hatchel Site and Paul Mitchell cemetery. *Caddoan Archeology Journal* 13 (2): 25–7.

Jackson, A. T., Goldstein, M. S. and Krieger, A. D. (2000) *The 1931 Excavations at the Sanders Site, Lamar County, Texas: Notes on the Fieldwork, Human Osteology, and Ceramics*. Archival Series 2. Texas Archeological Research Laboratory, University of Texas at Austin TX.

Jackson, H. E., Scott, S. L. and Schambach, F. F. (2012) At the House of the Priest: faunal remains from the Crenshaw Site (3MI6), southwest Arkansas. In *The Archaeology of the Caddo*, ed. T. K. Perttula and C. P. Walker: 47–85. University of Nebraska Press, Lincoln NE.

Jackson, J. (1999) *Shooting the Sun: Cartographic Results of Military Activities in Texas, 1689–1829* (2 vols). Book Club of Texas, Lubbock TX.

Jackson, M. K., Middlebrook, T., Avery, G., Shafer, H. and Meissner, B. (2012) *Trade and Cultural Interaction along El Camino Real de los Tejas During the Spanish Colonial and Republic Periods in Nacogdoches County, Texas* (2 vols). Nine Flags Museum, Nacogdoches TX.

Jackson, R. H. (2004) Congregation and depopulation: demographic patterns in the Texas Missions. *Journal of South Texas* 17 (2): 7–38.

Jackson, R. H. (2005) *Missions and the Frontiers of Spanish America: A Comparative Study of the Impact of Environmental, Economic, Political, and Socio-cultural Variations on the Missions in the Rio de la Plata Region and on the Northern Frontier of New Spain*. Pentacle Press, Scottsdale AZ.

Jelks, E. B. (1961) *Excavations at Texarkana Reservoir, Sulphur River, Texas*. River Basin Surveys Papers 21, Bureau of Ethnology Bulletin 179. Smithsonian Institution, Washington DC.

Jelks, E. B. (1965) The Archeology of McGee Bend Reservoir, Texas. Ph.D. dissertation, Department of Anthropology, The University of Texas at Austin.

Jelks, E. B. and Tunnell, C. D. (1959) *The Harroun Site, A Fulton Aspect Component of the Caddoan Area, Upshur*

County, Texas. Archaeology Series 2. Department of Anthropology, University of Texas at Austin TX.

Johannessen, S. (1984) Plant remains from the Edelhart Phase. In *The BBB Motor Site*, T. E. Emerson and D. E. Jackson: 169–89. American Bottom Archaeology FAI-270 Report 6. University of Illinois Press, Champaign IL.

Johnson, L., Jr. (1962) The Yarbrough and Miller Sites of northeastern Texas, with a preliminary definition of the LaHarpe aspect. *Bulletin of the Texas Archeological Society* 32: 141–284.

Jones, B. C. (1968) The Kinsloe Focus: A Study of Seven Historic Caddoan Sites in Northeast Texas. Master's thesis, Department of Anthropology, University of Oklahoma, Norman.

Jones, E. E. (2014) Spatiotemporal analysis of Old World diseases in North America, A.D. 1519–1807. *American Antiquity* 79 (3): 487–506.

Jones, V. H. (1949) Maize from the Davis Site: its nature and interpretation. In Newell and Krieger 1949: 241–9.

Kay, M. and Sabo, G. III (2006) Mortuary ritual and winter solstice imagery of the Harlan-style charnel house. *Southeastern Archaeology* 25 (1): 29–47.

Kelley, D. B. (2006) *The Burnitt Site: A Late Caddoan Occupation in the Uplands of the Sabine River Basin of Louisiana*. Coastal Environments Inc, Baton Rouge LA.

Kelley, D. B. (2012) The Belcher Phase: sixteenth- and seventeenth-century Caddo occupation of the Red River Valley in northwest Louisiana and southwest Arkansas. In *The Archaeology of the Caddo*, eds T. K. Perttula and C. P. Walker: 411–30. University of Nebraska Press, Lincoln NE.

Kelley, D. B., Hunter, D. G., Roberts, K. M., Scott, S. L. and Haley, B. S. (2010) The Burnitt Site (16SA204): a Late Caddoan occupation in the uplands of the Sabine River Basin. *Louisiana Archaeology* 31: 4–33.

Kemp, L. (2015) Regional considerations and drought history. In McKee *et al.* 2015: 415–31.

Kenmotsu, N. A. (1992) The Mayhew Site: a possible Hasinai farmstead, Nacogdoches County, Texas. *Bulletin of the Texas Archeological Society* 63: 135–73.

Kenmotsu, N. A. (2006) *Investigations at the Salt Well Slough Site (41RR204), a Salt Making Site in Red River County, Texas*. Archaeological Reports Series 4. Texas Historical Commission, Austin TX.

Kenmotsu, N. A., Bruseth, J. E. and Corbin, J. E. (1993) Moscoso and the route in Texas: a reconstruction. In Young and Hoffman (eds) 1993: 106–31.

Kidder, T. R. (1998) Re-thinking Caddoan-Lower Mississippi Valley interaction. In *The Native History of the Caddo: Their Place in Southeastern Archeology and Ethnohistory*, ed. T. K. Perttula and J. E. Bruseth: 129–44. Studies in Archeology 30. Texas Archeological Research Laboratory, University of Texas at Austin TX.

Kidder, T. R. and Sherwood, S. C. (2016) Look to the earth: the search for ritual in the context of mound construction. *Archaeological and Anthropological Sciences*, DOI:10.1007/s12520-016-0369-1.

King, A. (2006) Leadership strategies and the nature of Mississippian chiefdoms in northern Georgia. In *Leadership and Polity in Mississippian Society*, eds B. M. Butler and P. D. Welch: 73–90. Occasional Paper 33. Center for Archaeological Investigations, Southern Illinois University, Carbondale IL.

Kintigh, K. W., Altschul, J. H., Beaudry, M. C., Drennan, R. D., Kinzig, A. P., Kohler, T. A., Limp, W. F., Maschner, H. D. G., Michener, W. K., Pauketat, T. R., Peregrine, P., Sabloff, J. A., Wilkinson, T. J., Wright, H. T. and Zeder, M. A. (2014) Grand challenges for archaeology. *American Antiquity* 79 (1): 5–24.

Kiwat Hasinay Foundation (2001) *Nusht'uhti?ti? Hasinay Caddo Phrasebook: Handy Words and Phrases as used in Real Life*. Kiwat Hasinay Foundation, Binger OK.

Kleinschmidt, U. K. W. (1982) Review and Analysis of the A. C. Saunders Site, 41AN19, Anderson County, Texas. Master's thesis, Department of Anthropology, University of Texas at Austin.

Knight, V. J. (2001) Feasting and the emergence of Platform Mound ceremonialism in eastern North America. In *Feasts: Archaeological and Ethnographic Perspectives on Food, Politics, and Power*, eds M. Dietler and B. Hayden: 311–33. Smithsonian Institution Press, Washington DC.

Krieger, A. D. (1946) *Culture Complexes and Chronology in Northern Texas, with Extensions of Puebloan Datings to the Mississippi Valley*. Publication 4640. University of Texas, Austin TX.

Krieger, A. D. (1947) The eastward extension of Puebloan datings toward cultures of the Mississippi Valley. *American Antiquity* 12 (3): 141–8.

Krieger, A. D. (1948) Importance of the "Gilmore Corridor" in culture contacts between Middle America and the eastern United States. *Bulletin of the Texas Archeological and Paleontological Society* 19: 155–78.

Krieger, A. D. (2000) The pottery of the Sanders Farm. In Jackson *et al.* 2000: 131–44.

Krieger, A. D. (2009) *Archaeological Horizons in the So-Called Caddo Area*. Archival Series 3, Texas Archeological Research Laboratory, University of Texas at Austin TX.

La Vere, D. (1998) *Life Among the Texas Indians: The WPA Narratives*. Texas A&M University Press, College Station TX.

Lankford, G. E. (2007) The Great Serpent in eastern North America. In *Ancient Objects and Sacred Realms: Interpretations of Mississippian Iconography*, eds F. K. Reilly III and J. F. Garber: 174–212. University of Texas Press, Austin TX.

Lankford, G. E. (2008) *Looking for Lost Lore: Studies in Folklore, Ethnology, and Iconography.* University of Alabama Press, Tuscaloosa AL.

Lankford, G. E. (2012) Weeding out the noded. *Arkansas Archeologist* 50: 50–68.

Lee, C. (1997) Paleopathology of the Hatchel-Mitchell-Moores Sites, Bowie County, Texas. *Bulletin of the Texas Archeological Society* 68: 161–77.

Lemley, H. J. (1936) Discoveries indicating a Pre-Caddo culture on Red River in Arkansas. *Bulletin of the Texas Archeological and Paleontological Society* 8: 25–55.

Loomis, N. M. and Nasatir, A. P. (1965) *Pedro Vial and the Roads to Santa Fe.* University of Oklahoma Press, Norman OK.

Mallouf, R. J. (1976) *Archeological Investigations at Proposed Big Pine Lake, 1974-1975: Lamar and Red River Counties, Texas.* Archeological Survey Report 18. Office of the State Archeologist, Texas Historical Commission, Austin TX.

Marceaux, P. S. 2011) The Archaeology and Ethnohistory of the Hasinai Caddo: Material Culture and the Course of European Contact. Ph.D. dissertation, Department of Anthropology, University of Texas at Austin.

Marceaux, P. S. and Perttula, T. K. (2010) Negotiating borders: the southern Caddo and their relationships with colonial governments in east Texas. In *American Indians and the Market Economy, 1775-1850*, eds L. Greene and M. R. Plane: 80–97. University of Alabama Press, Tuscaloosa AL.

Marceaux, P. S. and Wade, M. F. (2014) Missions untenable: experiences of the Hasinai Caddo and the Spanish in east Texas. In *Indigenous Landscapes and Spanish Missions: New Perspectives from Archaeology and Ethnohistory*, ed L. M. Panich and T. D. Schneider: 57–75. University of Arizona Press, Tucson AZ.

Martin, G. (1936) Supplementary Field Notes by Glenn Martin, Paul Mitchell Place, Bowie County, Texas, Sunday, November 22, 1936. MS on file, Texas Archeological Research Laboratory, University of Texas at Austin.

Mathews, W. H., Jr. (1935) Catalog of Prehistoric Indian Pottery Excavated by Wm. H. Mathews, Jr., Texarkana, Texas. MS on file, Texas Archeological Research Laboratory, University of Texas at Austin.

McClurkan, B. B., Field, W. T. and Woodall J. N. (1966) *Excavations in Toledo Bend Reservoir, 1964-65.* Papers of the Texas Archeological Salvage Project 8. Texas Archeological Salvage Project, University of Texas at Austin TX.

McClurkan, B. B., Jelks, E. B. and Jensen, H. P. (1980) Jonas Short and Coral Snake Mounds: a comparison. *Louisiana Archaeology* 6: 173–206.

McKee, A., Frederick, C. D., Perttula, T. K., Selden, R. Z., Bush, L., Kemp, L., Gregory, B., Yost, C., Scott Cummings, L., Ferguson, J. R., Glascock, M. D., Tomka, S., Cecil, L., Masiello, C., Gao, X., Goodmaster, C. and Beasley, V. III (2015) *Data Recovery Investigations: Murvaul Creek Site (41PN175), Panola County, Texas.* Archeological Studies Program Report 165. Texas Department of Transportation, Environmental Affairs Division, Austin TX.

McKinnon, D. P. (2013) Landscape as a ritual object: exploring some thoughts on organized space in the Great Bend region of southwestern Arkansas. *Caddo Archeology Journal* 23: 67–84.

McKinnon, D. P. (2015) Zoomorphic effigy pendants: an examination of style, medium, and distribution in the Caddo area. *Southeastern Archaeology* 34 (2): 116–135.

McKinnon, D. P. (2016) *Report on Magnetic Gradient Surveys at Four Caddo Sites in East Texas.* Department of Anthropology, University of Central Arkansas, Conway AR.

Means, B. K. (2013) Introduction: "Alphabet Soup" and American archaeology. In *Shovel Ready: Archaeology and Roosevelt's New Deal for America*, ed. B. K. Means: 1–18. University of Alabama Press, Tuscaloosa AL.

Middlebrook, T. (1994) An update of archaeological investigations at the Tyson Site (41SY92). *Journal of Northeast Texas Archaeology* 3: 1–36.

Middlebrook, T. (2007) A survey of Historic Caddo sites in Nacogdoches County. *Journal of Northeast Texas Archaeology* 26: 99–115.

Middlebrook, T. (2014) Early European descriptions of Hasinai elites and understanding prehistoric Caddo mortuary practices in Shelby County, Texas. *Bulletin of the Texas Archeological Society* 85: 83–110.

Miller, J. (1996) Changing moons: a history of Caddo religion. *Plains Anthropologist* 41 (157): 243–59.

Miller, J. (2015) *Ancestral Mounds: Vitality and Volatility of Native America.* University of Nebraska Press, Lincoln NE.

Mills, B. J., Peeples, M. A., Haas, Jr., W. R., Borck, L., Clark, J. J. and Roberts, J. M. Jr. (2015) Multiscalar perspectives on social networks in the late Prehispanic Southwest. *American Antiquity* 80 (1): 3–24.

Milner, G. R. (2015) Population decline and culture change in the American Midcontinent: bridging the prehistoric and historic divide. In *Beyond Germs: Native Depopulation in North America*, eds C. M. Cameron, P. Kelton and A. C. Swedlund: 50–73. University of Arizona Press, Tucson AZ.

Milner, G. R. and Chaplin, G. (2010) Eastern North American population at A.D. 1500. *American Antiquity* 75: 707–26.

Milner, G. R., Chaplin, G. and Zavodny, E. (2013) Conflict and societal change in late prehistoric Eastern North America. *Evolutionary Anthropology* 22: 96–102.

Miroir, M. E., Harris, R. K., Blaine, J. C. and McVay, J. (1973) Bernard de la Harpe and the Nassonite Post. *Bulletin of the Texas Archeological Society* 44: 113–67.

Monaghan, G. W., Schilling, T., Krus, A. M. and Peebles, C. S. (2013) Mound construction chronology at Angel Mounds: episodic mound construction and ceremonial events. *Midcontinental Journal of Archaeology* 38 (2): 155–70.

Moore, C. B. (1912) Some Aboriginal sites on Red River. *Journal of the Academy of Natural Sciences of Philadelphia* 14 (4): 526–636.

Neighbours, K. E. (1973) *Indian Exodus: Texas Indian Affairs, 1835–1859*. Nortex Offset Publications, Quannah TX.

Neighbours, K. E. (1975) *Robert Simpson Neighbors and the Texas Frontier, 1836–1859*. Texian Press, Waco TX.

Newell, H. P. and Krieger, A. D. (1949) *The George C. Davis Site, Cherokee County, Texas*. Memoir 5. Published jointly by the Society for American Archaeology and the University of Texas, Menasha WI.

Newkumet, V. B. and Meredith, H. L. (1988) *Ha: A Traditional History of the Caddo Confederacy*. Texas A&M University Press, College Station TX.

Norenzayan, A. (2013) *Big Gods: How Religion Transformed Cooperation and Conflict*. Princeton University Press, Princeton NJ.

Oates, S. B. (ed.) (1963) *Rip Ford's Texas*. University of Texas Press, Austin TX.

O'Brien, M. J. and Lyman, R. L. (1999) *Seriation, Stratigraphy, and Index Fossils: The Backbone of Archaeological Dating*. Kluwer Academic/Plenum, New York.

Ondaatje, M. (1999) *Handwriting*. Knopf, New York.

Osburn, T., Bruseth, J. and Pierson, W. (2008) Magnetometer investigations at the George C. Davis site, a prehistoric Caddo village. *Bulletin of the Texas Archeological Society* 79: 191–200.

Parsons, E. C. (1941) *Notes on the Caddo*. Number 57, Memoirs of the American Anthropological Association and Supplement to *American Anthropologist* 43. Menasha WI.

Parsons, M. L. (2015) *Archeological Investigations at Lake Gilmer, Upshur County, Texas Mitigation Phase*. Archeology Reports Series 6. Texas Historical Commission, Austin TX.

Parsons, M. L., Bruseth, J. E., Bagur, J., Goldborer, S. E. and McCrocklin, C. (2002) *Finding Sha'chahdinnih (Timber Hill): The Last Village of the Kadohadacho in the Caddo Homeland*. Archeological Reports Series 3. Texas Historical Commission, Austin TX.

Pauketat, T. R. (2007) *Chiefdoms and other Archaeological Delusions*. AltaMira Press, Lanham MD.

Pauketat, T. R. (2013) *An Archaeology of the Cosmos: Rethinking Agency and Religion in Ancient America*. Routledge, London and New York.

Pauketat, T. R. (2015) The Caddo conundrum. In *Medieval Mississippians: The Cahokian World*, eds T. R. Pauketat and S. M. Alt: 14. School for Advanced Research Press, Santa Fe NM.

Pauketat, T. R. (forthcoming) Illuminating triangulations: moonlight and the Mississippian world. In *The Oxford Handbook of Light in Archaeology*, eds C. Papadopoulos and G. Earl. Oxford University Press, Oxford.

Pauketat, T. R., Alt, S. M. and Kruchten, J. D. (2017) The emerald acropolis: elevating the moon and water in the rise of Cahokia. *Antiquity* 91 (355): 207–22.

Peeples, M. A. and Roberts, J. M. Jr. (2013) To binarize or not to binarize: relational data and the construction of archaeological networks. *Journal of Archaeological Science* 40: 3001–10.

Perino, G. (1995) The Dan Holdeman Site (41RR11), Red River County, Texas. *Journal of Northeast Texas Archaeology* 6: 3–65.

Perttula, T. K. (1991) European contact and its effects on Aboriginal Caddoan populations between A.D. 1520 and A.D. 1680. In *Columbian Consequences, Vol. 3, The Spanish Borderlands in Pan-American Perspective*, ed. D. H. Thomas: 501–18. Smithsonian Institution Press, Washington DC.

Perttula, T. K. (1992) *"The Caddo Nation": Archaeological and Ethnohistoric Perspectives*. University of Texas Press, Austin TX.

Perttula, T. K. (1993a) Kee-Oh-Na-Wah'-Wah: the effects of European contact on the Caddoan Indians of Texas, Louisiana, Arkansas and Oklahoma. In *Ethnohistory and Archaeology: Approaches to Postcontact Change in the Americas*, eds J. D. Rogers and S. M. Wilson: 89–109. Plenum Press, New York.

Perttula, T. K. (1993b) The long-term consequences and effects of the de Soto Entrada on Aboriginal Caddoan populations. In Young and Hoffman (eds) 1993: 237–54.

Perttula, T. K. (1993c) The development of agriculture in northeast Texas before A.D. 1600. In *Archeology in the Eastern Planning Region, Texas: A Planning Document*, eds N. A. Kenmotsu and T. K. Perttula: 121–46. Cultural Resource Management Report 3. Department of Antiquities Protection, Texas Historical Commission, Austin TX.

Perttula, T. K. (ed.) (1999) *The Hurricane Hill Site (41HP106): The Archaeology of a Late Archaic/Early Ceramic and Early-Middle Caddoan Settlement in Northeast Texas* (2 vols). Special Publication 4. Friends of Northeast Texas Archaeology, Pittsburg and Austin TX.

Perttula, T. K. (2000) Functional and stylistic analyses of ceramic vessels from mortuary features at a 15th and 16th century Caddo site in northeast Texas. *Midcontinental Journal of Archaeology* 25 (1): 101–51.

Perttula, T. K. (2001) Three mid-1800s Caddo vessels from the Brazos Reserve. *Journal of Northeast Texas Archaeology* 14: 31–6.

Perttula, T. K. (2002) Archaeological evidence for the long-distance exchange of Caddo Indian ceramics in the Southern Plains, Midwest, and Southeastern

United States. In *Geochemical Evidence for Long-Distance Exchange*, ed. M. D. Glascock: 89–107. Bergin and Garvey, Westport CT.

Perttula, T. K. (2004a) The prehistoric and Caddoan archeology of the northeast Texas pineywoods. In *The Prehistory of Texas*, ed. T. K. Perttula: 370–407. Texas A&M University Press, College Station TX.

Perttula, T. K. (2004b), with contributions by T. E. Emerson and R. E. Hughes, 41HO64/41HO65, late 17th to early 18th century Caddo sites on San Pedro Creek in Houston County, Texas. *Bulletin of the Texas Archeological Society* 75: 85–103.

Perttula, T. K. (2005a) 1938–1939 WPA excavations at the Hatchel Site (41BW3) on the Red River in Bowie County, Texas. *Southeastern Archaeology* 24 (2): 180–98.

Perttula, T. K. (ed.) (2005b) *Archeological Investigations at the Pilgrim's Pride Site (41CP304), a Titus Phase Community in the Big Cypress Creek Basin, Camp County, Texas* (2 vols). Report of Investigations 30. Archeological & Environmental Consultants, LLC, Austin and Pittsburg TX.

Perttula, T. K. (2006) Winston's Mound and Shawnee Town: mound explorations by the Bureau of American Ethnology in Texas, 1882–1884. *Bulletin of the Texas Archeological Society* 76: 183–7.

Perttula, T. K. (2008a) Caddo agriculture on the Western Frontier of the eastern woodlands. *Plains Anthropologist* 53 (205): 79–105.

Perttula, T. K. (ed.) (2008b) *Lake Naconiche Archeology, Nacogdoches County, Texas: Results of the Data Recovery Excavations at Five Prehistoric Archeological Sites* (2 vols). Report of Investigations 60. Archeological & Environmental Consultants, LLC, Austin TX.

Perttula, T. K. (ed.) (2008c) The archeology of the Roitsch Site (41RR16), an Early to Historic Caddo Period village on the Red River in northeast Texas. In *Collected Papers from Past Texas Archeological Society Summer Field Schools*, ed. T. K. Perttula: 313–628. Special Publication 5. Texas Archeological Society, San Antonio TX.

Perttula, T. K. (2008d) Archeological survey of the Roitsch Farm and adjoining lands, 1991 and 1992 Texas Archeological Society Field School, Red River County, Texas. In *Collected Papers from Past Texas Archeological Society Summer Field Schools*, ed. T. K. Perttula: 173–312. Special Publication 5. Texas Archeological Society, San Antonio TX.

Perttula, T. K. (2009a) Extended entranceway structures in the Caddo archaeological area. *Southeastern Archaeology* 28 (1): 27–42.

Perttula, T. K. (2009b) Caddo ceramic and lithic artifacts from the Washington Square Mound Site (41NA49) in Nacogdoches County, Texas: 1985 Texas Archeological Field School Investigations. *Bulletin of the Texas Archeological Society* 80: 145–93.

Perttula, T. K. (assembler) (2011a) *Archaeological and Archaeogeophysical Investigations at an Early Caddo Mound Center in the Sabine River Basin of East Texas*, Special Publication 15. Friends of Northeast Texas Archaeology, Austin and Pittsburg TX.

Perttula, T. K. (2011b) Analysis of the prehistoric artifacts from the Pace McDonald Site (41AN51), Anderson County, Texas. *Journal of Northeast Texas Archaeology* 34: 35–54.

Perttula, T. K. (2012a) The archaeology of the Caddo in southwest Arkansas, northwest Louisiana, eastern Oklahoma, and east Texas: an introduction to the volume. In *The Archaeology of the Caddo*, eds T. K. Perttula and C. P. Walker: 1–25. University of Nebraska Press, Lincoln, NE.

Perttula, T. K. (2012b) The character of 15th to 17th century Caddo communities in the Big Cypress Creek Basin of northeastern Texas. In *Archaeology of the Caddo*, eds T. K. Perttula and C. P. Walker: 36–410. University of Nebraska Press, Lincoln NE.

Perttula, T. K. (2013) Caddo ceramics in East Texas. *Bulletin of the Texas Archeological Society* 84: 181–212.

Perttula, T. K. (2014a) *Archaeological Studies of the Hatchel Site (41BW3) on the Red River in Bowie County, Texas*. Special Publication 23. Friends of Northeast Texas Archaeology, Austin and Pittsburg TX.

Perttula, T. K. (2014b) *The Mitchell Site (41BW4): An Ancestral Caddo Settlement and Cemetery on McKinney Bayou, Bowie County, Texas*. Special Publication 32. Friends of Northeast Texas Archaeology, Pittsburg and Austin TX.

Perttula, T. K. (2014c) *The Hale and Keith Mounds in the Big Cypress Creek Basin in East Texas*. Special Publication 33. Friends of Northeast Texas Archaeology, Austin and Pittsburg TX.

Perttula, T. K. (2014d) *The Caddo Archaeology of the Musgano Site (41RK19) in the Sabine River Basin of East Texas*. Special Publication 28. Friends of Northeast Texas Archaeology, Austin Austin and Pittsburg TX.

Perttula, T. K. (ed.) (2014e) *The Eli Moores Site, a 17th to early 18th Century Caddo Site on the Red River, Bowie County, Texas*. Special Publication 31. Friends of Northeast Texas Archaeology, Austin and Pittsburg TX.

Perttula, T. K. (2015a) *Caddo Ceramic Vessels from the Hatchel Site (41BW3) on the Red River in Bowie County, Texas*. Special Publication 39. Friends of Northeast Texas Archaeology, Austin and Pittsburg TX.

Perttula, T. K. (2015b) Caddo sites on Patroon, Palo Gaucho, and Housen Bayous in Sabine County in the Sabine River Basin of East Texas. *Journal of Northeast Texas Archaeology* 54: 63–91.

Perttula, T. K. (2016a), with contributions by W. Troell, The A. S. Mann (41HE7/41AN201) and M. S. Roberts (41HE8) Sites in the Upper Neches River Basin, Henderson

County, Texas. *Journal of Northeast Texas Archaeology* 59: 1–24.

Perttula, T. K. (2016b) Utility ware ceramic metrics and Hasinai Caddo archaeology in east Texas. *Journal of Northeast Texas Archaeology* 70: 61–8.

Perttula, T. K. and Bruseth, J. E. (1983) Early Caddoan subsistence strategies, Sabine River Basin, east Texas. *Plains Anthropologist* 28 (99): 9–22.

Perttula, T. K. and Ellis, L. W. (2012) *The Hickory Hill Site (41CP408): Archeological Investigations at a Middle Caddo Site in the Little Cypress Creek Basin in East Texas.* Document 120055, Atkins North America Inc., Austin TX.

Perttula, T. K. and Nelson, B. (2001) *Archeological Investigations at the Camp Joy Mound (41UR144): A Titus Phase Earthen Mound at Lake O' the Pines, Upshur County, Texas.* Report of Investigations 44. Archeological and Environmental Consultants and Friends of Northeast Texas Archaeology, Austin and Pittsburg TX.

Perttula, T. K. and Nelson, B. (2003) *Archeological Investigations of Village Areas at the Hatchel Site (41BW3), Bowie County, Texas.* Report of Investigations 58. Archeological & Environmental Consultants, LLC, Austin and Pittsburg TX.

Perttula, T. K. and Nelson, B. (2004) *Archaeological Investigations at the Shelby Site (41CP71) on Greasy Creek, Camp County, Texas.* Special Publication 5. Friends of Northeast Texas Archaeology, Austin and Pittsburg TX.

Perttula, T. K. and Nelson, B. (2006) *Test Excavations at Three Caddo Sites at Mission Tejas State Park, Houston County, Texas.* Report of Investigations 76. Archeological & Environmental Consultants, LLC, Austin and Pittsburg TX.

Perttula, T. K. and Nelson, B. (2007) *Archeological Survey Investigations and Test Excavations at 41CE354 at the North and South lake areas of the H.R.C. Cherokee Tree Farm, L. P. Project, Cherokee County, Texas.* Report of Investigations 80. Archeological & Environmental Consultants, LLC, Austin and Pittsburg TX.

Perttula, T. K. and Nelson, B. (2013) *Two Middle Caddo Period Habitation Sites and Cemeteries in the Sabine River Basin, Gregg County, Texas.* Special Publication 27. Friends of Northeast Texas Archaeology, Pittsburg and Austin TX.

Perttula, T. K. and Nelson, B. (2016) Further surface collecting and shovel testing investigations at the Sanders Site (41LR2), Lamar County, Texas. *Journal of Northeast Texas Archaeology* 60: 53–65.

Perttula, T. K. and Rogers, R. (2007) The evolution of a Caddo community in northeastern Texas: the Oak Hill Village Site (41RK214), Rusk County, Texas. *American Antiquity* 72 (1): 71–94.

Perttula, T. K. and Rogers, R. (2012) The evolution of a Caddo community in northeast Texas. In *The Archaeology of the Caddo*, eds T. K. Perttula and C. P. Walker: 209–38. University of Nebraska Press, Lincoln NE.

Perttula, T. K. and Selden, R. Z. Jr. (2014) New radiocarbon dates from east Texas Caddo sites. *Journal of Northeast Texas Archaeology* 47: 1–8.

Perttual, t. K. and Selden, R. Z. (2015) Additional radiocarbon dates from east Texas Caddo sites. *Journal of Northeast Texas Archaeology* 52: 39–41.

Perttula, T. K. and Sherman, D. L. (2009) *Data Recovery Investigations at the Ear Spool Site (41TT653), Titus County, Texas.* Document 070205. PBS&J, Austin TX.

Perttula, T. K. and Skiles, B. D. (1989) Another look at an eighteenth century archaeological site in Wood County, Texas. *Southwestern Historical Quarterly* 92 (3): 417–35.

Perttula, T. K. and Skiles, B. D. (2014) The construction and eventual burning of the experimental Caddo house structure at the George C. Davis Site (41CE19) in east Texas. *Bulletin of the Texas Archeological Society* 85: 33–47.

Perttula, T. K. and Walker, C. P. (2008) *The History of Archaeological Investigations and Geophysical Survey at the Jamestown Mound Site (41SM54), an Archaeological Conservancy Preserve in Smith County, Texas.* Archeological & Environmental Consultants, LLC and Archaeo-Geophysical Associates, LLC, Austin TX.

Perttula, T. K. and Wilson, D. E. (2000), with contributions by M. Walters, An Early Caddoan Period cremation from the Boxed Springs Mound Site (41UR30) in Upshur County, Texas, and a report on previous archaeological investigations. *Journal of Northeast Texas Archaeology* 12: 31–71.

Perttula, T. K., Bruseth, J. E., Kenmotsu, N. A. and Martin, W. A. (1995) *Archeological Testing at the Cabe Mounds (41BW14), Bowie County, Texas.* Cultural Resource Management Report 8. Department of Antiquities Protection, Texas Historical Commission, Austin TX.

Perttula, T. K., Bush, L. L., Schniebs, L., Middlebrook, T. and Marceaux, P. S. (2010c) *An Early Historic Caddo Farmstead at the Henry M. Site (41NA60) in Nacogdoches County, Texas.* Stephen F. Austin State University Press, Nacogdoches TX.

Perttula, T. K., Cast, R., Gonzalez, B. and Nelson, B. (2009) *Documentation of Unassociated and Culturally Unidentifiable Funerary Objects in the U.S. Army Corps of Engineers, Fort Worth District Collections Housed at the Texas Archeological Research Laboratory at the University of Texas at Austin.* Special Publication 13. Friends of Northeast Texas Archaeology, Pittsburg and Austin TX.

Perttula, T. K., Kelley D. B. and Ricklis R. A. (assemblers and eds) (2011) *Archeological Investigations at the Lang Pasture Site (41AN38) in the Upper Neches River Basin of East Texas.* Report 129. Texas Department of Transportation, Archeological Studies Program, Environmental Affairs Division, Austin TX.

Perttula, T. K., Lee, D. B. and Cast, R. (2008) The first people of the Red River: the Caddo before and after Freeman and Custis. In *Freeman and Custis Red River Expedition of 1806: Two Hundred Years Later*, ed. L. M. Hardy: 81–110. Bulletin of the Museum of Life Sciences 14. Museum of Life Sciences, Louisiana State University in Shreveport LA.

Perttula, T. K., Nelson, B. and Walters, M. (2012c) *Caddo Archaeology at the Henry Spencer Site (41UR315) in the Little Cypress Creek Basin of East Texas*. Special Publication 20. Friends of Northeast Texas Archaeology, Pittsburg and Austin TX.

Perttula, T. K., Nelson, B. and Walters, M. (2014c) Renewed archaeologica investigations at the Sanders Site (41LR2), Lamar County, Texas. *Journal of Northeast Texas Archaeology* 47: 25–30.

Perttula, T. K., Nelson, B. and Walters, M. (2016a) *Caddo Ceramic Vessels from the Paul Mitchell Site (41BW4) on the Red River, Bowie County, Texas*. Special Publication 44. Friends of Northeast Texas Archaeology, Austin and Pittsburg TX.

Perttula, T. K., Nelson, B., Cast, R. L. and Gonzalez, B. (2010a) *The Clements Site (41CS25): A Late 17th to Early 18th-Century Nasoni Caddo Settlement and Cemetery*. Anthropological Papers 92. American Museum of Natural History, New York.

Perttula, T. K., Nelson, B., Walters, M. and Cast, R. (2014b) *Documentation of Caddo Funerary Objects from the Crenshaw Site (3MI6) in the Gilcrease Museum Collections*. Special Publication 19. Friends of Northeast Texas Archaeology, Pittsburg and Austin TX.

Perttula, T. K., Nelson, B., Walters, M. and Selden, R. Z. Jr. (2015) The Sanders Site (41LR2): a Middle to Historic Caddo settlement and mound center on the Red River in Lamar County, Texas. *Journal of Northeast Texas Archaeology* 50: 1–87.

Perttula, T. K., Selden, R. Z. Jr and Wilson, D. (2014a) Corn is life: temporal trends in the use of corn (*Zea mays*) by Caddo peoples from radiocarbon-dated samples and stable isotope analyses. *Bulletin of the Texas Archeological Society* 85: 159–81.

Perttula, T. K., Tate, M. Neff, H., Cogswell, J. W., Glascock, M. D., Skokan, E., Mulholland, S., Rogers, R. and Nelson, B. (1998) *Analysis of the Titus Phase Mortuary Assemblage at the Mockingbird Site, "Kahbakayammaahin" (41TT550)*. Document 970849, Espey, Huston & Associates Inc., Austin TX.

Perttula, T. K., Trubitt, M. B. and Girard, J. S. (2012a) The use of shell-tempered pottery in the Caddo area of the Southeastern United States. *Southeastern Archaeology* 30 (2): 242–67.

Perttula, T. K., Walters, M. and Nelson, B. (2012b) *Archeological Investigations at the Pace McDonald Site (41AN51): A Middle Caddo Mound Center in the Neches River Basin in East Texas*. Special Publication 21. Friends of Northeast Texas Archaeology, Pittsburg and Austin TX.

Perttula, T. K., Walters, M. and Nelson, B. (2016c) *Caddo Ceramic Vessels from the T. M. Sanders Site (41LR2) on the Red River in Lamar County, Texas*. Special Publication 41. Friends of Northeast Texas Archaeology, Austin and Pittsburg TX.

Perttula, T. K., Walters, M., Nelson, B. and McKee, A. (2016d) The M. S. Roberts Site (41HE8): Archaeological Investigations at a Caddo Mound Site in the Upper Neches River Basin in East Texas. *Journal of Northeast Texas Archaeology* 71 (in press).

Perttula, T. K., Walters, M., Nelson, B., Gonzalez, B. and Cast, R. (2010b), with a contribution by R. G. Franciscus, *Documentation of Associated and Unassociated Funerary Objects in the Stephen F. Austin State University Collections, Nacogdoches, Texas*. Stephen F. Austin State University Press, Nacogdoches TX.

Phillips, P. (1970) *Archaeological Survey in the Lower Yazoo Basin, Mississippi, 1949-1955*. Papers of the Peabody Museum of Archaeology and Ethnology 60. Harvard University, Cambridge MA.

Pinkerton, G. L. (2016) *Trammel's Trace: The First Road to Texas from the North*. Texas A&M University Press, College Station TX.

Powell, G. S. and Lopinot, N. H. (2000) Archeological plant remains from the Helm Site. In *Data Recovery at the Helm Site, 3HS449, Hot Spring County, Arkansas*, by R. H. Lafferty, A. Early, M. C. Sierzchula, M. C. Hill, G. S. Powell, N. H. Lopinot, L. S. Cummings, S. L. Scott, S. K. Nash, and T. K. Perttula: 187–229. MCRA Report 2000–1, Mid-Continental Research Associates, Lowell AR.

Prikryl, D. J. (2008) The 1991 and 1992 Texas Archeological Society Field School Excavations at the Fasken Site (41RR14), Red River County, Texas. In *Collected Papers from Past Texas Archaeological Society Summer Field Schools*, ed. T. K. Perttula: 125–71. Special Publication 5. Texas Archeological Society, San Antonio TX.

Rafferty, J. (2015) Owl Creek, Thelma, and Bessemer Mounds: large peripheral Mississippian mound groups and bet-hedging. In *Exploring Southeastern Archaeology*, eds P. Galloway and E. Peacock: 189–215. University Press of Mississippi, Jackson MS.

Rafferty, S. M. (2004) "They pass their lives in smoke, and at death fall into the fire": smoking pipes and mortuary ritual during the Early Woodland Period. In *Smoking and Culture: The Archaeology of Tobacco Pipes in Eastern North America*, eds S. Rafferty and R. Mann: 1–41. University of Tennessee Press, Knoxville TN.

Rafferty, S. M. and Mann, R. (2004) Introduction: Smoking Pipes and Culture. In *Smoking and Culture: The Archaeology of Tobacco Pipes in Eastern North America*, eds S. Rafferty and R. Mann: xi–xx. University of Tennessee Press, Knoxville TN.

Regnier, A. L., Hammerstedt, S. W. and Beale, N. H. (2014) The Grobin Davis Site: archaeogeophysics and settlement patterns at Caddo mound centers in southeastern Oklahoma. *Southeastern Archaeology* 33: 87–107.

Rodning, C. (2010) Place, landscape, and environment: anthropological archaeology in 2009. *American Anthropologist* 112 (2):180–90.

Rodning, C. B. and Mehta, J. M. (2016) Resilience and persistent places in the Mississippi River delta of southeastern Louisiana. In *Beyond Collapse: Archaeological Perspectives on Resilience, Revitalization, and Transformation in Complex Societies*, ed. R. K. Faulseit: 342–79. Occasional Paper 42. Center for Archaeological Investigations, Southern Illinois University, Carbondale IL.

Rogers, J. D. (1982) *Spiro Archaeology: 1980 Research*. Studies in Oklahoma's Past 9. Oklahoma Archeological Survey, Norman OK.

Rogers, J. D. (2011) Stable isotope analysis and diet in eastern Oklahoma. *Southeastern Archaeology* 30 (1): 96–107.

Rogers, J. D. and Sabo, G. III (2004) Caddo. In *Southeast, Volume 14, Handbook of the North American Indians*, ed. R. D. Fogelson: 616–31. Smithsonian Institution, Washington DC.

Rogers, R. and Perttula, T. K. (2004) *The Oak Hill Village (41RK214), Rusk County, Texas*. Document 030083. PBS&J, Austin TX.

Rogers, R., Cliff, M. B., Perttula, T. K., Rutenberg, G., Victor, S., Dering, P. and Malainey, M. (2003) *Excavations at the Alex Justiss Site, 41TT13, Titus County, Texas*. Report 36. Archeological Studies Program, Texas Department of Transportation, Austin TX.

Rogers, R., Nash, M. A. and Perttula, T. K. (2001) *Excavations at the Herman Bellew Site (41RK222), Rusk County, Texas*. Document 000021. PBS&J, Austin TX.

Romain, W. F. (2009) *Shamans of the Lost World: A Cognitive Approach to the Prehistoric Religion of the Ohio Hopewell*. AltaMira Press, Lanham MD.

Romain, W. F. (2015) Moonwatchers of Cahokia. In *Medieval Mississippians: The Cahokian World*, eds T. R. Pauketat and S. M. Alt: 33–41. School for Advanced Research Press, Santa Fe NM.

Rose, J. C., Hoffman, M. P., Burnett, B. A., Harmon, A. M. and Barnes, J. E. (1998) Skeletal biology of the prehistoric Caddo. In *The Native History of the Caddo: Their Place in Southeastern Archeology and Ethnohistory*, eds T. K. Perttula and J. E. Bruseth: 113–126. Studies in Archeology 30. Texas Archeological Research Laboratory, University of Texas at Austin TX.

Sabo, G., III (1998) The structure of Caddo leadership in the Colonial Era. In *The Native History of the Caddo: Their Place in Southeastern Archeology and Ethnohistory*, eds T. K. Perttula and J. E. Bruseth: 159–74. Studies in Archeology 30. Texas Archeological Research Laboratory, The University of Texas at Austin TX.

Sabo, G. III (2012) The Teran map and Caddo cosmology. In *The Archaeology of the Caddo*, eds T. K. Perttula and C. P. Walker: 431–47. University of Nebraska Press, Lincoln NE.

Sahlins, M. (2013) *What Kinship Is—And is Not*. University of Chicago Press, Chicago IL.

Samuelsen, J. R. (2014) AMS and radiocarbon dating of the Crenshaw Site (3MI6). *Arkansas Archeologist* 52: 17–35.

Saramago, J. (2012) *The Lives of Things*. Verso, London and New York.

Scarry, C. M. and Scarry, J. F. (2005) Native American 'garden horticulture' in southeastern North America. *World Archaeology* 37 (2): 259–74.

Schachner, G. (2015) Ancestral Pueblo archaeology: the value of synthesis. *Journal of Archaeological Research* 23 (1): 49–113.

Schambach, F. F. (1972) Preliminary report on the 1972 excavations at the Ferguson Site (3HE63). *Arkansas Archeologist* 13 (1–2): 1–13.

Schambach, F. F. (1982a) An outline of Fourche Maline Culture in southwest Arkansas. In *Arkansas Archeology in Review*, eds N. L. Trubowitz and M. D. Jeter: 132–97. Research Series 15. Arkansas Archeological Survey, Fayetteville AR.

Schambach, F. F. (1982b) The archeology of the Great Bend region in Arkansas. In *Contributions to the Archeology of the Great Bend Region*, eds F. F. Schambach and F. Rackerby: 1–11. Research Series 22. Arkansas Archeological Survey, Fayetteville AR.

Schambach, F. F. (1989) The end of the trail: the route of Hernando De Soto's Army through southwest Arkansas and east Texas. *Arkansas Archeologist* 27/28: 9–33.

Schambach, F. F. (1993a) A summary of the history of the Caddo People. *Notes on Northeast Texas Archaeology* 2: 1–7.

Schambach, F. F. (1993) Some new interpretations of Spiroan Culture history. In *Archaeology of Eastern North America: Papers in Honor of Stephens Williams*, ed. J. B. Stoltman: 187–230. Archaeological Report 25. Mississippi Department of Archives and History, Jackson MS.

Schambach, F. F. (1993c) The end of the trail: reconstruction of the route of Hernando de Soto's Army through southwest Arkansas and east Texas. In Young and Hoffman (eds) 1993: 78–105.

Schambach, F. F. (1996) Mounds, Embankments, and ceremonialism in the trans-Mississippi south. In *Mounds, Embankments, and Ceremonialism in the Midsouth*, eds R. C. Mainfort and R. Walling: 36–43. Research Series 46. Arkansas Archeological Survey, Fayetteville AR.

Schambach, F. F. (1997) Continuing the discussion of the Spiroans and their entrepots: a reply to Brooks' critique of my new paradigm for the archeology of the Arkansas Valley. *Caddoan Archeology* 7(4): 17–46.

Schambach, F. F. (1998) *Pre-Caddoan Cultures in the Trans-Mississippi South: A Beginning Sequence.* Research Series 53, Arkansas Archeological Survey, Fayetteville AR.

Schambach, F. F. (2000) Spiroan traders, the Sanders Site, and the Plains interaction sphere: a reply to Bruseth, Wilson, and Perttula. *Plains Anthropologist* 45 (171): 17–33.

Schambach, F. F. (2001) Fourche Maline and its neighbors: observations on an important Woodland Period culture of the trans-Mississippi south. *Arkansas Archeologist* 40: 21–50.

Schambach, F. F. (2002) Fourche Maline: a Woodland Period culture of the trans-Mississippi south. In *The Woodland Southeast*, eds D. G. Anderson and R. C. Mainfort, Jr: 91–112. University of Alabama Press, Tuscaloosa AL.

Schambach, F. F. (2003) Osage orange bows, Indian horses, and the Blackland Prairie of northeastern Texas. In *Blackland Prairies of the Gulf Coastal Plain: Nature, Culture, and Sustainability*, eds E. Peacock and T. Schauwecker: 212–36. University of Alabama Press, Tuscaloosa AL.

Schambach, F. F., Trubowitz, N. L., Rackerby, F., Hemmings, E. T., Limp, W. F. and Miller, J. E. III (1982) Test excavations at the Cedar Grove Site (3LA97): a Late Caddo farmstead in the Great Bend region, southwest Arkansas. In *Contributions to the Archeology of the Great Bend Region*, eds F. F. Schambach and F. Rackerby: 90–140. Research Series 22. Arkansas Archeological Survey, Fayetteville AR.

Schoeninger, M. J., Sattenspiel, L. and Schurr, M. R. (2000) Transitions at Moundville: A question of collapse. In *Bioarchaeological Studies of Life in the Age of Agriculture: A View from the Southeast*, ed. P. M. Lambert: 63–77. University of Alabama Press, Tuscaloosa AL.

Schultz, T. C. (2010) *Architectural Variability in the Caddo Area of Eastern Texas.* Special Publication 16. Friends of Northeast Texas Archaeology, Pittsburg and Austin TX.

Scurlock, J. D. (1962) A Historic Caddo Site Near Marshall, Texas. MS on file, Texas Archeological Research Laboratory, The University of Texas at Austin.

Selden, R. Z., Jr. and Perttula, T. K. (2013) Radiocarbon trends and the east Texas Caddo tradition (ca. A.D. 800–1680). *Southeastern Archaeology* 32: 85–96.

Selden, R. Z. Jr and Perttula, T. K. (2014) At the confluence of GIS and geochemistry: identifying geochemical correlates of Ripley Engraved Caddo Ceramics. *Bulletin of the Texas Archeological Society* 85: 147–58.

Selden, R. Z. Jr., Perttula, T. K. and Carlson, D. L. (2014) INAA and the provenance of shell-tempered sherds in the ancestral Caddo region. *Journal of Archaeological Science* 47: 113–20.

Shafer, H. J. (1973) Lithic Technology at the George C. Davis Site, Cherokee County, Texas. Ph.D. dissertation, Department of Anthropology, University of Texas at Austin.

Shafer, H. J. (2011) Boxed Springs Mound Site (41UR30) lithic analysis. In Perttula 2011a: 78–111.

Skinner, S. A., Harris, R. K. and Anderson, K. M. (eds) (1969) *Archaeological Investigations at the Sam Kaufman Site, Red River County, Texas.* Contributions in Anthropology 5, Southern Methodist University, Department of Anthropology, Dallas TX.

Slater, P. A., Hedman, K. M. and Emerson, T. E. (2014) Immigrants at the Mississippian polity of Cahokia: strontium isotope evidence for population movement. *Journal of Archaeological Science* 44: 117–27.

Smith, B. D. (2015) A comparison of Niche Construction Theory and Diet Breadth Models as explanatory frameworks for the initial domestication of plants and animals. *Journal of Archaeological Research* 23 (3): 215–62.

Smith, B. D. and Cowan, C. W. (2003) Domesticated crop plants and the evolution of food production economies in eastern North America. In *People and Plants in Ancient Eastern North America*, ed. P. E. Minnis: 105–25. Smithsonian Books, Washington DC.

Smith, F. T. (2014) *Louisiana and the Gulf South Frontier, 1500–1821.* Louisiana State University Press, Baton Rouge LA.

Smith, N. G., Karasik, A., Narayanan, T., Olson, E. S., Smilansky, U. and Levy, T. E. (2014) The *Pottery Informatics Query Database*: a new method for mathematic and quantitative analyses of large regional ceramic datasets. *Journal of Archaeological Method and Theory* 21 (1): 212–50.

Solis, Fr. G. J. de (1931) Diary of a visit of inspection of the Texas Missions made by Father Gaspar Jose de Solis in the year 1767–1768. Trans. M. K. Kress. *Southwestern Historical Quarterly* 35: 28–76.

Spielmann, K. A. (2009) Ohio Hopewell ritual craft production. In *Footprints: In the Footprints of Squier and Davis: Archeological Fieldwork in Ross County, Ohio*, ed. M. J. Lynott: 179–88. Special Report 5. National Park Service, Midwest Archeological Center, Lincoln, Nebraska NE.

Spock, C. (1977) An Analysis of the Architectural and Related Features at the George C. Davis Site. Master's thesis, Department of Anthropology, University of Texas at Austin.

Stahle, D. W. and Dean, J. S. (2010) North American tree rings, climatic extremes, and social disasters. In *Dendro-climatology*, ed. M. K. Hughes: 297–327. Springer, New York.

Stahle, D. W., Cook, E. R., Cleaveland, M. K., Therrell, M. D., Meko, D. M., Grissino-Mayer, H. D., Watson, E.

and Luckman, B. H. (2000) Tree-ring data document 16th century megadrought over North America. *Eos Transactions, American Geophysical Union* 81 (12): 121.

Stark, M. T. (2003) Current issues in ceramic ethnoarchaeology. *Journal of Archaeological Research* 11 (3): 193–242.

Steponaitis, V. P. (1983) *Ceramics, Chronology, and Community Patterns: An Archaeological Study of Moundville*. Academic Press, New York.

Steponaitis, V. P., Kassabaum, M. C. and O'Hear, J. W. (2015) Cahokia's Coles Creek predecessors. In *Medieval Mississippians: The Cahokian World*, eds T. R. Pauketat and S. M. Alt: 13–19. School for Advanced Research Press, Santa Fe NM.

Story, D. A. (1990) Cultural History of the Native Americans. In *The Archeology and Bioarcheology of the Gulf Coastal Plain*, by D. A. Story, J. A. Guy, B. A. Burnett, M. D. Freeman, J. C. Rose, D. G. Steele, B. W. Olive, and K. J. Reinhard: 163–366. 2 Vols. Research Series No. 38. Arkansas Archeological Survey, Fayetteville AR.

Story, D. A. (1993) Alex D. Krieger. *American Antiquity* 58 (4): 614–21.

Story, D. A. (1997) 1968–1970 archeological investigations at the George C. Davis Site, Cherokee County, Texas. *Bulletin of the Texas Archeological Society* 68: 1–113.

Story, D. A. (1998) The George C. Davis Site: glimpses into Early Caddoan symbolism and ideology. In *The Native History of the Caddo: Their Place in Southeastern Archeology and Ethnohistory*, eds T. K. Perttula and J. E. Bruseth: 9–43. Studies in Archeology 30. Texas Archeological Research Laboratory, University of Texas at Austin TX.

Story, D. A. (2000) Introduction. In *The George C. Davis Site, Cherokee County, Texas*, by H. P. Newell and A. D. Krieger: 1–31 (2nd edn). Society for American Archaeology, Washington DC.

Story, D. A. (ed.) (1982) *The Deshazo Site, Nacogdoches County, Texas, Vol. 1*. Texas Antiquities Permit Series 7. Texas Antiquities Committee, Austin TX.

Story, D. A. (ed.) (1995) *The Deshazo Site, Nacogdoches County, Texas, Vol. 2: Artifacts of Native Manufacture*. Studies in Archeology 21. Texas Archeological Research Laboratory, University of Texas at Austin TX.

Story, D. A. and Creel, D. G. (1982) The cultural setting. In Story (ed.) 1982: 20–34.

Story, D. A. and Valastro, S. Jr. (1977) Radiocarbon dating and the George C. Davis Site, Texas. *Journal of Field Archaeology* 4 (1): 63–89.

Story, D. A., Barber, B., Cobb, E., Cobb, H., Coleman, R., Gilmore, K., Harris, R. K. and Hoffrichter, N. (1967) Pottery vessels. In The Gilbert Site: a Norteno focus site in northeast Texas, ed. E. B. Jelks. *Bulletin of the Texas Archeological Society* 37: 112–87.

Suhm, D. A. and Jelks, E. B. (eds) (1962) *Handbook of Texas Archeology: Type Descriptions*. Special Publication 1, Texas Archeological Society, and Bulletin 4, Texas Memorial Museum, Austin TX. Reprinted in 2009, Gustav's Library, Davenport IA.

Sullivan, L. P. and Mainfort, R. C. Jr. (2010) Mississippian mortuary practices and the quest for interpretation. In *Mississippian Mortuary Practices: beyond Hierarchy and the Representationist Perspective*, eds L. P. Sullivan and R. C. Mainfort Jr.: 1–13. University Press of Florida, Gainesville FL.

Sundermeyer, S. A., Penman, J. T. and Perttula, T. K. (2008) *Integrated Cultural Resources Investigations for the Bowie County Levee Realignment Project, Bowie County, Texas, and Little River County, Arkansas*. Miscellaneous Reports, Report of Investigations 29. LopezGarcia Group, Dallas TX.

Swanton, J. R. (1942) *Source Material on the History and Ethnology of the Caddo Indians*. Bulletin 132. Bureau of American Ethnology, Smithsonian Institution, Washington DC.

Thurmond, J. P. (1990) *Archeology of the Cypress Creek Drainage Basin, Northeastern Texas and Northwestern Louisiana*. Studies in Archeology 5. Texas Archeological Research Laboratory, University of Texas at Austin TX.

Tiller, J. (2007) The Shreveport Caddo, 1835–1838. *Journal of Northeast Texas Archaeology* 26: 159–67.

Tiller, J. (2008) Was Timber Hill the last Caddo village in the Caddo homeland? *Caddo Archeology Journal* 18: 11–21.

Tomka, S. A., Perttula, T. K., Middlebrook, T. and Jackson, M. K. (2013) Native-made historic ceramics of Texas. *Bulletin of the Texas Archeological Society* 84: 247–67.

Tous, G. (1930) The Espinosa-Olivares-Aguirre Expedition. *Preliminary Studies of the Texas Catholic Historical Society* 1(4) :2–24.

Trubitt, M. B. (2009) Burning and burying buildings: exploring variation in Caddo architecture in southwest Arkansas. *Southeastern Archaeology* 28 (2): 233–47.

Trubowitz, N. L. (ed.) (1984) *Cedar Grove: An Interdisciplinary Investigation of a Late Caddo Farmstead in the Red River Valley*. Research Series 23. Arkansas Archeological Survey, Fayetteville AR.

Tunnell, C. D. (1959) The Sam Roberts Site, Ferrell's Bridge Reservoir, Texas. MS on file, Texas Archeological Research Laboratory, The University of Texas at Austin.

Turner, R. L., Jr (1978) The Tuck Carpenter Site and its relation to other sites within the Titus Focus. *Bulletin of the Texas Archeological Society* 49: 1–110.

Turner, R. L. Jr (1992) *Prehistoric Mortuary Remains at the Tuck Carpenter Site, Camp County, Texas*. Studies in Archeology 10, Texas Archeological Research Laboratory, University of Texas at Austin TX.

Wade, M. F. (2008) *Missions, Missionaries, and Native Americans: Long-Term Processes and Daily Practices*. University Press of Florida, Gainesville FL.

Wade, M. F. (n.d.) Por Las Espaldas Se Nos Van Entrando Con Silencio: Fr. Hidalgo's Letter to the Viceroy. MS on file, University of Texas at Austin, University Extension, Thompson Conference Center, Austin.

Walker, C. P. (2009) Landscape Archaeogeophysics: A Study of Magnetometer Surveys from Etowah (9BW1), the George C. Davis Site (41CE19), and the Hill Farm Site (41BW169). Ph.D. dissertation, Department of Anthropology, The University of Texas at Austin.

Walker, C. P. and McKinnon, D. P. (2012) Exploring prehistoric Caddo communities through archaeogeophysics. In *The Archaeology of the Caddo*, eds T. K. Perttula and C. P. Walker: 177–208. University of Nebraska Press, Lincoln NE.

Walker, C. P. and Perttula, T. K. (2011) *Archaeogeophysics and Archaeological Investigations at a Historic Caddo Site Along El Camino Real de los Tejas: The J. T. King Site (41NA15) in Nacogdoches County, Texas*. Archaeo-Geophysical Associates, LLC and Archeological & Environmental Consultants, LLC, Austin TX.

Walters, M. (2006) The Lake Clear (41SM243) Site and *Crotalus horridus atricaudatus*. *Caddoan Archeology Journal* 15: 5–41.

Walters, M. (2009) The Henry Chapman Site (41SM56). *Journal of Northeast Texas Archaeology* 31: 11–35.

Walters, M. (2008), with contributions from L. G. Cecil, L. S. Cummings, J. P. Dering, J. R. Ferguson, M. D. Glascock, T. K. Perttula, L. Schniebs, H. J. Shafer, J. Todd, and C. P. Walker, Life on Jackson Creek, Smith County, Texas: archeological investigations of a 14th century Caddo domicile at the Leaning Rock Site (41SM325). *Caddo Archeology Journal* 17: 1–114.

Walters, M. (2010), with contributions by T. Middlebrook and T. K. Perttula, Redwine or Pie-Crust Mode forms in East Texas Caddo ceramics and comparisons with Sprocket-Rims of southwest Arkansas. *Caddo Archeology Journal* 20: 77–128.

Walters, M. and Haskins, P. (1998) Archaeological investigations at the Redwine Site (41SM193), Smith County, Texas. *Journal of Northeast Texas Archaeology* 11: 1–38.

Walters, M. and Haskins, P. (2000) The Bryan Hardy Site (41SM55), Smith County, Texas. *Journal of Northeast Texas Archaeology* 12: 1–26.

Webb, C. H. (1959) *The Belcher Mound: A Stratified Caddoan Site in Caddo Parish, Louisiana*. Memoir 16, Society for American Archaeology, Salt Lake City UT.

Webb, C. H. and Dodd, M. Jr (1939) Further excavations of the Gahagan Mound: connections with a Florida culture. *Bulletin of the Texas Archeological and Paleontological Society* 11: 92–126.

Webb, C. H. and McKinney, R. R. (1975) Mounds Plantation (16CD12), Caddo Parish, Louisiana. *Louisiana Archaeology* 2: 39–127.

Webb, C. H., Murphey, F. E., Ellis, W. G. and Green, H. R. (1969) The Resch Site, 41HS16, Harrison County, Texas. *Bulletin of the Texas Archeological Society* 40: 3–106.

Weddle, R. S. (2012) *Archival and Archaeological Research: Camino Real de los Tejas and Texas State Parks*. Texas Parks and Wildlife Department, Austin TX.

Wedel, M. M. (1978) *La Harpe's 1719 Post on Red River and Nearby Caddo Settlements*. Bulletin 30. Texas Memorial Museum, Austin TX.

Williams, J. M. (2007) GIS Aided Archaeological Research of *El Camino Real de Los Tejas* with Focus on the Landscape and River Crossings along *El Camino Carretera*. Masters thesis, Stephen F. Austin State University, Nacogdoches TX.

Willey, G. R. and Phillips, P. (1958) *Method and Theory in American Archaeology*. University of Chicago Press, Chicago IL.

Wilson, D. E. (2008) Human remains. In Perttula 2008b: 557–79.

Wilson, D. E. (2011) Analysis of Human Remains from the Lang Pasture Site. In Perttula *et al.* (eds) 2011: 381–401.

Wilson, D. E. (2012) Bioarchaeological evidence of subsistence strategies among the east Texas Caddo. In *The Archaeology of the Caddo*, eds T. K. Perttula and C. P. Walker: 86–116. University of Nebraska Press, Lincoln NE.

Wilson, D. and Perttula, T. K. (2013) Reconstructing the diet of the Caddo through stable isotopes. *American Antiquity* 78 (4): 702–23.

Wilson, D., Perttula, T. K. and Walters, M. (2012) Stable isotope analysis from a burial at the Pipe Site (41AN67) in Anderson County, Texas. *Journal of Northeast Texas Archaeology* 38: 79–85.

Winter, J. C. (2000a) From Earth Mother to Snake Woman: The role of tobacco in the evolution of Native American religious organization. In Winter (ed.) 2000b: 265–304.

Winter, J. C. (ed.) (2000b) *Tobacco Use by Native North Americans: Sacred Smoke and Sacred Killer*. University of Oklahoma Press, Norman OK.

Woodall, J. N. (1969) *Archeological Excavations in the Toledo Bend Reservoir, 1966*. Contributions in Anthropology 3. Department of Anthropology, Southern Methodist University, Dallas TX.

Wyckoff, D. G. and Baugh, T. G. (1980) Early historic Hasinai elites: A model for the material culture of governing elites. *Midcontinental Journal of Archaeology* 5: 225–83.

Young, G. A. and Hoffman, M. P. (eds) (1993) *The Expedition of Hernando de Soto West of the Mississippi, 1541–1543: Proceedings of the DeSoto Symposia, 1988 and 1990*. University of Arkansas Press, Fayetteville, AR.

Index of Sites

Page number in italics indicate pages with illustrations or tables

General index

Page numbers in italics denote pages with illustration or tables. All places, rivers and landforms are in (or predominantly in) Texas unless otherwise stated